KENMARE: HISTORY AND SURVIVAL

Fr John O'Sullivan and the Famine Poor

'The wild flower of Mangerton or a Kerry peasant child' by Matthew Wood, about 1845; engraved by George McCoy, Dublin, 1847.
Courtesy Prints & Photographs Division, Library of Congress.

Kenmare: History and Survival
Fr John O'Sullivan and the Famine Poor

Colum Kenny

East_wood_

First published by Eastwood Books, 2021
Dublin, Ireland

www.eastwoodbooks.com
www.wordwellbooks.com
@eastwoodbooks

Eastwood Books is an imprint of The Wordwell Group

Eastwood Books
The Wordwell Group
Unit 9, 78 Furze Road
Sandyford
Dublin, Ireland

© Colum Kenny, 2021

ISBN: 978-1-913934-15-6 (paperback)
ISBN: 978-1-913934-18-7 (ebook)

Front cover: View of Kenmare across Kenmare Bay, with the workhouse and fever hospital on extreme right. Also, Henry Street (also 'Sound Street'), Kenmare, with the steeple of Holy Cross Church. Both photographs *c.*1900. *Courtesy National Library of Ireland* [The Lawrence Collection L_ROY_04684 and L_CAB_06497]. Kindly colourised for this book by Prof. John Breslin, NUI Galway.

British Library Cataloguing in Publication Data.
A catalogue record for this book is available from the British Library.

Typeset in Ireland by Wordwell Ltd
Copy-editor: Myles McCionnaith
Cover design and artwork: Wordwell Ltd
Printed by: SprintPrint, Dublin

In memory of Catherine Connolly

– 'a little girl as he thought asleep on the road' –

who with her brothers Dan, John and Michael died of starvation
in the open air near Kenmare Bay on the night of
30–31 December 1847.

Contents

Foreword

If most people now live in cities, many of us are no more than a few generations removed from the land. And the land along the coast of Kenmare Bay is some of the most spectacularly beautiful in Europe. The story of how a town rose there, and of how local people have struggled to surmount adversity through war and famine, has something to say about survival to a world facing its own crises today.

I might never have written this book had I not happened to share an ancestor with the man who was the parish priest of Kenmare from 1839 to 1874. For it was the chance discovery of a copy of a printed letter from Fr John O'Sullivan to his parishioners, carefully transcribed by my Kerry-born grandmother and handed down after her death in 1972, that eventually led me to O'Sullivan's unpublished journals in the Kerry Diocesan Archives. Through these and other sources, his relationship with Lord Lansdowne – one of Britain's most influential politicians and one of Ireland's biggest landlords – became clear. So too did his remarkable service to the poorest of the poor, the workhouse paupers.

During the seventeenth century, Sir William Petty – a Cromwellian official – was granted thousands of acres of Kerry confiscated from the native Irish. In the late eighteenth century, his descendant and namesake – a sometime British prime minister – founded the town of Kenmare. Local men and women built it up, only to see it overwhelmed by misery during the great famine. The metal cock that O'Sullivan erected as a weathervane, on the spire of a fine church that he built there after the great famine, is a sign of its people's resilience. This is their story.

1

Smeared with Blood

She saw him 'standing over the sheep with his coat wrists turned up, his hand smeared with blood and a knife in it'. So wrote Fr John O'Sullivan of Kenmare, Co. Kerry, while events were still fresh in his memory.[1]

Just three days later in 1849, the man with the knife was sentenced to transportation for seven years. He had slaughtered one of O'Sullivan's nine sheep. The perpetrator was suspected of also killing a sheep belonging to Rev. Denis Mahony – a parson and landlord, and the proprietor of Dromore Castle.[2]

O'Sullivan, as he himself archly observed, was sometimes referred to as 'Father John that killed the Parson'. This was because Rev. Mahony, aged 55, collapsed and died in 1851, seven months after being roughly assaulted during a confrontation with O'Sullivan's parishioners. For over a decade there had been hostility between the two men, one a Catholic priest and the other a Protestant proselytiser.

This was the era of the great famine, a disaster for Ireland's poor. The stealing of sheep and the death of a clergyman were rooted in its horrors. The response of Fr John O'Sullivan and the plight of paupers in Kenmare's 'workhouse' (its poorhouse) are vivid illustrations of the challenges facing people then. A large underclass had become fatally dependent on the yield from small potato patches. In this and in other ways, the history of Kenmare is a history of survival. Starvation exacerbated older fault lines between rich and poor; landlord and tenant; Gaelic Irish, Anglo-Irish and English; Catholic and Protestant.

Sheep-stealers

The men who stole a sheep from O'Sullivan did so early one day in 1849 – from land, adjacent to his house, that he rented from Lord Lansdowne:

Honora O'Sullivan [...] servant maid to the Rev. John O'Sullivan recollects that on 2 April between the hours of nine and ten in the morning she got the alarm that one of the sheep was missing, ran down to the bottom of the farm where the sheep were and she saw there were eight only – there had been nine; saw the prisoner at the bar standing on the ditch and called to him to stand. He ran into the plantation and she followed him, where she saw the other prisoner standing over the sheep with his coat wrists turned up, his hand smeared with blood and a knife in it. Both prisoners then ran across the river and she followed them for about a half quarter of a mile when two neighbours joined her and the pair were made prisoners.[3]

The dizzying speed with which criminals were then dispatched is clear from this case. Within a week of being caught Daniel Brennan and his co-accused, named Sullivan, were sentenced to transportation to Australia. So too were seven other Kerrymen who appeared on charges at the current Quarter Sessions in Killarney, which were particularly busy due to many cases of sheep and cow stealing.[4]

Shortly after the trial ended, Fr John O'Sullivan wrote a brief account of it in his journal – an account that reveals the strength of his feelings about the offence. The theft was striking, because it was from a priest and it followed the men's earlier killing not only of Mahony's sheep but also of sheep belonging to two Protestant ministers whom O'Sullivan respected. He confides in his journal that he 'had to' prosecute the men and that 'I succeeded in getting them transported' – which expression Gerard Lyne has described as 'callous'.[5]

Nevertheless, although O'Sullivan was both a patriarchal priest and a member of the growing Catholic middle-class, he was not insensitive to hardship. Soon after the trial of the sheep-stealers, for example, he appealed to the Lord Lieutenant on behalf of a certain 'honest, inoffensive, industrious' man who had a disability and who had been sentenced to a year in jail for being found in possession of a single workhouse shirt that had been stolen. O'Sullivan also then expressed concern privately to Charles Trevelyan, his powerful acquaintance in London, about 'the immense influx into the little town' of paupers from the countryside who were 'now living at their wits end by begging, by plunder, by rapine [seizing property by force]'. As it happens, in that letter to Trevelyan he himself also used the term 'callous', doing so to describe the Poor Law Commission's inspectors. He told Trevelyan that he would go down on his knees to anyone if he could 'procure the discharge of the immense crowds by which the workhouse is thronged […] without shoes, without clothes in filthy rags and misery', and pleaded with him to send 'some humane person' to see for himself the state of about 1,800 'unfortunate inmates' in the workhouse.[6]

Nonetheless, O'Sullivan could not be thought to excuse sheep-stealers if he wished to persuade those in authority to do more to relieve the law-abiding poor. As it was, his mere willingness in court to acknowledge that distress drove people to crime brought him into conflict with Captain William Clarke, who was one of the inspectors appointed to supervise the administration of poor law relief. Clarke had earlier had an encounter with one of the same sheep-stealers:

> Clarke foolishly took it into his head that I was extenuating their crime and stood up in court to say that himself, the vice-guardian [of the workhouse] and the relieving officer had been put in bodily terror by one of the prisoners and thought to give me a hit in the business, but I retorted on him with a vengeance by saying it was a very bad proof to find a fellow of his [the prisoner's] kind, who though having a knife in his hand was captured by my servant maid, infuse such terror into a gallant colonel and his staff.[7]

O'Sullivan protested that he was neither excusing the accused nor palliating the crime, but added that the prosecution would never have arisen if Clarke had had the man arrested when he made the threat at the workhouse. O'Sullivan later thought it prudent to make a record of the proceedings, 'as it is possible the old colonel may hereafter refer to a whack I gave him at the Killarney quarter sessions'.

In O'Sullivan's notes of the hearing, there is a further jarring reminder of how assumptions change and evolve with time. Thus, while he was willing to refer in court to the men's state of desperation, he also agreed that deportation was an appropriate punishment for thieves who were 'bad characters and must of necessity be sent out of the country'. It was an era when three people found in possession of six sheets, nine shirts, one blanket and one petticoat – all stolen from Kenmare workhouse – were sentenced at Tralee to twelve months' imprisonment with hard labour.[8] Workhouse authorities marked workhouse clothing with 'red fluid', a sign of their ownership and of the paupers' shame.[9]

Fr John O'Sullivan was no plaster-cast saint, and Captain Clarke was no hard-hearted demon. Their clashes in court and elsewhere, like those between priest and pastor, were shaped by the context of Irish history. If Clarke was an obedient servant of the Crown who sought to see a public budget spent as his government intended, albeit a distant government in London with priorities beyond those of Ireland, O'Sullivan was a priest who belonged to a church headquartered in Rome that had its own ambitions for the island. Yet O'Sullivan also personified some of the contradictions in his society in a way that undermines simple binary accounts of Irish history. For he asserted the potential benefits of the union with Britain while barely supporting its repeal; saw his own family treated kindly by Protestants and had good relations with some Church of Ireland clergymen while bitterly opposing proselytism; praised landlords who improved their estates while engineering for himself an appearance before a parliamentary committee in London in order to support the continuing imposition of a workhouse rate on landowners under what he called 'the first law that was ever made for the poor'; and was critical of a powerful centralising hierarchy within the Catholic Church, of which he was a loyal member.

Voiceless and voice

The poor who suffered and died in the Irish great famine were seldom heard outside their own circles. Their voices were generally unrecorded. The paupers of Kenmare, like many hundreds of thousands of poor people across Ireland who perished from starvation and its related diseases between 1845 and 1852, had no association to represent them and could not elect members of parliament due to a property qualification for voting. Absent from archives and libraries are detailed memoirs by them. Even before they experienced the great hunger, their way of life was basic.

In recent decades the historiography of 'the great hunger' has flourished. The recently published *Atlas of the Great Irish Famine*, for example, bears witness broadly to the very many people who died and are buried in mass famine pits such as that in old Kenmare cemetery, or in fields and ditches, with little or nothing to mark their passing. It noted the centrality of the workhouse as a place of destitution.[10] The present volume is more specific, allowing a fuller understanding of the context and contradictions of the great famine through the exploration of relations between classes and cultures in one of the areas worst affected, and it does so in a manner that is accessible to the general reader while at the same time including a scholarly apparatus necessary to support its argument and findings appropriately. Ireland had certainly known famine before,[11] and was by no means the only European country to experience a serious shortfall in food supply during the 1840s,[12] but the great famine exposed social and religious relationships in Ireland in a particularly harsh manner that the story of Fr John O'Sullivan and the Kenmare paupers reveals.

Many Irish people lived in small mud cabins then, relying on a daily diet of potatoes and milk. Others spoke *about* them. This included members of parliament, whom the poor could not vote for or against because they did not own any or enough property to qualify for a vote; journalists, who wrote about them for papers that many poor people could not read because they were illiterate; and clergymen, who ministered to them on behalf of churches that had their own ideas of what was best for their faithful Irish flocks. One of the clergy was John O'Sullivan, parish priest of Kenmare during the great famine. He did not just minister to spiritual needs. He also lobbied bankers in London for aid, corresponded with powerful officials, gave evidence to a select committee of MPs and fiercely rebuffed Protestant 'soupers' who he believed were exploiting human misery. At times irascible, yet opposed to revolutionary violence, he held neglectful landlords largely responsible for the famine and personally organised the importation of food. Subsequently chosen by the priests of Kerry and the hierarchy of Munster to become their bishop, O'Sullivan was ultimately blocked from the appointment by higher church authorities due to his attitude and personality.

In 1839 O'Sullivan became the parish priest of Kenmare and Templenoe combined, an area stretching along the north side of Kenmare Bay to the little River Blackwater. In 1849 he told the House of Commons that the population of Kenmare and Templenoe combined was 10,028, 'and I would say that there cannot be more than 300 to 400 Protestants.'[13] His parish accounted for about one third of the population and about one quarter of the land of the broader 'Kenmare Union' – one of 130 'unions' created across Ireland under the Poor Law Act 1838 to administer, by means of the election of a local board of guardians, measures for the relief of poverty. The board set and collected a local poor tax or 'rate', and ran a local workhouse – which in this case was about to be built on the outskirts of Kenmare town. The Kenmare Union consisted of the districts of Kenmare, Templenoe, Ballybog (Sneem, with Bordoneen), Kilgarvan and – across the bridge at the narrow end of Kenmare Bay – Tuosist and

Bonane. Of 217,000 acres within the union, only about one in every twenty was planted with crops. The others were mainly rocky or rough pasture on which cattle, sheep or goats grazed – with much cold and spuey soil that had not been drained.[14] Poor people relied greatly on the potato to survive. Some migrated annually to work as labourers elsewhere, and some ostensibly to beg. Seeing labourers cross the mountains between Cork and Kerry, Mr and Mrs Hall were told that at one time Lord Lansdowne's agents 'stationed themselves at the old entrance into the county, to meet the beggars as they were returning homewards from Cork to Kerry, and received the rents of their cabins by taking from them the half-pence they had collected'. The Halls added reassuringly, if not entirely convincingly, 'This is no doubt a humorous exaggeration.'[15]

As O'Sullivan and other local priests worked hard before and after the great famine to build a network of new schools and other facilities for their parishioners, and to erect churches that complemented or replaced humbler chapels, they incidentally constructed a system that was to help the Catholic Church dominate the new Irish state after independence. The affinity of many priests with farmers and with the emerging middle-class, as well as their close personal knowledge of the labouring, landless class – due not least to their bringing the sacraments of baptism, confession, communion and the last rites by day or night during the famine to remote and appreciative rural families – allowed them to forge a close bond with Irish Catholic lay people.

O'Sullivan left behind handwritten journals that provide vivid insights into poverty, society and religion in early Victorian Ireland. Still unpublished and too seldom quoted, they are a valuable source of analysis and information about his life as a parish priest and about the lives of the people of Kenmare.

It would have been fascinating to have been present when he sat down not once but twice in Threadneedle Street with some of the most influential bankers in the city of London, including sympathetic Jewish millionaires, to seek aid for his hungry parishioners. It would have been likewise absorbing to see him dining as a private guest at the home of one of the most powerful civil servants in Whitehall, Charles Trevelyan; or giving evidence at Westminster to members of parliament about conditions in Kenmare; or meeting the Prime Minister of the United Kingdom in Dublin; or falling foul of archbishops Paul Cullen and John MacHale at the Synod of Thurles; or encountering the wealthy, influential and generally absent landlord of his parish, Henry Petty-Fitzmaurice, 3rd Marquess of Lansdowne, with whom he spoke in England about the condition of his tenants on the thousands of acres of his estate in Kerry. The latter was a Whig who is said to have been 'almost universally praised for his leadership in the house of lords between 1842 and his retirement in 1858'.[16] A newspaper in Kerry that was strongly Tory and Protestant in its sympathies accused O'Sullivan of being Lord Lansdowne's 'pet', yet the priest expressed to senior officials what Peter Gray has described as 'savagely anti-landlord views'.[17] He attended to the plight of the poor in deed as well as in word, once sacrificing a greatly desired opportunity to meet representatives of the prestigious London *Times* – who he hoped might be persuaded to change its tune on Ireland – because he wished to hurry back to his home country before an imminent outbreak of cholera took its toll on paupers at the Kenmare workhouse.

It would also have been fascinating, if unpleasant, to visit the overcrowded poorhouse with him while, in his capacity as its salaried chaplain, he braved its stench and disease to console the afflicted. Afterwards, one might have relaxed with him as he walked his beloved dog by the little River Finnihy, which he liked to do in the evenings, or have listened to him playing the piano in his parlour while sharing his whiskey. But one would always be conscious of the fact that he could be called away on a winter's night to make his way by foot or horse to console some gravely ill parishioner in a remote hillside cabin. Or perhaps, joyfully, one might have accompanied him through Killarney back to his hometown of Tralee to celebrate, as he did, the wedding of a child of his first cousin Anne Walsh and her husband John Murphy (also 'O'Murphy'). Their son Edward was father of the present author's grandmother Annette, who left to her own descendants her carefully handwritten copy of an open letter O'Sullivan addressed to his rival Denis Mahony in 1848. That copy was the genesis of this book.

O'Sullivan tried to help the impoverished and sometimes starving people when others who might have done more did not. Yet he was not the fiercest advocate of tenant rights, for his ultimate priorities were religious rather than social or political. Lyne has pointed out that Lansdowne let priests have land on more favourable terms than other tenants – a circumstance that may have encouraged them to stay aloof from tenant agitation, as O'Sullivan and some others usually did. It certainly left them open to insinuation.[18] Whatever the limits of his activism, O'Sullivan's journals allow us a view of the too-often-invisible lives of some of the poorest people in Ireland during a terrible famine. He wrote his journals half a century or more before the Anglo-Irish novelists Somerville and Ross published their well-known, amusing accounts of a fictional resident magistrate in the west of Ireland. O'Sullivan's random recollections of an actual Irish parish priest strike a plangent note but are not entirely lacking in humour. They provide a vivid and realistic insight into the most traumatic and transformative period in modern Irish history.

On confiscated O'Sullivan lands

Before coming to Kenmare, Fr John O'Sullivan's only long-term posting 'on the mission' – as even the domestic assignments of priests were then called – had been as a curate in Dingle during the 1830s. On that most westerly peninsula he and some friends made occasional excursions to its rocky tip, where a headland at Smerwick overlooks the Atlantic Ocean. It is a place for picnics, but in 1580 it was the site of the bloody English slaughter of a papal force of up to six hundred European mercenaries that had surrendered at Dún an Óir, along with some of their Irish allies. The massacre, after a large relieving force of Irishmen failed to materialise as expected, was part of a brutal phase in Irish history that came to a climax when the centralising ambitions of the Protestant government in London resulted in the defeat of Gaelic and Catholic resistance.

One of the last Gaelic chiefs to hold out against the English was Domhnall O'Sullivan Beare (1560–1618) on the Beara Peninsula, which constitutes the southern coast of Kenmare Bay. For generations the O'Sullivan, or Ó Súilleabháin, 'sept' (clan/family) had dominated both shores of the bay, and in that capacity they had dealings with the English in Ireland long before William Petty was granted lands there. In 1602 the English seized control of O'Sullivan Beare's Dunboy Castle, killing its defenders in battle or massacring them afterwards. Three hundred women, children and old people of the clan who had taken shelter on Dursey Island were also slaughtered. Domhnall O'Sullivan Beare and a thousand of his remaining followers embarked on a famous, long march to join the northern Gaelic chiefs of Ulster, but their journey ended in disappointment, and he fled to Spain – where a surviving portrait of him was painted. Other chieftains also went abroad. This 'flight of the earls', as it became known, left Gaelic Ireland rudderless and despondent. O'Sullivan Mór, chief of the O'Sullivan sept's other main branch in Kerry, was long remembered around

Kenmare for having defended the local O'Sullivan castles of Dunkerron and Cappanacush against the English.[19]

During the later seventeenth century, much of the O'Sullivan sept's land was granted to William Petty. Some of it continued to be occupied by O'Sullivans under long subleases. As late as the 1790s, for example, the O'Sullivans of Bonane and Creeveen resisted the Lansdowne estate's efforts to force new leases on them; they saw the attempt as contrary to their ancestors' favourable terms of agreement with Richard Orpen – who himself had earlier leased the same land directly from Petty.[20]

It would be wrong to idealise Gaelic society, which was no monolith but a complex web of kith and kin, and septs, with pre-Reformation values and its own inequalities. However, the social order that replaced it from the seventeenth century was dominated by English and Anglo-Irish Protestants with whom a nineteenth-century Kerry 'peasant' was unlikely to have much in common. While some poor Protestants lived in Kerry in Fr John O'Sullivan's day, the vast bulk of small farmers and labourers there were Catholics. Differences of class, religion and politics bitterly divided Ireland when the potato failed and the great famine began, with Catholics only having been permitted to sit in parliament or to be appointed to the higher civil service and judiciary as recently as 1829, and with only the wealthier classes of any religion being entitled to vote.

Although the great bulk of Irish land had passed from Catholic to Protestant hands by the early eighteenth century, the Protestant Anglo-Irish never felt completely secure in possession of it. The French Revolution and the crushed revolt of the United Irishmen in 1798 came as shocks and augured change. A union of Ireland with Britain would ensure that the Gaelic and Catholic Irish could never take control of an Irish parliament in the event of Catholic emancipation being granted (as it was to be in 1829). The Lord Chancellor of Ireland, 'Black Jack' Fitzgibbon, himself the son of a man who had conformed to the established Anglican Church in order to practise as a lawyer, unashamedly put the self-interested case for such an Act of Union as clearly and bluntly as possible on 10 February 1800. He was proposing its acceptance, and the consequent extinction of the hitherto independent and politically awkward – if entirely Protestant – Irish parliament in Dublin:

> The whole power and property of the country has been
> conferred by successive Monarchs of England upon an English

colony, composed of three sets of English adventurers who poured into this country at the termination of three successive rebellions. Confiscations is their common title; and from their first settlement they have been hemmed in on every side by the old inhabitants of the island, brooding over their discontents in sullen indignation. It is painful to me to go into this detail, but we have been for twenty years in a fever of intoxication, and must be stunned into sobriety.

What then was the security of the English settlers for their physical existence at the Revolution [when William of Orange superseded King James II]; and what is the security of their descendants at this day? The powerful and commanding protection of Great Britain. If by any fatality it fails you are at the mercy of the old inhabitants of the island.[21]

Many of the 'old inhabitants of the island', such as the O'Sullivans, lived on the western seaboard. If they were 'brooding [...] in sullen indignation' over their losses, looking daily upon land that had been taken by force from Catholics and even from their direct ancestors, their 'discontents' were exacerbated by knowing that some landlords only enjoyed their property because their families had converted to keep it. The Fitzmaurice ancestors of the lords Lansdowne had done so. Likewise, Denis Mahony's grandfather left the Catholic Church in order to retain former lands of the O'Sullivans that his family held under a sublease from William Petty – and to gain more land, as will be seen.

Denis Mahony's father was a colonel of the Dromore Volunteers and a delegate to the National Convention of Volunteers at Dungannon in 1782. The Volunteers were a Protestant militia formed to defend Ireland under the Crown but were also an expression of the confident ambitions of a Protestant Irish parliament that would be snuffed out by the Act of Union in 1800. A few Catholics were admitted surreptitiously into Volunteer companies, but the penal laws forbidding papists to hold arms were still in force. A French visitor to Kenmare in 1790 formed the impression that Mahony's company consisted of 'all Sullivans and all well-off men enjoying from £200 to £500 a year'. The same visitor noted that the region comprising Glanerought, Bantry and the whole of Kenmare Bay was Sullivan country, with between two and three hundred heads of families bearing the name, 'The Sullivans are full of personal vanity. They have their children taught English, which they speak with great purity, and they also speak Latin. They dress well and affect an air of good breeding and affluence that is quite astonishing.'[22]

In later life, in one of his more colourful or 'smashing' sermons – as that rambling broadside was described by the *Tralee Chronicle* – O'Sullivan ridiculed what seemed to him (he said) to be a firm belief 'among all classes from the farmer to the cowboy, that they are all "gentlemen born"', and he condemned 'the foolish nonsensical ideas of blood and lineage that so pervade all classes [...] fill them with pride, nonsense and vanity, and render them the laughing stock of every thinking person.' Although there were ruined castles and many religious sites, ancient and more recent, scattered about the countryside, he said, 'I see no old buildings, no old mansions, no old churches, no traces of old cultivation or civilisation, no monasteries whatever, nothing, positively nothing to lead me to believe there was ever anything like refinement, cultivation, or civilisation amongst us.' However, he notably qualified his dismissiveness, 'There are, to be sure, three old castles in the country, and singular enough, two of them are in Templenoe, the very parish in the [Kenmare] Union where the least noise is made of their ancestors and their cousins, and all that came before them.' These last two castles were the O'Sullivan Mór strongholds of Dunkerron and Cappanacush, the latter standing on lands that the Mahonys came to own only because they had conformed to the Anglican Church. Among those born at Cappanacush Castle, before he was sent to France at the age of 9, was one John Sullivan (*c.*1700–*c.*1762). He became, in effect, commander of the Jacobite army of Bonnie Prince Charles at Falkirk and Culloden.[23]

It is not known if Fr O'Sullivan's surname was a factor in his bishop's decision to appoint him as parish priest of Kenmare and Templenoe. Once there, the priest had a cordial relationship with Lord Lansdowne, who was the dominant if absentee Anglo-Irish landlord in the Kenmare area, even as O'Sullivan and Denis Mahony of Dromore Castle in Templenoe were contemptuous of each other. In his journals O'Sullivan gives no indication that he harboured bad feelings towards the absent Lord Lansdowne or even the present and proselytising Mahony on the grounds that they possessed much land once confiscated from O'Sullivans. Yet, according to John O'Hart, Fr John appears to have been a direct lineal descendant of Domhnall O'Sullivan Beare, whose daughter married a Sugrue ancestor of the priest's grandmother Anne Sugrue (the latter being also an ancestor of the present author).[24]

Ancient Kenmare and Glanerought

At the eastern, inland end of Kenmare Bay, the little River Roughty flows out from a glen called Gleann Ó Ruachta; this was anglicised to Glanerought and served as the name of the old 'barony', or former county division. Here, on the bay's south shore, near Sheen Falls, is an ancient holy well, a ruined church and the old Kenmare cemetery. On the north shore, from 1775, the present town of Kenmare was developed at a location previously known as (An) Neidín, or 'Nedeen'.

Kenmare Bay is also shown on maps as 'Kenmare River', although it is not in fact a river. It is bordered by two great peninsulas that extend west from Kenmare town for more than 50 kilometres into the Atlantic Ocean. While the bay's southern shore is the Beara Peninsula, on the northern side lies the Iveragh Peninsula ('The Ring of Kerry'). Here are Ireland's highest mountains, including Carrauntoohill and Mangerton. Kenmare House (later Killarney House), principal residence of the Browne family, Earls of Kenmare, was erected on the shore of Lough Leane about 35 kilometres north-east of Kenmare town. The Browne estate lay outside the Kenmare parish and poor law union districts.

People have settled around Kenmare Bay for millennia. Seán Ó Nualláin describes ancient stone circles lying in an arc from Kenmare town across to the Beara Peninsula as being of 'exceptional interest and importance', and draws attention to their proximity to copper deposits. One notable axis, no longer completely extant, extended north-eastwards from the 'Giant's Ring' or 'Druid's Circle' at Reennagappul on the western side of Kenmare town through a row of standing stones to Killowen – and on again to the former site of another fine stone circle and what, in 1841, O'Donovan described as 'a very remarkable *Gallán* or standing stone'. Surrounded by several smaller stones, this was Gallán na Cille Bige (i.e. 'the pillar of the small church').[25] The small church itself was one of a number of old Christian sites in the area; there are also the remains of castles and towers that were visited or sacked by English armies years before Kenmare town was founded. Older than these is Staigue Fort. The Anglo-Irish landlord on whose property this stone fort stood – 45 kilometres west of Kenmare – reported on it appreciatively in 1825 for the *Proceedings of the Royal Irish Academy*.[26] There is also a long history of local seafaring connections with Britain, Spain and other European coastal countries, and with the Americas. The Gaelic chiefs O'Sullivan Beare and O'Sullivan Mór partly sustained that trade, an account of which was given in the 1750s by an author believed to have been both an O'Sullivan from Kerry and a lay friar living in Louvain. Connections with Kerry that bypassed Britain persisted, with researchers still uncovering today their extent in soldiering, trade and smuggling, among other activities.[27]

The Ring of Kerry

When John O'Sullivan arrived in Kenmare in 1839, there was no easy way west around the coast of the Iveragh Peninsula – no clear 'Ring of Kerry', as the later paved road would become known. The Frenchman entering Kerry near Kenmare in 1790 noticed the use of the *cárr slaodha*, a kind of sleigh, on terrain unsuited to wheels.[28] In 1807 Isaac Weld acknowledged that the horses he used locally near Kenmare were better adapted than some finer specimens to the rough terrain, but in 1829 the Romantic poet William Wordsworth wrote irritably of riding from Kenmare to Glengarriff 'on a vile Irish hack horse [...] over vile roads'.[29]

In 1822, a surgeon coming from Cork met 'a great many little farmers driving their stunted horses with back-loads of butter, three casks each, to the Cork market. In this way, almost all the butter made in Kerry is conveyed to Cork, each horse carrying about three hundredweight – a distance sometimes of more than a hundred miles.'[30] A Silesian prince and friend of Goethe visited Kenmare in 1828; he described in vivid terms his journey west from there on horseback, at night and in the rain, to visit Daniel O'Connell at Derrynane. It was a perilous journey of 30 miles that took him almost 8 hours. Much of Iveragh was impassable by wheeled cart, and on his return he met men with loads of stones, planks, beer and butter, all being conveyed on the backs of horses. He described the 'ingenious' means by which locals transported such goods.[31]

A modern road south from Kenmare into Co. Cork opened only just as O'Sullivan came to the town in 1839. Travellers setting out to use it crossed Kenmare Bay by a suspension bridge, which had been constructed against strong advice that a stone bridge would last longer.[32] This bridge over the sound allowed funerals to pass easily from the new town to old Kenmare cemetery near Sheen Falls. The new road south climbed over the mountains and through new tunnels, or 'galleries', to Bantry Bay. Among the earliest to travel its whole length, from Co. Cork to Kenmare, were Samuel Carter Hall and Anna Maria Hall, who emerged from the tunnels and observed sunlight gleaming on houses far below. They reported that, previously, people who had not wished to walk or ride ponies over the mountains were 'compelled to order carriages from Kenmare to meet them at the Kerry side of the mountain; or, as was usually done, hire five or six stout peasants from Glengarriff to carry the car on their shoulders over rocks and along precipices exceedingly dangerous from the want of a protecting wall'.[33]

The principal connection to Kenmare then was still from Killarney. Yet as late as 1846 it was only thanks to the services of a horse-drawn car that plied daily to Kenmare, leaving Killarney after the Dublin mail-coach arrived there, that the town could be reached from Dublin in just ... 25 hours![34]

2

Macaulay's Myth:
Settlers and 'Kerry Savages', 1655–1855

'I thought to have lain down and died under my Kerry calamities,' declared Sir William Petty in 1679.[35] From 1655, Petty – an English physician and administrator in Cromwellian Ireland – identified himself closely with the country's governor, who was Oliver Cromwell's son Henry. Petty was entrusted with planning and managing the redistribution of lands forfeited to the authorities by their Irish owners, and he personally benefited from that confiscation. He also survived the restoration of monarchy in 1660, being confirmed as a landlord of confiscated holdings around Kenmare Bay and elsewhere. The Kerry historian Mary Hickson thought that it was dangerous for a native Irish person even to be seen at times in the Iveragh Peninsula between 1650 and 1675.[36] One of Petty's contemporaries wrote that from Mangerton mountain, near Kenmare, Petty could now survey 50,000 acres of land of which he was master. That did not amount to even one fifth of all his land in Kerry.[37] He was a clever man, who was sketched by Edwin Sandys for the Dublin Philosophical Society in 1683.[38] Reputedly offered a noble title on condition that he would pay for it, he declined on the grounds that he would 'rather be a copper farthing of intrinsic value than a brass half-crown'.[39] However, his descendants accepted elevation to the peerage as the earls of Shelburne and lords Lansdowne. In 1849 Thomas Babington Macaulay, the popular English historian who owed his seat in parliament to the then Lord Lansdowne, was to forge for Kenmare, in his *History of England*, a foundation myth that flattered Petty and his decendants – as will be seen.

Sir William Petty (1623–1687) did not found the town of Kenmare, for which credit may be given to his descendant and namesake William Petty (1737–1805). Nevertheless, Sir William did create a British Protestant settlement in the area, where some of his settlers exploited fishery resources that had long provided employment and food, and had

Fig. 1. Sir William Petty (1623–1687), by Edwin Sandys, Dublin, 1683. From Hiberniae delineatio *(published London, 1685).*

been the basis of trade with Spain and France.[40] Others engaged in mining, an activity of which there is local evidence from prehistoric times. In 1666 Petty also directed his agent 'to bring in English and Protestant workmen in the greatest number possible' to build him ironworks in which furnaces were to be fed by big trees from the nearby great forests. His efforts were dogged by difficulties. Visiting the county and coping with its terrain and inhabitants soon wore him out.[41]

According to Richard Orpen, one of his leading settlers, Petty's Kerry colony amounted to about 815 people at its very peak. Most of these were driven out during the wars of the late 1680s. Petty was not seen in Ireland thereafter. His descendants, although big landlords of Kerry, were rarely to visit the county. Some of his colonists returned to Kerry after William of Orange defeated King James at the Battle of the Boyne, but in 1694 'not above 75 of those Protestants were left in being' as farmers or landlords – in an uneasy relationship with the local people.[42] The latter still occupied much land around Kenmare Bay, although now in law as tenants or subtenants of Petty's family. From 1697 the principal tenants were Richard Orpen, who also functioned as Petty's agent, and one John O'Mahony. The latter was an unconverted Catholic, a member of an old family long resident in the area and thus liable to suffer confiscation. Accordingly, he arranged his interest by way of an informal trust that was in the Protestant Orpen's name. Later members of this O'Mahony/Mahony family conformed to the Anglican Church in order to consolidate and secure their extensive holdings, and one at Dromore Castle became Fr John O'Sullivan's foe.[43] Orpen also sublet land to local Catholic families by way of what became known as 'great leases', the terms of which suited all parties.[44] A large majority of the population around Kenmare Bay continued to be Gaelic in descent and, until the late nineteenth century, Irish-speaking.

The settler William Petty attempted to be fair about what other English adventurers represented as moral weakness in the defeated Irish population. In a remarkable passage he excused certain Irish Catholic behaviour that affronted worldly English Protestants, and he acknowledged both the impact of restraints on Irish trade and the uncertain manner in which landholders could be deprived of their rights and property:

> Their lazing seems to me to proceed rather from want of employment and encouragement to work, than from the natural abundance of flegm in their bowels and blood; for what need they to work, who can content themselves with potatoes, whereof the labour of one man can feed forty; and with milk, whereof one cow will, in summer time, give meat and drink enough for three men, when they can everywhere gather cockles, oysters, muscles, crabs, &c. with boats, nets, angles, or the art of fishing; can build an house in three days? And why should they desire to fare better, tho' with more labour, when they are taught that this way of living is more like the patriarchs of old, and the saints of later times, by whose prayers and merits they are to be reliev'd, and whose examples they are therefore to follow? And why should they breed more cattle, since 'tis penal to import them into England? Why should they raise more commodities, since there are not merchants sufficiently stock'd to take them of them, nor provided with other more pleasing foreign commodities, to give in exchange for them? And how should merchants have stock, since trade is prohibited and fetter'd by the statutes of England? And

why should men endeavour to get estates, where the legislative power is not agreed upon; and where tricks and words destroy natural Right and Property? They are accused also of much treachery, falseness, and thievery; none of all which, I conceive, is natural to them; for as to treachery, they are made believe that they all shall flourish again, after some time […] they have in their hearts, not only a grudging to see their old proprieties [landed property] enjoyed by foreigners, but a persuasion they shall be shortly restor'd.[45]

Petty's was an honest acknowledgement of the traumatic changes visited on Ireland by himself and other English adventurers in the seventeenth century. As time passed, not all who wrote about Kenmare's past were as interested in such details.

Macaulay's Kerry myth

Thomas Babington Macaulay was a prominent and popular English historian of his era and a Whig politician. He was a protégé of Lord Lansdowne, who had seen to it that his fellow Whig Macaulay was returned to parliament in 1830 for a borough in Wiltshire that was virtually in Lansdowne's gift. Macaulay was also a brother-in-law of Charles Trevelyan, the senior Treasury official central to Irish famine relief with whom Fr O'Sullivan stayed when visiting London in 1847, and in whose house the priest met two of Macaulay's sisters, as will be seen. Macaulay even lived with the Trevelyans for a while and is thought to have advised Trevelyan on the latter's signal article about the Irish crisis that was published in the *Edinburgh Review*. Macaulay found space in his four-volume *History of England* for an account of the colonisation of Kenmare that aligned progress in Ireland with the broader British imperialist enterprise and that sketched out a simplistic and linear version of the town's history.

Macaulay did not admire Ireland or the Irish; he gritted his teeth when visiting the country in August 1849, coming principally to inspect battle sites of the war between King James and William of Orange at Derry and the Boyne. He also briefly visited Cork, Killarney and Limerick. He had already published the first two volumes of his *History of England* to great acclaim in Britain.[46] The next two volumes, which included his account of Kenmare, were to appear in 1855. On Macaulay's arrival in 1849, the *Daily News* reported Irish scholarly claims that his first volumes contained errors about Ireland due to his reliance on a partisan text – namely King's *State of the Protestants,* 'that has ceased to be regarded as an authority for facts'.[47] Macaulay is thought to have undertaken little or no original research on sources in Ireland.[48] His account of Kenmare is one of brave and industrious English Protestants doing their best in the face of feckless and resentful Catholic natives. His narrative diminishes Gaelic culture in a manner that is at one with his attitude towards native populations in parts of the world, such as India, that were being colonised by the British as he wrote. Macaulay himself had already served in the imperial service in India. In his account of Kenmare, he ignored the impact of the great famine on Kerry; it was still devastating Ireland, though it lay outside the period about which he wrote. This is ironic given that, about this time, John Partridge painted Macaulay reading Canto 21 of the Inferno, which has Dante admitting that there are things 'of which I do not care to sing' even as he and Virgil gaze upon a scene in hell as black as pitch. Macaulay came to Kerry, gazed upon misery, but decided that neither the famine nor a version of Kenmare history unfavourable to British aspirations belonged in his work.

Half-naked savages

Macaulay was not writing a disinterested account of the past. His brother-in-law Charles Trevelyan, in Whitehall, had expressly urged him to make his Irish history instructive. What Macaulay wrote bolstered a contemporary narrative in Britain that saw progress and the expansion of empire as correlated.[49] He also defined Ireland possessively as a *British* island notwithstanding its distinct culture and history and its status within a united kingdom of Britain *and* Ireland:

> The southwestern part of Kerry is now well known as the most beautiful tract in the British isles. The mountains, the glens, the capes stretching far into the Atlantic, the crags on which the eagles build, the rivulets brawling down rocky passes, the lakes overhung by groves in which the wild deer find covert, attract every summer crowds of wanderers sated with the business and the pleasures of great cities. The beauties of that country are indeed too often hidden in the mist and rain which the west wind brings up from a boundless ocean.

His Kerry is exotic and wild, a part of Britain but not like it. His is the sort of 'remoteness' that can distance the metropolis from the consequences of its actions overseas; one is reminded of a Kerry land agent's joke about an Arctic explorer who 'had never been to Killarney because it was so far off'.[50] Kenmare is even further. Yet, as already noted, in and around Kenmare are many remnants of settlements and monuments, stretching back far more than a thousand years, that attest to a long history of mobility and change.

One notable visitor to Kerry before the arrival of Petty or Macaulay was Giovanni Battista Rinuccini, the pope's ambassador to the rebellious Irish Catholics of the Confederation of Kilkenny. He formed quite a different impression from that of Macaulay. In October 1645, five years before the Cromwellian William Petty first came to Ireland, Rinuccini landed in Kenmare Bay, having escaped pursuit by English vessels. He was making a dangerous and surreptitious journey from Rome to Kilkenny, but on the way he found respite in Kerry; here, he and his party were welcomed warmly by a large crowd of local people when they disembarked near the head of Kenmare Bay. He stayed the first night in a cabin in which some animals also sheltered, 'I however rejoiced greatly that fortune had brought me to a sterile and unknown part of the country [...] the most barren and unfrequented spot in Munster.'[51] Admiring the beauty of the area, one of his party wrote that the 'courtesy of the poor people' was 'unexampled', as they brought the visitors beef, mutton, pork, 'excellent fish and oysters of most prodiguous size in the utmost abundance', along with beer, butter and milk so delicious that 'I drank copiously of it.'[52]

Rinuccini had imported a large quantity of arms purchased in France for the rebels, and these were temporarily stored nearby at the MacFineen (MacFinian) MacCarthy castle of Ardtully – between Kenmare and Kilgarvan – from where he wrote to Rome. O'Sullivan Beare and O'Sullivan Mór came to greet Rinuccini, and armed men escorted him on his onward journey across the mountains. He was carried in a litter because he could not ride a horse on that terrain. His companion from Italy wrote that the country through which they passed as they left Kerry in 1645, 'being entirely pasture-land, is most abundantly stocked with cattle of every kind, interspersed with woods and groves; which as they are neither high nor densely planted, partake more of the agreeable than of the gloomy'.[53] Macaulay swept aside such history:

> During the greater part of the seventeenth century, this paradise
> was as little known to the civilised world as Spitzbergen or
> Greenland. If ever it was mentioned, it was mentioned as a
> horrible desert, a chaos of bogs, thickets, and precipices, where
> the she-wolf still littered, and where some half naked savages, who

could not speak a word of English, made themselves burrows in the mud, and lived on roots and sour milk.

Macaulay has deftly turned his glens, groves and 'crags on which the eagles build' – so sublime, so primitive, so picturesque for his contemporary tourists – into 'a horrible desert' domain of the she-wolf (her very uncontrolled femininity presumably more threatening than the masculine he-wolf). In Macaulay's version, Kerry awaited the civilising victory of English colonisers over 'half naked savages'.

Macaulay celebrated a special moment in the area's past: when Sir William Petty took possession of thousands of acres in Co. Kerry that later passed to the 3rd Marquess of Lansdowne – Macaulay's political patron (whom the historian described as 'a posterity worthy of such an ancestor'). In commemorating the event, Macaulay conflated Petty's seventeenth-century troubled settlement with the much later town of Kenmare:

> At length, in the year 1670, the benevolent and enlightened Sir William Petty determined to form an English settlement in this wild district. He possessed a large domain there, which has descended to a posterity worthy of such an ancestor. On the improvement of that domain he expended, it was said, not less than ten thousand pounds. The little town that he founded, named from the bay of Kenmare, stood at the head of that bay, under a mountain ridge, on the summit of which travellers now stop to gaze upon the loveliest of the three lakes of Killarney.

Sir William Petty did not found Kenmare town. Insofar as he founded any settlement, it consisted of some dwellings and a Protestant church at Killowen (Irish: Church of John), which was to the east of the later town of Kenmare and where the ruin of an earlier little chapel of St John the Baptist stood. Such English settlements were an aspect of what has been termed 'the westward enterprise' – that purportedly civilising expansion by England that embraced North America and its natives.[54] Macaulay wrote:

> Scarcely any village, built by an enterprising band of New Englanders, far from the dwellings of their countrymen, in the midst of the hunting grounds of the Red Indians, was more completely out of the pale of civilisation than Kenmare. Between Petty's settlement and the nearest English habitation the journey by land was of two days through a wild and dangerous country. Yet

the place prospered [...] The neighbourhood of Kenmare was then richly wooded; and Petty found it a gainful speculation to send ore thither [as well as mine it]. The lovers of the picturesque still regret the woods of oak and arbutus which were cut down to feed his furnaces.

Macaulay was explicitly writing a *History of England*. The readership that he aimed to impress was a British one that was benefiting greatly from its burgeoning empire. He offered no evidence that 'the place prospered' then, and Petty himself complained bitterly of the difficulties. In 1937 Petty's descendant, the 6th Marquess of Lansdowne, rejected Macaulay's implication that Petty 'found the country a forest and left it, as a result of his activities, a wilderness'. The marquess pointed out that there was abundant evidence that the woods were being cut down by the native Irish before Petty had arrived, and that the natives continued to take trees despite efforts to control their felling.[55] This was not simply virgin forest awaiting Petty's entrepreneurial hand. Between 1557 and 1668, for example, there had been 'a strange destruction of woods, and vast number of pipe hogshead and barrel stave exported'.[56] Nevertheless, Petty's ironworks did accelerate the process of deforestation begun by native entrepreneurs. Thus, John O'Donovan, in 1841, quoted a manuscript of 'about a century and a half since [i.e. *c.*1690]' which stated that Glanerought 'was formerly very woody, affording most stately timber, but now it is mostly destroyed by the devouring iron works'.[57]

Aliens and envy

In the 1680s – with King James II not yet deposed and replaced on the throne by King William, and with the decisive battle of the Boyne yet to be fought – 'natives' attacked the new settlement at Kenmare. As Hickson pointed out in 1872, 'the great historian' (as she deemed Macaulay) derived his information on this incident from a rare pamphlet attributed to Richard Orpen, 'one of the chief gentlemen of the colony' but scarcely an unbiased source.[58] While Macaulay acknowledged that there possibly was provocation on the English side, he turned this into a compliment to the colonists by attributing it to the temptation of 'superior intelligence'. He defined the land occupied by settlers around Kenmare, which had been in the hands of locals before they were dispossessed, as 'a booty of the children of the soil' when locals retrieved it:

In the eyes of the peasantry of Munster the colonists were aliens and heretics. The buildings, the boats, the machines, the granaries, the dairies, the furnaces, were doubtless contemplated by the native race with that mingled envy and contempt with which the ignorant naturally regard the triumphs of knowledge. Nor is it at all improbable that the emigrants had been guilty of those faults from which civilised men who settle among an uncivilised people are rarely free. The power derived from superior intelligence had, we may easily believe, been sometimes displayed with insolence, and sometimes exerted with injustice. Now therefore, when the news spread from altar to altar, and from cabin to cabin, that the strangers were to be driven out, and that their houses and lands were to be given as a booty to the children of the soil, a predatory war commenced.

Was this war any more 'predatory' than the one waged across Ireland that had yielded so many acres of Kerry to Petty and other adventurers? Surrounded at the 'White House' that had been built for Richard Orpen, and outnumbered, the colonists now surrendered. They were not slaughtered – as the women and children of followers of Domhnall O'Sullivan Beare on Dursey Island had been by the English, or the defenders of Drogheda had been by Petty's former chief, Oliver Cromwell – but were allowed to leave. The description of how they left, penned by Macaulay – who has been described by one biographer as 'artful' and 'cunning'[59] – insinuates a parallel with emotive accounts of those fleeing the great famine (as at the time that Macaulay visited Ireland, these emigrants, hungry and thirsty, were being crowded for six weeks or more into the holds of 'coffin-ships' sailing to America):

> The colonists were suffered to embark in a small vessel scantily supplied with food and water. They had no experienced navigator on board: but after a voyage of a fortnight, during which they were crowded together like slaves in a Guinea ship, and suffered the extremity of thirst and hunger, they reached Bristol in safety.

Macaulay's is an inexact rendering of Richard Orpen's own eyewitness version. For Orpen tells of two barques, not 'one small vessel'. Just thirty-six of forty-two remaining families boarded these. Orpen claimed that the settlers had been promised before surrendering that they could leave the kingdom of Ireland, but that they were subsequently kept in harbour for eight days, 'packed like fish upon one another', until forced to agree that they would sail only as far as Cork. His version cannot be independently verified. Nevertheless, Orpen wrote that, once on the ocean, he and the others chose to chance crossing the Irish Sea 'rather than come again under the hands of the Papists [at Cork], whose mercies are very Cruelties'. They had not been 'suffered' to go to Bristol. They went despite the fact that 'the masters of the ships were not expert in navigation, but were skilful only in coasting about those western [Irish] ports'; Orpen reported that three people died from exposure and hardship.[60] While Orpen's account makes a good story, and the colonists were undoubtedly fearful and aggrieved at being dispossessed, Macaulay has not just relied on a partisan source but also manipulated it.

Following the defeat of King James in 1690, a minority of Petty's settlers returned to Kenmare Bay, but Petty himself did not. However, Petty and his descendants, the lords Lansdowne, long continued as ultimate landlords in the Kenmare area. They sublet largely to local people who further sublet to undertenants. A second well-known polemical English historian, J.A. Froude, was also to come to Kerry in the nineteenth century. Citing Macaulay, Froude too addressed the local Cromwellian legacy for a British readership – doing so, as will be seen, in a manner that earned the scorn of Oscar Wilde.

Mother dead in workhouse

When he visited Kerry in 1849, Macaulay privately described people there as 'scarecrows'. He could not avoid seeing and 'almost touching' them. He found that 'the beggary is worse than that of the worst governed parts of the continent that I have ever seen', and thought that '"Give me a halfpenny" is the cry of the whole rising generation of Kerry.' Macaulay told his sister Hannah, wife of Charles Trevelyan, that children followed him everywhere crying, 'Give me a halfpenny – mother dead in workhouse.' Their strange appearance, he wrote, 'sometimes made me laugh, and yet I could hardly help crying. But what use is there in making oneself miserable.'

Despite witnessing such poverty in Kerry, Macaulay was not diverted into a critical analysis of past British actions, nor did he subvert the broader narrative of providential imperialism that he was to spin so persuasively for both his and future generations of Englishmen.[61] It is said that in his *History of England*, he enunciated a doctrine of co-operation in British politics 'to please Englishmen of both parties'.[62] His vignette of the history of Kenmare within that influential work presumably achieved the same end. Macaulay's history was no doubt reassuring to his patron Lord Lansdowne, who never once visited Kerry during the famine but whose family – according to Griffith's valuation of 1852 – still held some 96,800 acres of the county.

3

The Foundation of Kenmare Town, 1775–1839

In 1692 William Petty's only daughter Anne Petty married Thomas Fitzmaurice, who was later made 1st Earl of Kerry and who was the descendant of an Anglo-Norman or Cambro-Norman family long settled in Ireland. Since settling, its ancestral blood had been continually and thoroughly mixed through marriage with that of old Gaelic families. Anne and Thomas had a son, John, born in 1706. When grown to middle age, John ceased to use his surname, Fitzmaurice, and instead legally adopted that of his mother, Petty. He did so in 1751 because his mother's brother Henry Petty, the 2nd Earl of Shelburn (whose late brother Charles had been the 1st Earl of Shelburn), made this change a condition of John's inheriting Petty estates.

According to the Petty family in 1721, their estates in Kerry were 'for the most part inhabited by roman catholics, who living very far from courts of law, and justice, had hitherto acted without any regard to either'. The family gave lawlessness as the reason that it had not been possible for it to 'reclaim' the lands, on which there were 'considerable woods' that had been 'almost destroyed' by local people. Henry Petty had assured the King that 'he had nothing more at heart than the planting the said county with Protestants, and making the said papists in some measure amenable to the law.' As Anne's son John Fitzmaurice had complied with the terms of his uncle Henry's will by changing his surname, the King was pleased to advance this 'John Petty' to the title Viscount Fitz-Maurice and then, in 1753, to create him 1st Earl of Shelburne (with a last letter 'e' added to differentiate his new title from the 'Shelburn' earldom that Anne's brothers previously held).[63]

John's own son, William Petty (1737–1805), 2nd Earl of Shelburne and a Whig politician, briefly served as the British prime minister in 1782–83. Born in Dublin, his peers in London are said to have seen him as 'a pushy Irish upstart'. In 1784 William was created the 1st

Marquess of Lansdowne as a reward for his services in negotiating peace to end the American war of independence. He acquired Bowood estate in Wiltshire, which has served ever since as the Lansdowne family home.[64] Immensely wealthy, he seldom came to Ireland but occasionally took an active interest in the exploitation of his Irish acres. The reformer and philosopher Jeremy Bentham, William's acquaintance through the Bowood circle, thought that William was 'muddle-headed, with a tendency to embrace grand schemes without fully understanding them'. One of his schemes was the planning of Kenmare town.[65]

Founding a town at Neidín

No town stood on the site of modern Kenmare until the present one began to rise there from the late eighteenth century. In his history of Kerry published in the mid-eighteenth century, Charles Smith used the name Kenmare to refer only to a district or parish and to a stretch of water, not to a town. When Smith wrote, there was a small settlement at Killowen, a little east of the present town of Kenmare. It included a Protestant church, the rector of which was then Thomas Orpen (died 1768). He was the son of Petty's agent Richard Orpen, and of Isabelle Palmer, and lived by the shore in the 'White House' erected for his father. This was the building where forty-two settler families (consisting of 180 persons) are said to have sought shelter before most of them were driven out in the 1680s. It is a ruin today.[66] Reverend Thomas connived with the Petty family to deprive the leading tenants of Kenmare and Tuosist of the terms of the beneficial leases that Richard Orpen had agreed with them – a fact that demonstrates how such leases were not perpetual trusts.[67] Smith, writing in the 1750s, observed that Rev. Thomas Orpen was then living

> with a colony of Protestant families, consisting of shop-carpenters, rope-makers, smiths, &c. who are very necessary in supplying the fishing vessels that frequent the trade of this river; for it abounds with cod, hake, mackerel, ling, herring, and divers other kinds of fish; which are taken by a considerable number of boats, sometimes to the amount of an hundred, which assemble here from Kinsale, and the western coasts of Ireland; who fish about the island of the Durseys, and up Kenmare river, from April to September; and take and cure sometimes considerable quantities for foreign markets.[68]

The location of the present town of Kenmare and its contingent area, on the northern side of the bay, was then known generally as Neidín (also 'An Neidín', anglicised as 'Ned[h]een'); Patrick Joyce has translated this as 'little nest', with the last two letters being understood as the usual Irish diminutive.[69] Nevertheless, the late Sister Philomena McCarthy wrote, 'More than one historian believes that the name Nedeen is a corruption of Nead Fhionn – a place where Fionn rested.' Fionn Mac Cumhaill was the leader of the legendary Fianna, and Oisín was his son. She added that local tradition identifies one location (a rock at the Shrubberies in Kenmare) as 'Finn's Cradle', and she wrote that 'It is very likely that the River Sheen was originally *Abha Oisín*. The "O" disappeared in the translation as it did in Ballaghisheen (*Bealach Oisín*) the scenic mountain pass above Kenmare through which Oisín rode on his way to *Tír na nÓg*.' The names Fionan and Finghin were 'widely used' by McCarthys and O'Sullivans in the area.[70] The ancient holy spring, or 'well', that emerges onto the seashore below the old cemetery of Kenmare is known as St Finian's, reputedly after an early Irish Christian, and Finnihy is the name of a local river.[71]

The ancient ruined chapel in the old Kenmare cemetery has also been popularly known as St Finian's. However, during a dispute over access to the graveyard in 1858, Fr Denis O'Donoghue, curate of Kenmare and sometime secretary of the Munster section of the Royal Society of Antiquaries, described the 'crumbling ruin' as 'the old church of the Invention of the Holy Cross'.[72] When the scholarly John O'Donovan visited the old Kenmare site in 1841, he found that 'patterns' (traditional folk festivities associated with the patron, or figure, to whom a holy place is dedicated) had been held annually at it on 3 May and 14 September 'until 20 years since when they were abolished; but stations are nevertheless still performed at St Finan's [*sic*] well, and many diseases are cured by its sacred waters.'[73] On each of those particular dates, the Christian church in Europe used to celebrate the feast of the 'Invention' or finding (Latin: *invenire/inventus*) of the true cross of Jesus by Saint Helena, mother of Emperor Constantine, in the fourth century. The first was the older of the two feast days, and it coincided with the Celtic quarterly festival of Bealtaine at the start of May. The present church in Kenmare, which Fr John O'Sullivan built, is named Holy Cross.

Neidín was said to have been the location of a fort before Petty's arrival, and a barracks was built there in 1735 for a half company of soldiers. This was used only intermittently.[74] Besides this barracks –

before 1800 – there was only a small hamlet of houses to be found here. The editor of a guide to Britain and Ireland, published in Dublin in 1757, did not reference any settlement at Kenmare – merely a large bay of the sea 'vulgarly called Kilmare'.[75] Records before then show no town of that name.[76] Nevertheless, during the 1770s William Petty, 2nd Earl of Shelburne, envisaged improvements here. He thought the location of Neidín 'wonderfully calculated for trade'.[77] His new Kerry-born estate agent, Joseph Taylor, may have been unconvinced. After having taken up residence in nearby Dunkerron in 1773, Taylor reported, 'The Fair at Nedeen has been very indifferent – scarcely anything sold at it but sheep. The whole Country seems miserably poor [...] Beggars and Idle people without any kind of employment lounging about in filth and nastiness without thought or the least inclination to Labour or Industry.'[78]

Petty inspected his Kerry estate in 1764 and 1772, and again in 1775 when the construction of a substantial house, which he had commissioned more than a decade earlier and which later became known as 'Lansdowne Lodge', was finally completed at Neidín.[79] During that visit of 1775, he expressed the opinion that 'the poor people are oppress'd to the greatest degree, and are become in consequence timid and lying.' He took steps to improve the area, asking a Munster merchant, Thomas Trant, to draw up a plan for establishing a town at Neidín. Trant appears to have suggested to him that the name Neidín be changed to Shelburnstown, Kenmare, Bell Port or 'some English name in order to engage foreigners'. Petty now 'directed immediately the name of Nedeen, which I [Petty] found signified in Irish a Nest of Thieves, to be chang'd for that of Kenmare'. Petty's descendant, the 6th Marquess of Lansdowne, later observed, '"Nedeen" is the Irish for "little nest"; the suggestion that it meant a "nest of thieves" must have been made to please Shelburne!'[80] The English agricultural reformer Arthur Young did not register the recent change of name when he visited Kenmare later in the 1770s. He wrote simply, 'Nedeen is a little town, very well situated [...] there are but three or four good houses. Lord Shelburne, to whom the place belongs, has built one for his agent.'[81]

A visitor in 1809 wrote that Neidín was still the most common name locally for the 'small and straggling town'. Even the Office of Ordnance, when seeking tenders nationally, gave 'Neddeen' as an alternative for Kenmare – this was as late as 1823.[82] It continued to be used by Irish speakers with, as John Windele explained in 1839, 'Nad-

Fion, i.e. the cave or nest of Fion or Fingal; a cave near the town being still pointed out as the retreat of that redoubtable hero.'[83] Ireland and the western isles of Scotland were once steeped in a cycle of heroic stories about Fionn, the wise and noble warriors of the Fianna and their poet Oisín. Legends provided perspective and inspiration for people struggling against the imposition of an alien culture. That such tales long survived as part of an oral tradition is not surprising; the written word scarcely impinged on most of the population, and its effect was even more marginal on the poor in Kerry. During the 1930s the Folklore Commission found stories of Fionn still extant locally.[84] Even today the official Irish name of Kenmare is 'Neidín'.[85]

Shortly after Petty named his planned town Kenmare in 1775, he approved the development of a central triangular block constituted by three new streets named William (now Main), Shelburne and Sound (also Henry). He noted that 'the priest wants a Mass House or leave to build one, which requires consideration.'[86] The Frenchman visiting in 1790 found still fewer than twenty houses there. He also met the local parish priest, James Kennedy, whom he described as an excellent man. Kennedy's only chapel then was a converted ruin in the old burial ground out in Templenoe, 7 kilometres distant. He eventually received permission for a 'Mass House'; to this end, a new chapel of St John the Baptist was constructed a little south of Shelburne Street.[87]

In Weld's account of Kerry, published in 1807, a map showed the 'principal place of trade' on Kenmare Bay only as 'Nedheen', although the book's text gave both 'Nedheen' and 'Kenmare-town' as alternatives. Arriving late one night, Weld found himself in 'a miserable public house: It is a very small town; and, though we observed some new houses, has, on the whole, an appearance of decay.' Yet the place was changing, and in 1809 a visiting British naturalist and porcelain manufacturer, Lewis Weston Dillwyn, saw the chapel 'nearly finished', thinking it 'handsome'.[88] The subsequent development of the town was driven by the rise of a merchant class in Ireland that had the resources to invest in building there.

The 3rd Marquess of Lansdowne

When William Petty, 2nd Earl of Shelburne, was also made the 1st Marquess of Lansdowne in 1784, his family's properties became known as the Lansdowne estate. The estate allowed Fr James Kennedy 20 acres just outside Kenmare, rent free, for a presbytery. It was here that Fr John O'Sullivan would live when he came to Kenmare in 1839.[89]

O'Sullivan later wrote that he had heard many curious stories of
Kennedy:

> He was one of the first that condescended to give his curates a
> glass of punch after dinner and that was only on Sunday evening.
> They would then so draw the poor man out that more would be
> drunk in the one night than is now drunk by us for the week. He
> was an oddity but he must have had the spirit of the Priesthood.[90]

Scattered throughout O'Sullivan's journals are many such lively
references to Kerry priests, some of them sharp pen-pictures.

In 1805 William Petty died and was succeeded by his son John. John
himself died in 1809, aged just 44, and was succeeded in turn by his half-
brother Henry (1780–1863), who thus became the 3rd Marquess of
Lansdowne as known to Fr John O'Sullivan. By styling himself Petty-
Fitzmaurice, Henry now readopted the Fitzmaurice family name that his
father's father had changed to Petty in order to qualify for an
inheritance. Henry appears to have visited his Kerry properties only five
times, the last occasion being in 1840 – more than two decades before
he died. In 1858 it was said, 'Even still those who recollect the fine, stately,
courteous and affable gentleman, who eighteen years ago paid a visit to
his Kerry property, cling to the belief that, did he thoroughly understand
how matters really are, he would prefer sacrificing a small portion of his
great wealth, to having it wrung as it is from the misery of his poor
dependents.'[91] He spent his days far removed from Kenmare, between
London and his country home in Wiltshire. Appointed Chancellor of
the Exchequer in his mid-twenties, he became a senior and sophisticated
Whig politician who was unconstrained by strict party lines. His
reputation and social position 'enabled him to facilitate the larger,
constitutional process of government in which success was measured in
terms of the smooth interaction of all parts of the mixed constitution'.[92]
A later Lansdowne descendant wrote a very readable account of his
ancestors' involvement in the Kenmare area. This was the 6th Marquess
of Lansdowne, also named Henry Petty-Fitzmaurice, who was a respected
historian in his own right and once read a paper before the Royal Irish
Academy. He was also a member of the senate of the Irish Free State
from 1922 to 1929.[93]

A middle-class

The town itself grew gradually. Its development owed at least as much
to an expanding Irish bourgeoisie – Catholic as well as Protestant – as

it did to the Lansdownes. Prominent among middle-class businessmen and shopkeepers who helped to build it was the merchant and smuggler Eugene Downing. His mother was an O'Sullivan of Dunkerron in Templenoe, and he had broad commercial interests. In 1817 he decorated his house in the town in what was described as a 'conspicuously brilliant' manner in order to welcome Sir Francis Burdett, the radical MP and supporter of Catholic rights. Over Downing's balcony 'was placed a transparency, representing the Genius of Ireland, reclining on a Harp'. One newspaper reported that Burdett was met at Kenmare by eighty young girls dressed in white and some five hundred men sporting laurel branches in their hats, and was serenaded by fiddlers and pipers and 'presented with a shamrock wreath by a very pretty boy'. It is a rare and vibrant glimpse of life in the new town at this time. Catholics and Protestants joined in festivities for Burdett that lasted late into the night; 'the town was in a blaze of light' emitted by a burning pyramid of turf surmounted by a tar barrel and other illuminations.[94] In the 1820s and 1830s, Eugene Downing and his brother Simon undertook much of the construction in Kenmare. The children of Eugene and his wife Helena (Nellie) McCarthy included the attorneys Francis Henry Downing (Lord Lansdowne's legal adviser) and Timothy McCarthy Downing MP.[95] Some fifty merchants and tradesmen were listed under Kenmare in Pigot's *Provincial Directory* of 1824.

The old barracks was acquired by the 1st Lord Lansdowne for use as an estate revenue office but came to serve, as Samuel Lewis noted, as 'a commodious court-house, in which the assistant barrister of the county holds sessions twice a year, and the seneschal, also, his court'.[96] In 1837 Lewis wrote that 'The town, formerly called Nedeen [...] consists chiefly of one wide street of neat and well-built houses, from which another diverges towards [the new suspension bridge across] the sound. The number of houses in 1831 was 170, and since that period several others have been erected.' In 1839, the year in which O'Sullivan arrived as parish priest, Windele observed that until recently Kenmare had 'remained little better than a miserable village', but that it 'is at this day, a thriving and increasing town [...] its growth has been of very great rapidity.'[97] The famine was to stunt that growth, with the 1851 census finding 201 houses, an increase of just 31 in twenty years.[98]

4

John O'Sullivan: A Tralee Youth, 1807–1830

'I was born on 23rd of January 1807 in the town of Tralee in Bridge Street.' So Fr John O'Sullivan began his 'Random Recollections and Effusions' in 1843. The Act of Union had been passed just seven years before his birth. A great famine lay ahead. More than once, he was to ask God to be taken.[99]

John O'Sullivan's father, also named John, was a house painter 'much addicted to reading and possessor of a good library'. This painter had married Elizabeth Walsh on 12 November 1805. She was the daughter of Stephen Walsh of Dingle, a ship's captain of the merchant service, and of Walsh's second wife, Anne Sugrue, who was thought to be a descendant of Domhnall O'Sullivan Beare.[100] Fr John O'Sullivan wrote that his grandfather Walsh's drowning left his grandmother in great need. He mentioned this when his bishop asked him, in 1849, to deal with a deed by which a woman named Murphy wished to convey to the diocese thousands of pounds for the poor of Dingle:

> Her father John Murphy of Dingle began this world with very little, acquired a considerable fortune by dishonesty and his descendants have the fruit of it. My maternal grandfather Captain Stephen Walsh of Dingle was joined in trade with him. The trade (butter) was then direct to Lisbon from Dingle. Jack Murphy had the money, was the sleeping partner and remained at home. My grandfather went to sea and the ship he built himself called the *Nicholas Connolly* after Jack's eldest son was dashed to pieces on his last voyage, the very voyage he promised himself would be the last, having as he thought put up a competency.[101] When the news of his death arrived old Jack Murphy would not give my grandmother as much as one kissogue; and she with her two children – my mother and my uncle Stephen[102] – was forced to take refuge in the house of the Rev. Mr Day, then rector of Kilgobbin near Tralee

(Protestant of course), her own cousin germain, but a good, kind, charitable, honest, well-meaning man.[103]

O'Sullivan wrote that 'both my father and mother, though poor, were most respectably connected'[104] – although precisely how their son was a 'near relative' of Daniel O'Connell's family, as he was to inform both Lord Lansdowne and William Fagan MP, is unclear.[105] He asserted that one of the O'Connells was his great-great paternal grandfather. His grandmother Anne is said to have been a great-grandnephew of Thomas Sugrue, a former captain in the French Army who became a priest and canon of Kerry and whose mother was Elizabeth Fitzmaurice, niece to the Earl of Kerry. He admitted that his habit of calling his arch-rival Denis Mahony his 'friend and cousin' was 'more to annoy him, for he took great umbrage at my claiming relationship 'tho we were in truth distantly related'.[106]

Saved from a workshop

One of Fr John O'Sullivan's earliest memories was of the Presentation nuns who established a convent in Tralee soon after he was born, 'My father and mother were alive to serve them, and I was daily, being then about four years of age, at the convent.' He recalled the reverend mother joking with him, handing him some salt with the promise that he could catch any bird on whose tail he succeeded in putting it. He credited the nuns with encouraging his calling as a priest, 'I would even then say Mass for them with a surplice they had made for me and an egg cup for a chalice.'[107]

His father and his father's 'cousin' Daniel 'Splinter' O'Connell, an attorney in Tralee, were 'inseparable friends'. The latter was 'a wild, reckless fellow – married a sister of the illustrious Daniel O'Connell and she [Ellen] was forced to separate from him'. When dying, 'Splinter' called his friend's son John to his bedside and made the future priest a gift of 'a great portion of the classics', books which the boy subsequently used to learn Latin.[108]

Not long afterwards John O'Sullivan senior died of a fever. He left his widow Elizabeth with three young children. John was the eldest, just six and a half years old. Money was tight, so 'my mother having no prospect of being able to forward me took me from school with a view to binding me to my uncle [and her brother] Stephen Walsh, then an eminent and wealthy cabinet-maker in Tralee.'[109] Some friends of the family – including the future 'Liberator' and member of parliament

Daniel O'Connell – prevailed on his mother to let John continue his schooling for a while, he wrote, and thus 'I was saved from my uncle's workshop.' He claimed that O'Connell even undertook to pay for his tuition. Nonetheless, John's schoolmaster, 'poor, honest Bob Slattery, one of the most beautiful scholars that ever taught in Kerry, took such a fancy to me that he never asked nor accepted of a farthing for my tuition, may he rest in peace. He was a splendid scholar and a most eccentric man.'

There were in Tralee some small private schools – the preserve of one teacher in some cases – to which aspiring parents might send their children. Slattery's was one. It was a 'mixed' school, and the Protestant Kerry historian Mary Hickson was to write in the 1870s that O'Sullivan was fond of recalling those days spent 'with many of the sons of the Protestant gentry of Kerry, some of them his relatives', and that he believed he had derived benefits 'from a free intercourse with young companions of another creed who in after life continued as his friends'.[110] A local priest, Dan McCarthy, also came to the boy's home to teach him Greek and Latin.[111] Classicism in Kerry was highly regarded; Latin helped to equip John for a possible priestly vocation, as it helped other Kerrymen to move in European diplomatic and military circles. In 1808 in Tralee, one Eugene O'Sullivan, 'a celebrated poet and professor', reportedly gave evidence in Latin.[112]

School friends

One of O'Sullivan's acquaintances at school was Edward Godfrey, whose father William was to be rector of Kenmare when O'Sullivan later arrived there as parish priest and whom O'Sullivan always respected.[113] Another was David Peter Thompson, son of a late treasurer of Kerry and 'my old school fellow and inveterate enemy', who 'had more perhaps of my company than I had of my own brother's' but with whom O'Sullivan later clashed bitterly in Dingle. Thompson's mother's great-grandfather Garrett Wellesley was a great-granduncle of Arthur, 1st Duke of Wellington.[114] John and his school friends would divide into two groups around a pool at the quarry and drench one another when throwing stones at a piece of wood that they each sought to drive to the other's side. They swam, flew kites in Thompson's field and played ball at the old chapel.[115] In 1851 O'Sullivan recalled his Tralee boyhood and how he liked, among other things, to go out to the Spa and pick up shellfish on the strand:

Was there a happier or a merrier soul in the world them days? I firmly believe not. Then the White Wall where we used to come from school everyday to bathe, the race in the fields after, '*puris naturalibus*' [Latin: in a pure state (i.e. stark naked)] – and who took anything evil or sinful therefrom? No one, not a bit of it. At least I did not. Was there ever such enjoyment as teaching a big country fellow to swim and giving him a good ducking at the end of the lesson, then swimming out beyond his depth where we knew he could not follow us, and making all manner of game with him on his rising up frightened and bewildered at the sousing. Then the races, oh the races. What with getting old Bob Slattery [their school master] to give us the play-day. What with mustering pence for mutton pies, and the mutton pies that one would cock their nose at now, how delicious they were in them days, in a tent too. By jove, they were sweeter than the honey or the honeycomb. Apples and gingerbread, and all the regaling from chance friends, uncles and aunts, etc. – such a saturnalia as the Tralee races were. Will I ever take such interest in any amusement again? I believe not.[116]

According to himself, O'Sullivan was a proficient and talented pupil, 'at the half yearly examinations I uniformly got the first place, though I must say I made very little exertion for it, and was very unconscious of the notice I was attracting.' He read the classics for about a decade, 'and had read all the Trinity College entrance course besides, and various other authors seldom studied in schools – including Longinus, Epictetus, Anacreon and Persius, together with English and logic'. Nevertheless, 'I never would or could learn Irish in Tralee.'[117] At that time Irish was still widely spoken, especially in Kerry, so this is a remarkable reminder of variations in familial and local practice in respect to its use. O'Sullivan's lack of fluency appears to have been no barrier to a happy childhood in the town, although it was to delay briefly his posting as a curate in Dingle, as will be seen. He could not recollect having ever, as a boy, 'given expression to an immodest word, or thought of or done any immodest act', and he wrote that the effect on him of once swearing was such that he still remembered it. One wonders how many such virtuous youths then lived in Kerry.[118]

Going to Maynooth

When John was about 17 years old, a Protestant clergyman named Nash, who lived just outside the town, applied to John's teacher for a young

man to instruct Nash's family, and the teacher recommended him. His
mother insisted that he consult the local parish priest, Cornelius Egan,
who was soon to be consecrated bishop of their diocese. Egan advised
the boy to go but not to contract with Nash for a long period in the first
instance. O'Sullivan formed the impression that Egan was then trying to
get him a place in Maynooth College, the national seminary. Meanwhile,
he was in for a shock:

> In the month of May 1824 I went out to parson Nash's and a salary
> of £12 or £14 per annum. They had no bed in the house for me
> but had fitted up a room in an old castle near the gate in which
> the porter lived. The place was so lonesome, so gloomy and so
> dismal – and the hordes of rats that tramped all night about the
> room were so alarming – that I never closed my eyes all night with
> crying. After a few days I went in to see my mother and she would
> not hear of my continuing there any longer. So I had to pack up
> my things and take my leave of the parson.[119]

He returned home to Tralee, but was not back long before Egan sent
word for him to prepare to go to Maynooth in August. The bishop
arranged for him an application to a local endowment known as the
O'Sullivan Burse, created by a Kerryman who 'got a classical education
at home and went to America like many beside him to seek his fortune'
and who became a medical doctor. The fund assisted students at
Maynooth.[120] This, according to O'Sullivan, was 'the happiest hour of
my life':

> I was going playing goal one day when Mahony of Listowel, then
> curate in Tralee, called me to say Mr and now Dr Egan had written
> from Killarney for my claim on the Byrse [O'Sullivan Burse] in
> Maynooth. In three or four days after, as I was reading as was my
> habit ever and always in bed, Dan McCarthy then a priest came
> up to tell me I had got a place in Maynooth and to prepare for it
> immediately.[121]

Cornelius Egan was consecrated bishop of Kerry on 25 July 1824;
afterwards, he gave O'Sullivan his blessing and forty shillings for the
journey to Maynooth.[122] Catholics were still not permitted to hold senior
civil, military and judicial offices or to sit in parliament, but the
government had allowed Irish bishops to open a national seminary in
Maynooth, Co. Kildare, and also endowed it. College authorities adopted
a rigorous, even rigid, approach to moral issues and an overtly loyal

attitude towards the King. Both positions were facilitated by the French influence that arose from the college employing émigré French priests and Irish teachers who had been educated abroad in the Gallican royalist tradition. It is even said that, in the early nineteenth century, French was the customary language of the professors' dining table – except for one end, where Irish was spoken. Staff at Maynooth took an oath of allegiance to the monarch. Students had to promise and declare that they were not and would not be 'concerned in any latent conspiracy'.[123] Before long, priests emerging from Maynooth became the spearhead of a burgeoning phalanx of clerics, monks and nuns – with the total number of these rising throughout the nineteenth century. That total was to reach five thousand for a Catholic population of five million in 1850, and fourteen thousand for just over three million Catholics left in Ireland by 1900 – after years of massive emigration.[124]

O'Sullivan's teachers at Maynooth College included François Anglade (1758–1834), one of the French émigrés from revolution who had been employed to teach at the college soon after it was established. An official report of 1827 indicates what academic life was like on the campus when O'Sullivan was a student.[125] One fellow student was to stick in his mind for an unforgivable reason. This was James Hampston, later a priest in Castletown Bearhaven, who 'looked down upon all the Kerrymen so that he never would walk or associate with us. He always kept company with the Corkmen.'[126]

O'Sullivan claimed to have studied hard at Maynooth:

> The same success attended me in college as at school. I generally got the first premiums in all my classes and had so distinguished myself in Natural Philosophy that the president, Doctor [Bartholomew] Crotty, now bishop of Cloyne, told me it one time, in the event of Callan's retiring as was then expected, he would use all his influence to procure me the physics chair.

O'Sullivan believed that Callan was ill. Nicholas Callan, known as the inventor of the induction coil, had been appointed professor of experimental physics as recently as September 1826 and was to have a long and distinguished career. Even if Callan had retired then, which he did not, it seems surprising that someone as inexperienced as O'Sullivan thought that he had a chance of replacing Callan.[127] In later life O'Sullivan was to teach elementary physics to schoolchildren in Kenmare, 'with a special emphasis on electricity', and some of the models that he used (including a 'Callan coil') long survived. O'Sullivan later used his practical skills to carve a baptismal font for his church and to make rough tables for the first convent school; he also designed objects such as a folding altar for the workhouse and a portable confessional to take with him sometimes when saying Mass in a parishioner's home.[128]

His sister dies

Meanwhile, John's sister Ann, who he thought 'possessed a high order of talent', had remained in Tralee. Her promising career was cut short:

> She too in consideration of her abilities was gratuitously educated by a Miss Giles, a cousin of ours, a Protestant who for many years kept an eminent boarding school in Tralee [on Nelson Street]. She [Giles] retired having acquired five or six thousand pounds and handed over the concern to my sister. She was getting on rapidly in a fair way for realising a similar fortune when it pleased God to take her to himself after giving birth to her first child [...] I asked and obtained leave to go home in the last week of Lent [...] My sister died a few days after my return and blasted all the hopes of my dear mother.[129]

Their brother Stephen later secured a clerkship in the National Bank through the influence of Daniel O'Connell MP, one of its founding directors in 1835. But having been promoted to manager of a branch in Athlone, Stephen left the bank under a cloud and caused O'Sullivan embarrassment, as will be seen.[130]

After his sister's funeral, O'Sullivan had hoped to return to Maynooth for some years, believing that its president had promised him a place 'on the Dunboyne', but Bishop Egan decided that his services were needed in Kerry as soon as possible. The Dunboyne scholarships, funded partly by a bequest from Lord Dunboyne and partly (after 1813) by parliament, were intended to provide a further three years of study for twenty students who 'exhibited more than ordinary talent and good conduct'. However, in 1827 a parliamentary committee found only eleven individuals in that group and was informed that 'the demand for priests, particularly in the province of Ulster, had been lately so urgent, as not to admit of the Dunboyne students completing their additional course of three years within the College.'[131] That same year, Bishop Egan of Kerry was 'grieved' to inform Daniel O'Connell MP that 'I am unable, from a scarcity of priests, to supply the wants of some parishes in my diocese.'[132] Yet despite his pressing need, the bishop felt unable to ordain

O'Sullivan immediately, insisting that he first study for some months the native language widely spoken in Kerry. He had not learnt Irish as a boy, and after Professor Paul O'Brien's early death in 1820, Maynooth College appears to have neglected the Irish language. O'Sullivan wrote, 'I could not speak nor understand a single word of Irish […] I had never spoken a single word of Irish until I was ordained.' He served as a deacon before being ordained.[133]

O'Sullivan was now living through an optimistic time for Irish Catholics, who had long been oppressed by penal and discriminatory legislation. In April 1829 the campaign for emancipation led by Daniel O'Connell secured the passing of a relief act enabling Catholics to enter parliament, to belong to any corporation and to hold many but not all higher political offices from which they had long been excluded. O'Connell himself entered parliament as its member for Co. Clare that same year. Though the electoral franchise was substantially restricted to men who owned property of a certain value, many people of all classes in Ireland saw O'Connell's victory as a great breakthrough. Their beloved 'Liberator' would later launch a campaign for repeal of the Act of Union.

Ordained a priest

On 10 July 1830 O'Sullivan was ordained in Killarney. He would never again live in Tralee, but throughout his life he kept in touch with his first cousins there – the children of his mother's only brother, Stephen Walsh. In 1841, for example, he made the 70-kilometre journey back from Kenmare to officiate at the wedding of Ann, Stephen's daughter, to John Murphy (also O'Murphy), as witnessed by Thomas Pembroke and John Mulchinock, sons of two of Tralee's leading merchant families. In January 1849, during the famine, O'Sullivan wrote, 'I have another letter from my cousins, the Walshs asking my advice as to the only unmarried girl Maria's marriage with Tade [Timothy] Scanlan, many years first clerk in John Mulchinock's. Scanlan is no doubt a good husband and she will prove I think a good wife for him.' The following month he went again to Tralee, no short journey in the days before motors, to wed Maria to Tade – 'a good match for her, he being a steady man worth some money'. The marriage took place at the Walsh home in The Square. Passing through Tralee after the famine, the priest paid visits to the family. He was again present in Tralee in 1863 when Anne's first child, Elizabeth, a namesake of his own mother, became a nun – and in 1865, to officiate at the marriage of Anne's third child, Mary, to John Reardon.[134]

5

Piping and Proselytism: Dingle, 1831–1839

O'Sullivan's first and only posting as a curate was in Dingle town on the most westerly peninsula of Ireland. Before going there, he spent six weeks as a new priest assisting at a parish across Dingle Bay:

> The very morning I was ordained, such was the exigency of the mission, I was sent to Caherciveen [...] The morning after I arrived the Parish Priest left home, leaving word for me to go to town to say Mass and marry a couple. I knew the ceremonies of Mass very well but I had never even seen a couple married, and thus I was thrown on my own resources as to the performance of the ceremony.[135]

A 'precious specimen'

O'Sullivan watched for a chance to cross the bay from Caherciveen and visit the town where he was due to be stationed. A remarkable opportunity presented itself:

> We were informed that the Hon'ble and Reverend Frederick Mullins, uncle to the present [3rd] Lord Ventry, was in the harbour in his schooner. Frederick was always more at home with priests and enjoyed their society more than any others except women, for he was a terrible, dissolute debauchee. We got a boat and pulled alongside and asked for Parson Mullins. 'Not on board sir – impossible – not on board Sir I assure you.' We had seen him on deck. 'Tell him the parish priest and curate of Caherciveen want a passage over to Dingle and would feel obliged by getting it.' 'Damn your blood,' cried Frederick who had been listening on. 'Come up. I took ye for a pair of Methodist preachers as ye neared the ship and I told my men to send away the vagabonds for I detest them. It is a treat to have

your company over; we sail in an hour, dine in an hour after and we shall be in Dingle for tea.'[136]

Frederick Mullins (1778–1832) was a 'precious specimen of the clergy of the Established Church', according to O'Sullivan. He was the sixth son of Thomas, 1st Baron Ventry, who had been elevated to the peerage in 1800 because the family supported the Act of Union. This family (which would, in 1841, change the form of its surname to de Moleyns) owned large tracts of the Dingle Peninsula, having first been granted Irish lands in the troubled seventeenth century.[137] Frederick belonged to a generation of parsons that enjoyed an income from tithes, which were a tax levied on members of any or no faith to support the established Protestant Church. O'Sullivan claimed that Frederick, although rector of Killiney near Castlegregory – about 20 kilometres north-east of Dingle town – never lived there for more than three months each year. Frederick now sat at the stern of his yacht, 'with a huge jug of punch between his knees, dispensing it in the greatest profusion to guests and sailors, and if I sang one song I think I sang at least half a dozen, so that we walked in all at once to the parson's good graces.' They did not in fact get to Dingle in time for tea, for the yacht was becalmed and it took all night to reach their destination. On arrival there, the two Catholic priests promised to dine with the parson that evening in Petries, the town's 'Protestant hotel'. Their meal turned into a party when, afterwards, as many as forty men and women came and danced to the music of fiddle, drum and tambourine until well past midnight. When later living in Dingle, O'Sullivan would visit Frederick, who was then lodging in a thatched public house at Castlegregory.[138]

Curate in Dingle

From September 1830 until March 1839, O'Sullivan served as curate in Dingle, a town of about seven hundred dwellings. He wrote that 'Dingle was a happy place' when he arrived.[139] Nevertheless, soon afterwards, an international cholera pandemic changed that:

> Dingle was the Haceldoma [Aceldama, or 'field of blood'] of Kerry that year. The cholera raged there with greater fury than in any other part of the diocese. It was not an unusual thing for one of us to go out at night and not return till nine or ten the following morning, moving from house to house preparing the dying. I was

myself taken out of bed thirteen successive nights to prepare cholera patients, and so little fear or concern had I about the sickness ultimately, that I recollect on a fine morning being rapped up to a sick-call at West Minard some eight miles from Dingle. The road was then very bad, so I left my horse at the chapel and walked across the mountain. The poor man was in a state of collapse; I suppose he died before the evening. Not one of the people in the village would come near me, for cholera had been confined almost exclusively to the west of Dingle. I had some laudanum with me, the most effective for the complaint at the time, and after giving him a dose of it I began to think of myself. I could not return without eating something and the poor woman, having informed me that she had some tea and bread, I desired her get them ready and with the greatest disregard for contagion sat down and ate my breakfast alongside of the cholera patient in his cabin – for it was a mere cabin – from the very bowl that he had been using ten minutes before: such is habit!!![140]

He wrote that there was great panic, with Dingle town being deserted and two hundred deaths in hospital reported in one month, 'We could not account for the number that died in the country. In one village, Ballymore, I recollect going out about ten at night and until eight the following morning I did nothing but going from house to house anointing the unfortunate victims of cholera.'[141] It was a preparation for what he was to experience in Kenmare during the great famine.

There were also sectarian tensions. He dined with Captain Collis, port surveyor of Dingle, and George Woodhouse, an inspector of fisheries from whom O'Sullivan bought his first horse:

When Woodhouse had taken five or six tumblers he verified Horace's 'In vino veritas' [Latin: In wine is the truth] and he gave 'The Boyne Water' in the true chant of an Orangeman. I walked out of the room and Collis made Woodhouse come and apologise to me on the following morning.[142]

That ballad celebrated the Protestant William of Orange's defeat of the Catholic King James. But worse was to come.

Bible war

During the 1830s the Catholic Church grew concerned about Protestant evangelical activities in the west of Ireland conducted through the medium of the Irish language, and particularly about Protestant 'colonies' on Achill Island and the Dingle Peninsula. These settlements provided a supportive environment for Catholics who chose to convert, or 'go to church' – as opposed to 'going to Mass', or 'to the chapel'.[143] The evangelisers saw the cholera pandemic of the early 1830s as providential. 'The Lord gave a fearful opportunity of effecting his purpose in this respect,' wrote one chronicler of their efforts.[144] Some Catholic priests were paternalistic and proprietorial when it came to protecting 'their' flocks against what they saw as an offensively opportunistic assault on their church and its most vulnerable members.

The establishment of a Protestant 'colony' at Ventry in Dingle was facilitated by the existence of a remote coastguard station where some sympathetic Protestants worked; it was also enabled by the arrival, in 1833, of Charles Gayer as chaplain on Lord Ventry's estate. Ventry's agent at this time was David Peter Thompson, who had known O'Sullivan well as a schoolboy in Tralee. He lived at Ventry's Burnham House, which Lewis, in 1837, described as 'the principal seat in the vicinity'. Thompson married his first cousin, Anne Thompson of Clonskeagh Castle, Co. Dublin; she promoted the Anglican evangelism that was beginning to make headway in Dingle and later wrote a short local history of that controversial, ill-fated movement. She painted an unflattering depiction of Catholic priests on the Dingle Peninsula, alleging that a number abandoned parishes when cholera struck and accusing some of stirring up hatred and even violence against converts.[145]

Fig. 2. View of the Protestant missionary settlement at Ventry, Co. Kerry. From a lithographed report by Charles Gayer, 26 Sept. 1839. Courtesy National Library of Ireland *[MS 24,445].*

Fig. 3. View of Dingle, Co. Kerry. From Report of the Colony at Dingle *(Dublin: White, 1842).*

O'Sullivan, the new young curate, played a prominent role in rebuffing proselytisers. He was quite possibly the unnamed priest said to have forbidden Catholics from buying soup from a certain Protestant, 'a benevolent lady of the town', who offered it to the hungry. 'All who did avail themselves of it were henceforth branded "soupers",' he recalled later.[146] Much later, a man in Kenmare even credited O'Sullivan with having coined the widely used term 'souper' to describe proselytisers.[147] The priest himself wrote:

> When souperism began first to spread in Dingle the whole burden of its opposition fell upon me. I was continually pelting and pounding them. A woman named Ellen Waters sent her children to Church though professing to be a staunch Catholic herself, and I got leave from the bishop to excommunicate her, which I did in due form, bell, book and candlelight, leaving no tailoring on the business. Ellen was in consequence shunned and avoided by the whole community and the parsons thought they had a fine ground for prosecution [...] the prosecution in the end waivered and faltered, '*et sic servatus est*' [Latin: and thus was protected] Father John.[148]

In an open letter published in 1839, a few months after O'Sullivan left Tralee to become parish priest in Kenmare, Charles Gayer wrote, 'The priest who most violently opposed the work at Ventry, and who by his harangues stirred up the people to insult and ill treat the converts, has been removed, and our enemies are comparatively at peace with us.'[149] Yet the bitter contest over conversions in Dingle rumbled on. A teacher, one James Glaster, or Gloster, who lived with his family out on the tip of the Dingle Peninsula, near Ballyferriter and Dún Chaoin, told a court in 1845 what had happened since he converted in the 1830s – through contact with Protestant coastguards whose children he taught – and became a scripture reader:

> When I became a convert, the thatch of my house was taken off, and my windows were broken; those who were my dearest friends became my bitterest enemies, and not one of them would speak to me. One of my cousins [...] passes me almost every day, and yet he never speaks a word to me except he'd call out 'soup' or some other nickname after me; stones were often flung at me and clods; when I was a Roman Catholic I kept a school, and my wife was a mantua-maker; but I lost the favour of my friends; my family have often stones thrown at them.[150]

Before converting, he had started to read a bible belonging to one of the coastguards and 'was for some time in doubt whether the Protestant Bible was true'. By the time that coastguard had departed, Glaster had replaced his 'Protestant Bible' with one of a number of Douay testaments that a parson had sent to Ballydavid, near Murreagh. The Douay was a Catholic edition prepared, in the late sixteenth century, by members of the English college at Douai in Flanders in order to further the Counter-Reformation. When Glaster compared Protestant and Catholic editions, he 'found very little difference between them'. Glaster said, 'I asked Mr. Casey, the [Catholic] priest and he gave me leave to buy one [...] I had no falling out with Mr. Casey.'[151] Casey was to fall out with Fr O'Sullivan's friends.

The Kerry historian Bryan MacMahon has recently turned his attention to the evangelical campaign in Dingle then.[152] Amongst others who have also studied the 'Protestant crusade' of those years, as it became known, was Desmond Bowen (1921–1998), an Irish-Canadian and a minister in the Anglican Church. He thought that a 'myth' grew around 'souperism' that resulted in it being regarded by Irish Catholics as more widespread within the Church of Ireland than it actually was. He instanced abuses by lay and clerical evangelicals during the famine but also recalled the good work done by local Protestant clergymen, some of whom died while trying to help starving people regardless of denomination. Fr John O'Sullivan himself, from time to time, made a similar distinction between Protestant clergy. Bowen, in his volume on 'souperism' and his other work on 'the Protestant crusade' between 1800 and 1870, mentions neither O'Sullivan nor the violent sectarian confrontation in Kenmare and Templenoe considered later.[153]

The 1835 election

During the general election campaign of 1835, O'Sullivan was tempted to intervene against Maurice Fitzgerald, Knight of Kerry, who had voted for the Act of Union in 1800 and who had been returned to the House of Commons in London in the three decades that followed. Fitzgerald made a fortune from slate quarried on Valentia Island, a scheme that preoccupied him until his friendship with Lord Lansdowne brought him back more frequently to London from 1827.[154] The priest came to regret his involvement:

> I induced some of Lord Ventry's freeholders to vote against the Knight of Kerry and for years after, when any of them would be persecuted by the agent, the harpy [David Peter] Thompson, they would come [...] to me and lay the whole blame at my door. I could not stand it. I made up my mind never again to interfere in politics.[155]

It was claimed that at Mass in Dingle chapel:

> Father John O'Sullivan said from the altar before the election that any person that would vote for that *renegado* the Knight of Kerry he would not prepare him for death, but he would let him die like a beast; neither would he baptise his children, and that they deserved to be pelted as they went along, any person that voted for the Knight of Kerry.

It was further alleged that the priest had said that people should neither buy from nor sell to any person who would vote for the knight.[156] Accusations and denials flew.[157] According to O'Sullivan, Thompson pretended not to know him when they met in Dingle, and even insulted him. Vengeful towards those who he thought had voted against the Knight of Kerry in accordance with O'Sullivan's wishes, Thompson reportedly told worried freeholders to 'go to Father John [...] and see what help can he give you now.' O'Sullivan felt obliged to spend money to get such people legal advice. He was still smarting years later when he wrote, 'I never took an active part in an election since, nor will I.'[158]

A drop of port

It was not all cholera and confrontation for O'Sullivan in Dingle. Captain John Hickson of The Grove, Dingle, who was both a justice of the peace and deputy governor of Kerry, and his brother Sam were attentive to local priests. Sam had recently built Ballintaggart House near Dingle, which still stands today. O'Sullivan wrote in 1851 that 'the only drop of the *Lady Nelson* I ever tasted was at his house, and it was then a great rarity.' He noted:

> That ship was smashed to pieces on the Skellig rock, and the most of her cargo, port wine expressly made for George IV was sent in on the Dingle coast. Many made a fortune of it, particularly Jack Neligan of Tralee, father to the present attorney of that name residing in Tralee and a brother to the present William in this town that met Napper Tandy.[159]

On 14 October 1809 the *Lady Nelson*, on its way from Oporto to London, had gone down with the loss of almost all of its crew and cargo. Visiting Dingle in the 1830s, Lady Chatterton found some of its 'stranded' cargo, which had included no fewer than four hundred and fifty pipes of port (each pipe cask typically containing 477 litres), being offered as a '*bonne bouche*' (French: good mouth, i.e. a treat).[160]

James Hickson, a brother of John and Sam, became 'a particular friend' of O'Sullivan in Dingle.[161] Described by Mary Hickson as 'a most popular and respected country gentleman', he and the priest were to have many dealings with one another in Kenmare, because James was agent for the Lansdowne estate in Kerry from 1818 until 1849. On the other hand, John Hickson had married Barbara, a sister of O'Sullivan's future opponent, Denis Mahony of Dromore Castle, while yet another Hickson married Mahony's second sister, Agnes.[162]

O'Sullivan was also friendly with that William Neligan, an apothecary, who had 'met Napper Tandy' of the United Irishmen. Neligan taught both the priest and John O'Connell MP a song about Tandy and other rebels of 1798 – a version of 'The Wearing of the Green'. In Neligan's house, wrote O'Sullivan, 'I spent many a pleasant day when a curate', and he would later sleep there when visiting Dingle with Bishop Egan.[163] Presumably Neligan was the person of whom Lady Chatterton learnt on her visit to Dingle in 1838 when she enquired about reports that the town of some five thousand inhabitants had neither a doctor nor an attorney, 'Oh, we have an excellent apothecary here; and when he sees much danger, why he sends to Tralee for help

– and so most of the people, you see, die easy, without troubling the doctor.'[164] That is to say, unless they consulted a certain 'Doctor Griffin' in Dingle, whom O'Sullivan described:

> A curious old fellow was Doctor Griffin, used to call to Moll regularly for some of the '*aquam puram*' [Latin: clear/pure water (i.e. poteen?)]. Such was the confidence the people had in the medicine he gave them that he was at one time seriously interfering with William Neligan at whose instance the Apothecaries Hall had him prosecuted for compounding medicine, but it having been proven that the Doctor was compounding and vending for forty years, and before the passing of the Apothecaries Hall Act [1791], he was acquitted.

Griffin ministered to the soul as to the body, continued O'Sullivan:

> The Doctor when I first went to Dingle was selling orations, printed ones, and they ensured the safety of every house from fire, of every vessel from wreck, of every woman in danger from childbirth, all for twopence. He was then going down the hill fast and had scarcely anything else to look up, and as he had been selling these for some years without the priests either coming to hear of it, or, if they did, to prevent it, we had a good deal to do to make him give it up.[165]

Ballyferriter: 'a famous dinner'

O'Sullivan and his friend Neligan occasionally walked 15 kilometres from Dingle town out to Ballyferriter and Dún Chaoin. There, at the end of the peninsula, they sometimes met Fr John Casey. In 1851 O'Sullivan recalled that 'Father Casey was parish priest of the western parish in my time, a mighty simple primitive old man.' He added, 'Casey was a deadly enemy of pipers and card players. He pursued them with dreadful invectuary [invective].'[166] Fortunately, Pádraig de Brún has left us two fine articles about Casey and his work. Born in Kerry, the priest was over 60 years of age when O'Sullivan and his party encountered him. He was a respected scholar and a pioneer of research on ogham script; he worked with John Windele and others to unravel the early history of Dingle, and he joined antiquarian societies. In his little thatched house on the tip of Dingle, he kept a library of old volumes and manuscripts in a number of languages. While O'Sullivan refers to him as 'simple' and 'primitive', another contemporary used

the words 'plain and unaffected'. The Irish that Casey spoke was both
fluent and beautiful, and it was the first language of his parish. He
actively discouraged people from believing in what are called in Irish
'*na slúagh sídhe*' (spirit people).[167]

Asenath Nicholson, an American who distributed bibles in Ireland
during the famine and who later published a well-known account of
her trip, visited this 'learned priest', as she called him. He received her
with 'the greatest kindness'. He sat by the fire 'surrounded with Latin
authors of various descriptions, and piles on piles of the most
antiquated looking books in Hebrew, Greek and Latin'. She refers to
his 'simple urbanity of manners' and calls him a 'benevolent gentleman
[...] retired in that desolate part of the earth, buried in his musty
books'.[168] His benevolence was sorely tried by Neligan's visit.

Casey, wrote Fr John O'Sullivan, came into Dingle town every week
or two and stayed with the Neligan family, 'where he was always
entertained comfortably. The only return they ever sought or asked
from him was the privilege of carrying a dinner to his house sometime
in the summer and enjoying a day in the country.' One such Neligan
outing was undertaken with relatives and friends, including O'Sullivan,
'Some thirty or forty of the townspeople, having contributed their
quota of drink or provisions, we all set off early for Father Casey's. It
was a splendid day.' Out at Ballyferriter, the young people headed for
Dún an Óir, while O'Sullivan, Neligan and a few others sat down to play
a game of cards at Casey's house – where a pair of old English
cannonballs sat on top of the gate's pillars.

The visitors had brought their own cards, 'knowing we had no
chance of them from Casey'. Casey's parlour was very small and the day
very fine, so they brought the table into his garden.[169] Lady Chatterton,
who visited Casey on her tour of southern Ireland in 1838, described
his 'little sitting-room, which was ornamented with a few portraits of
saints, and a small picture of Saint Patrick [...] The furniture was scanty
and poor – a rumpled sofa, a quaint side-board, upon which stood a
few jugs, plates and candle-sticks, four chairs, and a round table made
up the simple inventory.'[170] Having taken Casey's table to the garden
and sat around it, O'Sullivan and his friends were engrossed 'in the
midst of a most exciting game of spoil five'. Father Casey walked in and
was thunderstruck:

> The idea of the cards he had been denouncing with such a
> vengeance all his life being played not only in his own house but
> there before the public '*sub dio*' was too much for him. He

clapped his hands expressively, poor man, but he did not like to prevent us. The game accordingly went on more for the sake of the amusement we had with Casey than anything else, when a funeral passed by the garden on its way to Kilmalkedar Church. We fortunately had seen it approaching and put the cards under the cloth, but continued sitting round the table. The novelty of the sight would of course attract the attention of people in a less civilised place than Ferriter, but here they actually laid the coffin down, climbed up on the garden hedge all round and remained looking for half an hour at the party gathered round the card table, wondering of course what in the world they [the party] could be at or about; and I verily believe they would have left the dead to bury the dead and remained until night had we continued to occupy our places at the table. We had at length to dissolve and found Casey inside more like a lunatic than a man in his senses, fancying that the card-playing was going on all the time in the presence of his flock and despairing of ever again being able to denounce a card-player in his parish.[171]

O'Sullivan's reference to the behavior of 'people in a less civilised place' seems difficult to interpret as other than sarcasm. How civilised was his own party to remain seated instead of standing as a mark of respect, or dispersing, while the funeral passed? If they had 'at length to dissolve', they were soon seated again:

We dined in the garden, and a famous dinner we had and plenty to drink after it, but the measure of poor Casey's troubles was not yet filled up. The young people should have a dance and they had taken care before dinner to send to Dingle parish for a piper, on the bounds of which one lived who would now and then make an incursion into Casey's territory in spite of him.

There was no use in Casey's objections. The piper evidently in bodily fear of Casey was induced to strike up, the jigs, reels and country dances were carried on with great vigour, the funeral people being now on the return perched all round on the garden hedge and enjoying vastly such an incident, for incident it was in that remote sequestered parish.

It seems an insult as much as 'an incident', for there was, according to O'Sullivan, 'no use in Casey's objections' to people entering his home and taking pleasure in behaving in a manner that they knew this man in his sixties would find offensive. He was renowned for standing on ceremony. Casey is said to have once told a nun that he had taken lessons from celebrated dancing masters and that this informed the manner of his stately approach to the altar in her convent. ('the Sisters had ample leisure to indulge their piety,' as O'Sullivan nicely put it.) When he was given a broad hint to hurry up, he replied, 'No, no, Madame. I have no intention of making a fox-hunter's jig of the Mass.'[172] This was the man asked now to baptise a dying child who was brought to his kitchen while the party from Dingle jigged in his garden. O'Sullivan continued:

> Neligan got up to dance but was so tipsy that he fell flat on the ground three times; his young son John who was equally so began to cry for having his father so tipsy; the mirth and humour began to increase when Doctors Hickson and Fagan got up on a table to dance a jig on it, at which the shouting and cheering and laughing rose beyond all bounds so much so as completely to bother and confuse old Casey who was baptising the child in the kitchen. He ran out in a fury with his stole on him when he saw the two doctors on the table, his whole parish again gathered about and beholding the profanation; his anger knew no bounds, he rushed over, laid hold of the innocent and unfortunate piper, kicked, cuffed, and beat him most unmercifully, broke his pipes and completely dispersed the whole assembly. We had to make a collection for the poor piper who freely admitted 'he'd wished them broke tomorrow again on the same terms'.[173]

The party left for Dingle as it was getting dark, some in horse-drawn cars; they made for Neligan's house, where there was more drinking, cards and piping – 'and some of them I believe kept footing it until morning.'[174] There is not a word of sympathy or understanding, let alone apology, in O'Sullivan's record of events that day, although de Brún uses the word 'friend' to describe the priest's relationship with Casey. In 1851 both became members of the respected Kilkenny Archaeological Society – the body that later became the Royal Society of Antiquaries of Ireland. By then Casey had left Dingle and was chaplain to the Sisters of Mercy in Killarney.[175]

Speaking Irish

Bishop Egan had delayed O'Sullivan going 'on the mission' to Dingle for his first assignment after ordination due to the priest's weakness in the Irish language, which was still widely used on that peninsula. Once settled in Dingle, O'Sullivan became close friends with another curate there, John Naughten, and 'derived much benefit from his instruction in Irish when I first began to try my hand in that most unprepossessing branch of science'.[176] Although he was to spend between eight and nine years in Dingle, his command of the native language remained imperfect. Yet he slowly learnt it and, on returning there with Bishop Egan in the 1850s, would remark, 'When I first came to Dingle without a word of Irish in my jaw what little expectation I had of ever being the man to accompany the Bishop on his visitation and to catechise every day in Irish, yet such is perseverance.'[177]

O'Sullivan confessed, in 1852, that his Irish was still 'very, extremely indifferent' and that some people 'banter me on it'. On another visit to Dingle, he remarked, 'I know many of the priests are laughing at my Irish, but let them laugh away.' Far from lamenting its gradual disappearance in daily usage, he welcomed the convenience of everyone speaking English:

> English again but the bishop was now becoming reconciled to it. The doom of Irish is sealed, some dozen years will root it out altogether and he [Bishop Egan] may as well bear with it, and a great ease it would be to the clergy who at present require to be '*au fait*' at two languages.[178]

He was by no means alone at this time in noting the gradual disuse of Irish, with Daniel O'Connell too, for example, earlier acknowledging the utility of English.[179] Yet Irish was still spoken by many in Kerry then – even if Tralee and its hinterlands appear to have led its decline in use. Indeed, in 1851 almost one in three inhabitants of the barony of Glanerought, where Kenmare lies, and more than half of the people of the adjacent barony of Iveragh were found to speak *only* Irish.[180]

The pre-Christian past

O'Sullivan, at least in his journals, also displayed little regard for old Gaelic culture or folklore; Catholic authorities looked upon these traditions with suspicion, regarding them as a repository of pagan practices and superstition. At times he was to prove himself an able advocate for the paupers of the workhouse and the poor country people around Kenmare, but he grew up in the town of Tralee and belonged socially to an evolving nationalist middle-class.[181]

Yet, even though he did not share Fr John Casey's great interest in aspects of local culture such as ogham stones and old Irish manuscripts, it is difficult to take at face value O'Sullivan's ostensible ignorance of one of Dingle's annual events, long recognised by local people for its connection with pre-Christian beliefs (as the folklore collection in University College Dublin amply testifies). This was the annual 'pattern', or patron, day on Mount Brandon, that great peak on the Dingle Peninsula frequently shrouded in mist. Such patterns were an intrinsic part of rural life.[182] At the end of July in Dingle each year ('the last Sunday in summer'), a pilgrimage was held to honour St Brendan; it was a Christian adaptation of a much older harvest celebration (Lughnasa), which was one of the four quarterly festivals of Celtic Ireland and honoured the god Bran.[183] Back on the Dingle Peninsula briefly in July 1850, accompanying Bishop Egan on an episcopal 'visitation', O'Sullivan made his way from Dingle town up towards the Connor Pass on a journey of about 15 kilometres to Cloghane (An Clochán), near Mount Brandon:

> Horses sulked as we got out of town and were near backing us out or rather into the dyke had I not jumped out and caught the horses' heads. I walked the whole way to the top and nearly to Kilmore at this side of Connor Hill, the horses being unable to make any way by reason of the roughness of the road, it having been lately covered with pounded stones and gravel. We arrive at the chapel at 12 exactly. It is a pattern day there, the last Sunday in summer and called by the people 'lá Crom Dhuv' – for what reason, 'tho we made several enquiries, we could not at all discover.[184]

This pattern of Cloghane was the great assembly of the year in Dingle. Even if O'Sullivan and Egan did not understand why the festival was called 'lá Crom Dhuv', would locals not have shared with them some of their folk tales? Máire MacNeill includes a good variety of such stories in her magisterial book on the feast of Lughnasa. She firmly identifies a deity known as Crom Dubh with the origins of the pattern at Cloghane. Crom Dubh ('Black Stoop') was said to have brought the first sheaf of wheat to Ireland and was regarded as a harvest god until displaced when successfully challenged. If in many places the Christian challenger was said to be St Patrick, in Dingle it was St Brendan of Mount Brandon.[185]

O'Sullivan elsewhere wrote that one of the reasons he liked to go on walks was so that he could fall into conversation with people along the way and 'thereby learn much of the state of the parish, their habits and their manners'.[186] Nevertheless, he did not record much of their lore in his journals.

He was keen to make a definite distinction between superstitions and genuine country cures – a separation that some people might not understand as such. More than once, he wrote, people had been accused of the serious sin of consulting a magician or fortune-teller for merely 'using an infusion of dandelions which I was using myself for many years and is a most powerful tonic'. His advice for young priests was that they discover the real intention of people accused of such a sin, 'Ascertain what their feelings were on the matter, and if they thought they were really renouncing their allegiance to God Almighty or consulting the Evil One.' He likewise felt that the relating of one's dreams should not necessarily be condemned, unless some kind of charmer was consulted about them.[187]

Riding to Kenmare

While he was a curate in Dingle, O'Sullivan began to travel by gig in preference to riding on horseback, especially when he developed a hernia, 'I had never even crossed a horse until I was ordained and I was sure to get a fall at least once a week until I became so nervous and frightened as to be in a continued state of excitement from the time I got on horseback until I got off again.'[188] He was about to become the first parish priest of Kenmare to have his own light two-wheeled carriage.

6

The Poor of Kenmare

The accommodation of very many Irish people before the famine was remarkably basic. In 1808 one writer described it graphically in the course of what purported to be his 'unbought and unbigoted opinion on the measure of Catholic emancipation', then being debated – but not ultimately conceded until 1829. The author saw little similarity between Irish Catholics and Catholics elsewhere in Europe. He had reservations about granting equal civil rights, based partly on the degraded social conditions of many Irish Catholics:

> Their dwellings are of primitive and easy construction – the walls and floors of clay, the roof of sod or thatch: within are two unequal divisions; in the smaller, filthy and unfurnished, you would hardly suppose the whole family to sleep; in the larger, on a hearth, without grate or chimney, a scanty fire warms rather by its smoke than by its blaze, and discolours whatever it warms. Glazed windows there are none, the open door amply sufficing for light and air, to those who are careless of either. Furniture they neither have, nor want; their food and preparation are simple – potatoes or oaten cakes, sour milk, and sometimes salted fish. In drink they are not so temperate: of all spirituous liquors they are immoderately fond, but most of whiskey, the distilled extract of fermented corn [...] Their dress is mean and squalid [...] Both sexes wear, in winter and summer, long woolen coats, or cloaks derived from, and similar to, the sagum [cloak] of their ancestors.

The writer advised that

> The religion of such a people is not to be confounded with one of the same name professed by the enlightened nations of Europe. The University of Paris has some tenets in common,

perhaps, with the Irish Papist; but does it believe that water [of 'holy wells'] restores the cripple, enlightens the blind, or purifies the guilty?[189]

The water of St Finian's Well in Kenmare reputedly healed eye ailments.

Investigating poverty

In 1833 the government appointed a Royal Commission on the Poorer Classes to establish the nature of poverty in Ireland; in 1836, the commissioners issued a report. Their principal sources were local individuals with social standing, such as clergymen or landlords. The report provides unique glimpses of how the poor lived at the time.[190] In the Kenmare Union, for example, the Catholic priest Daniel Garvin of Kilgarvan believed that in his parish there were about five hundred families; he claimed that one-fifth of these families depended on breadwinners who worked as labourers – 'of whom few (if any) have constant employment'. Thomas Taylor, a widely respected doctor who later became medical officer of the Kenmare workhouse, thought that two-thirds of the male population in Templenoe were labourers, with only one in every hundred in constant employment.

In seeking to determine the landlords of the cottages or cabins in which poor people lived, the commissioners established that by no means did all the poor hold directly from large landlords. In Kilcrohane, for example, they had been allowed on land by 'a very miserable description of persons'. James Hickson, Lansdowne's agent in Kenmare and Tuosist, replied, 'The landlords of cabins are generally farmers, and shopkeepers of the town.' The Church of Ireland clergyman in Kenmare, William Godfrey, thought that the landlords of cabins were chiefly 'under-tenants or small farmers in the country, and in the town of Kenmare people in business'. It might suit a head landlord to turn a blind eye to formal or informal subletting by his Catholic and Protestant tenants so long as he received what was due to him at the top of the chain. One landlord – Francis C. Bland of Derriquin, Kilcrohane, whose estate was west of that of Denis Mahony of Dromore Castle in Templenoe – claimed that many cabins were built on the outskirts of his demesne 'without *leave* or *licence* [original italics]'. He criticised the mountain farmers:

> The mountaineers' wealth consists in stock or cattle, and some
> have ten, twenty, or thirty cows, and even considerably more: they

do not live much better than the poorer people of the lowlands, and are not one bit cleaner in their habits: they have more milk, butter, curds, and goat's flesh, but less potatoes; and some of them live for a part of the year almost entirely on milk and curds: their luxury is whiskey, and almost all feuds and riots originate with this class: they sleep a great deal: they contribute nothing whatsoever to defray the expenses of the commonwealth by their industry or consumption, except in the article of whiskey.

The cabins of labourers were far from luxurious, as respondents in the Kenmare Union observed, 'They are very miserable buildings, and more miserably furnished. They have no bedsteads, and little or no bedding.' They were 'of the very worst description, without furniture, bedding or bedsteads'. Rev. Godfrey noted that even when stone was used outside, it did not guarantee comfort inside, 'The cabins are stone-built; sometimes one apartment, sometimes two; furniture miserable; bedding wretched, and often supplied by their day-clothing. A few stakes supporting a rough frame sometimes serve to keep the pallet of straw from the floor. I speak of cabins held from under-tenants.' Rev. Samuel Mathews of Kilcrohane thought there were 'a great many instances of two families residing in the same cabin', although Godfrey did not think that this was so in the parish of Kenmare.

The diet and garments of the poor were very simple in Kenmare Union, as elsewhere. According to Fr Daniel Galvin, 'Their clothing is of the very worst description, yet not a sufficiency of it: their ordinary diet potatoes alone, for in winter they seldom taste milk; in summer they get a little from the farmers, their neighbours.' Dr Taylor reported that they had 'wholesome potatoes, with generally (sometimes without) milk or fish: clothing warm frieze'. Denis Mahony of Templenoe reported, 'Potatoes and milk their diet: their clothing very bad, wool being scarce in consequence of thieves and foxes.' There was agreement that the area had been remarkably quiet since the rebellion of 1798, although there had been some trouble locally in 1822 when the potato failed and one or two persons were deported for Whiteboyism (agrarian violence).[191] Respondents thought that the illicit distillation of alcohol was rare, but whiskey was sold from some unlicensed huts and cabins. Most respondents thought that the general condition of the poorer classes had improved around Kenmare since 1815. The opinion of the poorer classes themselves went unrecorded.

Housing and the census of 1841

The census of 1841 was the first effort to classify types of Irish housing nationally. The editor of a gazetteer welcomed this, because 'so much is usually said, both vaguely and violently, by tourists, declaimers and politicians of all classes respecting the house-accommodation of the Irish'.[192] The authors of the census chose certain indicators of a house's worth, adopting four classes:

> The lowest, or fourth class, were comprised all mud cabins having only one room – in the third, a better description of cottage, still built of mud, but varying from two to four rooms and windows – in the second, a good farmhouse or, in towns, a house in a small street, having from five to nine rooms and windows – and in the first, all houses of a better description than the preceding classes.[193]

The finding of the census nationally was as follows:

	Number of families	Number of houses
1st Class	67,224	40,030
2nd Class	321,925	264,184
3rd Class	566,659	533,297
4th Class	516,931	491,278
Total	**1,472,739**	**1,328,789**

In rural districts of Ireland, 43.5 per cent of families lived in the lowest class of housing ('mud cabins having only one room') and 40 per cent in the second lowest ('still built of mud, but varying from two to four rooms and windows'). Thus, the authors of the census wrote, 'Nearly half of the families of the rural population, and somewhat more than one-third of the families of the civic population, are living in the lowest state, being possessed of accommodation equivalent to a cabin consisting but of a single room.' In this context it is also worth bearing in mind that the *average* number of persons in an Irish family then was 5.5, and that many families in mud cabins were larger than that.[194]

The London *Times* in Kenmare

A decade after the Poor Law Commissioners published their report of 1836, a correspondent for the London *Times* came to Killarney and Kenmare. The potato had begun to fail, but the full extent of the

Fig. 4. An Irish cabin in Derrynane Beg, Iveragh. Pictorial Times, *7 Feb. 1846.*
Courtesy 'Views of the Famine' website.

unfolding disaster was not yet apparent. The *Times* was unsympathetic to
Ireland, and its correspondent, Thomas Campbell Foster, was on his way
west to Derrynane to write an article about Daniel O'Connell's tenantry:

> Westward, however, of Killarney but few visitors journey. There
> is no commerce, an infinitely sub-divided and pauper tenantry,
> who (excepting a little butter, which they manufacture to pay
> their rents) create nothing beyond their consumption. The
> planting of potatoes and the churning of butter bounds their
> knowledge; the selling of a firkin of butter a year to some Cork
> merchant is the extent of their intercourse with the rest of the
> world. Here then we may expect to find all the peculiarities of
> the Irish character strongly marked, and their habits still after
> their own hearts; and we do find them.[195]

Much of that butter was exported from Cork, including to London,
where – according to Weld, in 1807 – it was 'deprived' of its conserving
salt and sold as the product of Epping in Essex, 'Many a worthy citizen,
who would spurn the idea of breakfasting upon the produce of the
Irish mountains, devours it without perceiving the difference.'[196]

Foster of the *Times* did not admire those in Kerry whom he
described as 'the half-naked and potato-fed people' in their 'miserable
hovels', although he acknowledged that their landlords were not much
help to them:

In filthiness and squalid poverty, starving on a rood of land with miles of wasteland around him, which the application of knowledge and industry would make teem with plenty, the poor Kerry farmer exists in contented wretchedness. Neglected by his landlord, he knows nothing beyond the growing of potatoes; oppressed by the hard-fisted middle-man, who lives by squeezing another rent out of his industry, he is steeped in hopeless poverty; cheated and robbed by the bailiffs and drivers, who extort from him his last sixpence for rent, and their fees; and pounced upon by the middle-man for an increased rent, if he improves an acre of land; he learns cheating and extortion from his betters, and practises both on the wretched being who labours on his farm. In a hovel like a pigsty, in which it is impossible to stand upright, without chimney and without window, with but one room, an iron pot, and a rude bedstead, with some straw litter, as the only furniture, bed, or bed-clothes, the labourer, in the midst of half a dozen nearly naked children, with his barefooted wife, sits squatted on the mud floor round the peat fire. A garden plot of potatoes is their whole subsistence, and for this patch of land, and the hovel which shelters him and his family, his labour is sold to some farmer, who lets him his land and hovel, for a year.[197]

Such was the sub-division of holdings that most families on them 'have not more than a cow's grass a piece to live upon'. Foster offered this 'clue' to their poverty:

A cow on fair good land in this part of Kerry will yield a firkin and a half of butter a year. A firkin of butter is worth £2.15s; a firkin and a half of butter will therefore leave about £4 a year, and the rent is from £2 to £4 for this cow's grass. A patch of the land is manured with seaweed and shell-sand, which the poor barefooted women carry in hampers on their backs great distances, and on this they raise the potatoes for their year's consumption. The value of the butter barely pays their rent, and the buttermilk and potatoes are the only food or means of subsistence which the small tenants have. The labourers are worse off; they have not the buttermilk.[198]

While the *Times* was no friend of Ireland, John O'Sullivan himself, in 1849, used quite similar graphic terms to describe the condition of poor people in the Kenmare Union before the great famine:

The habitations were the most indifferent; in one parish of mine I do not suppose there were six slated houses; in the parish of Templenoe few of the houses were even thatched with wheaten straw; the practice was to spend, say a fortnight, cutting a long grass that they call finane; this finane was fetched home, and a coat of it was put over the cabins; twisted ropes of the same material were then put over it, and stones were suspended from the roof; sometimes they procured strips of osiers or other twigs to stack it on the roof; the houses had no glazed windows and no chimneys; they were not plastered either inside or outside; there were scarcely any doors to keep out the inclemency of the weather, and they were of such a height inside as scarcely to admit of one standing up erect; there were no separate sleeping apartments, and scarcely enough of straw to supply them with a bed, and no covering to an extent that you would say was necessary. Then as regards clothing, the clothing was certainly not what we should say a farmer should enjoy; it was indifferent clothing, seldom a second suit, nothing at all like what we see on the farmers in Leinster, or in the northern part of Munster, or even on the farmers in the vicinity of Tralee and Killarney, in the same county; and the food was potatoes, and, *semper eadem* [Latin: always the same], worse and worse.[199]

The approaching catastrophe was still unforeseen when, in November 1845, the Kenmare workhouse opened as a resource for the destitute. Reporting to the Poor Law Commissioners in January 1846, its newly appointed guardians noted that the potato crop was 'above an average one'. This should have been very good news, but it was qualified by the fact that half of the crop was lost to disease.[200] William Steuart Trench, who later replaced James Hickson as Lansdowne's agent in Kenmare, once gave this pugnacious explanation for the extent of pauperism in Kenmare during the great famine:

No restraint whatever had been put upon the system of subdivision of land. Boys and girls intermarried unchecked, each at the age of seventeen or eighteen, without thinking it necessary to make any provision whatever for their future subsistence, beyond a shed to lie down in, and a small plot of land whereon to grow potatoes. Innumerable squatters had settled themselves, unquestioned, in huts on the mountain-sides and in the valleys, without any sufficient provision for their maintenance during the year. They sowed their patches of potatoes early in spring, using seaweed alone as manure. Then as the scarce seasons of spring and summer came on, they nailed up the doors of their huts, took all their children along with them, together with a few tin cans, and started on a migratory and piratical expedition over the counties of Kerry and Cork, trusting to their adroitness and good luck in begging to keep the family alive till the potato crop came in again. And thus, in consequence of the neglect or supineness of the agent, who – in direct violation of his lordship's instructions, and without his knowledge – allowed numbers of strangers and young married couples to settle on his estate, paying no rent, and almost without any visible means of subsistence, not only the finances, but the character and condition of the property, were at a very low ebb. The estate, in fact, was swamped with paupers.[201]

Trench described Hickson, his predecessor, as 'an elderly gentleman of easy habits; kind hearted and honourable; but scarcely capable of grappling with the serious difficulties which at that time surrounded him as responsible manager of so large and important a property'.[202] Hickson and O'Sullivan were friends, not least perhaps precisely because the agent was kind. On one occasion in London, O'Sullivan persuaded Lord Lansdowne to find jobs in the navy for two of Hickson's thirteen children.[203] Trench would apply a heavier hand than Hickson in managing the Kerry estate, thus benefiting Lansdowne but antagonising tenants.

Faction fights

In 1770 William Petty (1737–1805), 2nd Earl of Shelburne and the future 1st Lord Lansdowne, complained to the Lord Lieutenant in Dublin that Catholics around Kenmare were 'of fierce and uncultivated manners, accustomed to hate and despise civil government'. He claimed that the inhabitants formed various large groups with the object of 'terrifying men of different principles (who might introduce the Protestant Religion, attachment to Government, obedience to the Laws, Arts and Industry) from settling among them, or ruining such as have attempted it'. He lamented 'the habitual tendency of the natives to idleness and rioting'.[204]

Rioting in the form of faction fights was indeed habitual in parts of Ireland, including Kerry.[205] Seen in part as a transgressive form of recreation, such fighting with sticks was nonetheless deadly, with frequent casualties. The man who murdered Rev. Fitzgerald Tisdall at the Priest's Leap between Bantry and Kenmare, in 1809, was notorious for being 'regularly sent for, fed and paid according to his work' when factions fought at fairs.[206] In autumn 1828 Hermann Pückler-Muskau, a Silesian prince, visited:

> It was fair-time [fair day] when I arrived in Kenmare, and I could hardly penetrate through the bustling crowd with my one-horse vehicle, especially from the number of drunken men who would not – perhaps could not – get out of the way. One of them fell in an attempt to do so, and knocked his head so violently on the pavement that he was carried away senseless, – a thing of such common occurrence that it attracted no attention. The skulls of Irishmen appear to be universally of a more firm and massive construction than those of other people, probably because they are trained to receive shillelagh blows. While I dined, I had another opportunity of observing several affrays. First a knot of people collect, shouting and screaming; this rapidly thickens; and all at once, in the twinkling of an eye, a hundred shillelaghs [hard sticks used as weapons, typically blackthorn or oak] whirl in the air, and the thumps, – which are generally applied to the head, – bang and snap like the distant report of fire-arms, till one party has gained the victory. As I was now at the fountain-head, through the mediation of mine host I bought one of the finest specimens of this weapon, yet warm from the fight. It is as hard as iron, and that it may be sure to do execution it is also weighted at the end with lead.[207]

Fr John O'Sullivan was later to describe faction fights as 'the bane and the ruin of our unhappy country'. Although the priest thought that these 'cannot be dealt with too severely', they were a symptom of the complexity of cultural and economic relationships and were not easily suppressed.[208]

Notwithstanding such fighting and drunkenness, Prince Pückler-Muskau generally liked the 'merry humour and good-natured politeness' of those whom he met in Kenmare, 'I know no nation of which the lower classes appear so little selfish; so thankful for the least friendly word vouchsafed to them by a gentleman, without the least idea of gain. I really know no country in which I would rather be a large landed proprietor than here.' While deference to the gentry evidently had its charms for the Silesian aristocrat, he was impatient with what he saw as English intolerance and Protestant bigotry in Ireland.[209]

Literacy

The Iveragh poet Tomás Rua Ó Súilleabháin (1785–1848) was of humble origins in Derrynane and worked as a schoolmaster in the area. He built up and treasured a collection of books and manuscripts in the Irish language, but on taking new employment further west in Portmagee, he lost these when the boat transporting them there for him ran onto rocks. The loss inspired him to compose a heartfelt lament entitled 'Amhrán na Leabhar' (Song of the Books). Daniel O'Connell, who is said to have funded Ó Súilleabháin's training as a teacher at a Dublin institution – and whose praises the poet sang – thought that the vast majority of people who spoke the Irish language in his day could not read it.[210] According to the 1841 census, 71 per cent of Kerry people aged over 5 years could neither read nor write *any* language, while only 17 per cent of those between the ages of 5 and 15 were attending school. By 1851 the figures improved (illiteracy falling to 64 per cent and schooling on the rise to 27 per cent). It may be noted that rates in the Kenmare Union were below the Kerry average. In 1861, in a thundering sermon that he delivered in Kenmare, Fr John O'Sullivan scolded his congregation:

> Now how many listening to me can read and write? I'm ashamed to say it, but for your own good I must – I am quite sure not one-half, and this very one-half perhaps the loudest in chanting the glories of their ancestors. What value is any man that cannot read and write? What claim has he on being looked upon as a civilised being at all?

He declared that he had worked hard for years 'to educate all under my charge, and try and put a better face on our poor county'.[211]

Class interests

About 1791, the settler William Petty's descendant and namesake – the 2nd Earl of Shelburne and 1st Lord Lansdowne, who had founded Kenmare town – observed that

> The history of Ireland is in fact a history of the policy of England in regard to Ireland [...] It will be found to have always been the shame of England, as Sicily was of Rome and is now of Naples,

and Corsica was of Genoa. God never intended one country to govern another.[212]

If the catastrophe of a terrible famine had occurred in England, would the UK government have responded more actively than it did to the Irish great famine of the 1840s? Cormac Ó Gráda is scathing about historians who, in his opinion, have not attributed to those in power responsibility for the scale of the disaster.[213] A Whig administration in London was very reluctant to interfere with the mechanisms of the market place, being slow even to release supplies from its food depots. The prevailing philosophy of political economy placed great emphasis on free trade as a solution to social ills. Government ideology rationalised imperial and class self-interest, leaving the poor exposed.

However, there were also class distinctions between, and within, the Protestant and Catholic populations of Ireland that meant certain Irish people fared much worse than others when the potato blight came. Middle-class Catholic merchants, for example, worked with local Protestant land agents and might benefit from business connections while remaining neutral on issues such as rural tenant rights. Struggling farmers and labourers alike watched the emergence and growth of a professional middle-class, becoming sceptical of the role of traders, doctors and priests. This scepticism was expressed during the great famine, for example, in verses entitled 'The Kenmare Committee':

> The farmers are taxed every quarter,
> As a means to keep paupers secure,
>
> But doctors, priests, parsons and guardians,
> Have plundered it all from the poor.[214]

There were differences of interest between landlords and tenants no matter what their nationality, religion or social level. On the Catholic side, too, there were various political perspectives, with demands to repeal the Act of Union of 1800 certainly not commanding unanimous support. Although O'Sullivan had supported Catholic emancipation, he thought the subsequent campaign for repeal of the union of Britain and Ireland a distraction, 'a farce and a humbug', and described himself as a 'bare repealer'.[215] Anglo-Irish landlords and Catholic bishops looked at European developments and feared the influence of egalitarian revolts there on Irish society. Many parish priests condemned both agrarian violence and radical organisations such as Young Ireland and the Fenians.

Middlemen

A significant factor in rural life was the constant exploitation by 'middlemen' farmers, or profiteers, of those poorer than themselves – a phenomenon that predated the great famine. Indeed, in 1937 the 6th Marquess of Lansdowne, by then a former member of Seanad Éireann (the Irish senate), observed that the system of middlemen under his ancestors 'was scarcely a new one'. He thought that 'it continued in an altered form that [system] under which the former [Gaelic] overlords and their tributary chieftains had each exacted what they could from those beneath them. It was always those at the bottom of the scale who suffered.'[216]

Middlemen earned a bad reputation in general. They stood between a head landlord, from whom they rented, and tenants, to whom they sublet either some or all of the land leased to themselves in the first instance. In Kerry, as elsewhere, some were native Irish Catholics, including members of families that had been resident in the area before the English confiscated local land. They primarily constituted a sort of residual and reduced Gaelic gentry rather than a mercantile bourgeoisie, although some also had businesses in towns. Such old Irish families were mocked for their social pretensions and habits, which rubbed salt into the wounds of their native kith and kin regardless of class.[217] As Eoghan Rua Ó Súilleabháin (O'Sullivan), the eighteenth-century Kerry poet who was ever conscious of changed circumstances, is reputed to have said when directed to sit on a pile of turf, 'Ní insan ainnise is measa linn bheith síos go deo, ach an tarcaisne do leanas sinn i ndiaig na leon.' (It's not being down that's worst, but the scorn that goes with it.)[218]

While some prominent middlemen around Kenmare prided themselves on being sprung from the blood of O'Sullivan chieftains and other prestigious Gaelic families, their standing was firmly qualified by that of an ultimate Anglo-Irish or English landlord – backed up, if necessary, by legal and military systems that were firmly in Anglo-Irish and English Protestant hands. Sometimes there were layers of middlemen, and often, at the bottom, there was a precarious tenant who in turn might allow labourers or other 'squatters'[219] to live on a tiny plot without any security. Even before the famine, landlords in Kerry won an unenviable reputation as 'the worst in the country'.

They were said to have rack-rented the farmers to such an extent that those at the end of the leasehold line were little better off than the labourers under them, 'Tenants of from one to ten acres were only nominally superior in their material position to labourers, and they were continually sinking to the status of labourers through being dispossessed of their holdings.'[220]

These layers of class might be obscured by how formally one chose to define a middleman. Did it include someone allowed to occupy land without a written agreement? Fr O'Sullivan told a select committee of the House of Commons that there was only one middleman on the Lansdowne estate in his own parish. However, tenant farmers permitted some labourers to hold a small plot without any formal lease; and O'Sullivan certainly complained about how farmers treated labourers, 'They are the most wretched people upon the face of the globe. I do not believe that any race upon the face of the earth would suffer the privations they do under the farmers.' Yet Rev. Denis Mahony of Dromore Castle thought that many local farmers did not merit the security of a lease, for 'they are a pastoral people who live by their herds and flocks. They are a lazy people, and I do not think of giving a lease to them […] they are naturally an indolent people, and do not like any innovation.' Without a lease, such farmers might be deemed not to be tenants in law.[221]

Small farmers and labourers could be driven by want to the workhouse, or to desperate measures such as sheep-stealing, not only by the failure of the potato crop but also partly by the exactions of Protestant or Catholic middlemen and tenant farmers in a society where class complicated religious and national identities.[222] In 1805 Henry Petty, later 3rd Marquess of Lansdowne, wrote to Francis Horner MP:

The only instance in which a middleman (in this or any other trade) can contribute to improvement, is being enabled from situation, industry, or capital, to do that which neither the proprietor nor the immediate holder of the land can do, or can do without inconvenience. This is not the case with the Irish middleman; he is generally a sort of small needy gentleman, who finding his means inadequate to his expenses, takes the lease or in other words the agency of a district from the great proprietor [head landlord], collects the rents and puts a part of them in his pocket. In this district he expends neither capital nor industry, unless that activity can be called industry which he exerts driving for rents, and goading the tenantry to overwork the land and overwork themselves [...] and the farm, in which he has of course no permanent interest, comes out of his hands with a diminished value [...] the subdivision of land among the peasantry is too minute, and the country consequently overstocked with population.[223]

Identifying, as other observers did, the 'minute' subdivision of land as a major Irish problem, Henry pointed to the clearances of families off land in Scotland as a remedy, 'though the task is distressing from the prediliction they [tenants] have for situations to which they are accustomed, and the reluctance one naturally feels in dispossessing them so much against their inclination.' Clearances in Scotland, where many dispossessed tenants had little option but to emigrate, were indeed one way to change the form of agriculture. But if Lansdowne blamed middlemen, there were critics in England as well as Ireland who thought that absentee landlords were also responsible for the poor use of land in Ireland. After all, what Robert MacCarthy has written of Trinity College Dublin in relation to middlemen on its estate at Glanerought in Kenmare might be said of many landlords who used middlemen to escape close involvement with the ultimate tenants on their land:

> The practice relieved a college of a number of responsibilities. The lessee bore all the risks inseparable from land ownership: of failing to find a tenant in times of rural distress, or of loss by bankrupt or absconding tenants; and he performed the necessary detailed supervision for which the college would otherwise have had to employ an administrative staff.[224]

Without adequate reforms, Ireland was then poorly equipped to cope with an economic crisis such as a great famine.

7

A New Priest and Old Whiskey, 1839–1844

In April 1839, when John O'Sullivan arrived in Kenmare as its new parish priest, the area was largely rural.[225] Although born in the town of Tralee, O'Sullivan bore a surname that had a particular resonance for people around Kenmare. On each side of Kenmare Bay, as seen earlier, lie lands once under the control of the O'Sullivan sept.[226]

Parish 'chapels of mud walls'

O'Sullivan was responsible for the combined parish of Kenmare and Templenoe, with a chapel at each location. The road from Kenmare to Templenoe is known today as part of the Ring of Kerry, running west near the coast of Kenmare Bay and out past the ruined O'Sullivan Mór stronghold of Dunkerron Castle towards Sneem. One turns left after Reen crossroads, down a small lane, to find the remains of Templenoe chapel. While the place name is formed by Irish words meaning 'new church', by the nineteenth century the original structure was already ruined and a makeshift building was thrown up against its remains. A source from the 1750s indicates that the original was said to have been part of a settlement once much frequented by Spanish traders:

> I very well remember to hear antient people tell, about sixty years ago, that they had it for truth from other antient people, about eighty years before, that, at the little village that was at Templenoe Church for about sixty years after the building thereof, and about the like term before the declination of said Spanish trading, that a gallon of rich Spanish wine could be purchased there for a fresh salmon, and a good many gallons for a green hide.[227]

Until Kenmare town developed in the nineteenth century, Templenoe chapel remained a centre of pastoral activity. By the time O'Sullivan arrived as parish priest, it was in a very poor state – as John O'Donovan of the Ordnance Survey observed about that time.[228] An anonymous author in an English-Catholic journal of 1841 wrote that a great number of existing Irish chapels were 'in a condition utterly disgraceful to any nation affecting to call itself civilised', and that 'in some parts of Kerry and Mayo chapels of mud walls and thatched roofs, which freely admit the snow and the rain, are by no means uncommon spectacles.'[229] Indeed, O'Sullivan described the chapel at Templenoe as an 'old thatched cabin with the rain pouring down […] and the people lying in on me while saying Mass'.[230] He wrote that it was 'a source of great uneasiness and trouble to me for eight long years':

> It was a wretched hovel; the rain poured down through the rotten roof, the whole floor of the chapel was inundated every wet Sunday. The merest cabin in the country was preferable to this wretched edifice alongside the old church of Templenoe. I was not many months in the country when I applied to the Rev. Denis Mahony for a site somewhere west of the New Church and the scoundrel would not condescend to reply to my letter.

He added that it took him a few years more to obtain a suitable site for a new chapel, north of the main road west, 'the foundation stone of which I laid on the 18th May 1846, and said my first Mass therein on the 15th of December of the same year. *Deo Gratias* [Latin: Thanks be to God].'[231] His new chapel was to be substantially reconstructed and reduced in size in 1960, but fortunately, an old printed photograph of people arriving at it survives.[232]

By 1847 O'Sullivan had also enlarged the chapel built at Kenmare earier in the century. This continued to serve until he erected the present Holy Cross Church in the town. Locals say that the former was fitted with *súgán* (straw) chairs, for women, rather than the hard benches later used in many Irish churches, and that flat stones were provided on which men knelt on wet days to keep their trousers dry.

The new parish priest purported to desire good relations with those Protestants who looked for the same with him; as was seen, Protestants had been good to his widowed mother and his sister. In 1841, at a meeting in Kenmare attended by local Protestant dignitaries, he expressed pleasure at how well Catholics and Protestants were getting on in Kenmare, 'as it had been his fault perhaps as well as his misfortune to stand on very different terms with those who differed with him in religion, as well as in politics in another place [Dingle]'.

He reportedly added that 'without at all intending to blame those with whom he had the misfortune to differ', it was not entirely from 'the pugnacity of his own disposition' that such differences had arisen.[233]

O'Sullivan thought that his experience of preaching in Irish in Dingle was of limited value in Kenmare town:

> At the first Mass in Kenmare it would be a positive insult to the great people there, aye and to the low ones, to address them in the Irish language. They never will forget the affront put upon them by my predecessor, Michael Devine, who was there only three months, by giving out the Rosary in Irish.[234]

Yet many of his parishioners spoke Irish as their daily language, and the workhouse nurse was required to have it. In 1850 he was to describe Irish as an 'obstacle to progress and to civilisation'; he asserted that 'any two languages in a country must embarrass'.[235] Nevertheless, it is clear from references in his journals that he continued to use Irish on his diocesan travels with the bishop of Kerry, even as he found it a tiring tongue in which to preach.[236]

At sea: 'a most miraculous escape'

O'Sullivan got on well with Cornelius Egan, the bishop of Kerry who had personally encouraged his vocation. In 1839 Egan made him vicar-general as well as parish priest, and he soon began to have O'Sullivan accompany him on some of the annual visitations that saw the bishop tour his diocese and confirm children. He did so first in 1841, when both the bishop and John Quill, parish priest of Milltown, stopped a while with O'Sullivan in Kenmare:

> We had some merry nights at my house, so much so that the bishop whose bedroom was over where we sat had to send down to tell us to behave ourselves. We did so by adjourning to another room. Not that we drank anything but Quill, who was a mighty pleasant man, would stay up until morning upon the good and long-established principle of 'quoniam convenimus' [Latin: since we are met]. I never went a pleasanter visitation; we had no black potatoes, no soupers in those days save in Dingle, unhappy Dingle.[237]

The visitations were not entirely pleasant:

> At Sneem, Quill and I had to sleep together and that on a sofa in the bit of a parlour in which we dined. The heat was

intolerable and tho' we left the window down and threw off all the bedclothes save the sheet, we could not close our eyes with the heat. The bishop slept in a miserable bedroom inside us.[238]

On another occasion, across Kenmare Bay, the whole visitation party boarded boats to get to a very remote part of the parish on the Beara Peninsula:

The day was beautiful on our going out, the sea like a sheet of glass, but all of a sudden it turned to blow, the waves became nearly mountains high, so high that the two boats though within a few perches were often out of each other's view. The bishop was awfully sick. 'Devil mend him' said *young* Sheahan when he saw him from the other boat stretched out at full length, 'many a man he made sick himself'. Sheahan was a regular Diogenes carping at and gnawing the whole world. When the bishop heard what he said he was amused beyond measure. *Old* Sheahan in our boat, a fine venerable respectable old man [...] was quite paralyzed with terror. Tho' he had all the playfulness of youth or a kitten in the morning, he became all of a sudden as mute and as dumb as an idiot.

Rounding a headland, they shipped several breakers and O'Sullivan's boat 'opened out at bottom from stem to stern'. He and his party had what he described as 'a most miraculous escape'. The bishop refused to return by sea.[239] Much of Kerry was still unsuited to a ride by gig, even where there was a basic road. Nevertheless, on two early visitations on which O'Sullivan accompanied his bishop, the priest went at least part of the way in his gig while the bishop rode on horseback, as was long his custom.[240] What local people made of the anomaly is unknown.

As a trusted vicar-general of the diocese, O'Sullivan participated in its local *concursus*, examining candidates for the priesthood. Its three other members had been doing the job alone for years, 'until Euclid and Algebra were also required, and none of the three "having read so far", I was added to the bench of judges'. His principle was 'to vote for the boy I see young, intelligent and smart in himself even though he may not have been so precise and accurate as more advanced and elderly fellows'. He wrote that he opposed nepotism, on one occasion offending his old Greek and Latin teacher, Dan McCarthy, by refusing to use his own influence to have McCarthy's nephew sent to Maynooth without competing in a *concursus*.[241]

The stations

One of the duties of a rural parish priest was to go on 'the stations', a once-common, weeks-long round of visits to homes at Easter and Christmas each year. Farmers who were better off than their neighbours took turns hosting at their own houses the celebration of Mass, the hearing of confessions, and baptisms – followed usually by a meal for any priests present.

The custom of stations had grown up in Ireland from the middle of the eighteenth century, partly because there were too few Catholic chapels to serve the large and widely dispersed Catholic population. O'Sullivan also identified an additional factor: that some of the poor old people had no clothes suitable to wear to church. At the stations, priests also collected 'dues' or donations that largely supported them and their church, an organisation that had long struggled financially because of the poverty of so many of its burgeoning Irish flock.[242] O'Sullivan later told a parliamentary committee that, as a priest, he would benefit from a consolidation of farms because 'one good farmer would contribute more to my support than twenty of the small farmers. We never get anything worth talking of from the small farmers; what we get comes chiefly from larger farmers and from people in business.' He added that he had 'not the slightest objection' to consolidation 'provided there were no clearances, that is to say, provided the tenants were not turned out and sent into the towns'.[243] His statement indicates that parish priests depended on bigger farmers and shopkeepers to support them.

Fig. 5. Sketch of a 'station' by W.H. Brooke. From Carleton, Traits and Stories of the Irish Peasantry *(1830).*

Going on the stations sometimes involved strenuous travel in bad weather, and there was no guarantee of comfort upon arrival. After moving to Kenmare, O'Sullivan had a fraught first round in 'the Glens'. This was the elevated northern part of Templenoe, about 17 kilometres from Kenmare. He had learnt that his predecessors always dined and slept in the house where they were to hold the station on the following day, and he decided to do the same now:

> My first station was at Béaldarg [near Lough Brin]. The rain was pouring down in all directions, the storm was howling and when the moon began to rise all was bright as day. Dan Healy [his curate] was snoring in the same bed, or rather bundle of straw with me. I never closed my eyes that night.

He fared better on the next two nights, but not on the fourth at Direendarragh (*doirín darrach*, or 'little oak wood'), by the upper River Blackwater:

> I was dead tired, was sound asleep when Dan Healy awoke me by jumping out of bed and wishing hearty bad luck to the whole of them. To whom I did not understand until I found my whole person pinched and gnawed and mangled by a host of vermin. I had to follow him. It was just 3 o'clock, in the month of June. I walked along the banks of the river until the people assembled, and when I sat down to hear confessions the stock I brought with me from the unlucky bed so tormented me that I had to get up three times and take off my stockings and shake the cattle out. I never slept in their house since. We take up two beds and come every night to a farmer's house in Direendarragh.[244]

Three or four years later, at that same farmer's house in Direendarragh, O'Sullivan enjoyed an unusual encounter, which was all the more pleasing because he guessed that it would annoy his foe Denis Mahony to learn of it. Mahony was away but had allowed Rev. George Henry Hely-Hutchinson, a son of the Cork City member of parliament Christopher – and a second cousin of Mahony, according to O'Sullivan – to stay at Dromore Castle in his absence. Hutchinson's 'living', or endowed position, as an Anglican clergyman was in England. His wife Alicia and his Anglican curate were travelling with him. According to O'Sullivan, Alicia was a daughter of the Rev. Robert Morritt of Co. Cork. Morritt had gained a reputation for his harsh treatment of tenants but, when prosecuted on one occasion, retained Daniel

O'Connell as counsel to indicate that he was not prejudiced against Catholics.[245] Alicia had become a Catholic, according to O'Sullivan. While at Dromore, she used to attend Mass weekly at his chapel in Templenoe:

> Having learned one day that we had stations at Lough Brin she never stopt until she brought the parson and his curate to our station dinner at the lake. They liked the thing vastly, took two or three tumblers of punch and upon their way home readily consented to turn in and take another one with us in our lodge at Direendarragh. The whiskey was very old, some I brought from home, and what with singing and playing on the accordion and drinking punch my two parsons and the lady never left us until near one o'clock – and two wolves and two lambs coming together could not be more talked about for years after than the meeting of the priests and the parsons.[246]

It is not known what Mahony made of all this, if he learnt of it, but he certainly grew no fonder of O'Sullivan as time passed.

O'Sullivan came to regard the stations as a vital part of his mission as a parish priest, believing that they kept him closely in touch with his parishioners and also gave people a chance that they would not otherwise conveniently have to participate in the sacraments. Nevertheless, some bishops regarded the Irish stations as unorthodox, and even unseemly, and wished to bring Irish practices more into line with those in other countries where a local church building was the focus of sacramental life.

Diary of a country priest

On 1 March 1842 Fr John O'Sullivan's maternal grandmother, 'the relict of the late Captain Stephen Walsh of the merchant's service', died at Tralee, aged 90, in the former home of her late son Stephen in The Square (where Stephen's own son then lived). A local paper described her disposition as 'friendly and affectionate', and reported that she had 'retained her memory unimpaired, and her mental faculties to the last'.[247]

Death was also the spur for O'Sullivan's decision, during 1843, to begin a book of occasional 'recollections and effusions'. He wanted 'some record of my care of this parish', having lingered the previous day before Mass in the burial ground at Templenoe by the graves of two priests, O'Quirke and Falvey. They had lived 'more than a century since', and 'were regarded as saints after their death'. The oldest people living in the area told him that, in medieval style, the graves of the two revered priests had been opened 'and their bones carried away for the purpose of effecting cures'. He could find out no more about them, 'Had those Rev. Fathers taken the trouble of committing to paper a few facts connected with the mission in those parishes […] how highly interesting would they not appear now and what precious relics would they not be considered.' He thought that perhaps 'the random sketches' that he was about to commence might be of interest to a successor; that they could induce the future priest to remember him at the altar, 'and pray the God of Mercy to overlook the many faults I am daily liable to'. He wrote at the outset that upon his death the diary should be handed over to his successor without anyone else reading it in the interim.[248]

The first few pages of his recollections are devoted to some details of his life up to that point. Then comes the first dated entry, on 10 October 1843. He had just returned from pastoral work to read in a newspaper that the great national movement of Daniel O'Connell MP – for the repeal of the Act of Union between Britain and Ireland – was being faced down by the government. According to O'Sullivan, O'Connell had offered to fund his education as a child and had secured a job in a bank for his brother. Having earlier won Catholic emancipation, O'Connell was now convening what were described as 'monster' open-air meetings to demonstrate peaceful support for his repeal campaign. However, the government prohibited his next gathering, scheduled for 8 October at Clontarf near Dublin, and O'Connell then confirmed its cancellation to avoid violent confrontation. O'Sullivan wrote, 'The newspaper brings an account of the Repeal meeting at Clontarf being put down by proclamation. I have not given in my adhesion to [i.e. declared support for] the Repeal cause for many reasons.' He identified just two such reasons. The first was his bad experience of the complications that arose when he encouraged parishioners in Dingle to vote a certain way in 1835. The second was that he felt that taking an overt political stance would weaken him strategically in his efforts to limit the ambitions of the local landlord and clergyman Denis Mahony. Mahony had threatened him with legal proceedings:

> I consider then that by abstaining from politics that I put him in the wrong by being able to show that I acted only in defence of my religion and in the discharge of my duty – which I trust in God has been my only motive and ever shall. I will not therefore take

any part in the Repeal Movement at least until after the opening of the [Law] Term in Dublin when I shall see if the Rev[eren]d Denis shall proceed against me. I rather think he will not.

O'Sullivan added, 'The priests of this district, all are repealers.'[249]

Paying for parish and presbytery

The parish priest's house stood a little outside Kenmare town, on the Dromneavane Road a couple of kilometres from his chapel on Shelburne Street. It was not in good repair when he arrived. Fr Richard Fitzmaurice, his immediate predecessor but one, was 'a good innocent man' who had neglected the place, even while living in it, and had allowed his sisters to reside there too:

> For twenty years he and his curate slept in one room over the miserable little parlour at the right hand side as you enter. His sisters slept in the corresponding room, and the small parlour and kitchen – which stood where the parlour we use now is – were the only apartments in the house. There was no stable but an old thatched cabin without a pane of glass in it, to the west of the garden. The garden itself scarcely deserved the name of one. The whole concern was in a shocking condition.[250]

Remarking that the Marquess of Lansdowne was 'very kind to me', O'Sullivan wrote that James Hickson, who was Lansdowne's agent and 'as good a man as ever lived', had advised him to apply to the marquess – 'and he at once made me a grant of £100 towards the improvement of the house.' The priest matched that amount for renovations and also rented 10 acres, 'adjoining the glebe' and running down to the little River Finnihy, from Lansdowne for farming purposes.[251] He might have moved into town but, certainly in 1843, there was a limit to his desire for the company of the Kenmare faithful:

> I consider it would be less expensive and I would wish to be more among the parishioners, [but] not in the way of dining with them or spending my evenings with them. I feel much happier away at home from them, but there is a vast deal of vice in that little town that I could perhaps restrain, and look after more effectually by being among them. I have no wish for the society of any one of the parishioners. They are without exceptions a selfish, grudging, narrow-minded people. I cannot feel among them as I did in Dingle but I must for religion's sake keep them

on hands and be civil to them, and may God give me the grace
to be able to do so.[252]

One wonders what was the 'vast deal of vice' in a very small Irish town.

That same year the English novelist William Makepeace Thackeray
published his unflattering impression of Kenmare, noting sarcastically
that 'it is approached by a little hanging-bridge, which seems to be a
wonder in these parts' and that 'it is a miserable little place when you
enter it.' He conceded that 'a splendid luncheon of all sorts of meat
and excellent cold salmon may sometimes be had for a shilling at the
hotel of the place.' He thought the hotel was 'a great vacant house, like
the rest of them, and would frighten people in England, but after a few
days one grows used to the Castle Rackrent style [...] among these
blustering, blundering waiters.' Samuel Lewis had recently found the
same hotel 'commodious and excellent'. Going on to the races at
Killarney, Thackeray liked 'the young female peasantry' but
encountered old, ugly and 'loathsome' beggars and thought it 'a shame
that such horrible figures are allowed to appear in public'.[253]

O'Sullivan later declared that donations to his parish came 'chiefly
from larger farmers and from people in business', but before the
famine he also thanked others:

> How well the poor people pay in general. How thankful I should
> be to God for His goodness to me at all times. I often fear that
> the prosperity I enjoy in this world may be sadly reversed in the
> next world. I certainly enjoy more real independence than many
> established gentlemen about me. God Almighty has visited me
> with few what may be called real crosses and this often alarms
> me.[254]

He thought then, 'I would be very ungrateful were I not to devote my
whole soul to the poor people who deserve so well of me.' Of the
money they donated, he wrote, 'It is certainly painful to me to be taking
it from them, but if I do not, those who can afford it will make a pretext
of my kindness for not paying me. I would to God that I had an
independence or that we had the government pension.'[255] By a
'pension' he meant a state income similar to that enjoyed by members
of the established Church of Ireland, and some other priests agreed
with him on the point. His blunt statement of approval for this
controversial idea, which was long in the air, appears to have been the
last entry in his journal of recollections for three and a half years. He
was busy, adding to his duties (and the parish income) by taking up

the statutory position of Roman Catholic chaplain at the new workhouse. He also hired a labourer to work the land rented beside the parish house, and (as he saw it) set the Kenmare Union an example of how to reclaim land and provide employment.

Lord Devon and Kenmare

In Kenmare on 7 September 1844, Fr John O'Sullivan was one of a small number of men who gave evidence to the Commission on the Law and Practice in Respect to the Occupation of Land in Ireland, chaired by Lord Devon. These witnesses clearly identified problems that left not just Kerry but also much of Ireland exposed to the full impact of a serial failure of the potato crop, and their evidence is very informative. Tenants had a precarious hold on their homes, and labourers were especially vulnerable. Year-to-year leases were common; they were often made orally and with no right of renewal. There was a limited incentive to improve one's property, as there was no guarantee of a proportionate return on the improving investment. Unfortunately, it was now too late to right such wrongs and avoid the imminent catastrophe.[256]

Nevertheless, despite the great famine, O'Sullivan came to like living in Kenmare. When the possibility of his moving to Tralee as parish priest arose early in 1848, he lay awake in bed and

> rolled about from side to side, excited, tormented, agitated at the prospect of leaving my quiet home and immersing myself in an unhealthy, dirty town. I walked down the farm and tears came to my eyes at parting with the fields I had just brought to such cultivation, where I had spent so many evenings down by the riverside with my dog Rover. No crowned prince was ever half so happy.[257]

In the end he was not moved to Tralee. When the parish priest of Dingle died of cholera in 1849, O'Sullivan reassured himself that 'my deficiency in the Irish [language], to which I would be exclusively confined in Dingle', was an argument against his moving there – despite the fact that he had learnt enough Irish to manage in Dingle when he was a curate in the 1830s. As it transpired, he was to stay in Kenmare until his death in 1874.[258]

He seldom if ever rode a horse; he walked to any station within 4 miles, even if the road was good enough for his gig:

> I like to saunter betimes on the road and admire the beautiful
> wild flowers that I have several times sought to cultivate in the
> garden but in vain. I fall into conversation too with the people
> and thereby learn much of the state of the parish, their habits
> and their manners. I enjoy a walk very much. I am never as much
> at home as when on my legs and it so conduces to my health as
> well. I feel so cold and so chilly in that gig.[259]

Sympathising with his cousin Anne's husband, who had been ill, he
suggested that 'want of exercise' may have been a cause of it, 'I don't
think I'd live twelve months myself but for all I walk.' He wrote, 'Above
all things I fancy a walk over a mountain, and alone though I had two
or three escapes from bulls on such occasions; but the dog is a great
protection.'[260] He was conscious of some of his personal shortcomings:

> I am too cold, too proud, too distant to engage the affections of
> the people; the only hope I have is that my principle study, '*non
> quaero gloriam meam sed gloriam ejus qui misit me*' [Latin: I seek not
> mine own glory, but the glory of him who sent me], – God grant
> it – be the truth.[261]

Pipe and whiskey

It is possible that John O'Sullivan trained his beloved dog to hold a pipe
in its mouth. The allegation that he did so was later used against him by
Archbishop Paul Cullen when local priests wanted O'Sullivan to succeed
Egan as bishop of Kerry – such a trick being deemed undignified.
O'Sullivan wrote that he himself abominated tobacco smoking and snuff,
'and since I was born a pinch of snuff I have not taken nor smoked a
pipe or cigar.' At least once he denounced the habit from the altar. In
April 1854 he also wrote in his journal, 'I don't drink, snuff nor smoke'
– a statement that may have reflected his position on that date, but he
did in fact drink alcohol at other times.[262] Just a month earlier, for
example, he had mentioned that he sometimes took 'a tumbler of
punch', and while a curate in Dingle in the 1830s, he had enjoyed
'stranded' port wine from the wreck of the *Lady Nelson*.[263] He made
punch from whiskey, some of it 'very old'.[264] It must have been tempting
to pack a hipflask when riding out in all weathers on annual visitations
or when trudging on a winter's night to a distant and dying parishioner,
especially during the horrors of the great famine.

Working out his possible expenses for 1849, at a time when the
famine had resulted in his income from parishioners dropping

substantially, O'Sullivan allowed the sum of £6 'for twenty gallons of whiskey'. This compared to £3 for fourteen pounds of tea and £4 for wine, including altar wine. His total household budget that year was £170; out of this, he not only had to feed himself but also had to pay two curates, his farm labourer, the parish clerk, a steward, two maids and a housekeeper.[265]

Priests who provided hospitality to the bishop and O'Sullivan on their annual diocesan visitation sometimes offered punch too. After enjoying such hospitality one night, O'Sullivan rose at four o'clock in the morning, 'my head splitting with aches from the salmon we had yesterday at Denis's'. But, recalling a query he had seen in *Punch* magazine asking if one ever saw a man complaining of headache in the morning who would not put the blame on the fish instead of the punch, he added, 'I took only two at Denis's but those two were perhaps two too many.' A dose of magnesia relieved his condition. When he was at lunch later that day and the host opened both a bottle of brandy and a bottle of wine, O'Sullivan partook of neither.[266]

He was also known to drink a glass of wine when he was not feeling well, but there is no indication that he drank to excess; it is clear from his journals that he was well aware of the dangers of priests and others abusing alcohol.[267] Returning to Dingle on a visitation with the bishop in 1851, he learnt that Patt Gray, once wealthy and generous to the clergy, 'now walks the streets shunned by everyone, with scarcely a coat to his back, his fine house an auxiliary workhouse and himself in a miserable cabin'. O'Sullivan exclaimed, 'What whiskey will do!'[268]

Fr Mathew and temperance

O'Sullivan was reluctant to promise to abstain from alcohol while at the same time believing that 'I would be wanting to my flock were I not to encourage them by all possible means to take the pledge, the blessings that flow therefrom are so immense, so incalculable.'[269] Nevertheless:

> I have not taken the pledge though I seldom, very seldom, exceed one tumbler of punch and I do not see why I should deny myself so much; but I am influenced more by the fear that I should be hereafter obliged to break through it [the pledge] and thereby cause a great shame of disedification.[270]

Catholics and Protestants were attracted to temperance movements, which were flourishing about the time that O'Sullivan moved to

Kenmare. The Catholic movement was led by Theobald Mathew (1790–1856), a Capuchin priest known as 'the Apostle of Temperance' whom O'Sullivan did not like much. In April 1841 Fr Mathew visited Kerry to administer the pledge, and teetotallers held a tea party in Kenmare. O'Sullivan took the chair for speeches by local civic and church leaders, 'The room was tastefully illuminated and ornamented with flowers and evergreens, the music was animating, contentment and happiness beamed on the countenance of all.' Tea, coffee, cakes, bread and butter were served in abundance. One newspaper editor held up the meeting as 'a brilliant example for imitation'. James Hickson, Lansdowne's agent, was present and indicated that Lansdowne had not initially welcomed the society but had 'changed his mind when they had seen their error and put themselves entirely under the guidance of his reverend friend in the chair [O'Sullivan]'.[271] This may signify that while some unionists saw the Catholic temperance movement as a potential form of nationalist mobilisation, Lansdowne trusted O'Sullivan to keep the local society in check. Fr Mathew himself was pointedly non-partisan.[272]

O'Sullivan thought that because the temperance movement embraced all creeds, the pledge to abstain from intoxicating liquor was one that could be violated without sin the moment that a person wished to cease being a member, 'I propounded this at the bishop's table in the presence of fourteen or fifteen priests, and the bishop turned on me most angrily to the evident satisfaction of some few who did not grudge the favourite to come in for a reproof.'[273] Perhaps as a reaction to this reproof, O'Sullivan firmly refused the sacrament of communion to a few young men who confessed to breaking the pledge. In February 1843 these men 'had the folly to bring whiskey to a party at the Temperance Hall' in Kenmare. They subsequently went to Cork to renew their pledge with Fr Mathew but were still refused the sacrament on their return. So they went back to Cork, and their second trip elicited a letter from Mathew to O'Sullivan; he pointed out 'the great cost and expense' of the parishioners' double journey and interceded for them on the grounds of their youth and sincere sorrow. Mathew wrote that he was fully aware of O'Sullivan's 'great exertions to uphold our glorious cause in Kenmare'. O'Sullivan retorted that the men had transgressed 'under rather aggravated circumstances', but he relented.

The Kerry editor who published the correspondence between O'Sullivan and Mathew endorsed the former's severity, 'as it is to be feared the facility of renewing the pledge with some clergymen on the spot is too often an inducement with some poor fellows to take a fling from which they perhaps may never recover'.[274] This incident, like the alleged pipe-smoking dog trick, was used against O'Sullivan to suggest poor judgement. When Mathew's letter and O'Sullivan's reply were published, the matter was 'brought before the authorities in Rome and was it not for the explanation the bishop was able to give of my motives and my character, I would have been cited over at no small cost and inconvenience.'[275]

Overall, Mathew has enjoyed a good reputation, and in April 1841 O'Sullivan himself praised him to the heights amid 'tremendous' cheering at the temperance meeting that Fr Mathew attended in Kenmare. Nonetheless, the parish priest subsequently confided to his journal:

> I am very much prejudiced too against Mathew. I have taken up an opinion that there is an immense share of acting and humbugging about him and I cannot look on him with the same eyes that the public do.[276]

Margaret Anna Cusack, 'the Nun of Kenmare', knew and liked O'Sullivan and also wrote a history of Kerry, but her admiring biography of Fr Mathew mentions neither his visit to the county nor O'Sullivan's reservations about him.[277] O'Sullivan's journals certainly show him ready to discern feet of clay under any priest, and he may have found Mathew too intense about the pledge.[278] Nevertheless, he extended hospitality to 'the Apostle of Temperance', who, arriving on a dark December night in 1845 on a second visit to Kenmare, went straight to O'Sullivan's house and stayed there. The following morning Mathew celebrated Mass in Kenmare chapel while O'Sullivan delivered a lengthy sermon on the great evils of intemperance. Mathew himself also spoke, and it was reported that more than three thousand people that day took the pledge. Non-alcoholic celebrations were held that night at the Lansdowne Arms Hotel and the Temperance Hall, where Mathew was presented with an address in which both Lansdowne and O'Sullivan were also praised for having 'added much to the advancement of the great cause in this locality'. Airs played at the soirée included 'We'll Never Get Drunk Again', 'The Liberator' and 'The Lord of the Soil: The Marquis of Lansdowne'. [279]

O'Sullivan occasionally played cards with Mathew's brother Charles, who sometimes visited Kenmare to audit the accounts of the workhouse and who became unwell in the town on one occasion:

Charles Mathew, brother of the famous Fr Mathew lies ill here, in fever. The Priest [Mathew] is come to see him. I do not like that man at all. I never did like him. The manner in which he hears confessions, the untheological decisions he gives, the whole private life of the man has greatly prejudiced me against him.[280]

O'Sullivan felt differently about Charles, whom he described as 'a very fair, honest man'. He appreciated the fact that Charles dined with him every time he came to Kenmare.[281]

Pl.1–Domhnall O'Sullivan Beare (1560–1618), artist unknown, Spain 1613. *Courtesy St Patrick's College, Maynooth.*

Pl. 2–'A Kerry Peasant'. *Courtesy National Library of Ireland* [L_ROY_09233].

Pl. 3–The 'Giant's Ring' or 'Druid's Circle', Kenmare, *c.*1900. One of a range of ancient monuments in the vicinity, a number of which have been destroyed. *Courtesy National Library of Ireland* [PD 1975 TX (50)].

Pl. 4 (above)–Suspension Bridge, The Sound, Kenmare Bay. Erected 1839–40. Replaced 1933. Linking Kenmare Town and Templenoe on the Iveragh Peninsula to old Kenmare cemetery and Tuosist on the Beara Peninsula. *Courtesy National Library of Ireland* [L_ROY_04691].

Pl. 5 (right)–Thomas Babington Macaulay (1800–1859). Photograph by Antoine Claudet, in *Miscellaneous Writings of Lord Macaulay* (London: Longman, 1860). *Image courtesy King's Inns Library.*

RUINS OF WHITE HOUSE. KENMARE. 6504.W.L.

Pl. 6 (above)–Ruins of the White House, Kenmare, *c.*1905. Petty's settlers surrendered here in the 1680s. It had been built for his agent Richard Orpen. *Courtesy National Library of Ireland* [L_ROY_02753].

Pl. 7 (left)–William Petty (1737–1805), future 1st Lord Lansdowne and Prime Minister of Britain 1782–3. He founded and named the town of Kenmare in the late 1700s. Sketch attributed to James Sayers, published 1782. *Courtesy National Library of Ireland* [PD LANS-WI (2) I].

Pl. 8 (above)–Old
Kenmare holy well ('St
Finian's').

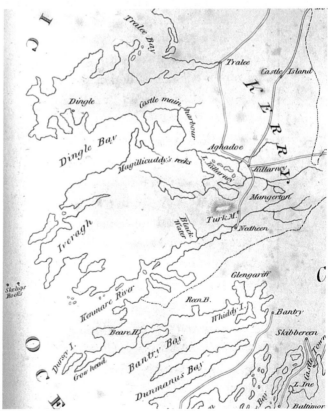

Pl. 9 (right)–A section
of Weld's map of
Kerry, giving still, in
1807, the approximate
location of Kenmare
town by its older name
'Ned[h]een' ([An]
Neidín). From Weld,
Illustrations.

Pl. 10–Lansdowne Lodge *c.*1900. Constructed by 1775 for the 1st Lord Lansdowne. The Lansdowne estate agents Hickson and Trench lived here. *Courtesy National Library of Ireland* [L-CAB-06388].

Pl. 11–The Square, Kenmare, at the bottom of Main (formerly William) Street, *c.*1900. The three-storey building facing the photographer is the Neidín military barracks, built in 1735 but converted to 'a commodious courthouse' by 1842. A floor over the court served as a crowded workhouse dormitory during the great famine. The building on the left with three arches is the Market House, constructed by the 3rd Lord Lansdowne, with a later butter market under the curved roof just past it. *Courtesy National Library of Ireland* [EAS_2233].

Pl. 12–The Square, Tralee, *c.*1900, where Fr John O'Sullivan's maternal uncle Stephen Walsh and family long lived, and where, as a priest, O'Sullivan married Stephen's daughter Maria to Tade Scanlan during the great famine. *Postcard.*

Pl. 13–Nelson Street, Tralee, *c.*1900, where Fr John O'Sullivan's sister Ann taught before her early death. *Courtesy National Library of Ireland* [L_CAB_08477].

Pl. 14 (left)–A Kerry family between 1860 and 1883. *Courtesy National Library of Ireland* [STP 0922].

Pl. 15–The new chapel that Fr John O'Sullivan built at Templenoe in 1846. Photograph before 1929. In 1960 this chapel was significantly restructured and reduced in size.

8

Paupers and Potatoes, 1845–1846

'Before the potato failed entirely', wrote O'Sullivan, 'every third or fourth year there was a partial failure in our own locality, and then fever was sure to follow in its train.'[282] The consequences for families could be dire. There was no extensive system of social welfare or state support for the poor – nothing resembling the kind of welfare with which Europeans would become familiar in the twentieth century. The destitute depended largely on charity.[283]

The workhouse system, introduced first in England and then adapted to Ireland in 1838, was a grudging concession to the economically deprived and desperate paupers. It was extended to Ireland against the best available advice as to what was actually required in Irish circumstances. Workhouse regimes were designed to deter those capable of working outside them, but as Ó Gráda puts it, 'Ireland was too poor for the principle of "less eligibility" to bite; in other words, a relief regime harsher than the least attractive alternative could not be devised.'[284] If in England an able-bodied destitute man might reasonably be expected to find a job to support himself, this was not always possible in Ireland – and especially not during the great famine. A system that gave relief only to people who were destitute or desperate enough to live in an unattractive workhouse was based on the premise that better options were ultimately available, and that was not so during the famine. As a result, workhouses were soon overwhelmed.

The new national network of workhouses (also known as 'poorhouses') was administered locally by boards of guardians, with each board being partly elected by ratepayers and partly filled by designated office-holders. To discharge their statutory duty of relieving the destitute poor in their 'union', particularly by means of a workhouse, each board was required to set a local tax or 'rate' and to collect it from the occupiers of properties in its area.[285] This put a great burden on the poor districts worst hit by famine, including Kenmare, and led to disputes.

Kenmare workhouse opens, 1845

The minutes of the Kenmare board of guardians have survived.[286] It first met in the town's Lansdowne Inn on 16 December 1840, nearly five years before the local workhouse was actually built and opened. Lord Lansdowne's agent, James Hickson, was unanimously elected chairman, and James F. Bland and Edward Godfrey were elected vice-chairmen. The Blands were landlords and descendants of a Yorkshire family that had settled in Kerry in the early eighteenth century. Edward was the only son of William, Church of Ireland rector of Kenmare, and the grandson of Sir William Godfrey of Kilcolman Abbey; he was descended from seventeenth-century settlers. Richard B. Orpen, Henry Orpen and Duckett Maybury, each of them also descended from those English settlers who had returned after the victory of William of Orange, were on the board too. So was Maurice O'Connell.

There was no sense then of the terrible disaster to come, and the system was not designed to withstand such a shock. According to O'Sullivan, the situation before the great famine was that 'the farmers had plenty of potatoes and milk whereon to live' and the destitute were supported 'by the farmers and by the middling classes in society; that is, by the shopkeepers and by persons in my sphere of life; that is having the same means; for the support of the poor was wholly unknown to the rich and landlords at that time.'[287]

At the very outset there were administrative difficulties, with the government's Poor Law Commissioners rejecting – 'on the ground of their inexperience' and on the basis of their high tenders – the Kenmare guardians' choice of persons to value local land for the purpose of setting a poor law rate. The commissioners likewise rejected the Kenmare guardians' first choice of clerk, John Maybury, in favour of a more experienced candidate.[288] Local doctors were at first unwilling to implement a new scheme of vaccination against smallpox; the plan was introduced for the whole population of Britain and Ireland, and the guardians were made responsible for it on a local level. The fee for each vaccination was at issue. The guardians resented bearing the cost.[289]

Kenmare was far from being the only district where problems – regarding the poor law rate, suspicions of jobbery and other matters – delayed the opening of a local workhouse. There are said to have been 'numerous and widespread instances of maladministration' of the new Irish workhouses before the great famine.[290] By the end of 1842, just over half of the 130 workhouses planned for Ireland were operating. Kenmare was not among them.

Mr and Mrs Hall, the two contemporary tourists and writers, were very impressed by the idea of these establishments, which were larger than those in England and differed in other details. The Halls, whose account appeared before Kenmare workhouse opened, singled out for praise Irish workhouse bedsteads – 'which are of a kind different from those used in any other buildings, and very conducive to order and cleanliness' (as well as being a lot cheaper than the English type). The paupers were divided into wards for men and women; they were further separated according to whether they were over or under fifteen years of age. According to the Halls, part of the building was 'reserved for male and female idiots – a class of inmates unprovided for in buildings of the kind in England, and whose location here greatly relieves the lunatic institutions of the country'. Moreover, every boy and girl 'obtains an education'. Able-bodied inmates were not to be idle but were to work within the confines of the workhouse – although workhouses struggled to find meaningful labour for them all.

The Halls thought that the standard of meals was possibly as good as what labourers got at home (but was designed to be no better), 'The diet varies in particular Unions, chiefly depending on the condition of the poor in the neighbourhood, the object being to give such diet to the inmates of the workhouse as shall not be superior to that obtained by the independent labourer.' Yet despite these efforts to assist them, some of the Irish paupers seemed determined to be unhygienic – a fact that provided light relief for the Halls. They noted that a 'poor old woman' decried a proposal to let in some air, which she said 'would be sure to give me the toothache, if I had any teeth left'.[291]

The ratepayers who had been elected as guardians of the Kenmare Union were not happy. They decided, before even opening their workhouse just outside the town, that the new system was 'a curse to the land' and – as administered in Ireland – likely to demoralise the poor. Early in 1843 they agreed to petition parliament, claiming that the system had already 'entirely failed', not least because – as they asserted – in order to fund it, the government was taxing most heavily in proportion to its means 'the class by whose labours and capital the entire community is principally supported and so reduces the grade immediately above pauperism to its level'. The guardians were 'most willing to contribute by every means in their power to any system for the relief of the diseased, the aged and the infirm, while they feel it a grievance to support those able to work in idleness out of the hard earned means of the industrious'. Lord Lansdowne was asked to present the petition to the Lords, and William Browne to the Commons, with Morgan John O'Connell being requested to support Browne there.[292]

O'Sullivan later recalled that when the local workhouse finally opened in October 1845, a representative of the Poor Law Commissioners who was present asked, 'Mr O'Sullivan, do you think that you will ever see this house half full; do you think you will ever see 250 in the house?' He had replied, 'I do not think you ever will.' He thought, and expressed the idea more than once, that no able-bodied person would choose to live in a workhouse unless absolutely desperate.[293]

For breakfast in the new workhouse, men were allowed a half pint of milk and 8 ounces of oatmeal in stirabout, while women got a half pint of milk and 7 ounces of stirabout. For dinner, men got one pint of milk and three and a half pounds of potatoes; women got one pint of milk and three pounds of potatoes.[294] An unvaried diet of milk and potatoes for dinner strikes one today as not just monotonous but also inadequate. At that time, it was the basic daily diet of a large proportion of the Irish population, very occasionally supplemented by a little seafood or meat. The potato crop's failure hit hard many who so heavily depended on that vegetable.

Blight strikes

Before 1845, the new Irish poor law system slowly bedded down.[295] Blight struck the potato during 1845, and that year is given frequently as the starting date of the great hunger. However, the high yield harvested during the summer was good enough to compensate for some of the loss. Between personal reserves and charitable donations, people in general managed to get by. Nevertheless, by November 1845 there were growing problems in Kenmare. The medical officer reported that a case of fever had been taken into the workhouse and communicated to four other paupers:

> The wards of the infirmary are not calculated for fever patients [...] the floors being of clay imbibe and retain all liquid excretions thrown on them by the fever patients and are really

instrumental in fostering and propagating contagion. The nurse attending these patients is calculated to communicate fever in every other part of the infirmary, where her services be required.[296]

Within a fortnight the master of the workhouse himself had contracted the fever and the guardians declined to inspect his books, lest it 'might tend to spread contagion'. In December the guardians agreed to construct a fever hospital adjacent to the workhouse. That same month, a visitor for the Poor Law Commission found Kenmare workhouse 'in a dirty state'.[297] The famine had struck Kenmare Union early, and it would linger late; local ratepayers felt hard-pressed to meet demands to pay for the relief of the starving there.[298]

The law required the appointment of chaplains for each workhouse, and in late 1845, Fr John O'Sullivan became the Roman Catholic chaplain of Kenmare's workhouse – at a yearly salary of £40.[299] In 1848 he was to write, 'It is a hard post to fill, and a most unpleasant duty to discharge – that of chaplain to a workhouse', and he saw his job as 'a poor unfortunate country Parish Priest' as requiring him

> To get between the pallets of the poor victims of persecution and misrule, to hang over and imbibe the infection that exhales from every pore, to listen in patience to the tales of woe, to the unheard of cruelties [...] to reconcile them to forgive and to pray for the men and the system that reduced them to that level.[300]

O'Sullivan was then responding to the local landlord Rev. Denis Mahony of Dromore Castle, who had snidely commented when O'Sullivan accepted the workhouse chaplain's salary.

Terrible 'alarm of losses' in 1846

Children came into the Kenmare workhouse with their parents. The guardians asked Fr O'Sullivan to apply to the Board of Education for stationery. Children were taught for three or four hours daily, and at other times were 'to be kept at such work they may be competent to do'.[301] Just over a year later, the Commissioners for Education were to report on 'the backward state of the children in the [Kenmare] workhouse' and 'the want of books, paper, call rolls etc.' In 1851 the guardians found it 'utterly impossible for the schoolmistress to control and educate the very large numbers of children' there.[302]

By the summer of 1846, the potato crop was again diseased, with no compensating high yield likely this time and with people's reserves depleted. Conditions at the workhouse deteriorated. Gruel was to be given to paupers 'until potatoes can be purchased'. Patients in the infirmary were suffering from the want of a proper supply of fuel. Residents could also no longer enjoy the cream of milk supplied to the workhouse, as the guardians had decided that cream was to be 'turned to profitable account by being converted into butter and sent to market'. A doctor warned that their diet of two meals of gruel or stirabout daily was 'very prejudicial to the paupers' health'.[303] In August 1846 the guardians of the workhouse indicated that there was then no realistic prospect of repaying even part of a building loan that had been received from public monies, because

> it would be impossible under existing circumstances in this part
> of the country to collect so large a sum from the ratepayers in
> addition to the other unavoidable expenses of the union which
> cannot be raised without great difficulty or in many instances
> causing great distress, which unhappily the failure of the potato
> crop is certain to increase.[304]

In September 1846 a local paper reported that one of the Kenmare guardians had found that milk given to the paupers was bad, and a report book mentioned inmates dying 'from want'. The paper raised questions about the appropriate use of imported Indian meal in the daily diet at the workhouse. Its Kenmare correspondent added, 'It is a telling fact that in these times of distress poor creatures are seen to leave after a few days reception, declaring they could not live on the food they got.' The correspondent reported that new milk delivered to the workhouse was being 'hoarded up and butter made from it [for sale] before the paupers should be treated with such a good draught in a poor-house'.[305] One of the workhouse guardians, Edward Godfrey, 'always thought the new milk ought to be furnished the paupers as bought for the house; that such saving was not worth making'. However, a guardian named Nathaniel Irvine was said to have contended that 'the sour milk furnished the paupers was as good as they ought to get.'[306]

The guardians thought that a large proportion of ratepayers in the Kenmare Union consisted of a class of person who, with the destruction of the potato crop, 'will shortly be, if not already, in as distressed a position as that portion of the population solely depending on daily

Fig. 6. 'Destitution in Ireland', Pictorial Times, 22 Aug. 1846. Courtesy National Library of Ireland *[PD A17].*

labour'. Seeing the line of need blurring between smaller farmers and labourers, they thought it would not be possible to provide workhouse relief to any but the 'aged, the infirm and the utterly destitute poor'.[307]

The poor depended partly on voluntary relief or charity, but not enough aid reached Kenmare.[308] Relief committees in each union gave advice and helped to dispense food or supervise public works. On 16 October 1846 a group of men, including Fr John O'Sullivan and the Rev. James Going, met at the workhouse and formed a relief committee to seek further help for Kenmare. O'Sullivan proposed that the chairman, James Hickson, call a public meeting to canvass for public subscriptions to relieve distress, but his idea was rejected, ostensibly because some of those present feared the consequences of assembling a public meeting at that point. It was reported next day that only 40 out of 103 'starved looking' paupers who came to the workhouse were admitted.[309]

The Kenmare correspondent of the *Kerry Examiner* reported a terrible 'alarm of losses' and of rising food prices; the writer identified a tension between traders who were concerned that intervention in the market might undermine their business and starving people who were now desperate, 'It is true food was brought in by a committee named a relief one, but in their sale of the food they charged the same price as the poor dealer who strove to live by his traffic.' The correspondent thought this approach favoured better off people and was inadequate to meet the needs of labourers, and complained that the latter were being oppressed, 'The refusal of the labourer in the locality at first to work at a reduced hire was turned into a cause for refusing him work after he was driven by a starving family to require it.'[310]

Coffee for babies

As numbers at the workhouse grew, the guardians ordered more clothing and bedding while holding creditors at bay. They had problems retaining staff. Bread they purchased was deemed by the visiting committee to be 'sour and bad', while milk was unavailable or 'of the worst description'. By November 1846 the medical officer warned that the workhouse was reaching capacity and that to admit more than the maximum of five hundred persons for which it was designed 'would be so to congregate human beings that pestilential disease would most assuredly be generated'. Already it was hard to cope with contagious fever in the workhouse. Food quality, hygiene and rats were to continue to present problems.[311]

Outside the workhouse, hunger abounded. Rev. James Going, vicar of Kilgarvan, a few miles east of Kenmare town, wrote publicly of one family with five children that had nothing to eat one day except two small heads of cabbage.[312] On 11 December 1846, Maurice O'Connell wrote to his father Daniel about a delay in sanctioning relief funds to construct roads around some property that the O'Connells had bought in Lacka townland in Templenoe parish (in the Kenmare Poor Law Union), 'They are most necessary and would employ a very poor and large population. Want is very great in that neighbourhood. A poor woman, wife of a cottier on Denis Mahony's property, has died of starvation. The roads I mention would absorb all the needy in that vicinity.'[313]

As Christmas 1846 approached, the *Kerry Evening Post* regretted to state that famine, 'gaunt, lean and hollow-eyed', was stalking the country and 'hunger has already elected his victims from the patient peasantry of Kerry.' Yet, in this crisis, 'the Whigs have chosen to maintain the principles of political economy.' The writer thought, 'Famine may bring desolation and death to the hovel of the Irish peasant, but the "paternal Whigs" will not interfere with private speculation.' Famished people could smell India meal heating in government depots, where it was locked up pending future distribution.[314]

Conditions in Kenmare workhouse were grim. Infants aged 2 and 3 who were suffering from fever were given coffee instead of milk. 'In a medical point of view nothing could have been more improper,' thought the medical officer. A week later he found coffee being given to fever patients generally and denounced this as 'improper' and 'cruel', because 'the patients are tormented with thirst which coffee will not quench, as such a drink retards recovery and promotes a fatal termination'. Shockingly, 'Florence Sullivan born in the house on the 9th inst., the mother having no suck, received coffee instead of milk and perished in seven days.'[315]

9

Famine: 'immeasurably worse', 1847

'I now come to, I fear, an important era for the true faith in this parish, and not only for this parish but for the whole of Ireland.' After a break of more than three years, John O'Sullivan had made a new entry in his journal. It is dated May 1847.[316] The potato crop had again failed, and the poor had few if any reserves left after the previous year. That he framed the looming catastrophe as a challenge to 'the true faith' reflected his particular perspective. For many it was primarily a matter of physical survival.

The priest provider

O'Sullivan had gone to Lansdowne's agent in October 1846 to seek money for relief. Lansdowne subscribed £200 and also gave a loan of £500 to the Kenmare Relief Committee. O'Sullivan extravagantly said publicly, 'no father could be more solicitous for the welfare of his children than Lord Lansdowne for the poor people of Kerry.'[317] If this was fawning, it was a flattery intended to prise money for the poor from a man who owned vast estates in Britain and Ireland but who was to remain absent from his Kerry lands for the entire famine.

O'Sullivan now repeated a strategy he had first deployed during hard times in Dingle: using relief money to buy food and selling it at cost, and then using the income again to keep a supply chain open. In less than six months, £10,000 of food had arrived in this manner. He wrote that the government looked favourably on his scheme, and he claimed that this fact excited 'the envy and the hatred of all the landlords about here', ostensibly because it kept prices down when it came to them selling food locally.[318] His scheme primarily helped those who needed access to an alternative food supply and who could afford to buy it; he did not regard it as the best way to relieve destitution – for the very simple reason that (as he told a parliamentary committee in 1849) 'it gave the poor no established right to relief' and was entirely dependant on the voluntary efforts of individuals.[319] This concept of an 'established right' to social assistance was progressive.

The *Kerry Evening Post* reported, in early 1847, that Kenmare was almost drained of provisions, with no prospect of immediate relief except that afforded by the local relief committee – and this was said to have just £230 left. The Board of Works had started to fund some public schemes in Ireland in order to provide men with an income, thus following precedents set during earlier but less extensive food shortages. This time the board's scheme was not adequate to meet the needs of Kerry – where a family of five persons was said to have lived two days on one hen, and another family made four meals of a starving goose.[320]

Dr Thomas Taylor

The local poor law guardians appointed Dr Thomas Taylor of Dunkerron, Templenoe, as medical officer of Kenmare workhouse, which he had been attending daily since mid-November 1846. Said to have been born on board a boat on the River Ganges, he was the son of an Indian mother known as 'Poor Begum' and a Kerry major in the Bengal artillery of the East India Company – who himself was the son of the former Lansdowne agent at Kenmare, Joseph Taylor. Dr Taylor was a Unitarian whose work as a botanist and physician has merited entries in both the *Dictionary of Irish Biography* and the *Dictionary of National Biography*. Before coming to live among his Taylor relatives in Dunkerron, he had acquired great experience at Sir Patrick Dun's Hospital in Dublin during the fever epidemic of 1817–18.[321] The guardians complimented him on his 'humanity and exertions to arrest fever' in Kenmare Union during the preceding few months. A member of the Royal Irish Academy, Dr Taylor was to help to open a new fever hospital that stood adjacent to the workhouse. Its builder was pressed to correct deficiencies. One ton of coal was ordered to light fires and air the hospital until it opened. Finances were stretched, with outstanding bills for bread and Indian meal now going unpaid by the guardians. On 9 January 1847, Taylor reported that 119 inmates had fever:

> Two, three and even four fever patients are put into one bed for want of straw. The convalescent from fever in the House cannot rise for want of fire. Sometimes they cannot rise for want of clothes. Coffee continues to be substituted for milk – in many cases of fever patients. The poor in fever suffer greatly for want of

proper nurses. Fever patients in the house lie on the ground and
not on bedsteads […] The bedclothes of the fever beds not always
changed, and often dirty when new patients are put in them. The
want of milk continues to be severely felt.[322]

The guardians thought it 'absurd' to imagine that rates could be raised
in the area at a level sufficient to meet local needs, and they requested
greater government support. They called on ratepayers who had not paid
their rates to do so; it was said that collectors were being forcibly
obstructed and even assaulted in some cases.[323] O'Sullivan later told a
committee of members of parliament that nobody anticipated the
demand that a sustained famine was to impose on the workhouse. He
said that the workhouse did not begin to fill until the potatoes failed in
September 1846, 'The house has been crowded ever since.'[324]

In London at the British Association

In January 1847, 'when famine was staring us in the face', the Kenmare
Relief Committee deputed both Parson James Going of the
neighbouring parish of Kilgarvan and O'Sullivan himself to go to
London and lay the state of the Kenmare Union before the
government.[325] Going and O'Sullivan did so, meeting Charles Trevelyan,
who was the senior Treasury official and the most influential civil servant
in respect to famine policy:

> We came to London and waited upon Sir Charles Trevelyan, not
> for the purpose of asking for assistance, but to show how
> impossible it was to continue such importations unless we got a
> means of transit; and after some parleying upon the matter in
> London, we succeeded in getting a depot established. I was
> prepared to continue the same importation if they would give us
> a transit by steam. It was, however, rather difficult to apply steamers
> to that particular purpose, but they consented to establish a depot
> at Kenmare upon one condition, for we objected to a depot being
> established unless they would make a promise that we should get
> six tons of meal daily at the depot at the government price.[326]

O'Sullivan and Going also succeeded in being received in person by the
committee of the recently formed British Association for the Relief of
Distress in Ireland and the Highlands of Scotland, which was to play a
central role in helping to co-ordinate the government's response to

famine that year. It had been established by a group of rich private individuals, including very powerful and busy bankers such as Samuel Jones-Lloyd, Moses Montefiore, Baron Lionel de Rothschild and his brother Mayer, Thomas Baring and Samuel Gurney. A letter from Nicholas Cummins of Cork to the London *Times* in December had been the catalyst for the formation of the association. His uncle James John Cummins, a London banker, was one of two members of the association's committee who came from Ireland. Nicholas's letter followed a visit to Skibbereen and was partly why that Cork town became a byword for famine.[327] Nevertheless, there is no reason to believe that the effects of the famine were not felt equally or worse in a number of other districts. Indeed, by the end of the year Deputy Commissary General John Saumarez Dobree reported to Trevelyan that Kenmare was the most miserable and destitute union in Ireland.[328]

The British Association first met on 1 January 1847 and moved quickly to organise ships to bring meal, potatoes and large quantities of peas to Ireland, together with some clothing and blankets. 'Nothing can be better than peas in any shape,' as Randolph Routh, the famine relief superintendent for Ireland, told Trevelyan that month, 'and the Indian corn meal shipped from America is not infrequently mixed with pea-flour. Even alone it makes good bread.'[329] David Salomons, a future Lord Mayor of London with whom O'Sullivan was to establish a rapport, joined the committee on 6 January and sat on its subcommittee examining applications for assistance. It was already receiving many petitions for aid from Ireland, but it had permitted only two witnesses related to these appeals to attend in person. These were Marshal Cummins of Glanmire, who spoke particularly to 'the condition of the peasantry' around Skibbereen, and Rev. George Hazelwood, who wished the association to direct some of its aid through an evangelical group in Ireland. However, the bankers were anxious not to be accused of religious bias.[330]

The British Association worked closely with transport companies on the logistics of the relief operation, and Queen Victoria donated £2,000 to its efforts. It met on no fewer than twenty-five days during its first month in existence. O'Sullivan and Going were permitted to appear before the association at the beginning of February; the meeting was held at South Sea House in Threadneedle Street. The fact that they met the committee once was an achievement – that O'Sullivan was brought back on a second day was remarkable, given that it had heard from only two other petitioners in person since its foundation. The first of the meetings at which O'Sullivan was present was chaired by Samuel Jones-Lloyd and attended by the Lord Mayor of London, John Kinnersley Hooper, who was also a member of 'The Honorable Irish Society', established in the seventeenth century to assist in the plantation of Ulster:

> The Rev. J. Going and the Rev. J. O'Sullivan, the Protestant and Roman Catholic clergymen of Kenmare attended the committee, and made statements respecting the distress existing in that district. It was resolved that Mr Raikes Currie [of the bank Curries & Co.] and Mr Henry Kingscote [another banker] do form a delegation to see the Marquess of Lansdowne on this subject.[331]

Two days later, having met with Lansdowne, this deputation reported back at the second meeting of the association that O'Sullivan attended. Baron de Rothschild personally put an additional vessel at the association's disposal, and the association's Applications Committee reported on the district of Kenmare. The committee resolved that one hundred tons of meal be loaded and 'dispatched to Kenmare to the Rev. John O'Sullivan – the said one hundred tons of meal to be sold by him at such price as he may deem advisable and a further five tons sent for gratuitous [free] distribution by him'.[332] O'Sullivan wrote:

> There they were, sitting every night – men with millions of money – to whom every moment was of the greatest importance – there they were night after night, listening to our details of the state of our unfortunate country. If a prince of the blood came there, he could not be treated with more deference or courtesy than we, the humble representatives of our suffering poor.[333]

O'Sullivan believed that what he and Going achieved in London that week ultimately saved thousands of lives.[334] O'Sullivan felt vindicated in his efforts to remain on good terms with Lansdowne, as they only got what they wanted after that powerful local landlord and influential politician was consulted.

Matters 'immeasurably worse'

In the meantime, conditions at home were deteriorating. O'Sullivan wrote to Trevelyan some days after he returned to Kenmare:

> Bad as matters were when we left home, they were immeasurably worse on our return. The mortality, the havoc, that death is making among the poor creatures is more than the most

hardened can endure; it is calculated to unman, to unnerve, the most obdurate. The cries of starving hundreds that besiege me from morning until night actually ring in my ears during the night, and if God Almighty, in his wisdom, be pleased to continue so heavy a hand on us, the whole face of the land must needs be desolate.

A few days since my curate prepared an unfortunate man, whose wife died of starvation, and at either side of him lay two children – one dead two days, the other some nine or ten hours. I attended myself a poor woman, whose infant, dead two days, lay at the foot of the bed, and four others nearly dead in the same bed; and, horrible to relate, a famished cat got up on the corpse of the poor infant and was about to gnaw it, but for my interference. I could tell you such tales of woe without end; such is not my object. Our common duty is to try and mitigate the evil, to try and propitiate the offended Deity by our exertions for our fellow men.[335]

Nonetheless, there was some good news on the evening of 25 February when a steamship, *Blazer*, finally reached Kenmare with forty tons of meal on board. The commodore immediately sent word to O'Sullivan that he would land the meal very early on the following morning. A schooner was also approaching with another hundred tons of meal. The authorities worried that this government assistance might induce O'Sullivan and others to relax their own efforts to feed local people – efforts 'worthy of imitation by other localities'.[336] Correspondence from Trevelyan to O'Sullivan in 1847 shows that O'Sullivan kept up pressure to ensure that aid reached Kenmare and that the possibility of a government depot there was kept open.[337]

The child in the cask

In March 1847 John Dillon Croker of Mallow, Co. Cork, came to Kenmare on business. He had invested in mining in the area and was embroiled in litigation with Richard T. Orpen concerning certain land. Croker – an uncle of the future 'Boss Croker' of Tammany Hall, then an infant – was shocked by what he found in Kenmare and described it as incomparably worse than even Skibbereen. In an open letter to the absent Lord Lansdowne, he catalogued gruesome incidents of starving people dying in the streets, as Kerry newspapers also did about that time.[338] However, it was not an episode that he directly witnessed but one related to him by the owner of the Lansdowne Arms Hotel, and other people, that has been remembered by locals down the years. It suggests divine retribution for those who are wilfully unkind in a famine. Croker prefaced his account with a warning to the editor of the London *Times*, lest 'the heavy judgment of a just God' fall on the editor's head for the 'venom, malice and base libels' published in that paper:

> A mason was engaged to build a pair of piers at the chapel gates of Kenmare, just opposite the hotel; an empty sugar hogshead [or cask] was used to support the scaffold; a poor boy was stretched on the steps of the inn, apparently dying; Dr McCarthy pronounced him to be in famine-fever; he was a stranger, had no hope, no friends, nor was there an hospital to receive him into; no person would admit a case of the kind into their house; the hostess of the inn directed some men to take the hogshead into a remote corner of the chapel-yard, make a bed of straw and cover it so as to prevent the rain from getting through, put in the child, and cover him with rugs or blankets supplied; they did so, and this humane woman ministered to his wants. After some days the little creature began to recover; but the mason, who had been absent, returned to his work. He required that the hogshead should be forthwith put back in its place. Offers were made to provide a substitute, and not inhumanly dislodge its inmate; but all in vain; he threw the child out of his tenement, and left him under the canopy of Heaven. The hogshead had been borrowed from a grocer in the town, who, on hearing it, instantly had the boy restored to his habitation. This monster [the mason] was father of three children, one of them a boy that he idealised. The day after his barbarous treatment to a perishing stranger, his wife left her children alone in her house while she was going to the market. On her return her only son, her husband's favourite, was found a corpse, having fallen into the fire and burnt to death. This Mr Sullivan, the proprietor of the hotel, assured me of. The famine-stricken one the Lord has pleased to recover, and awfully and suddenly taken the offspring of one who did not deserve blessing.[339]

The old chapel for which that mason was building square gateposts is long gone. The gateway itself is blocked up, the outline of its pillars still visible in the wall directly across Shelburne Street from the Lansdowne Arms Hotel, being just north of the present entrance to the Park Hotel. Entirely factual or partly mythical, the tale restores some order to a world torn apart by fate. Narratives of the famine, if and when it was remembered, could become a thick stirabout of anger, blame, trauma and survivor guilt. Everyday scenes were not easily erased from the mind. Croker himself thought that 'the faint but piercing cry of perishing children, mingled with the moan of despair and grief of the mother, who held her dead or dying child in her arms' was likely 'for years to tingle in my ears'. He wrote of a man employed in Kenmare to break stone in order to earn public relief who simply sat down, lay back on the road and expired; of 'a walking spectre' who struggled towards the graveyard with a basket on his back in which was doubled up the body of his sister, the fourth member of his family to die; of a father who made the same journey, his son's corpse thrown across a horse; of a man who dropped in the streets and lay a corpse there until evening, when some person paid for a coffin in which he continued to lie unburied; of forty to fifty people each day who stood by the hotel doors, 'not one of which, I firmly believe, will be alive in a week'. He wrote, 'I saw one woman (herself nearly dead) trying to hide the corpse of her child, though hugging it to her breast.' The details are numbing.

A local paper reported, from Tuosist, an eyewitness account of men on the public relief programme burying dead members of their families without coffins; they could not afford to miss a day's work and so buried their deceased in the potato patches beside their cabins until they could remove them to the cemetery at weekends. The newspaper also raised a common cry of 'jobbing', directing it in particular in this case at the guardians of Kenmare workhouse. This was amid suspicions across Ireland that local traders and others profiteered from the expenditure of relief funds and that some people even abused the emergency distribution of food.[340] A ballad survives that expressed this idea bitterly with reference to Kenmare.[341] Even today one hears such rumours quietly repeated.

Dillon Croker managed an optimistic postscript to his long appeal to Lord Lansdowne; in concluding, he noted that by the morning he left Kenmare, a vessel had docked there with boilers (in which to make soup or stirabout for mass feeding). It also brought tons of meal, flour and biscuit. Yet notwithstanding such shipments from the government and charities, circumstances around Kenmare in 1847 remained dire.

The guardians expressed regret that they were unable to provide enough fuel to take care of the sick – as required by the doctor, who attributed the death of patients to its want.

So many paupers were dying at the workhouse that the guardians decided to dispense with burying corpses in coffins. They said that this practice had become 'very general' throughout Kenmare Union. They ordered that graves in such cases were to be at least four and a half feet deep. Each pauper employed in preparing graves and bringing bodies to the cemetery from the workhouse – through the town and across the suspension bridge – was given three pence worth of tobacco or snuff daily 'as a preventative to contagion'. Those cleaning workhouse cesspools got a halfpenny worth of tobacco and one glass of whiskey daily.[342] William Bennett, an English Quaker who was inspired to distribute vegetable seeds in Ireland and who wrote a book about his visit, arrived in Kenmare town late one evening in April. Among the sights that upset him was that of a boy in a cask, although whether or not it was the same boy as above is unknown:

> We were beset immediately with the most terrific details of the want and sufferings of the people: indeed it could not be concealed. The sounds of woe and wailing resounded in the streets throughout the night. I felt extremely ill, and was almost overcome.
>
> In the morning I was credibly informed that NINE DEATHS had taken place during the night, *in the open streets*, from sheer want and exhaustion. The poor people came in from the rural districts in such numbers, in the hopes of getting some relief, that it was utterly impossible to meet their most urgent exigencies, and therefore they came in literally to die; and I might see several families lying about in the open streets, actually dying of starvation and fever, within a stone's throw of the inn. I went out accordingly. In the corner of an old enclosure, to which my steps were directed, on the bare ground, under the open heaven, was a remnant *of three*. One had just been carted away who had died in the night; the father had died before; the rest could not long survive. A little further on, in a cask placed like a dog-kennel, was a poor boy who had lain there some time, in high fever, without friends or relatives. I proceeded down the main street. In the middle of it, on a little straw, under an open erection made by placing two uprights and a board across them, were two

women, horrible to behold, in the last stages of consumptive fever, brought on by evident starvation. The town itself is overwhelmed with poverty; and the swollen limbs, emaciated countenances, and other hideous forms of disease to be seen about, were innumerable. In no other part of Ireland had I seen people falling on their knees to beg. It was difficult to sit over breakfast after this.[343]

Charles P. Thomas and another clergyman, along with Captain George Herbert, a local relief inspector, met Bennett and brought him to see other parts of Kenmare and Tuosist. While complimenting Lansdowne on the utility of the 'handsome' new bridge leading out of town to the south, Bennett noted pointedly that the influence of the Marquess of Lansdowne 'does not extend to the welfare of peasantry on his estates in the parish of Tuosist'. On that day, when they had gone about 10 miles along the coast of the Beara Peninsula from Kenmare, one of the clergymen remarked on the lives of people living there in poverty. The clergyman thought that out of a population of about thirty thousand, there were ten thousand who had no other means of subsistence, at that moment, than seaweed and shellfish from the rocks. He also thought, according to Bennett, that

> There existed considerable remains of clanship among these mountaineers. He [the clergyman] described them as a highly moral, a careless, but a peaceable and contented race, with great kindness and simple hospitality, and strong family attachments; but now the bonds of natural affection were fearfully broken and destroyed, under the pressure and sufferings of their present calamity. Their cattle, as in other places, had almost wholly disappeared.[344]

The population of Tuosist was to drop from 12,806 in 1841, before the famine, to 8,258 in 1851, immediately after it; and by 1871 it would be little more than half of what it had been thirty years earlier.[345]

With the situation desperate in such outlying areas, some people from Kenmare and elsewhere made for Killarney. A man named Sullivan had just lain down and died on the threshold of the county courthouse there, his wife pillowing his head in her bosom. A correspondent wrote that 'Death is busy in this town [...] terribly so among the stranger paupers', while people were 'dying like rotten sheep' in rural parts of Kerry.[346] Even in Killarney more than one hundred and forty people expired weekly in the workhouse and hospital, and fear of disease made people reluctant to help paupers on the street, 'the tale of woe which is uttered in too many instances, gets no credence, for (alas!) truth is too often perverted, and utterly disregarded by this class.'[347]

Better to be dead?

In May 1847 O'Sullivan wrote:

> fever and dysentery are ravaging every quarter of the parish. One hundred and twenty-four persons were buried in Old Kenmare between the first and the fourteenth of this month and it seems in no wise to be on the wane. The poorhouse is full, crowds of applicants are crying for admission every day and the whole state of the country is alarming, appalling.

The fever had taken, among other people that week, two Kerry curates. Five other curates were ill with it.[348]

Fr John O'Sullivan supported calls for a meeting of diocesan priests. This was, as he put it in, order 'to try and raise a cry against the landlords', amongst other objectives.[349] He also met Edmund Richards and Edward Fitt, two Quakers who were in Kerry to gather accurate information so that their society could distribute relief appropriately. They had just come from Sneem, on the western outskirts of the Kenmare Union:

> The appearance of the cabins from thence to Kenmare was very poor; at some we stopped, the inmates had not tasted food for a length of time, disease has added its ravages to famine [...] it was pitiable to see the expression of the poor children with whom we divided one loaf of bread; which was all we could purchase. Our usual supply of bread had been long since exhausted. The district from Sneem to Kenmare is really destitute, many squatters dispersed both on the roadside, and lower parts of the mountains.

On the following morning the Quakers met gentry and clergy in Kenmare, 'The P.P. [parish priest] O'Sullivan, waited on us; he appears to be very actively engaged in mitigating the suffering of those around him.' They found that 'the clergymen of both persuasions, generally speaking, are humanely engaged in this arduous undertaking. Godfrey [at] Templenoe has a soup kitchen near his residence where daily gratuitous distribution is made.'[350] A number of the big cauldrons used in such kitchens – in which food was cooked for mass distribution in Kenmare Union during the famine – survive.

In May 1847 the medical officer of the Kenmare workhouse reported:

> The workhouse now is not only a great hospital, for which it was never intended or adapted, but an engine for producing disease and death; a fearful proportion of those admitted in health falling, in a few days, victims to the epidemic [...] the dormitories of the Poor House are crowded with the sick.[351]

The following month, as the potato harvest approached, O'Sullivan made a dreadful discovery. He read in the *Dublin Evening Post* 'a most alarming account of the reappearing of the potato disease' and thereupon dug a few stalks of his own potatoes. He found, at the junction of the root with the tuber, the symptoms described in the paper, 'The only ones quite free from it in my mind are the few I got from London from the eminent Jew, David Salomons, and the four sacks I got from Cork from John Mahony – being Jersey potatoes. These are still doubtful.'[352] It appears from this that David Salomons of the British Association had sent him some potatoes that he thought might grow well in Kenmare. The priest and the banker were to keep in contact.

During that summer of 1847 the weather grew 'dreadfully hot', wrote O'Sullivan, and there was a constant wind from the north. Even gooseberries and young ash trees and flowers turned black. He hastened out to the potato field after dinner and found it all 'blasted, blighted, withered'. He exclaimed, 'Good God, what a store of misery awaits us for twelve, fifteen months more. Will His anger be ever appeased?' He walked down to the riverside and lay flat on his back, begging God to take him.[353] His parishioners were getting on his nerves:

> Fever rages through the parish. I must constantly be on foot and notwithstanding all my exertion mental and bodily, the ingratitude and unthankfulness of the people is most disheartening; the only thing to bear me up is the reflection that I cannot look for or expect a better return than Our Blessed Saviour met with for all his services and good deeds.

The outlook was grim, 'The potatoes without any manner of doubt are again blasted and the prospect for the coming year is truly frightful. May God Almighty speedily take me to Himself; the ordeal we will again have to go through is truly terrific, but God's will be done.'[354] By October his worst fears were confirmed, 'The potatoes gone again, the people starving and no likelihood of public works being resumed. I feared for my unfortunate parishioners last year, but are not the prospects for the coming year a thousand times more gloomy?'[355]

It was about this time that the Royal Irish Art Union published a charming engraving of a Kerry peasant child tending four placid goats on Mangerton mountain near Kenmare (see frontispiece). Plump and well clad, she smiles sweetly.[356] The artist, Matthew Wood, had left Ireland in 1838 and worked for the post office in London. He appears to have drawn the scene just before the famine began in 1845, but if any of the art union's subscribers visited the area in 1847 – when the union made an award to the engraver of that drawing – they would have found children dying and any surviving goats closely guarded.[357] People were already emigrating, with the Kenmare guardians noting that a large portion of property in the Kenmare Union 'has changed hands or is altogether waste by the numbers of emigrants during the present season'.[358] In August they warned:

> Thousands of families whose whole dependence was on the potato planted in conacre ground, have no such support to carry them through the ensuing winter and spring, while the quantity planted by the class immediately above them is certainly not sufficient to carry them through four months of the year.[359]

In November 1847 O'Sullivan reflected on the continuing decline around Kenmare. He noted that the failure of the potato crop in 1845 had been 'alarming enough' but that the abundance of the crop that year compensated to a great extent for any loss:

> A more fatal blight destroyed it in the July of 1846 and so completely blighted them that the like misery and destitution was never before witnessed since the days of Titus before Jerusalem.

> The entire food of the population destroyed, the destitution that one can conceive ensued; nothing more usual than to find four or five dead bodies on the street every morning. They would remain dead in their home unburied until putrefaction would ensue, had we not employed three men to go about and convey them to the graveyard. Theft and plunder and robbery became so universal that every man's hand seemed to be lifted up against his neighbour.[360]

He found 'the frightful condition of the people [...] more than flesh and blood can bear up against':

> Tears come to my eyes when I think on their melancholy destitution and condition. I often bethink of taking myself to some other country rather than see with my eyes and hear with my ears the melancholy spectacles and the direful wailing of the gaunt spectres that persecute and crowd about me from morning until night imploring for some assistance. Through my English acquaintances I have been able to collect £80 for their relief – and my having afforded assistance to a good many thereby it has brought such hordes of distressed people around me that I know not what to do or how to manage [...] I pray to God – with more fervour than I ever asked for anything I believe – to speedily take me from it to Himself. Thank God such was my prayer in the best of times. I never set my heart on this world or its vanities.[361]

But God did not take him then. Instead, the priest went again to England and met Lansdowne and Trevelyan.

London and Trevelyan again

O'Sullivan crossed to London in November 1847, sailing from Dublin. He went because, as he later explained to a parliamentary committee, 'I found that we did much good to our locality by coming here [in February 1847], and [...] I thought there would be no harm in coming over again to see what they were about, that we might be first in the field if anything was going.'[362] He had gone to Dublin to prevent the return to Kenmare of a particular inspector under the Temporary Relief Act – one whom he thought 'did all he could in a covert way to play the game of the parsons and to put anything he could in their way [...] I got my lad sent off to Donegal as a reward for his manoeuvering with the parsons.'[363] O'Sullivan was referring to Capt. George Herbert of the Royal Navy, who had been given charge of the arrangements for British Association relief supplies at Kenmare.[364] Having gone so far as Dublin to get rid of Herbert, wrote O'Sullivan, 'I determined on taking a turn to London again.' There he met Lord Lansdowne, amongst others. In London Trevelyan invited him to his home, where they dined with Trevelyan's wife Hannah and one of her sisters. O'Sullivan afterwards sent a message to the two women, whose brother was Thomas Babington Macaulay. Trevelyan drafted a reply, 'The next time you come to London I hope you will again give us the pleasure of your company.'[365]

Trouble with Captain Ommanney

Back in Kenmare, O'Sullivan found that his difficulties with relief officers, or inspectors, were not over. Herbert was replaced by Captain Erasmus Ommanney, who was assigned to Kenmare in October 1847, when Herbert went to Donegal.[366] Ommanney was a grandson and nephew of admirals and the son of a former MP for Barnstable; he already had a distinguished naval career. In 1877 he was to be knighted for scientific work in the Arctic.[367] He and O'Sullivan did not hit it off:

> He evidently seems determined to cut me. I showed him a few letters from the Treasury to give him some notion of my position with them, but he seems to have been already poisoned against me. I must be very cautious in my dealings with the little noodle.[368]

Trevelyan wrote twice to O'Sullivan in December 1847, saying that he relied upon the priest 'giving Captain Ommanney the support he requires to enable him to execute his difficult task' and disagreeing with the priest about how the British Association's money was being spent.[369] Ommanney let O'Sullivan know that he had appointed a committee to manage matters at the schools to which the British Association was about to send bread on a daily basis – a committee that was Protestant and had Denis Mahony at its head. O'Sullivan replied to Ommanney 'at great length' and sent copies of his reply to the Treasury and Dublin Castle, 'The step has been so openly absurd and preposterous that I must of necessity upset him.' However, he thought, 'I am in a heap of trouble. I pray to God daily to release me.'

Meanwhile, O'Sullivan sent to the Catholic national schools – that he himself had founded – some meal stored from a supply delivered to him during the previous summer; he intended it to fend off food supplies from those whom he suspected of proselytising. According to him, he very soon got his way regarding the administration of aid to the schools, thanks partly to Trevelyan. In particular, he secured control of aid at the school that he built in Templenoe – 'in spite of Ommanney and his ugly wife'. He thought that he had Ommanney 'hampered', but the latter remained in Kenmare until August 1848, and the guardians and others paid him a very warm tribute on his departure. O'Sullivan appears to have named one of his dogs Ommanney.[370]

In December 1847 Ommanney, while still in Kenmare, set about having the workhouse cleared of people now entitled to 'outdoor-relief', which was given in the form of cash; he sought, in accordance with a new scheme, to have those people replaced within the workhouse by certain 'destitute able-bodied' men. Returning from an inspection in Tuosist just before Christmas 1847, he told the Poor Law Commissioners that the people there were 'suffering from all the miseries of famine; nor can I conceive it possible for them to endure their privations much longer.' He added that many local ratepayers were in dire straits, and that 'it is hopeless to look to them for the means of supporting the dreadful amount of pauperism.'[371] He helped to ensure that an oven was installed at the workhouse to bake bread. Before he left Kenmare, he informed the British Association, on 16 February 1848, that the benefits of the relief aid it sent were now manifest:

> When I contrast the aspect of the children when I first came to the Union, with the present time, the result of my trouble is most satisfactory. Instead of numbers of emaciated children, straggling all over the country, there are but very few to be seen now, in the middle of the day.

He added, 'I also perceive a very great improvement in the appearance and condition of the children.'[372] However, in hindsight, his view of developments seems unduly rosy.

He was succeeded as inspector by Captain William A. Clarke, previously assigned to Caherciveen.[373] Clarke was to prove even more difficult for O'Sullivan, who felt that these inspectors did not give him enough respect. Strains between the priest and inspectors were indicative of tensions between the rising Catholic middle-class in Ireland and the government in England.

10

Crawling and Rising, 1848

Charles Trevelyan, in London, was aware that conditions were difficult in Kenmare; he was also conscious that some people were criticising Lord Lansdowne for not doing more to help in Kerry. Given Lansdowne's prominence in the corridors of power, as Lord President of the Council in Russell's Whig cabinet, it was a risky matter for any career civil servant to raise. However, while Trevelyan had (as he informed Lansdowne in January 1848) 'studiously avoided giving encouragement to any of our officers [such as Ommanney] to make remarks on the local management of your estate and influence there' – and now confessed to the marquess that he was 'in a very delicate position towards you in regard to Kenmare' – he did indicate to Lansdowne that he felt more must be done. In response to the criticism, a 'furious' Lansdowne blamed a drainage inspector for holding up his application for a public works loan.[374]

Four dead children

As the year 1848 dawned, it also brought to light the tragic circumstances of a mother and her children. Catherine Connolly was admitted to the workhouse in August 1847, where her husband and one of her six children died. On 29 December 1847, under new poor law criteria for determining who might receive relief within and outside workhouses, she and the surviving children were put out. At a coroner's inquest in Kenmare in January 1848, George Phelan, master of the workhouse, gave evidence that

> Connolly and her children went much against their will; they left the house from 12 to 2 o'clock, after breakfasting; when putting out those classes [the master of the Kenmare workhouse] has never been directed to give them any rations for the purpose of supporting them until they arrived at home.[375]

Victoria Robertson, matron of the workhouse, remembered seeing Connolly 'in tears at leaving, as the children were almost naked; their old clothes were very ragged; desired the porter to search for the clothes of her husband, who had died in the workhouse, to give to her, but the porter could not find them.'[376] Examined also at this inquest, Daniel Sullivan of Derrynamucklagh townland said that he saw the deceased children, Michael, John, Daniel and Catherine Connolly, on the evening of Thursday, 30 December 1847, off the high road near Glaninchaquin (Gleninchiquin). In this townland, on the Beara side of Kenmare Bay, about 17 kilometres from the workhouse, the children's mother formerly had a home. Sullivan recalled that

> the two eldest [children] had the two youngest on their backs; asked them if they were going home – they answered yes, that · they had been turned out of the poorhouse; they were crawling on the road, falling from side to side; asked what was the matter with them, they answered they were hungry; asked where their mother was, they said she went to Dourus [Dawros] to get relief from Mr McSwiney, the relieving officer, who promised it to her; they said they would wait on the road for their mother. Witness said, he supposed she would not come that night; they answered, if she did not, they would die on the road. [Timothy Sullivan of Derrynamucklagh added that he] got up about 7 o'clock on Friday morning; went up the road towards Currageen [Cooryeen townland], where he saw a little girl as he thought asleep on the road; went up to her, found she was dead. It was Catherine Connolly. Found [her brothers] Dan and John Connolly about one-eight of a mile further on, on the roadside dead, and further on still, Michael Connolly, also dead.[377]

Catherine Connolly, the children's mother, herself gave evidence. 'The poor woman wept most bitterly', and after some time told a 'melancholy tale'. She said that the place where she left her children was 'about a couple of hours walk from her father's house', adding that 'the children would have had sufficient time to reach home, if they had had strength and food':[378]

> [She] parted with her children [at Feoramore townland] for the purpose of going [back] to Dourus to get her name put on the book of the relieving officer; thought the eldest boy would be able to take the rest home; he was about fifteen years old; she nor her five children did not eat anything from the time they left

Fig. 7–Left: Boy and girl at Cahera. Illustrated London News, *20 Feb. 1847.*
Fig. 8–Right: Woman with children. Illustrated London News, *22 Dec. 1849.*
Courtesy 'Views of the Famine' website.

the poor-house […] until she parted with them on Thursday evening, except one plate of gruel between them all, which she got in the house of John Harrington, of Muscua [Mucksna]; thinks it was hunger killed her children.[379]

There was disagreement as to whether or not she should have had a ticket for immediate relief before being discharged when she seemingly did not explicitly ask for one. Dr George Mayberry testified that he could find 'not a particle of food' in the stomach or intestines of her dead children. The inquest found that the children died 'in consequence of the neglect of Captain Erasmus Ommanney and the Board of Guardians', a verdict about which Ommanney complained to the Poor Law Commissioners.[380]

Rate collector beaten

Meanwhile, to add to Captain Ommanney's problems before he left Kenmare, the local assistant barrister dismissed many of the proceedings against people for non-payment of rates needed to fund the poor law system. Ommanney thought that these dismissals were made on narrow technical grounds, 'The result was received with great exultation by the public. The result will I fear be detrimental to the collection of the rate.' Asked for his legal opinion, Jonathan Henn Q.C. thought that the assistant barrister was mistaken.[381] Ommanney found 'a general feeling of opposition' to payment and wrote on 10 January, 'A collector was this day beaten in the town while distraining for poor-rates; a large number of the populace joined and rejoiced at their triumph.'[382] Ommanney took steps to make the workhouse shipshape, but need was overwhelming it:

> I cannot convey an adequate description of the miserable and wretched condition of the numerous unhappy creatures who presented themselves at the house this day for admission; many had travelled a long distance in the hope of being admitted; the greater proportion were women with young children, whose emaciated appearance was shocking to behold. There were many at the house when I left at 6 o'clock, crying from the pangs of hunger [...] The workhouse being full, and the destitution so rapidly increasing, I fear the out-door relief will soon become incapable of supporting the mass of poverty. The relieving officers report generally that there are numbers in the greatest want who do not come under any of the classes now sanctioned to be on their lists; and they state that they know not what to do with the numbers applying for relief and admission to the workhouse [...] In recapitulation, the state of the [Kenmare] Union is this: there is no other support for the destitute but the Poor Law, which is inadequate to relieve the distress, and there is already about one-sixth of the population maintained by it.[383]

In January 1848 the Poor Law Commissioners issued an order dissolving the elected board of guardians in Kenmare; they replaced it with two paid officers, or 'vice-guardians' – a step that they had deemed necessary in a number of workhouses. O'Sullivan gave himself some of the credit for their dismissal, recording in his journal on 12 January 1848:

> The poor are suffering greatly owing to the neglect of the Board of Guardians. I called into them last Saturday to implore them to commence giving outdoor relief but in vain, upon which I wrote to the Poor Law Commissioners and by return post I have

an answer that they are dismissed and paid officers appointed in
their stead. God grant they may be Catholics.

One of them turned out to be, the other was definitely not. The vice-
guardians appointed were Charles Barnewall and Richard Robinson –
'the former a sincere Catholic, the latter a bigoted Orangeman,' wrote
O'Sullivan. He added, 'The moment he [Barnewall] arrived in town
little Ommanney waited on him and told him above all things to
beware of a terrible fellow in town called Fr John who was constantly
writing letters to the Castle.'[384]

Frog and bulls

Reading Captain Ommanney's reports from this period, one forms an
impression of him being a self-confident, dedicated and determined
man who tried to keep his vessel orderly and smart even as it was fatally
holed below the water line. He clearly had contempt for members of the
workhouse's dissolved board of guardians, whose failure even to pay all
their own rates he made explicit. There is little or no indication in his
reports of early 1848 that he cared what Fr John O'Sullivan or any other
local person had to say. This was probably a strategic error, as Trevelyan
had taken an interest in the relationship between captain and priest. He
was concerned that Ommanney might be sectarian. But Trevelyan did
not act immediately, and it was to be some months before the captain
was transferred. 'Remembering the Fable of the Frog in The Meadow',
as he told a member of the British Association, 'I did not venture to
interfere.'[385] Aesop's frog watching two bulls fight in a field and fearing
that he would be trampled was a facile metaphor for the clash of cultures
in Kenmare. The only ones actually dying in fields were victims of famine
such as the Connolly children, and London's response was inadequate
to save them.

Struggling to cope with the volume of people seeking relief, the
guardians rented additional accommodation in Kenmare that, in
January 1848, Captain Ommanney described as affording 'very
indifferent shelter for the inmates'.[386] O'Sullivan's curate Patrick
Hampston wrote to a newspaper in April 1848 to highlight an incident
of near-suffocation or 'paralysis and hysterics'. The case involved one
hundred or more female paupers who occupied an apartment that
served as an auxiliary workhouse dormitory; this was situated over the
courthouse at the old barracks building in The Square. He and some
others had rushed there when alarmed by loud shrieks and cries. The

only access was by 'a frail piece of plank which served as gangway from the road, a space of twenty feet'. A policeman had to break windows that had been nailed shut. Referring to the place as a 'slaughterhouse', Hampston attacked the Poor Law Commissioners and the Whig government in no uncertain terms.[387]

Meanwhile, the workhouse's respected medical officer, Dr Thomas Taylor, had – like many of its inmates – fallen victim to fever. He was to die of it, as he had predicted when he wrote that more than forty workhouse medical doctors had already perished of fever caught in the discharge of their duties. Sadly, his surviving family felt it necessary to threaten to sue for outstanding fees due to him. His nephew Dr Andrew Taylor succeeded him on a temporary basis; he too contracted fever on his last day there.[388]

In an initiative that indicates remarkable local ignorance of what vegetables could be grown besides potatoes, the vice-guardians set out to improve the workhouse diet by incorporating 'carrots or parsnips boiled and then mashed up [...] to bring into use veg. that may be grown in this country with great advantage, the culture and use of which are not at all understood'. They ordered the planting of parsnips, carrots, turnips, cabbage and leeks.[389] In March 1848 the workhouse's new medical officer, Dr George Mayberry, sounded optimistic – but just a few weeks later he regretted that contagious diseases were spreading fast in the workhouse, 'which is crowded in the extreme'. He noted that the milk given to fever patients was 'sour and apt to give dysentery'.[390] Fever was increasing so much that the vice-guardians hastily erected two fever sheds, each fifty feet long. In April smallpox was reported from many places.[391] The workhouse found 'much that was wrong' with a weighing mechanism used by Edward McSweeny to issue relief. In contrast, they were very pleased with the matron, singing her praises and supporting her application to the Poor Law Commissioners for a raise.[392]

By the end of 1848, two thousand Kenmare workhouse inmates would be spread across eight locations, the greatest number sleeping not at the workhouse itself but at the merchant Garrett Riordan's store – 'commonly called The Brewery'. Here, Holy Cross Church would later rise. While six hundred people stayed in the workhouse itself, eight hundred people, mainly children, slept at Riordan's converted store. Riordan permitted the pauper children to play in an adjoining field. For doing so he was later allowed to have 'the manure' on the premises, by which was meant ostensibly the human waste to use as fertiliser.[393] On many occasions paupers surrounded O'Sullivan's house, complaining of

being refused admission to the workhouse and entreating him to
intercede for them, which he did. As they struggled to maintain order,
the vice-guardians were informed that fences around the workhouse
itself were too low to prevent people coming and going irregularly. The
master of the workhouse had, from the outset, recorded instances of
people leaving without having returned workhouse clothing; however,
permission was given, in the case of some deaths, to allow the corpse to
be buried in a workhouse shirt. People who absconded with workhouse
clothes faced severe penalties, some being flogged on conviction and
some sentenced to three months' imprisonment in the county gaol with
ten hours of daily labour on the treadmill.[394]

The rising of 1848

During 1848 there were democratic and liberal revolutions across
Europe, including in Hungary and France, and Karl Marx's *Manifesto of
the Communist Party* was published. The government in London, as well
as the Irish Catholic hierarchy, feared a revolutionary reaction among
hungry people in Ireland. Some priests evinced radical views, including
O'Sullivan's curate Patrick Hampston. On Easter Sunday 1848 he was
one of a number of priests (not including John O'Sullivan) who were
prominent at a large meeting in Kenmare demanding repeal of the
union. Hampston moved the third resolution: that it was the privilege
of every citizen in a free country to carry arms. It was reported that 'He
did not of course tell them to take up arms against the Queen – they all
owed allegiance to Queen Victoria', and that 'When in the College of
Maynooth he took the oath of allegiance and would keep it.' He was
loudly cheered. That same week he wrote to a newspaper attacking the
Whig government and the Poor Law Commissioners. In May 1848, at a
meeting in Dublin, he was openly admitted as a member of the Young
Irelanders' Irish Confederation. Displayed at this meeting was a tricolour
in green, white and orange; this was given to Young Ireland leaders in
Paris in April, when they went there to deliver a congratulatory address
from the Confederate clubs to the new French revolutionary
government.[395] The tricolour was later adopted by the independent Irish
state as its national flag.

In early July 1848 William Smith O'Brien, a member of parliament
for Co. Limerick and one of those Young Ireland leaders, personally
visited Kenmare, the Beara Peninsula and Bantry; as he wrote, he was
'everywhere welcomed with the utmost enthusiasm'. Indeed, he found
local people 'even too hot in regard to the country'.[396] Feelings were

running high, but not high enough to sustain the short rebellion that followed later that month. The Young Ireland movement briefly staged a rising in some counties, believing that local priests would back them. However, their initiative quickly sputtered out, and the movement's leaders were arrested or went into hiding. Fearing a repeat of the bloodshed of 1798 and hostile to the revolutionary philosophy then exciting other European countries, a number of priests actually played a crucial role in dissuading people from supporting the rising. Fr John O'Sullivan claimed that he dampened down enthusiasm for the seizing of Denis Mahony's Dromore Castle in his parish (see Chapter 14).

While some of the Young Ireland leaders, such as Smith O'Brien, were arrested afterwards, others fled. Michael Doheny and James Stephens (with whom Doheny later founded the Fenians) made their way to Kerry and hid in houses in and about the Kenmare Union. They passed their time ranging from Mangerton mountain, above Kenmare and Kilgarvan, over to Tuosist across the sound of Kenmare Bay. Doheny's description of one particular Kerry 'cabin' in which he spent time provides an insight into common dwellings:

> In the house where I slept – as indeed in every house of the same character in the county – the whole stock of the family, consisting chiefly of cows and sheep, were locked in at night. Such was the extreme poverty of the people that they would not be otherwise safe. The weather was excessively wet, and, for the season, cold. There was a slight partition between the room where my bed was and the kitchen, where there were three cows, a man, his wife and four children. It is impossible to convey any idea of the sensations which crowd upon one in such a scene. I fell asleep at last, lulled by the heavy breathing and monotonous ruminating of the cows. Never was deeper sleep.[397]

Doheny now, as he later wrote, 'fondly indulged the last dream for our country', which was to collect 'between fifty and one hundred of the hardiest and most desperate mountaineers, whom we could easily place in ambush near the lakes, to seize on Lord John Russell, the prime minister who was at the time announced as a visitor to Killarney'. He intended to convey Russell into the 'inaccessible vastness' of the region and there demand the release of Young Irelanders from jail. As it transpired, Russell did not come to Killarney when he briefly visited Ireland in early September – and, as will be seen, met Fr John O'Sullivan in Dublin.

Doheny turned his attention to going abroad, 'We had interviews with clergymen and others, who discussed various projects of escape.' O'Sullivan happened to be in the town of Millstreet (in Co. Cork, but in the diocese of Kerry) when Crown forces raided the convent there in which Doheny's sister was a nun. According to O'Sullivan, 'My worthy curates had no small share in getting him out of the country.' One of those two curates was Patrick Hampston, who now had words with policemen when they wished to display a proclamation regarding the Young Irelander Smith O'Brien at Templenoe chapel.[398]

It is said that James Stephens escaped only because a woman under the pseudonym 'Christabel' crossed over to London with him; they arrived at her residence there late at night, and he sheltered in it. It is also said that she helped Doheny get away to America:[399]

> We spent several days rather agreeably, perambulating the ranges of hills between Kilfademore [Kilfadda More in Kilgarvan] and Templenoe, embracing a district about fifteen miles square. One night we slept in an empty cabin within a field of Kilfademore House, a fine old mansion, belonging to [Daniel McCarthy] the father of Christabel, the mountain poetess, which is now only inhabited by the tenant of the farm, while the whole available military and police force of the district were drawing their lines of circumvallation around this old house, which, as soon as they made the proper dispositions to prevent our escape, they burst into with the stealth and precipitancy of a robber band.[400]

'Christabel' was Mary McCarthy Downing (1815–1881), wife of Washington Downing, whose father Eugene was a prominent Kenmare merchant and an O'Connellite. Her husband was a parliamentary correspondent and journalist for the London *Daily News*.[401]

Marched to the workhouse

Meanwhile, that August, there was more bad news for Kenmare. The vice-guardians resolved that 'we deem it our duty to prepare for the ensuing season which from the present appearance of the potato crop we fear will be one of extreme difficulty.' They took steps to secure auxiliary accommodation and, 'as it will be more difficult than ever to secure straw', decided to fit sacks for bedding.[402] Within the workhouse, men were required to break stone for road-metalling and paths. A few spinning wheels were provided for women and boys to spin flax, wool and cotton by hand.[403]

Men who were assigned sleeping quarters at one of the workhouse's auxiliary buildings, which was situated near the suspension bridge in Kenmare, were assembled each morning and marched up to the workhouse, 'Any pauper who leaves the ranks to be brought before the vice-guardians for punishment.'[404] The author of an anonymous letter from Kenmare in the *Dublin Evening Post* on 17 December 1848 described conditions in and around the workhouse. This was, presumably, the letter that is known to have been sent anonymously by O'Sullivan about that time. Giving some credit to the vice-guardians for improvements, including the growth of various vegetables, the writer described three hundred and forty boys and three hundred and sixty girls packed so closely together in the two schoolrooms – each measuring about twenty-five feet square – that 'it was almost impossible to find standing room between them.' Another hundred little girls were outside cowering under a wall and 'literally gnashing their teeth with cold'. Elsewhere, two hundred and fifty stinking women, 'like so many squaws', were squatted on the bare floor 'as close as pigs in the hold of a steamer, without a spark of fire'.[405] O'Sullivan wrote that 'the poorhouse people' were much annoyed by his anonymous letter when it appeared in the paper, 'I wrote it with a view of sending it to Nicholls of Greenwich Hospital, the honestest Englishman that ever came to Ireland. He will take it to the Treasury and I think notice will be taken of it.' John W. Nicholls had been secretary to Rear-Admiral Sir Hugh Pigot at Cobh, 'He sent several steamers here with meal, was most attentive to me at all times.' O'Sullivan claimed that his support for Nicholls had helped the latter to get his current job in Greenwich, 'I dined with him the last time I was in London.'[406]

Meanwhile, the new vice-guardians of the workhouse reproved the master for permitting paupers to carry lighted candles in their hands around the dormitories and for failing to report that paupers were in the habit of sticking candles in the walls without sconces. All the same, they merely recorded the fact that they had found 256 persons sitting around tables in the dining hall 'at the late hour' of 10.30 p.m., 'most of them provisional cases – who had not been fed up to that time'. They were critical of their immediate predecessors as well, for not raising rates to generate enough revenue from local property in order to meet workhouse liabilities; they raised the rate while very optimistically intending to cap the number of workhouse inmates at one thousand five hundred. The vice-guardians also found 'a considerable deficiency of bread' in the workhouse, and 'this had to be supplied by stirabout, the quality of which was much complained about.'[407]

The provision of an adequate supply of both milk and bread of a good quality remained a challenge. Thus, for example, in 1851 the medical officer is found rejecting 'the coarse brown hard cake [made of a mixture of Indian Meal and one-way flour] as being too hard in nature for a class whose stomach may be weakened by debility and age and want of teeth'.[408]

11

Westminster and the Workhouse, 1849

In March 1849 John O'Sullivan gave evidence to a select committee of the House of Commons appointed to report to parliament on the Irish poor laws. It was a big moment for an Irish country priest, and he did well. He vividly evoked the plight of the poor while proposing long-term solutions to poverty – and was invited by the committee to return the next day.[409] His evidence was factual and closely argued, ranging from a discussion of land use through to a defence of the poor laws as a minimum safeguard.

Clarke's cold eye

One of the reasons that O'Sullivan wanted that platform in London for his views was that the latest 'temporary poor law inspector' for Kenmare was not just scathing about local society at every level but also seemed to the priest to threaten him directly. The inspector, Colonel William A. Clarke, made little secret of his suspicion that landlords and tenants alike were duping the government. He claimed to be 'credibly informed' that up to one thousand dwellings in the Kenmare Union had been levelled during 1848, 'and the unfortunate starving inmates thrown on the wide world with no shelter but the canopy of Heaven or the Union workhouse'. Clarke thought, 'A retributive justice appears to have fallen upon those who encouraged the subdivision of land and increased population, in order to extract the utmost penny it could be made to produce.'[410] By 'those' on whom he thought that retribution fell, he appears to have meant the occupiers of land now burdened with a rates bill to pay for poor relief.

He and O'Sullivan had soon clashed, especially over the inspector's refusal to admit men into the workhouse who he thought were fit enough to work but who O'Sullivan felt were not. Letters were exchanged, with O'Sullivan claiming that he had 'stung him to the quick' and that Clarke 'struck the table and swore he would show me who was king of the poorhouse'. The priest told William Fagan MP, in a letter, that he had objected to the exclusion by the vice-guardians of 'unfortunate paupers [who came] thirty miles from hence [...] on the plea that it was competent for them to go to John Mahony's drains [and work there]'. [411] O'Sullivan wrote in his journal, 'Clarke is a blackguard and it is very hard for me to have patience with his type.' The priest recognised the difficulty of confronting such an official, 'as it must involve me with Clarke who is a friend of the lord lieutenant and with whom it behoves me to stand fair; but I cannot help it.'[412] O'Sullivan championed in particular the application of James Murphy of Templenoe, 'with a wife and three children, disabled', who was refused entry to the workhouse a number of times. O'Sullivan complained that Murphy was crudely told 'to go to work or go into his a—s [arse] and kiss it'. He added that 'Murphy's case is one of many cases that have come before me of such severity on the part of the Relieving Officer [...] in truth, I could scarcely believe them.'[413]

Destitution

The numbers admitted to the workhouse continued to exceed by far the maximum of five hundred for which it was designed; in December 1848, between it and its auxiliary buildings, it was providing shelter for more than two thousand people. Hundreds more were being refused admission. Indeed, it was claimed that 'a great number' approached the workhouse and, 'when they saw by the number rejected how hopeless it was to apply, left without urging their claims'.[414] O'Sullivan told parliament in March 1849 that 'upon one occasion in this last year there were 2,400 paupers in the house'. Estimating six people to a family, he believed that such a total of inmates represented about four hundred families:

> The whole 2,400 were fed in the workhouse [...] It was the most horrifying spectacle that any person could cast his eyes upon [...] They have no clothes but the rags they come in with; they have no shoes and stockings, and they are in the most horrifying condition that one can possibly imagine.[415]

On 8 January 1849 William Clarke reported to the Poor Law Commissioners in terms that enraged O'Sullivan when he discovered them. The priest interpreted certain words (underlined below) to insinuate that he had made a pronouncement from the altar that people were entitled to relief without working for it. He denied having said so. Clarke wrote:

> I returned late on Saturday night from Kenmare, and regret to have to report to you that affairs continue there in a most unsatisfactory state; and no sooner is the workhouse relieved from its plethora of inmates under your sealed order, than a fresh batch of paupers present themselves, yelling and howling for admission.

> I do not mean by this to convey the impression that destitution does not exist; on the contrary, I know that it does to a fearful extent; but there is no assistance given to the vice-guardians by the rate-payers in checking those abuses which are known to exist, and <u>the doctrine has been publicly preached</u> that a man has no occasion to work unless it so pleases him, but has a right to support for himself and family in the workhouse.

> All principle of right and decency appears to have vanished since the out-door relief commenced; and the assistant-barrister who presided at the sessions most emphatically declared from the bench on Friday last that he had never witnessed such profligacy in wilful perjury as had been exhibited in that court during the entire session.[416]

Clarke complained further that people were in the habit of making wholesale charges 'without shadow of proof' against relieving officers, and he regretted a 'total want of discipline of the workhouse officers, and utter confusion of books and accounts of every description'.[417] In the course of their reply to him, the commissioners sternly stressed that 'destitution' or, in some cases, sickness formed the only grounds on which relief was to be given. They also emphasised that the requirement in the law to set inmates of the workhouse to work in order to earn relief should be interpreted as requiring labour that was 'unattractive' and strictly enforced.[418]

Writing again to the Poor Law Commissioners, on 23 January 1849, Clarke sketched out the number and categories of those receiving relief in Kenmare: 668 able-bodied men in the workhouse, 1,573 'other classes' therein, and 3,999 on outdoor relief. He expected the number to rise, 'for destitution is very general'. Even if all the arrears of rates due and the higher rates now set were to be collected, the total would fall far short of what was needed to meet the crisis. He reported that there was only one resident proprietor in the Kenmare Union who was not thought to be 'embarrassed' financially, while a great proportion of the others were insolvent. Then he delivered his *coup de grace*, which was an exercise in exculpating governments in London past or present:

> There is no social evil existing in any part of Ireland, save that of combining for deliberate assassination, that has not its ramifications in this union. Middlemen, with all the consequences of infinitesimal subletting; political agitation, which though now slumbering, has produced its demoralising effects; religious animosity; habits of idleness, with all their vicious fruits. These, combined with a state of semi-barbarism, consequent upon remoteness of geographical position and non-intercourse with the civilised world, are sufficiently evident causes of the existing destitution; and although it may be universally affirmed, that the failure of the potato crop is the true and only cause, I cannot but express my conviction that it only hastened that crisis, which was long since foreseen to be inevitable by every reflective man having a knowledge of the country.

For good measure, Clarke proceeded to suggest that there was actually a larger stock of potatoes in the Kenmare Union than was generally supposed – deducing this from 'the fact that there is very little retail demand for Indian meal; and that preparations are making on an extensive scale for again to try the experiment of their growth'. He thought that all those people not on relief 'must use them [potatoes] for food', and this suggested to him that there was an adequate supply generally.[419] Even the Poor Law Commissioners seemed to reject his suggestion, writing that from what they could ascertain, the stock of potatoes was very limited and confined almost entirely to the large occupiers and 'better class of farmers'. Nevertheless, they also lamented 'the thoughtless, improvident habits of the people'.[420]

By 20 February 1849 O'Sullivan learnt that what Clarke had told the Poor Law Commissioners about a 'doctrine' being 'publicly preached' in Kenmare had appeared subsequently in printed parliamentary papers. He was concerned because Lansdowne had written to his agent, James Hickson, about it, 'I must keep Lansdowne on my hands and I have accordingly written to Clarke.' He informed Clarke, 'I never heard such doctrine was either from altar or elsewhere

publicly preached and will be very much obliged by your informing me
[…] I look upon the poorhouse as the first step for the regeneration
of our unhappy country and it would grieve me immeasurably to find
any of the clergy of this Union place any obstacle in the way of its
successful operation.'[421] That same month, O'Sullivan published his
controversial letter to the people of Templenoe suggesting that, for
their own sake, they should emigrate (see Chapter 14). Then, in March
1849, he left Kenmare for London again. 'Blessed be He for the grace
He has given me to seek Him in most of my actions,' he wrote.[422]

O'Sullivan at Westminster, 1849

During 1848 it was proposed that a select parliamentary committee
examine the Irish poor laws, and such a committee was appointed in
February 1849. Trevelyan made it clear, in response to a letter from
O'Sullivan, that 'I have nothing whatsoever to do with the summoning
of the witnesses for the Committee on the Poor Law, and could not
with any propriety interfere.'[423] When he sailed for Britain from Dublin,
O'Sullivan still did not know if he would be called before the
committee:

> even though I fail my journey to England will frighten the bigots
> here and I possibly may yet get summoned [to parliament] and
> thus come by my expenses. I will go then in God's name. My two
> other trips thereto [in 1847] were of infinite use to me and who
> can tell what good may come out of the present.[424]

He also had another reason for going to London: to ask Lansdowne to
find a position for his brother, who had lost his job. On the way over,
the parish priest of Kenmare met Denis Shine Lawlor of Castlelough,
near Killarney, whose brother-in-law Edward Huddleston was the
Catholic parish priest of Stafford. Lawlor invited him to stay the night
there, and O'Sullivan used the opportunity to visit Stafford's
workhouse, jail and lunatic asylum the next day. Arriving later in
London, he called on Charles Trevelyan and 'learned from him that I
was on the list for a summons before the committee of the House of
Commons'.[425]

While he waited – for days – for official confirmation that he was to
give evidence, he visited twelve music shops, seeking a suitably priced
seraphine (keyboard) for the chapel of the Presentation Convent in
Tralee. He told one of the nuns there that he had had 'abundance of
time to look after one as I was a fortnight waiting to be examined' by

the parliamentary committee. He also sought out a society in London
that might take and sell products made by poor children at the nuns'
Tralee convent. While he was in London, John O'Connell MP invited
him to dinner, along with 'a good many Irish', and songs were sung
there.[426]

Appearing before the select committee on 16 and 19 March 1849,
O'Sullivan estimated that in addition to more than two thousand
paupers within the precincts of the workhouse, a further seven
thousand impoverished people were by now in receipt of outdoor relief
in the Kenmare Union. He added that there was not enough money
to provide clothing to paupers within the workhouse – and even when
it came to food, inmates there had depended for some time on
advances made by a flour factor in Killarney. Luckily, for some time
there had been 'a wonderful exemption from sickness' in the entire
Kenmare workhouse and union, but that was now changing. Within
the last two months fever and dysentery were beginning to set in and
the position was worsening. He did not think that the food given in the
workhouse was sufficient in quality or quantity; by now he had visited
English workhouses in Stafford and London, where the diet appeared
to be better than in Ireland, 'I take it that Irish paupers ought to be
fed as well as English every day in the year.' O'Sullivan thought that
the condition of people in Kenmare had been improving before the
famine. They had 'become more sober and industrious, and they were
advancing rapidly in civilisation until the failure of the potato.' Since
then, there was 'a decided retrogression both in condition and in
morals'. He thought:

> You cannot have discipline or order or regularity in a house that
> was built for 500 when you have 2,400 in it [...] Some of those
> persons who have come into the workhouse quite pure and
> untainted in morals, have become debased in morals to an
> extent which is incredible.

Work was found for only a very small proportion of those in the
workhouse. O'Sullivan described for the committee those who resorted
to the workhouse as being 'in great distress, emaciated, and filthy and
dirty [...] I do not think any pauper would go into the poorhouse till
all resources failed; but of course exceptions to that will arise.' He
noted that some people died rather than accepting relief in the
workhouse, 'I know that a protracted existence has frequently occurred
from their reluctance to enter the workhouse, and thus they have

wasted away by degree, till they have been like a candle that has blown out.' He was also aware of instances where the very poor had died sooner than accepting relief on the condition that they give up their land. Indeed, 'I have within the last four or five weeks, known four or five persons in great destitution who hold land, and who cling to it to the very last, rather than give it up.'[427]

No paupers gave evidence in the committee room at Westminster. O'Sullivan there defended them, and the Irish poor generally, against common prejudices:

> My opinion of the lower orders in Ireland is such, that they will not throw themselves upon the rates, even for out-door relief, if they can at all earn a livelihood otherwise [...] With regard to some who were supposed not to need relief, I found afterwards that I had wronged those people, and that if I had administered relief to them when I was in a condition to do so, I would have kept them in their status, and they would now have been in a condition to support themselves, instead of being paupers in the workhouse [...] my opinion is that no pauper will enter into the workhouse until he has been driven to it by the direst destitution [...] the readiness to submit to workhouse confinement is a sufficient test of the destitution of an Irish pauper, generally speaking [...] I take it to be a grievous calumny on the Irish people, to say that they prefer idleness in the workhouse to subsisting by labour outside, I am satisfied that it is, morally speaking, a positive test of a man's destitution to find him ready to submit to an Irish workhouse.[428]

He stressed that it was not just paupers within the workhouses but also men on outdoor relief work who were desperate, 'The families of some of them are lying down, even to my own knowledge, in fever, and they are themselves very emaciated, wretched, squalid-looking creatures.' He denied categorically the insinuation that he or some other priests had 'publicly preached that a man has no occasion to work unless it so pleases him', and he accepted that some people seeking outdoor relief made unfounded or exaggerated statements to get it.[429] He was prepared to give credit where it was due for measures to relieve famine:

> There would have been a great many more corpses in the streets in Kenmare than we had in 1846 and 1847, if it had not been for the poor law; I am convinced of that; It was an ordinary thing in February and March 1847 to find five or six dead bodies in the

streets of Kenmare every day. We had three men employed regularly, at 10*s*. 6*d*. a week each [more than twice the standard labourer's wage], and a horse and cart along with them, in conveying those dead bodies to the grave-yard [at old Kenmare]; and we had another man in the grave-yard engaged in digging a pit of a sufficient depth to receive those bodies, and all those bodies were huddled together into that pit, and that man was employed to cover them with a sufficient quantity of earth, to prevent the dead bodies being scratched up by the dogs, and to prevent effluvia escaping from those bodies. I am satisfied that we should have had the same thing occur again if it had not been for the introduction of the poor law [...] As soon as it was ascertained that the potatoes had failed at once the workhouse was crowded from that time, and the people began to fall in the streets.[430]

At times O'Sullivan appears to have been weighing up the committee and searching for ways to win it over. For example, he claimed that while local landlords in the Kenmare Union might complain about the poor rate that was struck in order to raise money from them, there had been no resistance by their tenant farmers who, as occupiers, also had to pay it. Yet the rate was clearly not enough to meet the need, for farmers were protesting that they were 'as much subject as ever to importunity for alms by persons begging'. O'Sullivan added, 'beggars go from door to door just as they used to do, and their excuse is that they get only a pound of meal a day, and that is quite insufficient for their support, for that they have to provide clothing, firing and other things which the pound of meal is unable to meet.' He recalled that he had 'begged' the farmers 'to pay the poor-rate cheerfully, with a view to put down begging'.[431] According to O'Sullivan, whenever the Vagrancy Act had been invoked as a threat against beggars, it far from upset them, 'we had hundreds of people imploring the police to put them in the Bridewell, in order that they might get a night's lodging and something to eat.' Some people were even committing crimes in order to be locked up, 'They have broken the church windows twice, and they have entered into and ransacked another church twice in order to get sent to gaol; the workhouse people have done that.'[432]

The 'first law that was ever made for the poor'

O'Sullivan told the select committee that he personally went to great lengths, when the rates were being collected, to impress on people how important the rates were, 'upon the principle of its being the first law that was ever made for the poor'.[433] He sounded a radical note, calling for the better use of Irish land by landlords, who ought to invest more in its reclamation and development. The way this could be encouraged, he thought, was by making poor rates so punitive that they would act as an incentive to landlords to invest in opportunities for employment. He surmised that this would attract people out of the workhouse:

> My view is that a workhouse ought to be made as expensive as possible to the landlords, and I do not think the landlords will ever move to support the people outside the workhouse till the support of the paupers inside the house shall be made so heavy that they must, in their own defence, cultivate the land.

This did not address the assertion that landlords were already so burdened by rates and other liabilities that they were left with nothing much to invest. Nevertheless, O'Sullivan thought, 'it is much more natural that the uncultivated lands, which are equal to the support of five times the population, should be cultivated, by employing the poor people on them, than that the paupers should be kept to such work within the workhouse.' This was a generous estimate of the amount of land available for new cultivation; it possibly included parcels on high mountains or in remote valleys. It was asserted polemically, countering suggestions that Ireland was already overpopulated. Having gone that far, O'Sullivan wished to assure the committee that he would not mollycoddle the poor:

> I would not spend beyond that which was necessary for the support of the paupers; I would not put silk stockings upon them, which would make them more expensive, but I would not go out of my way to take a burthen off the landlords which I conceive ought to be put on them, in order to induce them to cultivate the land, and employ the people.

He reassured members that there was no priest 'who stands better with the landlords of the district than myself, no one who has given less annoyance to the landlords'.[434]

As regards able-bodied men in the workhouse who would prefer to be working productively, he told the committee of 1849, 'I never see them in that way, rolling their wheel-barrows along, while thousands of acres which might be cultivated are at their doors, without feeling that it is enough to drive the people to desperation.' When Joseph Napier, the conservative member of parliament for Dublin University (Trinity College), asked him if he thought the legislature should take the unfarmed estate of one man for the purpose of supporting the pauperism on the estate of another, he answered simply 'Yes' and added that this would be just, 'because we are all brothers, and I do not see how it is unjust if any has land which he cannot cultivate to cultivate it instead.' He pointed out:

> If parties want land for a railroad, the legislature empowers them to take it away from the owner on paying him for it, and I propose to take the land for the purpose of supporting the people, which is of more importance than merely giving an easy drive by the construction of a railroad.

He thought that the landlords should be paid a full value for the land so taken.[435]

Invited back

O'Sullivan was called back before the committee on a second day, although according to him, 'the Tories wanted to have done with me.'[436] Its chairman, Sir John Young MP, as well as Joseph Napier MP and George Poulett Scrope MP, explored O'Sullivan's views on the balance between imposing financial obligations on landlords and encouraging them to invest in their holdings. O'Sullivan was not opposed to a suggestion raised by Scrope that one might exempt from the poor law rate, 'at least for the relief of the able-bodied, landlords who give full employment to the poor in proportion to the resources of their property'.[437] He thought that the Kenmare Union was highly capable of being improved by drainage. He gave as an example his own rented acres, some of which was 'the worst description of land'. Yet he had made something of it, 'I set about improving it; and at present I have plenty of hay and oats, and some to spare.'[438]

In the absence of firm data, he estimated that at least one thousand two hundred people had died of famine so far. He told the committee that, in October 1846, he had taken on trying to feed people by importing food and selling it at cost, 'I felt myself that it was an unusual business for a person in my sphere of life to turn flour merchant, but still somebody must have done it at the time.' He had drawn on his earlier experience as a curate in Dingle, where he worked with Lansdowne's agent, James Hickson, to relieve 'considerable pressure' there. Asked by William Fagan MP if the purchase and sale of provisions such as he had organised was a better mode of relieving destitution than the operation of the poor law, O'Sullivan replied firmly in the negative:

> Certainly not, because that was a thing that was entirely dependent upon the exertions of individuals. It gave the poor no established right to relief; it was a transient thing; a person may take it up today, and another may be unwilling to do it tomorrow.[439]

O'Sullivan also told the select committee about a 'want of confidence between the classes': Ireland was not functioning as a smooth economy, with investor, entrepreneur and farmer sharing common aims. The problem could only be solved ultimately by developmental policies and not by simply increasing taxation:

> The root and mainspring of all the evils in Ireland is the want of confidence between the classes [...] my idea is that you are trying to keep out the ocean with a pitchfork or a spoon in trying to amend the condition of the people of Ireland by fixing a maximum [poor law] rate; nothing will put Ireland upon her legs or right her till you come to the foundation of all our social evils, the want of confidence between the classes.[440]

O'Sullivan suggested that 'if the landlords could be induced to sell part of their waste lands, and to cut them up into lots [at £500 to £1,000 each], hundreds of persons in towns, who are possessed of some capital, would be delighted to make investments in such lands.' He thought:

> When persons who have been in business, and have made some little money in business, turn their attention to the purchase of land and the cultivation of it, there are no better landlords, or more spirited landlords in Ireland, and there are no persons more willing to employ the poor.

O'Sullivan wanted to see it made easy for tradesmen to buy holdings of 40 or 50 acres; he cited a case in Tralee where such an arrangement had turned out well for all involved, although he was challenged about this by Henry Herbert, member of parliament for Kerry, who suggested that 'the cottier population was turned off that land'. O'Sullivan pressed ahead with his ideas, sounding more like a reforming

economist than a rural parish priest and pressing the possibility of
compulsory purchase of land, albeit at a fair valuation.

> Looking to the quantity of wasteland in our union and the want
> of employment, one cannot understand how it is that people
> should be forced to go and cultivate the prairies of America
> when there is so much land at their doors upon which they might
> be profitably employed.

As regards the estate owned at Glanerought by Trinity College Dublin,
'In almost every instance there are two landlords between the college
and the occupier, and sometimes three.' He blamed this for the 'very
bad' state of property and its administration there.[441] Always slow to
criticise Lansdowne harshly, at least in public, O'Sullivan conceded that
there were also 'one or two' middlemen on Lansdowne's estate;
however, he claimed that Lansdowne was 'a good landlord'
notwithstanding evidence of impoverishment on his land and thought
that Lansdowne's tenants had 'tenant-right' there 'as complete as in
any part of Ulster':

> Any stranger passing through the country will immediately
> indicate where Lord Lansdowne's property lies; he will see good
> slated, substantial houses, and square fields, and good fences
> upon Lord Lansdowne's estate; but a good deal of the poverty
> upon Lord Lansdowne's estate arises from Lord Lansdowne's
> goodness and his unwillingness to exterminate; he was going to
> make room for all the people by allowing them lands which were
> too small for the subsistence of the people, but which would have
> been sufficiently ample for them if the potatoes had continued
> to grow.

O'Sullivan had remonstrated with Lansdowne's agent on the impolicy
of tenants taking in cottiers and letting ground to the cottiers as
undertenants. He did not now suggest to the committee that
Lansdowne or his agent had been 'allowing' such people lands for free.
Nevertheless, he thought that there were also some people coming
from other estates and squatting on Lord Lansdowne's land. O'Sullivan
added that he would not have the slightest objection to the
consolidation of farms so long as it did not result in evictions, for 'that
which causes such an outcry is the heart-rending scenes upon
witnessing those poor creatures being cleared out in the manner they
are.'[442]

Clashing with Clarke

O'Sullivan continued in his efforts to have Clarke, the poor law inspector, disciplined for claiming that he had 'preached' a doctrine of resistance, but he ultimately failed. He was assured, in April 1849, that Clarke would 'avoid in future similar terms which are liable to misconstruction'. But O'Sullivan would not drop it and kept up correspondence in the hope of damaging Clarke.[443] At some point he may have suspected that the dispute was partly defining him. Thus, he was irritated and embarrassed when his curate William Ahern's brother came to town to apply for the position of master of the workhouse. O'Sullivan told his journal that he expected that Ahern would press him to object if and when his brother John was turned down, bringing the parish priest 'into collision with these guardians whom I must endeavour to keep in my hands, as it must tell against me to have it told that I was fighting with every one of them as they succeeded.' Ahern actually got the job, although this master's 'melancholy death' by fever was recorded within two years.[444]

On his knees

O'Sullivan was troubled that the *Dublin Evening Mail* had given a 'version of what I did not say' at the select committee, and he informed Charles Trevelyan that he had written to another paper, the *Dublin Evening Post*, to correct it. He also told Trevelyan that due to reports of the select committee appearing in the papers, 'I am lauded and abused by my friends and my foes with as much zeal on one side and acrimony on the other as if on my humble testimony was depending the entire Poor Law.' He bared his heart to the Treasury official:

> If I could go on my knees to you or to anyone and by doing so procure the discharge of the immense crowds by which the workhouse is thronged I would not hesitate in doing so [...] There they are, 1,800 inmates in a house built for 500, without shoes, without clothes, in filthy rags and misery, the women squatted on the ground on the bare, cold, clay floor [...] unfortunate poor women on the naked clay floor, without as much as a stool to sit on [...] When you add to this the almost certainty of the cholera now in Ennis and Limerick it is frightful to reflect on the consequences.[445]

He added that 'the wretches have not the "animus" to combine', but if they had, 'they would have long since sacked or burned the town, or done something that would of necessity have caused them to be better cared and provided for than they are at present.' He also wrote to Lansdowne to express alarm at a significant increase in the population of the town of Kenmare, 'It consists entirely of those creatures who have been driven into town and all those are mainly living at their wits' end by plunder and rapine, and where things are to end God Almighty in His Goodness only knows.' He thought matters had 'not come to worst yet' and wrote, 'Seven poor people who were put out of the workhouse a few days ago on outdoor relief were found dead on the road to the west of Sneem on their way home to Bordoneen.'[446]

He sometimes allowed himself privately the terrible wish that the potatoes would fail yet again, 'to try if anything would bring about a radical change in the relations of society [...] a thing that in my opinion will never be effected if the potatoes return – and can be only secured while the landed proprietors are so frightened and while the pressure on them is great.'[447] Some advocates for the paupers felt mocked by those less sympathetic to people seeking relief. Morty Downing of the Skibbereen Union claimed to have seen hundreds of people in Kenmare left for months in the rags in which they had entered the workhouse, reporting that he was asked if he wanted 'to get the paupers dressed in top boots and to feed them with cakes'.[448] O'Sullivan told George Poulett Scrope MP, whom he met in London, 'If I am asked the question how the expense of keeping all these people alive is to be met, I would say that wherever it comes from, the thing ought to be met.' Conditions, as he explained to Scrope, were dreadful:

> In a corner you might be disgusted with the nakedness of some unfortunate wretch covered over with vermin and his unhappy comrades helping him to clean himself of some portion of it. Three and four of them sleep in a bed to which I believe they have no objection as they help to keep each other warm and the quantity of covering allowed them is no more than a mockery. They are wasting away by degrees; you could well imagine that a single breath would blow them into eternity.

> The most pitiful sight you could possibly witness is those poor children on the backs of others as sick and as emaciated as themselves, seeking to crawl from the auxiliary [workhouse dormitory] to the parent workhouse, to be prescribed for by the doctor. The auxiliary workshop stands a fair chance of being a

pest house to the town; with 500 children in it without sewerage, the stench from it is such – and the same in the case of the workhouse – that one is obliged to hold their breath when passing by them. The poor children have no one to look after them from nightfall till the following morning but a few of the grown paupers; and such was the abuse that one of them got that the poor child died of the beating. Five paupers were put out on outdoor relief the week before last and they were found dead on the road on their return to their cabins.[449]

At Tralee Assizes, Baron John Richards sentenced Patrick O'Shea, a labourer, to twelve months' imprisonment for receiving a stolen workhouse shirt. O'Sullivan appealed to Richards and Sir William Somerville for clemency for his parishioner, attesting to O'Shea's character, his partial disability and his industry at building dry walls ('such that even in the great dearth of employment he was never without it'). He pointed out that O'Shea's family, six in number, 'must now go into an already crowded workhouse – and the jail of Tralee at present has three times the number of prisoners for which it was built.' The prisoner was released early. O'Sullivan wrote, 'This is a satisfaction for me and will give no small annoyance to the Tories. It is a novel thing in their eyes for a priest to have as much influence.' However, his perceived influence resulted in great pressure on him by way of incessant applications for help. He again articulated what he feared was an awful truth:[450]

> Some infatuation seems to have seized the landlords. In the general crash they seek to keep up the old rents when the old prices are not to be had for anything, when there are neither potatoes nor pigs, when there is no price for cattle, for butter, for corn; the fools only vainly hope they can keep up a price for land. They cannot and will not, and though it is almost impious to pray the potatoes may not grow this year, on the whole I think it were better they would not as in the event of their not growing something decisive should be done to meet the crisis this year. Whereas let the potatoes grow again and with them will return all the misfortune and misery of score ground, rack rents and all the other evils in their train. That is my candid opinion.[451]

While he prayed from time to time to be taken by death, he also experienced a certain sense of guilt for thus far surviving the great famine in relative comfort, 'How it saddens me and makes me fear that

God's judgments are in store for me to find so many of my fellow creatures so shipwrecked and myself still comparatively safe.'[452]

The famine queen

From May 1849 there were signs of potato blight again in parts of Ireland. Walking out in a field to swim 'my honest dog Rover' in the river near his house, O'Sullivan discovered symptoms of it. He sent some diseased stalks to Charles Trevelyan at the Treasury in London, telling him of 'the destroying angel' and writing 'You can have no idea of the panic among all classes in consequence of its early appearance.'[453] O'Sullivan asked himself, 'What in the world is to become of the unhappy multitudes by whom I am surrounded and who are merely holding body and soul together in the hope of the potatoes growing again this year? God Almighty's ways are very inscrutable.' The thought of going to live in London often flashed across his mind, but he felt it would be mercenary of him to do so. In early June his cousin's husband wrote from Tralee with news of some deaths from cholera there; a week later cholera struck Kenmare workhouse. He thought that it wasn't the worst way to die, for he believed one kept one's mind to the end.[454]

In fact, some fields started to recover even that month. Nonetheless, blight was not completely banished, and for a long time many people were to remain in dire straits. Local parishioners complained bitterly that paupers from all parts of Kenmare Union who died in the workhouse were being taken for burial through the town and across the suspension bridge to the old cemetery – 'which is now so very much crowded as to make it offensive if not dangerous, and most particularly objectionable at the present time when cholera prevails, the road to the graveyard being through the public street'. This was along Sound Street, later Henry Street. An earlier decision to bury paupers without coffins in the workhouse grounds had been quickly abandoned, as the land there was found to be unfit. Locals now asked Lord Lansdowne to grant a suitable site near the workhouse for a new cemetery.[455]

A few weeks later, in August 1849, Queen Victoria visited Ireland. She landed in Co. Cork at Cobh port, which was renamed Queenstown in her honour (but later renamed Cobh). Remarking on the 'fine teeth' of the women of Cork city and the 'good-natured' crowd, she travelled on to Dublin and Belfast. She received polite and even warm welcomes, with a majority of the Catholic bishops deciding not to embarrass her by emphasising the recent sufferings. She avoided areas of Ireland worst hit by the great famine. An envisaged visit to Killarney was abandoned, although she was urged still to visit its lakes by dropping anchor in Kenmare Bay before Dromore Castle and taking the road north over 'the celebrated' Blackwater Bridge. She did not do so.[456] When in September the Lord Lieutenant passed through Kenmare on his way from Glengarriff, he recognised Fr John O'Sullivan from having earlier met him in Dublin and shook hands with him. O'Sullivan asked why he had not induced the Queen to visit Killarney; he was reportedly told in reply that Victoria would 'no doubt' return next year and make a more extended tour of the country.[457] She did not.

About the time that Victoria arrived and complimented Munster women on their teeth, the vice-guardians of Kenmare workhouse began the process of selecting some of its female inmates for emigration to Australia; this was under a new government scheme to increase the number of white women there. Meanwhile, the workhouse vice-guardians had accrued large debts at the expense of traders, including one for £3,000 for flour and meal; creditors threatened to charge interest or take other action.[458]

Fears of a recurrence of the blight faded slowly, and the union's minutes of 10 August 1849 recorded optimistically that what appeared to be the 'favourable appearance of the crops, more especially the potato crop, is sufficient to justify the expectation of a large supply of food, as well as employment'. Outdoor relief was discontinued, as was auxiliary accommodation outside the workhouse (although some rented spaces continued to be used for a while). The workhouse diet improved a little. But many people were still hungry and ill, and had few if any resources left. The vice-guardians expressed concern that 'a very great pressure is likely to arise during the coming winter.'[459] In November 1849 they agreed to purchase three and a half tons of flax that had been grown as a local initiative – so that paupers might be employed in preparing it under tutelage. Seven local people, including Fr John O'Sullivan and Mrs Mahony, had laid samples of the flax before the board.[460]

William Steuart Trench, who in late 1849 replaced Hickson as Lansdowne's agent, was to write eloquently of those who died of starvation or its effects in the Kenmare Union:

> They died on the roads, and they died in the fields; they died on the mountains, and they died in the glens; they died at the relief works, and they died in their houses; so that little 'streets' or

villages were left almost without an inhabitant; and at the last, some few, despairing of help in the country, crawled into the town, and died at the doors of the residents and outside the Union [workhouse] walls. Some were buried underground, and some were left unburied in the mountains where they died, there being no one able to bury them.[461]

Trench discovered on his arrival that the number of people receiving government relief in the union of Kenmare, inside and outside the workhouse, and including those from Lansdowne's large estate, was about ten thousand. He thought that in June 1849, six months prior to his coming, the number had reached its highest point, at about ten thousand four hundred persons.[462] By July 1850 he was to put the total number receiving relief in Kenmare as having dropped to 5,450, but the crisis was certainly not over.[463]

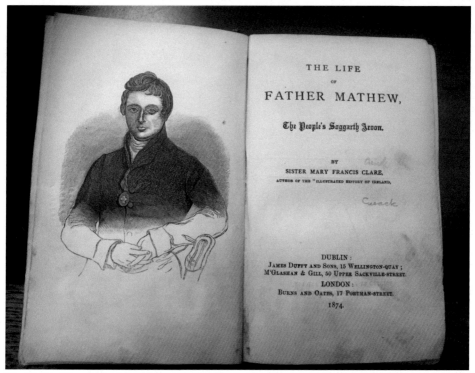

Pl. 16–Fr Theobald Mathew. Frontispiece and title-page from Mary ('the Nun of Kenmare') Cusack's *Life of Father Mathew* (Dublin: James Duffy, 1874).

Pl. 17–Kenmare about 1900, with the workhouse and fever hospital visible on the extreme right. *Courtesy National Library of Ireland [L_ROY_04684].*

Pl. 18–Kenmare workhouse (on left, now demolished) and fever hospital (now a private residence). *Courtesy National Library of Ireland* [detail of L_ROY_04684].

Pl. (19 left)–Fr John O'Sullivan. *Courtesy Holy Cross History 150 Group.*

Pl. 20 (above)–Sir Charles Trevelyan, From *The Drawing-Room Gallery of Eminent Personages* (4 vols, London: Tallis, 1859–62), vol. 4.

Pl. 21–A sailing ship at Kenmare quay, where famine aid was unloaded. *Courtesy National Library of Ireland* [EAS_2226].

Pl. 22–Henry Street (Sound Street), Kenmare, *c.*1900. This was the way from the workhouse to old Kenmare cemetery, and townspeople complained about pauper funerals passing along it. Where Holy Cross Church spire rises there once stood the old brewery, converted to house children during the great famine. *Courtesy National Library of Ireland* [L_CAB_06497].

Pl. 23–At a workhouse gate. From G.B. Smith, *The Life of William E. Gladstone* (2 vols, London: Cassell, Petter, Galpin, 1879).

Pl. 24–Dromore Castle, before 1914. *Courtesy National Library of Ireland* [L_CAB_01007].

Pl. 25–Famine soup cauldron, Templenoe, believed to have been used at Dromore Castle during the great famine. *Courtesy Mary O'Neill, Blackwater, Co. Kerry.*

Pl. 26–The Mahonys' former Church of Ireland place of worship in Templenoe. Now deconsecrated, then a site of confrontation.

A New Song entitled and called the

Parson's Lamentation!

Sung with great applause at the Theatre Royal, Liberty
Hall, by O'Gorman & Co.

Air.—" De night before Larry was stretched,

OH ! de night afore Dennis cut stick,
    And left yellow Kate to the rebels,
De report of de shots made him sick,
    For dey came as he tonght fast as pebbles.
De mountains seemed all in a blaze ;
    The bushes were swarming with pikemen ;
De clubs were on march fast apace,
    And dey marched to de fight very like men.
        Determined de Castle to take.

So Dennis calls up yallow Kate,
    Arrah, Katty, says he, you're my darling,
But the Priests and the rebels us hate,
    So I must be off before morning.
Lock up all de pewter and tin—
    Send 'em out to de yacht in de river,
And take care of poor Rose from big Tim,
    He'll have her as sure as I live, or,
        Faith maybe he'd rather yourself.

Musha Dennis, acushla, says she,
    Put your trust in your God and your bibles.
Your bible to blazes, quoth he,
    'Twas your stuff, your thrash, and your foibles,
That blew up the people about,
    Caused the vagabond Priests to excite dem,
And now I must clean turn out,
    Or dey'll pike me afore I take flight from
        Yourself and your rascally crew.

So Katty, poor lady fell flat
    As a flounder, while Dennis was packing,
'Till Rodney came in from de yat,
    And whipt Rose and herself in a crack in ;
But Dennis still hastened de more,
    And flew off in a fright, de old stager
Left the wife and de grawls at Dromore,
    To the care of the Lord and de Major,
        Who swore to protect 'em from Tim.

But horns are troublesome tings,
    And dey mighty disfigure one's noddle,
And dey some how or oder have wings,
    De quicker men's brain for to addle :
For no sooner did Dinney fly off,
    Than de Missus, whatever 'twould cost her,
Whoever may sneer or may scoff,
    Would have none but her dear darling Gloster,
        De angel so meek and so pure.

And Gloster, the broth of a boy,
    Was fast making up to the lady ;
Small blame to her sure—for what joy
    Could she e'er have with the old gaby ?
'Till the horns had gotten so long,
    And the Missus so fond of the preacher,
Dat in spite of the rebelly troug,
    He swore he'd come back and he'd teach her
        Dat he was still Lord of Dromore.

" And de poor fellow became quite plucky, and returned
determined to fight to the last," sooner than big Tim
should have his castle, or Gloster have his faded beauty—
long may he enjoy the one and the other ; but long as
Lord Landsdowne, and Father John, the vagabond, are
such friends, he can't expect much peace in the country.

        Ri tol de rol lol de rol la.

Pl. 27 (above)–The backward glance: A handbill
for *Mac na mná Déirce*, an Irish-language
production of *The Shuiler's Child* (1909) by
Seumas O'Kelly. The play features a workhouse
mother and her 'little lost child' left in the
'poorhouse'. *Courtesy National Library of Ireland*
[EPH E246].

**Pl. 28 (above) and Pl. 29
(left)**–Vitriolic verses aimed at
'Yellow Kate'. Anonymous.
*Courtesy Kerry Diocesan Archives,
O'Sullivan Papers.*

DROMORE PASTORALS.—No. 2.

From the New Opera, " The Siege of Dromore."

Air—" Kelvin's Grove."

Duet—GLOSTER AND YELLOW KATE.

GLOSTER TO KATTY.

Ugly Diu is gone to sea,
Dearest Katty O !
From the rebels fled away,
Lest they'd pike him O !
He's gone out in his yacht,
With that uglier devil Nott,
For whom hell wont be too hot,
    When there together O !
Spoken.—He is the old rawhead and
bloody bones. We could'nt stir that he
would'nt be peering over the wall with
his waitle and his old cambeen. A churn
of butter could't be made that he should'nt
be at the head and tail of it, for fear we'd
get a drink of the buttermilk.
    2.
And he's left you all alone,
Dearest Katty O !
To sigh and sob and moan,
In this cold Castle O !
For he's tired of you they say,
You're so withered, spent, and grey,
And like Bluebeard in the play
    He'd like another O !
Spoken.—He would in troth, for he's
just as wanton as a goat, and it is'nt of
late it came to him. Sure he's all his
life at it. Sure you'd find a young Ma-
hony in every bush on the mountain.
    3.

He's a miser and a knave,
I'd much sooner be a slave,
And the world wide I'd brave
    With you dear Gloster O !
Spoken.—He is the old rogue. Tho
very hens can't lay an egg unknown to
him. He must put his ugly nose under
every woman's apron that leaves hir
gazebo of a Castle for fear you or Pluck
or any of my darling converts should get
a bit to eat from us.
    6.
See how shamefully he ran
From his poor childer O !
Left them manage as they can
Amidst the rebels O !
Had'nt Rodney and his crew
Their protection round us threw
We'd be looking rather blue
    When there he left us O !
Spoken.—In troth and that we would.
Sure Rodney blew him up in the Parliament for leaving his poor wife and
childer to the rebels. But what made
him say the fellow is become more
plucky. What pluck he has. He'd
pluck a flea for the fat of it ; but devil a
a more I'm certain.
    7.
So Gloster now my darling,
If you'll take me O !

Pl. 30–Dancing at the crossroads, Blackwater Bridge, 1930s. O'Sullivan defended this very pastime to his bishop near here in 1851. *Courtesy Mary O'Neill and Sadie O'Sullivan, Blackwater, Co. Kerry.*

Pl. 31–Poor Clare Convent and Holy Cross Church, Kenmare, before 1914. *Courtesy National Library of Ireland* [L_ROY_02753].

Pl. 32 (above)–The original interior of Holy Cross Church, Kenmare, including its pulpit made by 'native tradesmen' but now gone. Immediately beside the altar are statues of Moses and Aaron, moved here from the old chapel but later sent to Templenoe chapel and subsequently buried there. *Courtesy National Library of Ireland* [STP_1339].

Pl. 33 (left)–Photograph of Fr John O'Sullivan in his vestments in later years. *Courtesy of the Poor Clare Sisters, Kenmare.*

Pl. 34 (left)– The famine pit in old Kenmare cemetery, with a surrounding wall made of stones collected by children from townlands of the Kenmare Union, 2016.

12

Panic and Exodus, 1849–1853

In January 1850 a child named Peter Shea fell from a dormitory window at the old brewery building, then an auxiliary or overflow workhouse in Kenmare. He died. A coroner's jury returned a verdict of accidental death.[464] A few weeks later another child, named James Sullivan, died. There were 'marks of a suspicious nature' on his body but no evidence of how exactly he met his end.[465] Clearly hunger was not the only danger that children faced. Yet, as Thomas Jordan has remarked, 'the young have rarely been considered as a focus' in studies of the Irish famine.[466]

If children were at risk physically, O'Sullivan was concerned about their spiritual welfare too. He thought that children lodged in the old brewery building were in a 'lamentable state of ignorance' concerning 'the first rudiments of Christianity'. Some boys in the house for six months 'cannot yet repeat the Lord's Prayer, nor the Apostle's Creed, and they must needs continue so while left under the exclusive care of paupers who feel themselves no responsibility.' He asked the vice-guardians to 'provide a suitable person to take charge of the boys'.[467] His priority was religious, and he expressly distinguished between the material and spiritual welfare of children when the Poor Law Commissioners asked for his opinion on premises in Green Lane (proposed as a location for girls then lodged in the old brewery). He replied:

> It does not appear to me to be any part of my duty to advert to the salubrity or the accommodation of 'Green Lane' workhouse. The vice-guardians have their duties to discharge in consulting for the children on such matters. I merely look to their religious instruction and education and the possibility of imparting such.[468]

He also worried about the spiritual needs of adults. The dangerously ill of Kenmare workhouse were lying in beds so close to other inmates that 'it is very difficult for the priest to take the confession of one of these without it being overheard by those in the beds convenient.'[469] Twenty years later J.A. Froude, the English historian who sometimes visited Kenmare and who was unsympathetic to Catholicism, was to write that 'Religion down here means right and wrong, and materially, perhaps, not much besides.'[470] O'Sullivan's notes show that even during the famine, he wanted children to learn the fundamentals of orthodox Christian faith and wanted adults to have the sacraments made available to them with dignity.

Trapped children

In May 1850 Lord Lansdowne's new agent for Kenmare, William Steuart Trench, heard a strange humming noise – 'as of the suppressed voices of many hundred people'. It came from the old brewery, which was not far from the agent's residence, Lansdowne Lodge. His servant rushed in to tell him that the building was on fire.[471] About three hundred 'pauper children' were lodged there. Trench went to the old brewery, meeting the schoolmaster. The master did not know what the matter was, but he was afraid to open the door because the children, he said, 'have become actually mad with fright; they would surely rush down the high stone steps, and half of them be killed in the panic':

> 'Is there only one way out for the whole three hundred children?' I asked.
>
> 'That is all,' replied he.
>
> 'Give me the key.'

Trench climbed the high stone steps onto a small flagged area outside the door. Pressing his foot against the low stone parapet on the opposite side of the flagged area, he carefully edged open the door and peered in:

> The sight which presented itself was strange and wild. Inside was a large room, in which as many children as it could possibly hold were crammed. The panic of the fire had seized them, and they were fast losing their senses with terror. The eyes of some were already staring wide, almost idiotic in expression. Others clenched their little fists, and ground their teeth, and threatened me in the most furious manner. And in some cases grown-up

women – nurses they appeared to be, with infants in their arms – cursed and swore at me, insisting that I was there to prevent their getting out, and that I was determined to burn them all together in the house. It was a dreadful scene of terror and despair, and the panic was evidently increasing.

He tried to calm the children and women but was met by a panic-stricken shriek. So he got himself outside again and ensured that the door could only open a few inches to prevent a rush that might have sent many children over the parapet, 'and thus, letting them out one by one, kicking, screaming, and some of them actually biting at my legs, they all got safely down the stone steps, and not a single one of them was hurt. I then went inside to examine the house for the fire. There was none: it was altogether a false alarm!'

On my return to the door, the scene in the courtyard below was a very curious one. About eighteen or twenty children, chiefly boys of about twelve years of age, were lying on the gravel, some with their eyes staring and their bodies working in hideous contortions, completely idiotic from the fright. Some were quite motionless, but doubled back as if under the influence of cramp or tetanus. Some were apparently dead. So strange a scene of killed and wounded I never saw in my life.

When the workhouse's medical officer arrived, his nonchalance surprised Trench. Dr George Mayberry reassured him that the children would soon recover, and in an hour or two 'most of them' did so, physically. The psychological state of the children can only be imagined, given their upbringing in mud cabins without locks, the trauma of famine and now their terrifying ordeal of being trapped in a crowded building that they believed was burning. Yet they were soon herded back to bed in the same big building, which had just one entrance and exit; it is not surprising to find Trench admitting that getting them inside it was achieved 'with some difficulty'. That being done, 'I walked all through the wards just as the children were going to rest, and it was curious to watch the starts and mutterings and convulsive sobs which numbers exhibited as they gradually dropped asleep.' Trench concluded his account of the incident at the former brewery by stating that he had never before seen a panic, although he had heard of the phenomenon, and he found it 'not by any means a pleasant thing to witness'.[472] How much more unpleasant it was for the children, whose own version of events is not recorded.

When Trench came to Kenmare in that winter of 1849–50, the worst of the potato failure may have been overcome in some parts of Ireland, yet times were still grim in the area. He wrote that

> The form of destitution had changed in some degree; but it was still very great. It is true that people no longer died of starvation; but they were dying nearly as fast of fever, dysentery, and scurvy within the walls of the workhouse. Food there now was in abundance; but to entitle the people to obtain it, they were compelled to go into the workhouse and 'auxiliary sheds', until these were crowded almost to suffocation. And although out-door relief had also been resorted to in consequence of the impossibility of finding room for the paupers in the houses, yet the quantity of food given was so small, and *the previous destitution through which they had passed was so severe* [Trench's italics] that nearly as many died now under the hands of the guardians, as had perished before by actual starvation.[473]

Trench claimed later that many deaths in Kenmare prior to his arrival could have been avoided if local people had been more competent and efficient. He contended that in the years before he himself became agent, Lansdowne had offered to provide 'money to any extent – in fact a *carte blanche*' for whatever food was needed for his tenants, with Trench claiming 'there was abundance of corn within a few miles distant'. It is hard to believe that O'Sullivan would not have taken Lansdowne's money if he had known that it was on offer, especially given the priest's unusual work in earlier importing and selling food at cost and his lobbying both government and politicians for further relief. Indeed, Trench somewhat qualified his claim in this respect when he subsequently wrote, albeit without explicitly acknowledging O'Sullivan's efforts:

> It may be true that large quantities of corn were *ultimately* imported, and a flotilla of abundance of food may from time to time have lain in the harbour of Kenmare. But either it was imported '*too late*' or the people did not get it *when most wanted*. Otherwise – why did 5,000 people die of starvation within the Union of Kenmare? [italics in original][474]

This was a question that, with considerable justification, might have been directed at their biggest landlord, Trench's own employer. If the marquess really did offer a '*carte blanche*', or blank cheque, to purchase necessary food, then he appears to have done too little to ensure that his offer was widely known or taken up.

Worse than Skibbereen?

In early 1849 one visitor, apparently from England, was struck by an ostensibly stark contrast between classes in Kenmare. The streets of the town were 'regularly laid out, wide, uniformly built, sideways flagged, and what is very uncommon in Ireland, the streets perfectly clean':

> Some twelve or thirteen gigs or jaunting cars containing well-dressed and respectable people passed and repassed. Two draper shops in the centre of the town with large windows and large panes in them, large enough for Regent-street [in London] immediately attracted my attention. Brass poles were ranged 'à la Piccadilly' along the whole outside, and within was displayed a goodly show of all manner and description of fineries, shawls, silks, satins, furs, boas, bonnets, caps, &c., &c. all arranged in a most tasteful and judicious manner. A crowd was collected about another window looking at a fresh importation of toys, pictures and playthings.[475]

Just outside the town he met 'a Mr. Riordan, owner of one of the corner shops above alluded to, a smart dapper little man', who was superintending men involved in draining and fencing fields. Riordan (presumably Garrett Riordan, the local cloth merchant) told the visitor that things were not as they might seem – that shops were not doing any business. He said he was 'tired of looking at his goods, and to avoid the importunity of the hordes of beggars that daily beset his doors, as well as to give some relief in the way of employment to his fellow-creatures', he had decided to spend some money draining the fields:

> While talking to Mr. Riordan a host of paupers came rolling as many wheelbarrows, with, perhaps, a shovelful of stones in each barrow, and they were reeling and staggering under that same. Heavens above what a spectacle! Can I ever put it out of my head? I was shocked in Skibbereen, Dunmanway, Bantry, but they were nothing to what was now before me [...] There they were. Not one of them in workhouse clothes, but in their own rags, in dirt, in filth, pale, squalid, emaciated poor worn things that one breath, you would say, would carry them like a feather, before the wind, or disperse them to its four quarters. Some of them, with ropes of

twisted straw about their middle to keep their tattered garments from being bandied about by the wind, more of them with smaller ropes of the same material, rolled over what once were shoes, hobbling along as if in a pair of skaits or Russian sabots. Bad as the Bantry paupers were, they were 'pampered rogues' in comparison to these poor creatures; 1,800 of them were in the [work]house, 7,000 were on outdoor relief [...] Spectres from the grave could not present a more ghastly, unearthly appearance; with what a vengeance the desolating Angel must have visited such a mass to reduce them to such a level. I was horrified and more alarmed when I ascertained that one of the vice-guardians was in fever in the very house in which I had put up, that the doctor was in fever, and I could easily understand that pestilence should, of necessity, follow in the wake of such an agglomeration of misery and wretchedness. The very thought of them in this moment sickens me.[476]

He returned to the hotel, checked out and fled Kenmare as quickly as possible.

Emigration

Fr John O'Sullivan advised his parishioners in Templenoe that emigration might well be the best option for them. Questioned about this in 1849 when he appeared before a select committee of the House of Commons, he said, 'I see no other way of avoiding the impending ruin, otherwise I should not give them that advice.' Asked if people were anxious to emigrate, he replied:

They are extremely anxious to emigrate; that is to say, they are anxious in a certain point of view; they are not anxious to emigrate if they have the wherewithal to support them at home. Every migrant leaves the country with a broken heart; and when they write back, sending for their friends, I see most of their letters, and every one of them breathes a hostile feeling to England; and I am convinced that if a rupture were to take place between this country [the United Kingdom] and America, the Irish emigrant would be the first man to handle a musket against the British empire.[477]

He thought that 'a man who has ten cows this year will not have five next year'. Yet he agreed with George Poulett Scrope MP that the Kenmare Union seemed quite capable of supporting its population, 'yes, and five times its population', if those in possession of the land adopted a different approach to its use. He added:

> I am not in favour of emigration at all; looking at it as regards the safety and well-being of the community, I am decidedly opposed to it; in the first place, because it is the healthiest and most industrious part of the community which will be the first to take advantage of it; those whom you want most here will be the first to leave. Secondly, because they will depart with hostile feelings to the people they leave at home; and thirdly, because there is quite sufficient employment for them at home. It is a preposterous thing, in my mind, to be sending people thousands of miles away while thousands of acres are at their doors upon which they might be profitably employed.[478]

The committee was concerned about reports of Irish landlords ejecting tenants against their wishes, but O'Sullivan thought that in his parish of Kenmare and Templenoe, 'not many' families had been evicted. Indeed, 'We have had no ejectments or clearances in our [Kenmare]

Fig. 9–'Here and There, or, Emigration A Remedy'. Punch, *18 July 1848.* Courtesy King's Inns Library.

Union that it would be worthwhile to enter into.' A few weeks later Fr John Fitzpatrick of Skibbereen, when called to give evidence before that same committee, wrote to O'Sullivan to ask him if he thought its members would 'allow me to name the exterminating landlords and the numbers ousted by them?' O'Sullivan replied, 'I had no exterminations to complain of but I could plainly see they were anxious for facts thereon and you will be readily listened to.'[479]

On 13 March 1849 the select committee had heard from Colonel Clarke – the poor law inspector – that upwards of one thousand dwellings in the Kenmare Union had been levelled to the ground in 1848, 'and the unfortunate starving inmates thrown on the wild world, with no shelter but the canopy of heaven or the union workhouse.'[480] O'Sullivan, who appeared before the committee later that month, questioned this information:

> If by levelling houses Colonel Clarke means knocking down the houses in spite of the occupiers, such a thing could not have occurred without my knowledge; but I can easily fancy that the persons may have come into the workhouses, and that upon their coming in the owners of the thousand houses may have knocked those houses down, because that is a thing which could be done without any noise, but if the parties had been put out against their will such a thing could not have occurred without my knowing it; and I think Colonel Clarke's report must allude to those parties who came in to workhouse and whose houses were then levelled; and I think it is perfectly just and proper for the landlords to knock the houses down in those cases [...] for those houses were little hovels that were not worth looking at, and which might be easily levelled.[481]

Those 'little hovels' had been the homes of families now in the workhouse who no longer had homes to which to return. It seems somewhat legalistic to regard the destruction of their cabins in their absence as anything but ejectment, even if the cabins were miserable and the families had no formal tenancy agreements. Noting that one thousand houses 'would certainly represent 6,000 persons, one fifth of the population', O'Sullivan wondered, 'What has become of the inmates?'[482] Did they exist or not? The inhabitants of such cabins might come and go without a recorded trace.

Another failed crop

As the winter of 1850–51 set in, the guardians grew frustrated, drawing attention to 'the crowded state of the House this autumn as compared with the past year' and blaming it on

> the almost total failure of the potato crop [...] the effect of which has been to drive the paupers into the House for want of food outside, while many were added to that unhappy class by the loss and waste of the little they possessed in a fruitless effort to raise the description of food which it has been the will of Providence to deprive them of.

They thought that fully one quarter of the population of the union were 'actual paupers', with 'two thirds of the residue closely bordering on the same state'. They complained that the burden of rates on better farmers was already unbearable, yet inadequate to meet local needs; that some of the best farmers were quitting the area and 'some of the best lands in the country' are lying waste.[483] The number of people in the workhouse and its rented auxiliary premises remained high, and this enticed ratepayers to support emigration rather than continuing to pay for local relief. Having fallen to under two thousand by Christmas 1849, the total number of inmates rose again during 1850 – at times that year exceeding three thousand – while sometimes in 1851, there were more than three thousand five hundred paupers there. That was about one seventh of the entire Kenmare Union population and more than twice the population of Kenmare town itself.[484] The medical officer referred to sixty-three deaths by disease in six months in 1850 as 'a small amount of mortality compared with the numbers in the house'.[485]

In November 1850 Trench crossed to England and spent five days at Bowood, Lansdowne's Wiltshire residence, discussing 'with that most enlightened and liberal statesman' his lordship's Kenmare Union estates. Trench argued that it made economic sense for his boss to pay people to go to America rather than have to continue to pay rates to support relief for large numbers in the workhouse. He believed that this was also better for the people, who – in his opinion – were otherwise condemned to uneconomic holdings or the workhouse. According to Trench, large numbers jumped at the chance to go, 'The announcement at first was scarcely credited; it was considered by the paupers to be too good news to be true. But when it began to be believed and appreciated, a rush was made to get away at once.'[486]

These emigrants departed in batches of two hundred. Within a little over a year, three thousand five hundred paupers had left Kenmare for North America, wrote Trench. Within four years the total reached four thousand six hundred. They went, he said, without any ejectments having been brought against them 'or the slightest pressure put upon them'. Only some fifty or sixty paupers were left in the workhouse to the charge of Lansdowne's estate. According to Trench, writing two decades later, almost everyone, 'down to the widows and children', found employment soon after landing and no ship carrying them ever met with an accident.[487] Nevertheless, Trench also wrote:

> It must be admitted that the paupers despatched to America on such a sudden pressure as this were of a very motley type; and a strange figure these wild batches of two hundred each – most of them speaking only the Irish language – made in the streets of Cork, as well as on the quays of Liverpool and America. There was great difficulty in keeping them from breaking loose from the ship not only in Cork but in Liverpool, where the ships touched before they left for the West.

Given half a chance, according to Trench, the emigrants would, on their way to a new life, 'hide all their good clothes which had been furnished them as an outfit' by the estate and then 'almost naked [...] delight in rushing through the streets of Cork and Liverpool in large bodies to the real terror of the inhabitants'. He seems to have thought that they were just having a bit of fun, for 'notwithstanding their apparent poverty, they were all in the most uproarious spirits; there was no crying nor lamentation, as is usual on such occasions; all was delight at having escaped the deadly workhouse.' Thousands took up his offer of assisted passage from Kenmare.[488] Those who departed sometimes remitted money that helped the local economy.[489]

One can only imagine what young girls going away to Australia thought as they set out, never having been outside Ireland before, or how Irish-speaking people reared in mud cabins on the coast of Kerry felt when they arrived in the cities of the United States or Canada. Many were destined for the Irish community at Five Points on Manhattan, which featured fictionally in Martin Scorsese's film *Gangs of New York* (2002), set in the early 1860s.[490] To those who complained that Lansdowne's agent was 'exterminating the people', he retorted that those 'people' knew well that those who cried loudest had given them no help when they so badly needed it. He wrote that Lansdowne's tenants 'rushed from the country like a panic-stricken throng, each only fearing that the funds at my disposal might fail before he and his family could get their passage'.[491] The version of events in his book *Realities of Irish Life* seems quite plausible, but it must be qualified by a reading of more recent work, including Lyne's detailed study of Trench's tenure as agent. Lyne remarks:

> In *Realities* Trench sought, by a process of suppression and distortion, not only to edit out of the story of his Kerry emigration scheme a whole dimension of human misery, but to turn it into a public triumph for his foresight, philanthropy and administrative skills. The scheme as it worked out initially, at least, would seem, in human terms, to have been something of a disaster.[492]

Trench rejected the idea that enough productive work could be found on the estate to provide a living for all its tenants, even with land reclamation. Before finally settling on the emigration scheme, he had organised some groups in draining, subsoiling, removing rocks and stones, and other such labour, but he decided that this was uneconomical. He and his son John Townsend Trench, who succeeded him as Lansdowne's agent, have not enjoyed good reputations among the people of Kenmare generally. Nonetheless, whatever the origins of land ownership and the politics of its usage in their day, it seems to have been impossible for land agents to square the circle of continuous subdivision in a manner that would yield a livelihood for everyone who might wish to live on some scrap of an estate. It was in the interest of neither landlord nor tenant to perpetuate unviable holdings. When the smaller class of tenantry left, especially those whose holdings were valued at £1 or less, the vacated plots could be acquired by adjoining tenants to make their holdings more viable. Trench wrote, 'Vast numbers of cottiers, or under-tenants also, as well as the small farmers, left; and at last a fair equilibrium was established between the demand and supply of labour. In short, the famine was over, and Lord Lansdowne's estate was righted.'[493]

His brother's keeper

O'Sullivan's journals show him acutely aware of issues that arose when other priests became too closely entangled with the needs of their families. Nevertheless, he himself felt bound to help his only surviving sibling. In doing so, he compromised his relationships with Lansdowne and Trevelyan, and crossed the O'Connells.

Reading in the *Dublin Evening Post*, in January 1848, that his brother

Stephen had 'married a Protestant in Athlone', O'Sullivan remarked, 'He must think very little about me when he would not condescend to write me a line about it, nor has he done so for the last two years.' Yet eight months later he was prepared to go to Athlone when his brother suffered some kind of 'paralysis'. [494] By Christmas Stephen, who had worked as a branch manager for the National Bank, was in big trouble:

> My brother Stephen is in great distress in Dublin. He ran a nice race of it in Athlone with balls and parties and neglected his business and got dismissed. Maurice O'Connell [MP, himself a director of the bank] promises to interest himself with the bank directors when he shall go over [to London] in February. He [Stephen] is bothering me with letters of his distress every day and urging me to procure a situation for him. However civil and complimentary the government and those great people may be to me I feel I have no claim on them and once I begin to importune them for situations they will not be as ready to listen to me on other matters. At all events I must try them sooner than let him starve.[495]

It appears that O'Sullivan's decision to travel to England again in 1849 was made partly on the basis of his brother's personal needs, although it was also the occasion for his appearance before the select committee of the House of Commons. He wrote:

> I will go to London […] the idea of my going will frighten the bigots here, and both my journeys there [in 1847] proved of such use that I anticipate much good from another. I have a very urgent invitation from David Salomons, one of the richest men in London, a Jew, to stop at his house. I expect Sir Charles Trevelyan of the Treasury may put me in the way of doing something for my unfortunate brother. I stayed at his [Trevelyan's] house the last time I was in London.[496]

When O'Sullivan made a will in January 1849, he left whatever he possessed, with one exception, to buy clothing for poor children and for the parish:

> My brother no doubt will be disappointed but I seek much more to please God Almighty. I leave him the house I have in Tralee [perhaps formerly his parents' home?] that used, until this last year, bring me £20 a year […] My brother never cared much for me but whether or no let me seek first the Kingdom of God and his glory.

Two months later he was 'greatly perplexed and annoyed' by his brother Stephen:

> He thinks I have nothing to do but to get a situation by asking it [...] Trevelyan of the Treasury may do something for me; Lansdowne may do something for me. If they do not my unfortunate brother will be a burden on me and I will not command the respect I have hitherto had or work my mission so efficiently. I will try them.[497]

But when he called on Trevelyan in March 1849, he found the official unwilling to intervene for his brother:

> I hoped Trevelyan would have done something for me in the way of procuring a situation for Stephen but he positively refused to interfere and recommended me to apply to Lord Lansdowne to get him out to the colonies. I went to Lansdowne expecting a refusal for I had much stronger hopes through Trevelyan but Lord Lansdowne promised me to speak to Lord Grey on his behalf. This would be a great matter for me, it would take the support of my brother off me and be a great ease to my mind.[498]

One can only guess how Lansdowne and Trevelyan regarded such lobbying, which could result in John O'Sullivan being perceived to owe them a favour.

O'Sullivan sometimes sent his brother money but feared that 'the more I send him the more I am likely to bring him on me.' Stephen's wife Mary was now ill, and the couple wished to move again. Where they were renting was 'underground on a level with the kitchen and coal' and 'so sunken a situation that I am sure the want of her usual good health was produced by it'. Stephen wrote that he and Mary were grateful for all that Fr John had done for them. He signed himself the priest's 'affectionate' brother. Fr John thought:

> You're neither grateful nor affectionate Master Stephen; for two years, and you in the enjoyment of your £300 a year you never dropped me as much as a line, you married a Protestant without ever paying me the compliment of advising me of it, and now you are besieging me with your letters.[499]

Stephen claimed that his wife Mary was the means of settling a Chancery suit between her father and a cousin, thus saving her father up to £2,000, 'yet he never offered her a farthing for having done so altho' she asked it.' This may indicate that Mary's family did not approve of her marriage to a Catholic.[500]

At one point the priest delayed pressing Lansdowne about his brother's prospects. This was because the relief inspector William Clarke, his local adversary, was then in London. O'Sullivan feared that Lansdowne, 'whom I could evidently see was favourably inclined to him', might show Clarke the letter and thus give Clarke something to use against the priest.[501] When O'Sullivan did write, he reminded Lansdowne of his promise to think about Stephen in respect to 'some employment in the Colonies'. He mentioned that his brother had got his job in the National Bank through the influence of Daniel O'Connell, whose wife was 'a near relative' of the family, and that he had been promoted after four years to the position of manager – 'in which position he continued to give the greatest satisfaction up to last Christmas twelve months'. He had then fallen into bad health, as a result of which 'some trivial errors' crept into his accounts and 'the bank most unceremoniously dismissed him from his £300 a year and with more inconsistency gave him a letter exonerating him from all manner of dishonesty.' The priest pleaded:

> The only way in which I can account for it is that the Inspector upon whose report he was dismissed was a violent Party man much opposed to O'Connell and from the fact of my brother being so near a relation he thought he ought be a partisan and co-politician when the very reverse was the fact.

There was a begging tone to his letter, 'It would relieve me of a burden that is grievously oppressing me when I can with difficulty procure the bare necessities of life for myself and my curates.'[502]

Stephen asked their cousin Anne Walsh-Murphy to lean on Fr John to send him more money. She wrote from Tralee to Kenmare:

> My Dear John, I had a letter from Stephen; he is in a most wretched state of distress, he may as well be walking in his vamps [the upper part of a boot] as to wear the boots he has on. He would have starved this last week only for a gentleman that lent him a few shillings. I can't tell you what I feel about him, and if I had the means of relieving him I would. For God's sake try and do something for him or he will have to go in to the Poorhouse. We are doing nothing. Business is very bad. Cholera is still here but not as bad as it was. I remain, my dear John, your affectionate cousin, Anne Murphy [born Walsh].[503]

O'Sullivan replied:

> My Dear Anne, Stephen I can conceive has been complaining of
> my not answering his letters. He applied to me for money the week
> after Easter. I sent him £3 making either £14 or £17 – I am not
> sure which – since November. In the course of ten days I had
> another application for more, to which I did not reply having none
> to send; he wrote to me again and so did his wife, to neither of
> which I replied. My own position, were he to know the difference,
> is just as critical as his. I have two curates who must be kept up as
> usual, and five servants, and not one shilling coming in to meet
> all the expenses attendant on such a retinue. I have my own station
> and dignity to uphold, and I will not plunge myself into debt or
> weigh myself down like many about me for any consideration. At
> a station, – where I used to get £2.17.0 – I got the other day three
> shillings. Were you to see the clothes and hat I wear here they
> would surprise you in no small degree; and it is near two years
> since I bought a suit of clothes until last week that I sold Garrett
> Riordan some oats and took clothes in exchange. Stephen cannot
> expect to get money from me any time he chooses to write for it.[504]

He was acutely aware that by canvassing Lord Lansdowne, he might
weaken his own standing, informing Anne, 'I wrote to Lord Lansdowne
on the 7th inst. [about the matter] and got no answer, and I have no
business urging him for fear my importunity would be more hurt than
good.' He asked her to 'tell Stephen what a predicament I am in myself
after passing through three succeeding famines. In truth he has no
business looking up to me. I sometimes am bewildered at the idea of
where matters are to end or what we are to come to.'[505]

O'Sullivan had earlier wanted Stephen to marry a woman called Kitty,
who 'would have been a much more desirable wife for him; the
O'Connells would have been so connected with him that he could not
fail.'[506] When a friend of the priest visited the married couple that same
year, in 1849, she wrote of Stephen's actual wife that 'barring the religion,
she is a very nice and – I believe – amiable young woman.'[507]

O'Sullivan felt somewhat humiliated when Lansdowne did not
respond quickly with an offer for his brother. The letter that eventually
came indicated that it might be possible to appoint Stephen as a
stipendiary magistrate on the Caribbean island of Grenada – at £300 a
year with some allowances. There was a sting in the tail, however.
Lansdowne, having explained that he had been speaking to Lord Henry

Grey, the Colonial Secretary, wrote:

> I think it but fair to add that whatever trouble it might give me I should think it my duty to institute an enquiry as to the cause of his leaving the bank before recommending him, as nothing would induce me to propose for a situation involving functions of a judicial nature any person whose character was not above all suspicion.[508]

The priest immediately contacted Stephen, urging him to get someone at the bank to answer Lansdowne's enquiries favourably. He also told him to improve his French, as this was required for the position.[509] He wrote to Lansdowne, signalling that his own efforts to 'uphold' the landlord in the past had caused his brother to lose out:

> Mr Maurice O'Connell [MP], my near relative and from whom I had the most distinct assurance of my brother's reinstatement, lately told my brother that I had better apply to Lord Lansdowne as I seemed to make a habit of upholding him at home, and disparaging every other landlord. Maurice is a Director of the bank, and the moment he saw the letter the Directors wrote my brother, he at once said [that] the moment he would go to London he would have him reinstated, but when my brother informed me of the reply he got, I made no further request of Mr O'Connell.

Beneath his own copy of this letter to Lansdowne, O'Sullivan noted with evident concern 'the obligations it will lay me under' to Lansdowne.[510] The latter appears to have accepted whatever assurances he was offered about why Stephen left the bank, for in July the Colonial Office informed Stephen that Earl Grey was pleased to appoint him as a stipendiary magistrate on the Caribbean island of Grenada. Immediately the couple looked for Fr John to send more money to help them make the long journey, but he suggested that they try her father.[511] They subsequently managed to get to the West Indies, only for Stephen's health to deteriorate. If he returns, mused John O'Sullivan, 'he will be a regular burden on me, but God's will be done.'[512]

O'Sullivan's concern about mixing family with politics is evident from his request to his brother, 'I beg of you not to be giving out that it was through the marquess you got the appointment.'[513] He confessed to his cousin Anne's husband, John Murphy, that by seeking the job for Stephen he placed himself 'under a compliment' to Lord Lansdowne.[514]

13

Fr John, Politics and Young Ireland

Fr John O'Sullivan's principal objectives were religious and social. Within that context he navigated political waters, but cautiously. He had had a bruising experience in Dingle as a young curate when, during a general election, he threw his weight against the Knight of Kerry in favour of candidates supported by Daniel O'Connell and was embroiled in the vindictive aftermath. Thereafter, as he told members of parliament in 1849:

> I never interfered in political matters except once in a public manner, and the way in which I was led to do so upon that occasion was this: my own parishioners had a row as to whether I should be a repealer or not, and I was afraid they were likely to come to an unpleasant termination; and I said, 'As I must be on one side or the other, here is for repeal'; but I never took any active part in it.

> [Question 2918] You are no politician?

> [Answer] No I am opposed to the repeal of the union if we could get any fair play from the British Government, which I do not think we have got.[515]

O'Sullivan openly expressed strong views on the needs of the poor and on land reform. When he thought that a landlord was interfering in religious matters, by proselytism for example, he was prepared to deploy publicly contentious economic, social, political and historical arguments against him.[516]

'I must look before me'

As he worked to persuade the government to help the Kenmare Union and sought to acquire land on which to build chapels and schools locally, the priest could not afford to incur the displeasure of the dominant local landlord, the Marquess of Lansdowne. Lansdowne had played an important role, in 1846, in the formation of the current government and was both Lord President of the Council and leader of the House of Lords. It was through him that O'Sullivan – when he first went to London in 1847, accompanied on that occasion by a local Anglican clergyman, James Going – came to meet Charles Trevelyan:

> A Treasury messenger was sent about with us to show us everything worthy to be seen – and Going being a diffident, gentlemanly fellow I had all my own way. I was proud of it beyond measure and thank God it was not because John O'Sullivan was the person they so complimented, but because it was the Parish Priest of Kenmare that was looked up to. We got all we wanted, all we sought for a depot here.[517]

Sir Charles Trevelyan was assistant secretary to the United Kingdom Treasury, being its highest-ranking civil servant under the Chancellor of the Exchequer and having immense influence over government policy on famine relief. This is reflected even today in a line of 'The Fields of Athenry', a popular song sung by Irish supporters at football internationals that mentions 'Trevelyan's corn'. His role was the subject of a substantial study in 2004, and his attitudes and motivation have excited conflicting opinions.[518] He certainly shared a contemporary and widespread view that inclined the UK government to minimise its intervention in the market, believing that free trade was the best mechanism for delivering affordable food to all. He and other officials in London were sceptical about all classes and interest groups in Ireland – not least about absentee landlords who failed to make the most of their lands. In an insightful if somewhat patronising article that he contributed anonymously to the *Edinburgh Review* in January 1848, he wrote:

> All classes 'make a poor mouth', as it is expressively called in Ireland. They conceal their advantages, exaggerate their difficulties, and relax their exertions. The cottier does not sow his holding, the proprietor does not employ his poor in improving his estate, because by doing so they would disentitle themselves to their 'share of the relief'.[519]

Trevelyan's brother-in-law, the historian Thomas Babington Macaulay, is thought to have had a significant input to the article.[520]

O'Sullivan first came to Trevelyan from a strong position, having personally taken measures to import badly needed food into Kenmare. He and Going waited on him, 'not for the purpose of asking for assistance' but to show how impossible it was to continue local importations without a satisfactory means of transit and a depot.[521] O'Sullivan noted that Trevelyan asked for him to write 'as often as my own good sense would say I ought. This from such a man was a great compliment.' A sustained exchange of correspondence developed.

Trevelyan invited the priest to stay at his home when O'Sullivan returned to London for a second visit during 1847.[522] George Villiers, 4th Earl of Clarendon, and Lord Lieutenant in Dublin, seemed particularly impressed by O'Sullivan. On one occasion Clarendon forwarded to Trevelyan a letter he had received from the priest and commended it as being both different in spirit from 'the letters which swarm every moment' and valuable when confronting Lord Kenmare over a difficulty in Kerry.[523] On another occasion O'Sullivan appears to have been instrumental in pushing Trevelyan into confronting Lansdowne over the condition of the latter's tenants – something that the priest himself could scarcely have done for fear of antagonising the local landlord.[524] He was not Trevelyan's only clerical correspondent. Others included Fr John Fitzpatrick, whose letters to London helped to make his parish of Skibbereen a byword for the great hunger, and the temperance advocate Fr Theobald Mathew.[525]

O'Sullivan heard that Sir John Tyrell MP had sneered that the priest had 'actually polished the doors of the Treasury by my repeated visits there since I came to town'. If so, it was an unintended compliment to O'Sullivan's tenacity.[526]

The need for caution was evident from an incident in May 1847. O'Sullivan was summoned in a pastoral capacity to Augustus Maybury of Clady – 'who was all his life a Protestant' but who married an aunt of Rev. Daniel McCarthy, then professor of rhetoric in Maynooth College.[527] O'Sullivan wrote that Maybury had earlier asked him to be his executor and now requested the priest to 'prepare' him for death. The local Protestant curate, Charles P. Thomas, 'charged me with tampering with him but nothing could be more untrue'. O'Sullivan added:

> Thomas I believe means well but he is crackt [*sic*] and only for Hickson [Lansdowne's agent] being his brother-in-law, I would have given him such a slating as would have kept him quiet for a while, but I must bide my time – partial as Lord Lansdowne is to

me, I am sure his bias and his feelings would lead him to join the minister in the event of our quarrelling, so I must look before me […] Thomas will, I am very sure, have to go to an asylum again and perhaps before long.[528]

O'Sullivan's visits to London enhanced his status at home. He later told a select committee that 'After some parleying upon the matter in London, we [he and Going] succeeded in getting a depot established' where imported meal could be stored in Kenmare before being distributed to relieve famine. He believed that the first visit alone 'was of the greatest importance to me and to my holy religion […] I made so many influential acquaintances.' As a result:

> officers of the vessels putting in here with Government provisions, shrewd fellows seeing these things, seek and enquire for me as the leading person in the country – to the no small dismay, annoyance and confusion of the '*Principis terra*' [Latin: the foremost] who were so much accustomed to have everything their own way.[529]

Back in Kenmare after his second trip to London in 1847, O'Sullivan wrote:

> My visit in February proved of such consequence and gives me such advantage over the lads here that I felt another visit needs be of use. Not having heard for some time from the people over, I was afraid some undercurrent had been setting in against me and I was determined to be satisfied of the truth. So I went a second time to London and have every reason to be proud of my visit. If my first reception was flattering, my second was doubly so. I was invited to dine and slept in the house of Trevelyan of the Treasury. The members of the British Association were equally glad to see me, and equally attentive and complimentary, and Lord Lansdowne himself apologised for Lady Lansdowne's absence from town in not asking me to dinner. This to be sure was all very flattering to the son of a humble man, and thank God it did not elevate me or puff me up, nor did I seek my own glory therein but the cause of my holy religion, nor had I any other feeling thereon than the satisfaction of a poor parish priest being received by such people with such deference and respect.[530]

While O'Sullivan worked carefully to increase the prestige of his church and the welfare of his parishioners, others were less patient and urged revolution.

Sedition, seduction and slander

During the summer of 1848, Ireland was gripped by news of Young Ireland, a more radical movement than that of the late Daniel O'Connell and one that the government feared might spark widespread violence in response to the great famine. In July and August there was a minor outbreak of rebellion in Munster led by William Smith O'Brien MP and others. Priests, including O'Sullivan, played a role in damping down the revolt then. Lord Lansdowne acknowledged that fact in the House of Lords on 21 July 1848:

> Some of the Roman Catholic clergy have taken the most effectual means of preventing the formation of clubs; and instances might be quoted in which, when circumstances were most favourable to the progress of sedition, the remedy has been found in the exhortations of the priests, who have warned their flocks against the dangers by which they were assailed. The Lord Lieutenant of Ireland is most anxious that it should be known, that if the great conflict shall come, which I fear is coming, though I trust it will be short, the Government of Ireland will be essentially sustained by the support of one part at least of that highly respectable and religious body.[531]

Nevertheless, O'Sullivan's curate Patrick Hampston got into trouble for objecting to the police posting a government proclamation concerning the Young Ireland leader Smith O'Brien on the chapel at Templenoe on 30 July 1848. The incident did not go unnoticed in London. O'Sullivan wrote:

> A Lord Rodney was lying in the bay in his yacht at the same time and he wrote a letter to Sir John Tyrell, a cracked, bigoted member of parliament [for North Essex] who makes a very foolish speech thereon in the House of Commons and brought Hampston into great notoriety.[532]

The letter that Tyrell read out during his speech was dated 6 August and was said to be 'from a friend [...] on board his yacht' in Kenmare Bay. It included criticism of Lansdowne. The writer may have mixed up Hampston with O'Sullivan, proclaiming:

> The vagabond priests ought to be exterminated, as there is not

a doubt but that in many cases they urge the people on, and, now they are frightened, pretend to try and quieten them [...] These are the scoundrels Lord Lansdowne praises in the House of Lords, and the very fellow who thus defied the Queen's proclamation is constantly with Lord Lansdowne when he comes here [to Kenmare] to see his property, so his [Lansdowne's] information cannot be very good respecting them; but it seems to be his main object, when here, to have no one but priests about him.[533]

John O'Connell MP rose on a point of order, 'He did not see what a letter written by some anonymous slanderer in a drunken moment had to do with diplomatic relations with Rome.'[534] Then Prime Minister John Russell spoke:

If we are to enter into the conduct of individuals we know that many priests of the Roman Catholic communion have exerted all their efforts and risked their influence with their flocks in order to prevent them from being led into the dangerous course to which they were incited by the rebels who were endeavouring to seduce them from their allegiance. What Lord Lansdowne may have done, and whom he lives with when he goes to Ireland, is hardly to the purpose; but Lord Lansdowne is a man who, when he finds good conduct, whether it be in Episcopalian, Presbyterian, or Roman Catholic, has that sense of justice and toleration that he would not allow a peculiar faith to separate him from such a person.[535]

O'Sullivan informed Charles Trevelyan that Tyrell's daughter had converted to Catholicism, thus suggesting an ulterior reason for Tyrell's anger.[536]

O'Sullivan, Russell and pensions

O'Sullivan went to Dublin a few weeks after the abortive Young Ireland rebellion. There he met both Lord Lieutenant Clarendon and Prime Minister Russell, reportedly having 'a long interview' with the two men at the viceregal lodge in the Phoenix Park, although O'Sullivan's journals are uninformative about its content. The meeting occurred on the same day that Russell and his young wife were entertained at the lodge by bands playing a polka and selections from operas, but 'there was not a single cheer given from any of the large crowds who had congregated to see the Prime Minister' as he rode through the streets of Dublin.[537] The priest noted in his journal, 'Had an interview with the Lord Lieutenant and Lord John Russell, now premier: both received me kindly. Had a regular row with Maurice Cross, one of the secretaries of the Education Board.'[538] While this suggests that schooling was discussed, the possibility of the government's 'pensioning of the priests of Rome' was said to be a prime consideration in Russell visiting Ireland in the aftermath of the 1848 rebellion,[539] and O'Sullivan supported such a controversial endowment.

A suggestion that the United Kingdom government might endow the clergy of the Catholic Church as it did those of the established church had long lain on the table, if only as a sop in the absence of Catholic emancipation before 1829. Parish priests and curates struggled financially to extract, from their parishioners, sufficient dues to support themselves, build chapels and provide other religious facilities, and there were some precedents elsewhere in Europe for such a state endowment of Catholicism. Moreover, the government had already endowed Maynooth College. However, the intertwined history of Britain and Ireland gave the question a particular twist, and priests and bishops were wary of the consequences of taking payments from London. It might appear to compromise them as much as it could help to free them from fundraising in order to devote more time to pastoral work. Donal Kerr has described the record of O'Sullivan's views as being 'the most interesting and fullest expression of opinion' by a priest on the matter.[540] A number of times in his journals, O'Sullivan makes his view clear. But when he did so in 1843, he did not then believe that most priests supported endowment:

> The Bishops to be sure and the greater part of the clergy are opposed to it. But, as for my own part, I do not think I would become more indolent or more inattentive to my duties. I work (at least I think so) more for my own salvation than for any emolument and I'm sure I would not relax by being in receipt of the pension. I think I would work as hard and my efforts would then have more of the appearance of disinterestedness.[541]

Yet by 1847 he thought that all the priests of Kerry diocese 'as far as I can ascertain are favourable to it, and in truth I think myself I have no other motive for wishing for it but with the view of making our labours more effective and have less the appearance of selfishness or self-interest.' He knew that some priests in wealthier parishes in Dublin did not want parish income to come from that source, but 'they had not to wring it from the poor creatures we have to deal with.' Poverty was not the only problem. He also faced parishioners whom he called 'the hard-fisted'.[542] During his second visit to London, in late 1847, O'Sullivan discussed with Lansdowne the idea of paying priests:

> I had a long conference with Lord Lansdowne on the subject of the pension for our clergy. I had been speaking to him about it before and I wrote to him on the subject before I left home. His answer came here [Kenmare] a few days after I left home.

That confidential letter cautiously outlined English political difficulties that lay in the way of endowing the Catholic Church. After reading it, the priest described Lansdowne as 'an old fox'.[543]

In 1848 Lord Lieutenant Clarendon concluded that many Irish curates were starving along with their parishioners, and that the clergy generally supported the suggestion that Catholic priests receive a payment or 'pension' from the state.[544] Ultimately, no such payments were approved.

Lobbying in London

In March 1849, on his third visit to London during the famine, O'Sullivan received a mild reproof from Trevelyan:

> Trevelyan astonished me by saying I should not be showing [to others] his letters [to me], from which I can easily perceive how the lords here are annoyed at my supposed influence with the government and why he hasn't replied to some of my letters lately. He asked me however to continue to write to him. I will, as he is in a way to do much good or evil and he must attach some importance to my communications when he seemed so anxious to get them.[545]

As he expanded on his meeting with Trevelyan, it became clear that he had reservations about the nature of the relationship:

> When parting with Trevelyan in London he asked me as a particular favour to write often to him, at the same time giving me to understand I was not to expect a reply but that he would send me all the Blue Books [published parliamentary papers] and all the papers connected with the poor law in return for my letters. He is evidently afraid of its going abroad that he would

be in correspondence with me and so much slipt from him the day he spoke to me about showing his letters. I was about to tell him indignantly that I would hold correspondence with no man in such terms but on reflection I may lose the opportunity of doing much good. He must have attached some importance to my communications – that being the third time he asked me to continue them, and his being evidently much mixed up with Irish affairs and looked up to thereon it may be of importance to my unhappy country to have the ear of such a man even though I do let myself down to a certain extent; along with that the fact of my getting all those Blue Books and parliamentary papers through the post office makes all the lads here think my influence must be unbounded and that contributes to awe them to a great extent.[546]

Trevelyan recommended that he talk to William Fagan, MP for Cork, or to John Bright, the reformist Liberal MP for Manchester and a Quaker. Each was in a position to help ensure that he was called to give evidence to the select committee, 'I could not find Bright but Fagan, an honest man and a good Catholic did everything I wished and I wanted.'[547] O'Sullivan subsequently told Fr John Fitzpatrick of Skibbereen that he 'preferred' Fagan, and that he had written out questions for Fagan to ask him at the hearing.[548]

He also had another meeting with David Salomons. Already referring to 'Salomons the Jew' as 'an old acquaintance' on the basis of his previous visits, O'Sullivan wrote that Salomons was 'as glad as ever to see me'. Besides being a member of the British Association for the Relief of Distress and a founder of the first joint-stock bank in London, Salomons was also a city alderman in the Liberal interest. As a professing Jew, he was prevented from occupying a seat in parliament, to which he was elected for Greenwich in 1851; however, he was to become the first Jewish Lord Mayor of London in 1855.[549] His continuing correspondence with O'Sullivan heartened the priest.

The select committee called O'Sullivan as a witness, as seen above. He was asked if other clergymen in Kerry took as active a part in the poor law as he did, and he replied that he did not think so:

The cause was that I was so mixed up with relief matters, and I had so much to do in working the relief committees; I had been in London twice, and residing near the workhouse, a pressure set in upon me that has not set in upon the other clergy. I got a

great deal of food through the charitable societies, which I
disbursed; and seeing me in a position to give so much, brought
a great influx of paupers upon me.[550]

He was examined over two days. John Tyrell MP, who had denounced
him and his curate in parliament, appears to have attended the whole
first day, although he was not a member of that committee. O'Sullivan
wrote that he had 'a good cohort' of MPs prepared in case of an attack
by Tyrell, including Morgan O'Connell (Kerry), John O'Connell
(Limerick), Henry Arthur Herbert (Kerry), John Reynolds (Dublin
City) and Henry Granville Fitzalan-Howard, an ardent Catholic and
the future 14th Duke of Norfolk (Arundel).[551]

    In London O'Sullivan also met George Poulett Scrope MP, a
geologist and political economist who was critical of the poor laws and
of Malthusian doctrines:

> Evidently a most kind, humane man but the preambles he made
> in putting a simple question, and the manner in which the
> chairman cut him off, took up the question and put it in a
> concise shape showed me he was a man – however well disposed
> – who had not much insight.[552]

Scrope was willing to help, 'He is an extremely well-disposed man and
seems to have a monomania against Irish landlords – or rascals as he
called them when talking to me in the corridor [at Westminster].' The
two men subsequently corresponded.[553] Reflecting on his appearance
before the select committee, O'Sullivan wrote:

> I never go to London that I don't feel that I do much good
> thereby. I really think the English people want not so much the
> disposition, but the knowledge of the wants of this miserable
> country. They seem to know as little about the real state of this
> country as if oceans instead of a channel were running between
> us.[554]

Melt down the regalia

O'Sullivan regretted that he had burned so much of his
correspondence in the past, and he resolved to make a record of it in
future. He could not afford to pay a clerk for the purpose, and 'nor
would I like to let one into many of the matters in which I have to
correspond.' So he began himself to copy letters into his 'Random
Recollections' journal – and ostensibly also into another book that is

lost, 'Curious enough my first entry is a letter I write this day to an eminent Jew [David Salomons MP]; if through him I can get introduced to the [London] *Times*, I will be able to do much good as they will attend to my communications.'[555] He explained that he had not dallied to meet, along with Salomons as was planned, 'two gentlemen of the *Times*', because he had been in a great hurry to get home to Kenmare before an expected outbreak of cholera. He had seen on his trips to London that 'the *Times* was England'. Indeed, 'I found the most extravagant, absurd, monstrous stories regarding my unhappy country received with implicit credence, simply because it was in *The Times* and I longed to make the acquaintance of some of the proprietors.' So much of what he saw of Irish affairs in English papers was, he thought, 'devoid of truth'.[556] Writing a long and poignant letter to George Poulett Scrope MP in April 1849, he delivered a powerful critique of the government's failure to come to terms with the great famine:

> If I am asked the question how the expense of keeping all these people alive is to be met, I would say that wherever it comes from, the thing ought to be met. Were it necessary to melt down the 'regalia' I would say it ought be done rather than have it told of the British Empire that her subjects were plague spots on her face and that such desolation should be allowed to stalk abroad in a rich, a prosperous, a civilised, a Christian country. I would have more patience were I see this Government grapple manfully with the difficulty and seek to lay down the foundations of such a state of society as would afford a fair prospect of being able to hope for fewer, if any recurrences of such calamities; but when I see them instead of facing the thing in such a spirit, peddling with their maximum rates and rates on annuities and jointures and every other measure they are now proposing I cannot but compare them to the physician who has recourse to gentle purgatives and fomentations, when his patient is convulsed and heaving and requiring the most prompt and the most active remedies.[557]

O'Sullivan lobbied Trevelyan to have John W. Nicholls, former secretary to Rear-Admiral Sir Hugh Pigot at Cobh, called to give evidence before the Poor Law Committee, and also his own 'intimate friend' John Mahony of Cork, whose lands included property in Templenoe and 'who I took the liberty of introducing to you at one time […] a landlord himself and intimately mixed up with the dealings of almost every landlord and tenant in the counties of Cork and Kerry.' He believed that Mahony, 'the most extensive butter merchant' in Cork, would talk of the misdeeds and oppressions of other landlords.[558]

Fr John O'Sullivan's public profile was now high enough for John Ball of the Poor Law Commission (and a future member of parliament) to write to him in July 1849 to say that the author, biographer and historian Thomas Carlyle was making a 'rapid tour' in Ireland and that Ball had taken the liberty of suggesting to Carlyle that he meet O'Sullivan. In the event, there appears to have been no such meeting; Carlyle went directly from Cork to Killarney.[559] Indeed, by the summer of 1849 O'Sullivan was beginning to worry that his profile was too high and his activities against the local proselytisers were raising eyebrows. 'I find of late considerable mistrust springing up among the gentry of Kerry towards me,' he wrote in his notebook. He told William Fagan MP, 'I know you think that I have been too violent and I am far from blaming you for your candor. Many besides you have told me that same, but had I not taken such a stand [against proselytising], I am satisfied Templenoe would be now another Dingle.'[560]

Lansdowne's 'own sweet pet'

Tensions between O'Sullivan and Denis Mahony concerning alleged proselytising boiled over into a mob assault in 1850. It was a chance for the *Kerry Evening Post* to take a sideswipe at both O'Sullivan and Lansdowne – and at O'Sullivan's support for a possible state endowment of Catholic priests. Two years earlier the Protestant paper had jeered at O'Sullivan as 'a great man these times' through his 'intercourse with great folks – such as Lord Lansdowne', and declared that 'we can recollect the bulky priest a *little shoneen*.'[561] It now returned to the attack:

> His Lordship has every facility of becoming acquainted with the state of things near Kenmare. Father John, who flourishes there, is his own sweet pet – thriving on the fat of his land – boasting the friendship of honourable and right honourables, nay (we are assured) cordially embraced by the hand (not very long ago) of his Excellency Lord [Lieutenant] Clarendon, on whose familiarity (it will be seen) this low-lived bully counts for disposal even of Church patronage![562]

The editor suggested that the Whig government provided no defence 'against the blood-thirsty and insatiable malice of persecuting Rome', complaining that Lansdowne had alleged 'aggressions' by some of those trying to convert Catholics. The editor thought that such people were simply 'preaching of the Gospel', and regretted that 'the voice of the President of Her Majesty's Council is raised to screen the instigators of the ungovernable fury of excited multitudes.' O'Sullivan responded by way of a letter published in the *Cork Examiner*.

> As regards all the farrago, all the nonsense, all the alarm, about my supposed intimacy with Lord Clarendon, and the unlimited sway I have over his party, was anything ever half so ridiculous? I had the honour, or rather the misfortune, of making his Excellency's acquaintanceship, and, to add to it, I had the additional mishap of shaking hands with him (oh horrible!!) and walking for a while with him when passing through here; and, as you are aware, the *Kerry Post* is ever since ringing changes on it; it is held up as a 'great Protestant grievance' and a greater crime on my part, than if I had been up in arms with Meagher and Doheny [of Young Ireland]. Make your minds easy, gentlemen. I know perhaps as little, maybe less, of his Excellency than you do yourselves. If I have been foremost in proclaiming my gratitude to the English people, for their kindness, hospitality, and munificence to me, when I went over to represent the wants of the starving poor of this union; if I unreservedly give expression to the opinion that the misgovernment of this country is owing more to an ignorance of its real state and condition than to a deliberate desire to keep it in a state of abject slavery; if I repeat that the country owes much to his Excellency for his coolness, steadiness and firmness in carrying it through the more than ticklish crisis we have passed; it is because I think and feel those things, and I lose no opportunity of giving expression to those sentiments.[563]

As he trod a path between political forces, O'Sullivan's life was complicated by his brother's problems.

The O'Connells of Derrynane

In 1849 O'Sullivan told William Fagan MP that he took no part in politics, though he was 'a near relative of the O'Connells'.[564] This did not stop him, before he entered the lions' den of Westminster to appear before a select committee, from arranging for both John O'Connell MP and Morgan John O'Connell MP, among others, to protect his back in the event of an anticipated parliamentary attack by Sir John Tyrell.

There are only some minor passing references to Daniel O'Connell in O'Sullivan's journals; in these, he acknowledges the great man's support of his schooling as a child. O'Connell died in May 1847. As seen earlier, the response of Daniel O'Connell's son Maurice to O'Sullivan's approaches about his brother Stephen, who had lost a job that Daniel O'Connell got him in the National Bank, irked O'Sullivan. He did not like Maurice, whose political career was not outstanding. The priest was also annoyed at having to sort out a problem concerning ownership of land in Caherciveen – land on which the O'Connells had allowed the Presentation Order to build its convent. When Maurice O'Connell wished to embroil O'Sullivan in his political ambitions in 1852, trying to get the priest 'to appear on the hustings with him', O'Sullivan avoided his scheme, describing him as 'a drunken, crackt, swob'. He noted, 'My principal position here being based on the fact of my being no politician until provoked by the attempts that were made at souperism. Maurice too was cavalier enough to my brother when dismissed from the National Bank.'[565] Nevertheless, Maurice was returned to parliament:

> The good or rather the silly people of Cahirciveen are almost frantic at the news, frantic with joy, drums playing, colours flying, men huraaing, brats screeching, an attempt at a band parading the town, tossing their hats in the air, waving green boughs and shaking handkerchiefs, hosannas and halleluiahs, such a bobbery!! – and all for a drunken swob that does not care one damn for the whole of them, a man that does not care for anyone, won't pay anyone, won't regard any principle or attend to any duty. God help poor Ireland while she has such men to make laws for her and to look after her interests. No wonder she should be what she is.[566]

High rents

Despite his protestations that he had eschewed overt political activity, O'Sullivan continued to play a role that sometimes had definite political implications. While he was undoubtedly reluctant to declare for any particular candidate or party, he had attended a repeal meeting rather than be thought to support the other side of that argument – and he dealt cannily with politicians in London when it suited his purposes. While he usually stood back from contention over tenant rights, in late December 1849 he made a speech that – as reported – showed him eager to support publicly major land reform. Addressing about five thousand farmers near the crossroads at Reen, between Kenmare and Templenoe, he strongly opposed high rents and the reintroduction of restrictions on trade that landlords supported. He explicitly disagreed with the views of Henry Arthur Herbert, a member of parliament for Kerry. O'Sullivan felt that Ireland was well able to support the current level of taxation that was required to finance the poor laws, claiming that these had helped the country.[567]

During the speech, he made a historical assertion that was remarkable, given the fact that the great famine had just devastated many families, 'there is not a man listening to me who, despite the visitation which has come upon the country [...] is not better fed, better housed, better in every way than were his fellow countrymen in 1784.' He said that there was once no baker in Kenmare, yet now there were seventeen, 'because every one eats bread, and much good may it do them (Cheers)'. He thought that landlords wanted to throw people back on potatoes; he claimed that the people now ate beef and mutton at Christmas – against the wishes of the landlords, who would see all livestock sold. He thought it 'melancholy' that 'we could never grow enough of food to support 33,000 people' in the Kenmare Union because the land remained untilled and unimproved. The behaviour of landlords reminded him of an old Irish joke, 'What are you doing, Paddy? Nothing Sir. What are you doing, Tim? Helping Paddy, Sir. (great laughter).' Yet he also carefully avoided alienating Lansdowne, claiming that tenants were treated well on his estate, provided they paid their rents. He added that Lansdowne, 'in his own parlour in London', had told O'Sullivan that 'after paying the poor rates and other encumbrances, he had not out of his own property in this district, for the last two years one penny.' A curate named Scanlan challenged O'Sullivan at the meeting on this benign view of the local landlord, pointing to the state of Lansdowne's tenants in Tuosist. O'Sullivan notably did not disagree with him; he said diplomatically that he could not contradict a colleague and spoke only of his own parish. O'Sullivan also recognised that he had stepped across the line of his religious and pastoral duties in addressing the crowd as he did:

I feel that I am not in my proper sphere in lecturing on these subjects. I would rather be addressing you on your moral and religious duties. I think that a priest goes out of his way, and is not minding of the duties of his profession when he goes talking at such length on such a public occasion as this. But, on the other hand, if the priest did not come forward, no one else would take it up (cheers) […] I say it is a bad sign of the times, because we would never have that power, unless you were ill-treated as you are. Therefore it is that we stand by you, as the only exponents of your wrongs and sufferings.[568]

It may be that his statement that 'no one else would take it up' was intended as a criticism of Maurice O'Connell, the local Catholic MP. O'Sullivan concluded his remarks by calling for three cheers for the Queen – a cry reportedly met by 'tremendous cheers'. In doing so, he may simply have wished to demonstrate that one was not being disloyal by calling for radical reform. But it should be remembered that modern nationalism was only slowly emerging into the mainstream at that time, and neither the recent repeal movement led by Daniel O'Connell nor the future Home Rule agitation envisaged Ireland standing independent of the Crown. Before 1800, when Ireland had its own parliament – being, constitutionally, a separate kingdom – its people had also been subjects of the monarch in London. In 1849 there was little or no reason to think that that particular relationship with the Crown would soon change. Regardless of those 'tremendous cheers', the *Kerry Evening Post*, never a friend of O'Sullivan's, attacked him and the other priests ('clerical spouters') whom it accused of fostering the meeting. He was 'that notorious clerical Whig agitator' who was very much mistaken about the weight of 'the resolutions of the ignorant serfs, whipped together by himself and his rev. coadjutors'.[569] O'Sullivan's speech received national attention, being printed, for example, on the front page of the *Northern Whig* in Belfast on 5 January 1850.

Phoenix and Fenians

Fr O'Sullivan's decision, in 1858, to inform Dublin Castle of the existence of an incipient revolutionary conspiracy in his parish was consistent with his opposition to agrarian and political violence. He rationalised his decision on the basis that he was protecting his flock from strife that could result in many young men getting into serious trouble. If his willingness during the famine to give credit to England for aid sent to Ireland was strategically necessary, he was later represented as sometimes giving comfort to Ireland's enemies.[570]

O'Sullivan's concerns in 1858 arose from the foundation of the Phoenix Society in Skibbereen by Jeremiah O'Donovan Rossa, later a Fenian hero, and from the related activities of its members. O'Donovan Rossa worked in Skibbereen for his first cousin's husband, Mortimer Downing from Kenmare. The latter was in the wool, cotton and flax business and occasionally had contracts for supplying the Kenmare workhouse, which O'Donovan Rossa then visited in the course of his employment. He used to stay with Mortimer's brother Dan, who ran the Washington Hotel in Kenmare, but it is not known if O'Donovan Rossa, on his visits to the workhouse, ever met Fr O'Sullivan.[571]

Towards the end of 1858 a number of priests in Munster had begun to speak out against what they saw as a growing conspiracy that was bound by an oath of secrecy.[572] The government soon made arrests, including that of O'Donovan Rossa. In 1885, in an article in a New York newspaper, O'Donovan Rossa was to claim that Dublin Castle blackmailed Fr O'Sullivan into not giving evidence that would have discredited one or two of the witnesses for the prosecution at the trial in 1858. He claimed that this was achieved by threatening to reveal the contents of letters ostensibly written by the priest to the authorities. He reprinted in his article what he identified as transcripts of those letters and of other letters from O'Sullivan to Matthew Barrington, Crown Solicitor, and Pat Jeffers BL, an old schoolfriend of the priest and a partner of Barrington. O'Donovan Rossa wrote that Morty Moynahan had copied the correspondence from a copy in the possession of the prisoners' Kenmare-born attorney, Timothy McCarthy Downing, whose chief clerk Moynihan was.[573] The senior lawyer representing the prisoners was Thomas O'Hagan, future Lord Chancellor of Ireland.

O'Sullivan does appear to have written on 5 October 1858 to Lord Naas (Richard Southwell Bourke, 6th Earl of Mayo and Chief Secretary for Ireland), outlining in his letter 'a good deal of the workings of the system' that he had denounced at Mass the preceding weekend. The correspondence as published indicates that O'Sullivan informed Naas that he had the names of some of those involved, and enclosed copies of two oaths administered by the conspirators. The government thereupon arrested a number of men and offered a reward to informers. O'Sullivan wrote again to Dublin Castle on 11 December to say that he believed that almost every one of those involved in the conspiracy in Kenmare had by now attended the sacraments of confession and communion in preparation for Christmas; he claimed that this was '*prima facie* evidence of their having solemnly pledged themselves to disconnect themselves from the society'. He added that nobody had joined the conspiracy since he first denounced it, and he asked the government to free 'these foolish boys – for boys they are'. He added that kindness would be wiser than pursuing a prosecution.[574]

Matters began to take a turn that O'Sullivan did not like. The public was agitated, and locals were rallying behind the young men. Some thought that O'Sullivan had provoked a Fenian scare to frighten Lansdowne's agent, Trench, because of the latter's continuing opposition to the establishment of a convent in the town. Magistrates investigating the alleged conspiracy heard from one Daniel Sullivan 'Goulah', a process server from Bonane, that he had taken oaths of secrecy and brotherhood and had drilled at the place where duels were fought at the Priest's Leap on the way from Kenmare to Bantry, 'when I went to the priest to confess, he refused to give me absolution till I'd break through them.' He added that the priest in Kenmare chapel who wished him to 'break through' his oaths of secrecy and brotherhood was John O'Sullivan.[575] On 26 December 1858, according to the correspondence as published, O'Sullivan again wrote to Lord Naas, claiming that 'The man never confessed to me: I never exchanged a word with him.' He advised Naas that there was likely to be trouble in Kenmare if the arrested men were not freed. He stated that by telling the authorities of the conspiracy, he had initially 'incurred much odium' – although 'all parties now admit I was their best friend.' He would, he said, be at the forefront in recommending prosecution if he thought it would 'tend more to the preservation of the peace and the dignity of the constitution' than the clemency that he was now suggesting. After some months, by agreement, the prisoners pleaded guilty and were released.[576]

In his New York article of 1885, O'Donovan Rossa condemned the manner in which O'Sullivan allegedly got copies of the Fenian oaths:

> He met in the confessional one of the men who were sworn in, he questioned him, he told the man to go out into the chapel yard and meet him there; the man went out, the priest went out after him, and in the chapel yard the priest got from the penitent a copy of the oath and afterwards sent it to Dublin Castle. This was getting it 'extra tribunal', as Father John 'technically' termed it [in one of the ostensible letters to Lord Naas], but I never met any priest to whom I told the story to approve of technicality of that kind in connection with the duties of the Catholic confessional.

O'Donovan Rossa claimed that Dublin Castle threatened to produce the whole correspondence from O'Sullivan and make the priest swear to it, and that O'Sullivan then decided not to give any evidence impugning the informer. Newspapers termed the prosecution 'The Phoenix Trials', although O'Donovan Rossa later indicated that the oath of secrecy was that of the Irish Republican Brotherhood and not the Phoenix Society, which was a literary club where attendees were sometimes recruited for the IRB. He wrote that O'Sullivan 'does not deny this correspondence; Indeed, I believe he justifies it.' He conceded that the priest 'no doubt' satisfied himself that he was doing the best thing he could do.[577]

Fr O'Sullivan certainly denounced the conspiracy, and the correspondence attributed to him has a ring of authenticity about it. Nevertheless, he was not in a position to respond to the 1885 article in the *Brooklyn Eagle* or to repeat his denial that he had heard Sullivan's confession. For by then he, McCarthy Downing and Morty Moynahan were all dead. O'Donovan Rossa exclaimed, 'I tell no lies of the dead', and in a reference to O'Sullivan added, 'It was his bishop – Bishop Moriarty – that said "Hell is not hot enough, nor eternity long enough" for the Fenians. God be good to them, both of them are dead.'[578]

14

Converts and Conflict at Dromore Castle

The relationship between Fr John O'Sullivan and Denis Mahony started as it would end: badly. O'Sullivan was not long in Kenmare when he wrote to the latter seeking a site on which to build a new chapel within his parish – at Templenoe, where Mahony was landlord, 'the scoundrel would not condescend to reply to my letter.'[579]

Castles

At the core of the bitterness was proselytism in general, and that of Mahony and his third wife in particular. The couple lived at Dromore Castle. In 1837 Samuel Lewis described their home as 'a noble edifice in the Gothic castellated style, lately erected on the shore of the bay'. He added that the demesne, 'which extends a considerable distance along the margin of the bay and the eastern bank of the Blackwater, has been much improved and extensively planted by the present proprietor [Denis Mahony]; within it are the ruins of Cappanacoss castle, formerly belonging to a branch of the O'Sullivans.'[580]

The Mahonys sprang from an ancient Gaelic Catholic family that long lived around the coasts of Kenmare Bay. Their O'Mahony ancestors (whose prefix 'O' was later dropped) gave allegiance to King James II, with Colonel Dermot O'Mahony dying at the Battle of Aughrim in 1691. With William of Orange victorious, the O'Mahony family suffered both fine and confiscation, and many of its members left Ireland. Among those remaining on the Iveragh Peninsula was one John O'Mahony, who prospered.[581] His second wife is said to have been a daughter of the then chief of the O'Sullivan Mór sept; through this marriage, he got the ruined O'Sullivan castle of Dunloe that he had earlier leased from her family and repaired.[582] The ruined castles of Dunkerron and Cappanacush had likewise belonged to the O'Sullivan Mórs. This John's son Donell O'Mahony (also known as Daniel of

Dunloe) came to dominate Iveragh in an uneasy relationship with the settler William Petty's family – chief absentee landlords of the area. Writing in the nineteenth century, Froude thought that the arrangement excluded the rule of law, 'The singular figure of Daniel Mahony is a specimen of the class of middlemen to whom the wild districts, now frequented by tourists and sportsmen, were surrendered for the greater part of the last century.' Donell was said to have had a large band of men at his disposal to enforce his will. He died in 1747.[583]

The convert of 1747

In the same year that Donell O'Mahony died, his brother's grandson Denis conformed to the established church.[584] Neither Burke nor McCarthy, in their accounts of the family, mentions this fact.[585] With penal laws in place against Catholics owning land, this conversion to Protestantism helped to secure the family's title to lands, including those in Templenoe and elsewhere that had been in O'Sullivan Mór hands. In the nineteenth century Ross O'Connell wrote of meeting a grandson of an 'illegitimate' son of the last O'Sullivan Mór, chief of the sept, who had died in 1762 without a legitimate heir. The grandson, a fisherman, told O'Connell that when he went to see his grandfather lying dead, he found not only his departed ancestor but also a great pile of old documents:

> maybe three feet high, mostly written on skins in Latin and Irish; and faith I was in dread they might fall into the hands of the Mahonys or some other new people in the country, and they might get more of the old O'Sullivan estates, so I burned them all myself.[586]

John Mahony, a son of the convert of 1747, and his second wife Margaret Day, a daughter of Archdeacon Day of Beaufort House, had two sons – the eldest Richard and youngest Denis (Fr O'Sullivan's future foe).[587] During the early nineteenth century the Mahonys contributed to the cost of erecting a new Protestant church at Templenoe, fitted up with teak wood from the wreck of a vessel.[588] Violent agrarian activists known as 'Rockites' tried unsuccessfully to burn this down in 1822 – one of a number of attacks in the area aimed against tithes and other grievances.[589] Lewis noted, in 1837, that there was also a Protestant school at Templenoe which Mahony supported, while another school was held in the Catholic chapel 'under the superintendence of the R.C. clergyman [O'Sullivan's predecessor]'.[590]

Archfiend, parson and wanton goat

On 10 October 1843, the day on which he began to write his 'Random Recollections', O'Sullivan referred to Denis Mahony as 'an archfiend'. His journal on that day leaves no room for doubting the strength of his feelings about the landlord and parson, 'His grandfather [also named Denis] was a Catholic, became a Protestant [in 1747], filed several Bills of Discovery against the surrounding [Catholic] gentry and thus became possessor of their property.' However, the latter's son John (Denis Mahony's father) 'was as good a man as ever lived, would have died a Catholic – it is supposed – had he any friendly one near him in his last illness.' John died in 1817:

> He left two sons, Richard and Denis. Richard had all the property, and for want of anything else they made a parson of Denis; but Richard unfortunately died and Denis is now in the enjoyment of the entire [estate]. Richard bore a great name and I believe deserved it. But Denis is a miser, a screw, a bigot, a tyrant, a man of no word, no principle, no honor – keeps faith with no one, falls out with everyone and would go to any length to subvert and undermine our Holy Religion. I went out of my way more than once to try and conciliate the fellow but in vain. I sought to get a place to build a chapel instead of this crazy old cabin we have at present, but to no purpose. I asked it of him at a time he must have felt himself under some obligation, but he would not condescend as much as a reply – and yet I thought it more prudent to say nothing about it, hoping always for the best, until he brought a fellow named Banks from Dingle to read the Bible to his workmen and to revile our Holy Religion.
>
> I had to denounce himself and Banks in the most unmeasured language; such was the fury of the townspeople that they nearly stoned Banks, and hosted after Denis – and the latter, I understand, is to proceed by law against me for what I said in the chapel.[591]

Making a parson of a son guaranteed that person an income at a time when even Catholics and Presbyterians were obliged to pay tithes for the support of the established Anglican Church. In 1838 the tithe levy was converted into a more acceptable rent charge, but as late as 1867, one independent clergyman observed that 'the social status of a gentleman is secured by being a minister of the Established Church, and the chances for curates intermarrying with the families of the gentry are numerous.'[592]

When Denis Mahony's older brother Richard died, the former's material prospects improved; O'Sullivan thought that this excited him, 'He unexpectedly tumbled into a fine fortune, and then in truth as the old song has it':

> He shut his book, his flock forsook,
> And threw away his gown Sir:
> He mounted his horse to hunt the fox
> Sing Tallyho the hounds Sir.

O'Sullivan added that Mahony 'did hunt with a vengeance, for he hunted all the young girls of the country and got children by them. He married two wives and buried them.'[593] Verses that seem to have been written by O'Sullivan himself uncharitably described Mahony as being 'as wanton as a goat' and asserted that he fathered children outside marriage, 'Sure you'd find a young Mahony under every bush on the mountain.'[594] It is thought locally that Mahony fathered at least three such children.[595]

Soupers

Notwithstanding O'Sullivan's caricature of Mahony, the latter became involved in the proselytising reform movement that manifested itself strongly within the Church of Ireland in the early decades of the nineteenth century. Around 1850 O'Sullivan was to draft this advice for priests:

> We have a very different class of people to contend with in the Protestant clergy of the present day. The old cursing, swearing, fox-hunting, drinking, gambling, whoreing [sic], pheasant-shooting Parsons have disappeared. As long as the Catholics were trodden under foot by the penal laws, as long as they could live only as it were on the sufferance of their Protestant neighbours, so long the Parsons cared not [...] for any one thing or duty in this world, save getting in of his tithes.[596]

Mahony's involvement in the movement was at least partly due to his third wife, whom he married in 1843, for she was to be remembered locally as a notorious proselytiser. This was Katherine, daughter of Matthew Franks of Merrion Square, Dublin.[597] As famine stalked Ireland, she and Denis responded. The *Kerry Evening Post* reported on

30 December 1846, 'The Rev. Denis Mahoney, of Dromore Castle, is daily distributing soup and vegetables to over 130 families in the neighbourhood of his residence.' O'Sullivan was incensed at Mahony, who, 'as if to make amends for all his previous vagabondising [...] set about a regular campaign on the faith of the poor people he had been all his life demoralising.'[598] When it became clear that the year 1847 was going to be even worse than 1846 for famine and hunger, O'Sullivan worried about Anglican clergy who were, as he saw it:

> constantly going about on the roads seeking to ingratiate themselves by promising employment on the work for anyone that chose to have recourse to them. They were heretofore a set of rakes, a set of rakes who sought to render themselves obnoxious to the people. They now began to play a different game and seek to conciliate.[599]

O'Sullivan denounced from the altar those Catholics who attended any Protestant service, 'I said first Mass in town and gave those unfortunate wretches that have gone to church a proper slating, but I fear to no purpose.'[600] He determined to resist their efforts, not least by building more schools in his combined parishes, including a temporary one at Direendarragh – 'as Denis Mahony will not give me a lease':

> It requires all my might to meet Denis Mahony and his viper of a wife. She has a school at Templenoe at which all the children are clothed and fed, and while they are starving it is next to an impossibility to keep them from going there. Still, it is not much frequented and on the whole I have much more confidence in the people than I had some time ago.[601]

He grew angry as Mahony brought Kerry converts into Templenoe to help to proselytise. One 'wretched turncoat' was named Sullivan, from Killarney. Another was 'Gloster', possibly that James Gloster, or Glaster, from Ballyferriter who had been active in Dingle when Fr O'Sullivan was opposing proselytism there. Mahony and his wife Katherine now had a schoolteacher and bible-readers going among the poor people and distributing food and clothes.[602] Deploying ridicule as a weapon, O'Sullivan had spiteful verses about 'Gloster' and Katherine printed on a handbill and circulated.[603] He thought Mahony's wife was 'far and away more zealous' than Denis himself and described her in vituperative terms, dubbing her 'Yellow Kate' – ostensibly because she had a sallow complexion. He worried too about Fr Dan Healy's flock on the Beara Peninsula, where 'the parsons are making a great hand' and Healy 'though doing his best is no match for them'.[604]

A rancorous meeting

Mahony was an active landlord as well as a proselytiser. It appears that during the Young Ireland troubles of 1848, his Dromore Castle was threatened. Going to its defence, Captain Manaton Pipon – brother-in-law of the 6th Baron Rodney, who O'Sullivan thought was on board a yacht in Kenmare Bay at the time – landed nearby with some men and reportedly came under fire.[605] Nevertheless, O'Sullivan told William Fagan MP that when he spoke to some local people who had met the landing party, they 'laughed at the idea of a shot being fired there' (which was not necessarily a denial). Scurrilous verses were circulated, jeering that Mahony had fled in fear of violence and left his wife and children to be protected by the sailors.[606] A local journalist defended him:

> He quitted his house to lay the state of the country before the Lord Lieutenant, and he had only gone as far as Killarney, some miles distant, with two of his children who were coming to England for education, when the report reached him that his castle was attacked; he hastened back and found that Lord Rodney had come to the assistance with guns and ammunition.[607]

In September 1848 the *Kerry Examiner* reported a meeting in Kenmare that was chaired by Mahony, 'surrounded by a troop of gentlemen much after his own heart, with the exception of two or three Catholic clergymen, who no doubt attended to watch the movements of their high Tory neighbours lay and clerical'. The meeting was called to consider subdividing the Kenmare Union into smaller units – as a means of reducing the poor law taxation rate in parts of it, thus leaving some landlords and middlemen with more to invest in creating local employment if they wished. Dramatically, as the meeting ended, O'Sullivan entered the room and denounced the proposal as 'a scheme for the extermination of the people'.[608] The Protestant *Kerry Evening Post* thought that everything was going 'merry as a bell' until Fr John O'Sullivan stormed in. It reported 'the violent and outrageous conduct of Mr O'Sullivan towards the gentlemen who had been so earnestly considering the state of the poor and the ratepayer'. The paper added, 'This gentleman, who is not the mildest of God's ministers, made a furious attack on some unnamed parties.' Reacting to O'Sullivan's

dramatic entrance, Richard T. Orpen, a descendant of one of William
Petty's settlers, commented, 'His [O'Sullivan's] temper, little used to
control, broke forth with redoubled violence.' The priest said he had
come 40 miles just to be there. The paper suggested that the priest was
motivated by 'a vindictive desire to annoy certain highly respectable
parties' rather than any concern for the poor, 'So bitter are Mr
O'Sullivan's feelings on this point that on Sunday last he made it the
subject of an altar harangue in his Chapel, abusing the gentry in the
most vehement manner.'[609]

The *Kerry Evening Post* further reported that O'Sullivan left Kenmare
after the meeting in order to oppose its objects, and that he soon had
an interview with the Lord Lieutenant on the subject, 'As he happens
to be a great favourite with the Marquis of Lansdowne, we fear that
much mischief may be the result of his presumptuous and meddling
interference.'[610]

Mahony, in turn, threw a spanner into the pastoral works of
O'Sullivan when it came to the Christmas stations. The priest and his
curate had to start out early and return from the Glens daily instead of
staying there for a week in a usually unoccupied lodge:

> To this house we came to sleep every evening, after dining at the
> several stations [held in a different home each day]. My friend
> Denis served us this year with a very summary ejectment by
> planting a Bible School therein. He had 85 for the first month
> but I took good care to be in time and so to threaten Ommanney
> [the poor law inspector] that he refused to send bread there and
> in consequence the numbers decreased gradually, so that for the
> last three months he had not more than three and last week they
> were obliged to break it up entirely and move to the west of
> Blackwater Bridge to my inexpressible satisfaction.[611]

O'Sullivan attributed his success to 'the terror of Father John in the
poor deluded people's minds'. That starving children had been
deprived of bread was secondary to O'Sullivan's defence of their
faith. One is reminded of the case of a priest elsewhere in Ireland
who used a sledge hammer to break up a boiler for porridge from
which a contemptuous Protestant landlord was doling out food. 'The
loss of the boiler may have meant the death of a considerable number
of people,' wrote Bowen. Nonetheless, Bowen also acknowledged that
bishops expected priests to repress efforts by proselytisers – who 'give
the poor a morsel of bread with one hand and kill their immortal

souls with the other', as Monsignor Tobias Kirby put it in 1847. Distinctions between 'legitimate and illegitimate' forms of religious persuasion, evangelism, mission, conversion and proselytism can be controversial.[612]

Two open letters

At Christmas 1848 O'Sullivan circulated a printed open letter rebutting accusations that Mahony ostensibly made against the priest.[613] O'Sullivan confided in his book of recollections:

> I have written and published a letter which I posted in here. It has turned a tide on Denis Mahony he never expected. I also attach a song got much circulation. Some wag enclosed it to the Lord Lieutenant in Denis's name complaining the police for allowing it to be sung in the street and for buying it. The Lord Lieutenant replied to express to Mr Mahony his regret at his family being insulted but that the law was open to him for redress and as far as the police were concerned that they should be made to account. By the same post the letter was sent down to the police for their explanation, and great was their surprise as well as Denis's when they read both letters. Denis says there is only one blackguard in the [Kenmare] Union who could think of the likes, and everybody knows who he means.[614]

That 'song' was probably one of the two anonymous and unpleasant compositions found on printed broadsheets among O'Sullivan's papers in the Kerry Diocesan Archives (box 1), these being 'A new song entitled and called The Parson's Lamentation!' and 'Dromore Pastoral No. 2, from the new opera *The Siege of Dromore*, duet – Gloster and Yellow Kate'.

After reading O'Sullivan's open letter, his friend Catherine Murphy wrote to him, 'I did not think you were half as wicked. I fancy they had better let you alone.'[615] Lyne holds O'Sullivan responsible for helping to spread a sectarian bitterness 'which finds echoes in local tradition to the present day'; with the benefit of hindsight, he suggests that 'any threat posed by the evangelicals to local Catholicism would probably not have outlasted the Famine.'[616] The parish priest resented what he saw as a humiliating exploitation of poor people in their desperation, with the assault on the faith of the majority exacerbated by the involvement of a local family that had benefited materially by its conversion.

The relationship between O'Sullivan and Mahony went from bad to worse as events unfolded. In February 1849 O'Sullivan published another controversial letter, this time recommending that the people of Templenoe emigrate.

> I publish it with great reluctance. It is a hazardous step to take. Should those unfortunate people not succeed in America great odium will devolve upon me, and in truth I write it not so much from a wish that they should go but with a view to annoy Denis Mahony. It has had such effect already. I can understand he is wild about it. It may induce him to desist from his attempts on the Faith of the poor people. He returned from Dublin about a fortnight since and brought four other Bible readers with him so that it behoves me to be alive. God, may He strengthen the poor unfortunate people against his assaults.[617]

When O'Sullivan appeared before a select committee of the House of Commons in 1849, he was asked if he was on good terms with his Protestant neighbours in the Kenmare Union. He replied, 'I am with every person in the union except with one gentleman, with whom I am at issue upon the point, *viz.* his seeking to draw my children to his schools.' To demonstrate that he usually got on well with Protestant clergy, he told the committee that he 'was never more surprised' than when the Protestants of Kenmare asked him to forward to the Lord Lieutenant their petition to have the local Protestant curate appointed in place of their minister who had died. He added that the petition that he had forwarded was successful.[618]

Apostles of turnip tops

Undaunted during the following month, O'Sullivan opened another front in his battle with Denis Mahony – one that shows how the poor might be caught between contending religious forces to their immediate material disadvantage. O'Sullivan had warmly welcomed an offer by the Royal Society for the Growth of Flax to send an instructor to Kenmare Union to teach people how to cultivate that crop. The offer was made to him with the support of Lord Lansdowne. However, about the same time O'Sullivan discovered that an instructor from the Royal Agricultural Society (RAS) was coming, under a different scheme, to Templenoe – on a visit initiated by Mahony without O'Sullivan's involvement. He took grave exception to the absence of any Catholic clergy on the committee established locally to supervise the latter instructor's work in Templenoe. He also rejected as inadequate the RAS's offer to send a second instructor to the Kenmare section of his parish if he would contribute some funding, as Mahony had in Templenoe.

O'Sullivan thought 'a deliberate move has been made to offer me a slight' and warned the society, 'Your instructor will not, cannot get on here without the active cooperation of the Catholic clergy and I am sorry to see him at the very outset placed in the hands of people who so studiously pass us over.' He thought the plan 'exclusive and sectarian', writing:

> Let me but give the people a hint of his being a hack of Denis Mahony and I warrant his lectures will meet with a very queer reception. This is all a move of Denis Mahony's who is now in Dublin, and I hope by my course to show him what little chance he has in a contest with me.

The RAS replied to him that it had sought and got the co-operation of Roman Catholic clergy in many other areas and that there was 'no plot or desire' to exclude anyone. O'Sullivan thought:

> Were you to know the lengths Denis Mahony goes to speak lightly of me and to tamper with my poor unfortunate flock you would not be surprised at what lengths I would go to oppose him. I promise him I will show him he is more in my power than I am in his.[619]

The secretary of the RAS resorted to sarcasm when replying to O'Sullivan, 'I am sorry that our poor apostle of turnip tops and thorough draining should have fallen foul of such troubled times in the Kenmare Union (of which I was totally unaware until I got your last).'[620] In O'Sullivan's eyes, Denis Mahony could do no right. When the latter tried to distribute turnip and parsnip seeds to needy farmers in Templenoe, the parish priest saw it as another ruse and had them spurned by his parishioners. He felt that he was winning and took a mean satisfaction in seeing a 'blackguard tailor', who had been employed to make clothes for children who attended the Protestant school, admitted to the workhouse. Yet he proclaimed in his journal, 'Would that I could make friends with the same Denis Mahony, I would be able to do much good for Templenoe.'[621] O'Sullivan estimated that Mahony had 20,000 acres and was worth £8–9,000 a year.[622]

On 14 December 1849 it was noted in the workhouse minutes, 'Rev.

Denis Mahony, a ratepayer, has undertaken to give employment to seven able bodied paupers of the House and give them three days pay in advance – accepted from Monday next.' Those paupers returned saying that no accommodation was provided, nor were there tools to work with. Nevertheless, they were not readmitted to the workhouse.

15

The Kicking and Death of
Rev. Denis Mahony

'That they were broke and the Parson beat within an inch of his life is a fact, but not by me [...] 'tho my language no doubt excited and stirred up the people,' conceded Fr John O'Sullivan. He added cagily, 'I took good care not to commit myself.'[623] O'Sullivan seemed to have few if any regrets about the beating of Denis Mahony in 1850. He wrote of Mahony, 'He would ride his hobby, whatever it may cost him, and he did ride it with a vengeance, until he was near paying dearly enough for it.'[624] When Mahony collapsed and died the following year, the parish priest came to be known by some as 'Father John that killed the Parson'.[625] This was the man whom Donal Kerr, when professor of ecclesiastical history at Maynooth, described as 'the moderate and broad-minded Archdeacon John O'Sullivan'.[626]

The death came as bitter relations between some Catholic priests and Protestant evangelicals reached fever pitch in Kenmare. Bad feelings were stirred by Mahony's proselytism; he brought in bible-readers and a schoolteacher and then James Rogers, a clergyman who resided at Dromore Castle and who incessantly tried to convert Catholics. O'Sullivan claimed that some of the proselytisers even insisted on entering houses of people to whom he had just administered the last rites. It was alleged too that Mahony's labourers were obliged to listen to visiting preachers in the hall of Dromore Castle. The parish priest thundered from the altar against Catholics 'going to church' (i.e. Protestant services) and advised that 'Catholic servants and domestics too who attend family prayers with a Protestant family are not to be absolved unless they promise to do it no longer.'[627]

In early 1849 O'Sullivan devised a plan to counter continuing proselytism. He envisaged himself going around to all of Mahony's tenants and compiling an inventory of their means and conditions, 'I think I will be able to draw such an other [unfavourable] picture of his tenants as the *Times* commissioner lately did of the tenants of our lamented Liberator [Daniel O'Connell].' He thought this would reflect so badly on local landlordism generally that other landlords would 'oblige that unfortunate "*diable*" [devil] Denis to stop short in his mad career'. However, the fact that he noted that he needed to reflect calmly on the idea was an indication that emotions were running dangerously high.[628] In fact, tensions were about to erupt in a confrontation at Reen crossroads.

Confrontation at Reen Cross

When the new Anglican curate at Templenoe, the evangelical preacher James Rogers, arrived into Kenmare from Killarney on the 'jingle' (horse-drawn carriage) in June 1849, O'Sullivan thought him 'a contemptible-looking, little thing'. The parish priest sighed, 'What a struggle I am to have with him [Mahony] again when I thought all was over.'[629]

Rogers entered Catholic homes to read the bible. Sleepless in bed one night, O'Sullivan devised a scheme to counter him. The parish priest would employ a

> queer bible-reader of my own to go about and watch Rogers and Pluck [a nickname for Mahony] with a bible under his arm, and as soon as he finds them offering to read the bible for any of my poor parishioners to pull out his own and ask the owner of the house whose bible will he have, the parson's or Father John's. This will annoy them very much and completely take the sting out of all their efforts.

He employed a 'queer little fellow' named Patrick Connor (also known as Paddy Keane) to do so, thinking that this would be for a month only. He was to retain his services much longer. Paddy was 'as hot as fire', and O'Sullivan thought, 'We will no doubt have royal sport of it between them, along with meeting the scoundrels on their own ground.'[630] His 'royal sport' seemed to make a mockery of reading the bible, although both James Going, the clergyman with whom O'Sullivan had gone to London for famine relief, and James Rogers purported to see it differently:

> When Paddy was first installed I met Going who seemed to be full of the glorious innovation. Tell me, said he, is it true that you have a bible-reader going about reading the word of God for

the people?! A fact, was the brief reply. Ah, bravo, but does the bishop know it? What care I, was my answer. Is it not the right of the people to get the word of God?! Bravo again said he, but you must admit you never gave it to them until the pressure was first upon you by us and the people began to get a taste for it. Well, said I, better go with the tide than against it, and left the dupe in his blessed ignorance about it.

In a letter to the people of Templenoe published in a local newspaper, Rogers wrote that his parishioners told him 'they have free permission to try and read the scriptures.' He added, 'I am delighted at this conversion of the Priest [...] I trust that my Roman Catholic friends will everywhere take advantage of what is now acknowledged to be your right by the Vicar General of this Diocese.' 'Dupe the second!!', exclaimed O'Sullivan.[631]

In July 1849 Fr William Ahern, curate of Kenmare and Templenoe, criticised from the altar the manner in which Rogers had begun to conduct his evangelical mission in the parish. Rogers challenged him to a public debate about the tenets of religion. Such debates had taken place elsewhere in Ireland, although some priests and bishops were distinctly reluctant to get involved in them. In 1824, in the Carlow area, there was a notable encounter when two evangelicals met and reputedly defeated four prominent priests in a discussion about 'indiscriminate reading of the Sacred Scriptures'. Bishop James Doyle of Kildare and Leighlin, the respected 'J.K.L.', forbade any further encounters of this kind, which might give publicity to the Protestants. The fact that the debate in Carlow also degenerated into a riot was a warning to Kenmare.[632]

O'Sullivan wrote to Sir Thomas Redington, Under-Secretary to the Lord Lieutenant, stating that Rogers 'has only just come to Templenoe, and seems disposed to follow a very different course from that of his two predecessors with whom the Catholic clergy of the Parish never had the slightest difference'. He warned that the challenge would lead to disruption and a breach of the peace. He suggested that 'Mr Mahony's fanaticism' made him unsuitable to remain a magistrate.[633] O'Sullivan also wrote to Lord Lansdowne to complain that Mahony, 'just now at the end of three years of famine chooses to begin anew, after all his efforts having proved a signal failure'. Once more, he pointed out that the priests had previously been 'on the most friendly terms with the Protestant curates of that parish'.[634] O'Sullivan later recalled:

[Ahern] was challenged to a public controversy [...] which of course I ridiculed and would not allow Ahern to accept of. Denis Mahony in whose castle he [Rogers] lived and Rogers made such a handle of our refusal and so dismayed were the ignorant poor people about it that to inspire him [Ahern] with confidence I caused him to accept the challenge. They would have none but an open air meeting, just the very thing we wanted and we were sure of having at least five or six thousand people there at which we were pretty sure Rogers would get no hearing.[635]

One Munster paper commented, 'Religious controversy of a public nature has for many years been a thing quite unheard of, and it remained for the parish of Kenmare to be the scene of its revival.' It reported that Rogers had been calling uninvited on Catholic families, upsetting them. The debate – which was planned for Thursday, 9 and Friday, 10 August at Reen Cross, between Kenmare town and Dromore Castle – excited attention across Kerry and west Cork.[636]

Dolly's Brae and dinner

Less than a month before the meeting at Reen Cross, there was a notable sectarian incident at Dolly's Brae, a Catholic village in Ulster, where a thousand Orange Order marchers and hundreds of Catholics clashed. Newspapers reported at least ten people dead and the homes of some Catholics burnt down.[637] On 1 August, in Kerry, Denis Mahony wrote to the authorities, describing himself in his letter as not just the only resident magistrate in the district but also 'an ordained minister of the Church of England'. He asked that a force be in attendance at the impending debate 'to overawe those who may be disposed to be turbulent'.[638]

When the day for debate came, it was sunny. Crowds thronged the beautiful spot. Food and drink were on sale as at a fair. One Catholic carried a banner laced with the sarcastic words, 'SOUP SOUP SOUP – HOT AND READY EVERY FRIDAY – APPLY TO PATRICK CONNOR SCRIPTURE READER'. Before the debate began, O'Sullivan addressed the crowd, claiming that 'up to this time the Roman Catholics and Protestants [...] were full of friendly feeling and kind disposition to one another' and naming a number of Protestant ministers with whom he said he had never had an angry disagreement. He claimed that every Protestant in that part of the country was on the most intimate terms with Catholics –

except that buck [Denis Mahony] in his bagpipe of a castle in the West (tremendous yelling) – a man that you can recollect when he had scarcely a coat to his back, and that you often saw carrying a keeler to Glencairn, when he had a dairy there (clamour). He chooses to create dissension and strife and disagreement amongst us.[639]

The *Kerry Evening Post* later singled out the role played in the affair by O'Sullivan, who, according to the paper, was 'aptly called "John of Kenmare"'. The *Post* accused him of 'drilling' his parishioners and of 'violent abuse of the Rev. Denis Mahony and others'. The *Cork Examiner* took O'Sullivan's side, describing him as 'a pious, able and determined pastor'. Rogers claimed later that the local Catholic priests had stirred up their flock in order to avoid a discussion that might not go their way, 'The low vulgarity, the mean and truculent disposition, the scandalous and audacious conduct of John O'Sullivan, P.P., fully justify the Apocalyptic sketch of the sanguinary harlot of Rome.' Yet Mahony's activities ran the risk of stirring up a reaction against the relatively small Protestant population around Kenmare Bay. The *Kerry Evening Post* could but

> express our wonder that a respectable gentleman, with a fine old Papistical name, and belonging to a fine old Catholic family, and having many Catholic relatives living, should take so unhappily a conspicuous part as he does in what his own good sense must assure him is a rank piece of folly – that is, a crusade against the Priests and the Faith of the People – of his own ancestors and relatives.[640]

The authorities had decided to pre-empt violence and sent police to intervene and stop the planned debate proceeding. After the police had done so, a large crowd marched back to Kenmare, carrying an effigy of Rogers, 'which they beat and trampled amid tremendous yelling, the bugle all the while sounding at their head'. On arriving in Kenmare from Reen, the crowd was addressed from a hotel window by the curate William Ahern. He again protested that they had previously had good relations with Protestants in Kenmare and, referring to the Dolly's Brae incident a few days earlier, asserted, 'If we were Orangemen and Denis Mahony a Catholic there would not be one stone of his castle left upon another this day (awful groaning and yelling which lasted some minutes).'

Following this, the Catholic clergy and others gave a dinner for

Ahern at the Lansdowne Arms, attended by more than thirty people. It was reported that a substantial meal including wine and whiskey concluded amid much jollity with songs. Lyne has drawn attention to the continuing presence of nearly two thousand paupers within the workhouse and its auxiliary buildings at the time, and has described the conduct of the diners and their chairman Fr John O'Sullivan on this occasion as 'grotesque' or 'almost surreal' in the circumstances.[641] His observations point up the social reality that some people fared worse than others during the great famine.

A case of conditional clothing

It was not just the doling out of soup to the hungry that angered Catholic priests. There was also the paid work for some adults if they converted and the special clothing for children if they attended Protestant schools. Children had to agree to return the clothes if and when they withdrew from the school.

Katherine Mahony stirred up a controversy – helping to earn herself an abiding and unfavourable reputation in local folklore[642] – when she pursued James Jones for clothes that he had been given as a pupil of the Protestant school that she helped to run near Dromore Castle. Jones sued when he was 'denuded' by the bible-reader Timothy Sullivan, whom Katherine despatched when Jones quit her school. The boy was described pathetically by the *Cork Examiner* as 'a miserable looking creature'.[643] Fr John O'Sullivan wrote, 'The poor child came into court in his sister's petticoats; he had nothing else to put on.'[644] Thade Murphy, a barrister from Killarney, represented the boy:

> Having obtained a set of clothes at the school, he ceased to frequent it; when Timothy Sullivan, the defendant, went to the house of the boy, and – if he was rightly instructed – with a stick in his hand threatened to beat him *as black as the stick*, if he would not strip and deliver up the clothes. He was prepared to show that Sullivan had no authority so to denude the poor creature, and the present action was brought for one pound, the value of the clothes, of which plaintiff was so unjustly denied.[645]

When Jones was called to give evidence, Timothy Sullivan's barrister immediately objected that this was 'more for effect and exhibition than anything else'. To which Murphy retorted, 'And a very pretty exhibition it is, and a fair specimen of the way in which the gospel is preached in Kerry.' Mary Laird, an Ulster woman and waiting maid to Mrs Mahony, gave evidence that Jones's sister had been handed the clothes for him and that forty children at the school had been clothed on the same express condition as Jones. 'God almighty!' exclaimed Murphy, 'Was ever anything so shameful heard of?' There ensued a bizarre series of interruptions to Laird's evidence – one by Fr John O'Sullivan himself, as reported in the press:

> Mr Murphy: Would you give me a coat if I went to school for a piece?
>
> Mr Joseph O'Riordan: I'd go too.
>
> Mr Morgan McSwiney: So would I.
>
> Rev. John O'Sullivan: I'd go myself for a spell if you promise me a good coat against the winter.
>
> ('So will I, so will I', from all parts of the court, amidst tremendous laughter).
>
> Cross-examination resumed [by] Mr Murphy: You spoke of the word of God, a while ago. In what part of it do you find it recommended to strip the orphan?

When Laird stepped down, the presiding assistant barrister, William McDermott QC, gave his decision. Noting that Jones had not received the clothes directly from the patrons of the school, and that there was no evidence that Jones was personally made aware of express conditions, McDermott held that the boy was wrongfully dispossessed. While praising the provision of education, McDermott concluded in a manner that cannot have pleased the Mahonys:

> But if it were to be clogged with the conditions they heard sworn to this day, and so opposed to the feelings of the great mass of the population, however repugnant it might be to his own and to Mrs Mahony's feelings, he should say it could prove to be no less than the bane and the curse of the country. He would therefore grant a decree against Sullivan for the whole amount claimed, and he thought he deserved it richly.

The *Cork Examiner* noted that 'The decision gave the most unmixed satisfaction to a crowded court.' The *Freeman's Journal* bluntly headed its report of the proceedings 'Gross Case of Proselytism'. On appeal, the court heard evidence that Jones had been expressly told in August, when he started in the school, that he must return the clothes if he quit and that he had only attended regularly for nine days. The tailor who made the clothes for Jones testified that he had heard Mrs Mahony inform Jones of the condition. Pressed to say who got him to come to court – 'What brought you here?' – the tailor repled, 'Wisha, then, my feet brought me here av course – (laughter) – I walked.' Some of the deficiencies in evidence for Timothy Sullivan were amended. Isaac Butt QC, a former professor of political economy at Trinity College Dublin, now spoke for Mrs Mahony:

> That lady living in a remote and populous district in this country, destitute of aid as regards the education of the poor in her immediate vicinity, some time since established a school, in which the children of the poor received instruction, and in furtherance of her benevolent intentions was in the habit of giving clothes to such children whose parents were not able to procure them. This, as his Lordship can easily understand, might easily open the door to an immediate degree of imposition, as it might offer an opportunity to get clothes under the pretext of receiving an education.

The court reduced the award to Jones by three quarters of the original £1, with the *Cork Examiner* reporting that the case had excited much public interest.[646]

Serious assault

If the encounter at Reen Cross and the court case had been tense, they were as nothing compared to the clash that took place on Sunday, 22 September 1850 in Templenoe. An outraged but anonymous 'Protestant' wrote to the *Cork Examiner*, giving one version of events. The writer explained that James Rogers, the Protestant curate of Templenoe, had been 'encouraged by the assurances of a vast number' of Catholics to announce that he would go to the Catholic chapel on the following Sunday and, near it, 'preach the truth as it is in Christ Jesus':

> The priests, to be sure, were alarmed. The archpriest [O'Sullivan], the headpiece, however, was away down at [the Synod of] Thurles, assisting in the freemasonry going on there, and the coadjutors were novices at getting up a demonstration. However, a considerable rabble was collected, headed by the priest's clerk, a crack't baker, a drunken tailor, and a few other

characters; and the Rev. Mr. Rogers, though accompanied by the Rev. Denis Mahony and his sons, saw it was in vain for him to expect a hearing, and, after repeated threats of violence [...] had to retire [...]

By the following Sunday (last Sunday) his reverence [O'Sullivan] returned from the Synod, and on Sunday morning delivered one of the most inflammatory harangues that ever fell from his lips.[647]

The *Kerry Evening Post*, never an admirer of O'Sullivan, reported what it claimed were 'the words used that very morning at Mass in Kenmare by the same Father John O'Sullivan. These were taken down on the spot and will be attested by the competent witness [unnamed].' The reported speech was as follows:

I heard sometime ago that Mr. Mahony was about giving up his folly in trying to force his religion on the people of Templenoe, and I was very glad of it; and I pledge you my solemn word, that for the last two or three months, I did not go to Templenoe, to give him every opportunity of doing so; but in place of that, on Sunday last, he and Rogers came down to the chapel gate of Templenoe, as the people came out from Masses yelling them they were all going to hell and damnation, and trying to induce them to abandon that religion, for which their forefathers suffered persecution and shed their blood. Look at this for work! I am sure there is not one here who would not suffer the same persecution and shed his blood as well as they, sooner than abandon his holy faith. *I wish I was at Templenoe* when Denis Mahony and Rogers came to my chapel gate, *and I promise you that Denis would not go home so quiet as he did on Sunday last.* How dare Rogers come to my chapel gate to insult my flock! Suppose now I went over there to the church as they were coming out, and told them they are all going to hell and damnation, why don't you think if I got a *good kicking* I would richly deserve it.[648] [italics in original]

The *Kerry Evening Post* claimed that neither Mahony nor Rogers had in fact done what was imputed to them – neither going to the chapel gate nor using the language ascribed. And the anonymous letter-writer painted a garish picture of O'Sullivan leading his flock along the road in Templenoe:

The mob followed the meek apostle in hundreds; many respectable people were forced to come by intimidation. A trumpeter headed the cavalcade, a huge idiot brought up the rear, a drunken woman of ill fame of Amazonian prowess moved to and fro, exciting the rabble, while the holy priest looked on with all complacency.

The Protestants inside their church at Templenoe were said to have heard stones rattling on its roof, 'and the most savage yells rending the air without'. Denis Mahony reportedly intervened and, initially, quelled the disturbance. However, as some of the Protestants emerged and made their way to the local Protestant schoolhouse 'for the usual monthly examination of the Sunday school the mob gathered with redoubled fury and more savage cries'. This was the same school that featured in the court case relating to the retrieval of clothing given to children there. The *Post* reported that Mahony, 'calculating on his influence with the peasantry, inconsiderately went among them to advise them to disperse'. They did not welcome this:

> While he was in the act of doing so, [he] received a severe kick from one of the ruffians in the crown [...] We regret to add that Mr Mahony has been suffering severely ever since [...] He received two kicks in the groin from which he is still suffering grievously, several kicks in the legs, various thumps and bruises, and with great difficulty escaped with his life in to our schoolhouse. His eldest son, one of the finest young men in the county of Kerry, was struck and kicked several times.[649]

The Mahony party took refuge in the schoolhouse. Yet, according to the *Kerry Evening Post*, 'the mob continued for some time yelling and crying for his blood':

> Their madness seems to have been stimulated by whiskey drinking – for there was not far distant a public-house, to which they occasionally repaired; and from the vicinity of which John O'Sullivan, the Parish Priest, at last emerged, and harangued the mob in most exciting, though ostensively [sic] soothing terms, telling them to despise, as he did, the proselytising soupers, for he would soon put an end to them; and by a letter from Dublin Castle, he would shortly prevent Parson Rogers from any further attempting on the faith of his flock.[650]

The *Cork Examiner*'s letter-writer claimed that O'Sullivan mounted a ditch opposite the schoolhouse in which the Mahonys were trapped, 'boasting that he had the lord of the soil caged up there, at his mercy', before finally urging people to go home quietly, 'which they did at once, taking him, no trifling burthen, on their shoulders'. However, several ruffians, 'and among them Father O'Sullivan's own clerk', allegedly broke into the grounds of Dromore Castle, 'tore up flowers, and committed other depredations, mounted on horseback, and blowing horns'. The writer also claimed that during the attack on the church, O'Sullivan and Callaghan McCarthy, the parish priest of Tuosist who had come over with parishioners by boat from the Beara Peninsula, 'took very good care to remain in the chapel yard, as if they had nothing to say to the business, well knowing how sure their dark designs were to succeed'.

O'Sullivan sent a long reply to the *Cork Examiner*. He denied some details of the account and claimed that it was one of Mahony's small group who struck the first blow. He had indeed been away at the synod in Thurles, 'I was there to represent our respected bishop, who was unable to attend.' Upon his return he had, at the first Mass in Kenmare, criticised the behaviour of Mahony and Rogers. When he went to Templenoe after that Mass, he had not the slightest notion that he would find 'the immense multitude of some four or five thousand persons' that had gathered. To say that it was his address at first Mass that collected them was 'monstrous'. In fact, he entreated the people to remain cool and to allow him to deal with Rogers. Nevertheless, they moved off towards the Protestant church and were met by Mahony, 'who in a very excited manner demanded their business and began to enquire their names to have them punished for an unlawful assembly'. With Mahony were his two sons and a few others:

> The first blow was struck by a souper of Mr Mahony's, who thought [that] a respectable farmer of the parish was not sufficiently courteous to that gentleman. This was the signal for a general scuffle. That Mr Mahony was kicked, and beat, and abused, I do not deny [...] But he brought it all on himself. He put his hand into a hornet's nest, and, well became the hornets, they quickly made him feel the consequences.

O'Sullivan told readers of the *Cork Examiner* that he personally only came on the scene when Mahony and his party had taken refuge in the Protestant schoolhouse, 'I verily believe the people would have sacked the school, had I not by a little tact diverted them from it.' He denied that he had threatened to throw people in the sea, or that he had them caged. But he also warned – or threatened – that 'If Mr Rogers be mad enough to avow his intention of public road-side preaching again, I could not control the people and would not undertake it.' He denied that his clerk rode a horse through Mrs Mahony's flower garden. The assertion that the Protestant place of worship was attacked, he wrote, was 'a vile calumny'. He claimed, 'An unthinking child threw a pebble on the roof of the church.'[651] An entry in his notebook made almost four years later was to indicate that more than a pebble was thrown:

> That they [the church door and windows] were broke and the Parson beat within an inch of his life is a fact, but not by me. He came three successive Sundays while I was at the National Synod of Thurles to preach to the people as they came out from Mass, and he paid for it the Sunday after I came home, but 'tho my language no doubt excited and stirred up the people I took good care not to commit myself.[652]

Writing about the incident later, O'Sullivan recalled that he had stayed away a Sunday longer than necessary 'to give the lads [Rogers and Mahony] more rope and more courage'. Of the assault itself, he said that the crowd of thousands 'closed in about them and so squeezed and crushed and kicked the latter that he was near losing his life to it. A huge foot gave him such a kick in the abdomen as would have killed him had that fellow had any shoes on' – a reminder that footwear was far from universal then.[653] 'Never did man get such a fright,' wrote O'Sullivan, about the assault, in April 1850. Nevertheless, he thought that there would be further trouble, 'Mahony is a fool and a fanatic and his ugly wife will soon make him forget the beating he got.' On the Sunday following the incident, a force of seventy police was drawn up outside the church, but Rogers did not appear and all was quiet.[654]

Ecclesiastical Titles Act 1851

Mahony was soon back in action. He sent one of a series of petitions that parliament received from across the United Kingdom 'when Lord John Russell's infamous Durham letter set all the bigots in England in a flame', as O'Sullivan wrote.[655] Russell had publicly attacked the pope for his 'aggression' in appointing a Catholic hierarchy in England for the first time since the Reformation. The passing of the Ecclesiastical Titles Act 1851 further inflamed sentiment by forbidding Catholics from using English place names in titles of members of the hierarchy of England. At a large public meeting in Kenmare on St Patrick's Day, O'Sullivan strongly opposed the legislation. In the event, the new law was a dead letter.[656]

The influence of Catholicism was growing in Britain, due partly to immigration from Ireland during the great famine, and it was being boosted intellectually by conversions that emerged from the Oxford Movement – including that of John Henry Newman. Russell struck a sectarian note in debates, including a reference to 'the mummeries of superstition' that encouraged the London *Times* and other intemperate voices – some of which extended their criticism to aspects of Catholicism in Ireland. If Ralls is right that Russell was 'badly miscast as the leader of No-Popery sentiment, for he had attacked the Tories for decades for mixing anti-Catholicism with politics', the affair was another example of Russell disappointing expectations that his Irish allies had once had of him.[657]

Mahony's sudden death

O'Sullivan remarked that in the parish of Templenoe, with thousands of Catholics and just 'some 50 or 60 Protestants', Mahony managed to muster for his anti-popery petition 168 signatures. The parish priest claimed that only forty-four of these were known anywhere in Kerry. He demanded that parliament enquire into the matter, given suspicions that many similar petitions from elsewhere were forged. Mahony felt obliged to have his eldest son go to London to discover what to expect in connection with this challenge to his petition's authenticity. Nobody anticipated what happened next to Mahony. O'Sullivan wrote:

> The old fellow got desperately alarmed. On Easter Monday he got up as well as ever, took a bath, eat [*sic*] his breakfast, got a fit immediately after, never spoke a word and in less than three hours was dead and – I was going to say damned! – God forgive me.[658]

Less than seven months after his beating, Denis Mahony died suddenly. On 23 April 1851 the *Kerry Evening Post* reported his death 'by apoplexy' at the age of 55. The paper described him as 'much respected' and reported that he had left a large young family 'to lament the loss of one of the best and kindest of parents'. Earlier, the writer of the letter signed by an anonymous 'Protestant' in the *Cork Examiner* had praised Mahony after the assault on him in Templenoe:

When I inform you, Mr Editor, that he – Rev. Mr. Mahony – is the owner of more than two-thirds of this extensive parish, in which his tenantry are conspicuous for their comfort and independence, that he spends all his time at home, gives constant daily employment to more than a hundred labourers, and his amiable wife and family are constantly employed in visiting, clothing and instructing the poor on his estate, to facilitate which he keeps the talented, pious and chivalrous minister, the Rev. Mr. Rogers, I leave you to judge what return has been made him for all his goodness and generosity.[659]

Hearing rumours later that his confrontation with Mahony was used in Rome to prevent him succeeding Egan as bishop of Kerry, O'Sullivan remarked, 'It surely would have been much easier and quieter for me to allow all the people to become Soupers than thus be snubbed for my violence.'[660] In November 1853 O'Sullivan recalled:

The death struck terror into the country the more so, because on the very Easter Sunday [20 April], in thundering away at him as usual from the altar, and explaining how I detected the forgeries, what a high offence it was in the eyes of the law &c &c, I pledged myself that before many days I would make a holy show of him, meaning of course the exposure he was sure to get before the House of Commons, so that when he met the sudden, the awfully sudden death on the very next day, the people were actually petrified with terror and consternation [...] and the thing will descend to their children. His second son died in a lunatic asylum before a year, his third son is now equally insane, his oldest son is nearly in consumption [TB], his other children in a very precarious way, and the people are not slow in attributing these [illegible word] crosses to the persecution, by the father, of their holy religion.[661]

Mahony's widow, 'Yellow Kate', soon left Kerry. His son Richard appeared to have no appetite for further proselytism and assisted Kerry converts to Protestantism to go to America. 'To my infinite satisfaction and delight, and to complete as it were my triumphs', wrote a gloating O'Sullivan, 'the vagabonds, every one of them with the exception of one, came to confession [in the Catholic chapel] fearing to cross the seas in their iniquity.'[662] O'Sullivan later acquired annual reports of a bible society of which Denis Mahony had been a committee member, but found nothing about his parish – although 'they were filled with the most extravagant stories of the good was being done [by proselytisers] at Dingle, Cape Clear and Connaught.'[663]

There is a hint of smug satisfaction in a detail he gave of a subsequent visit to Kenmare by one Mrs O'Reilly Dease and her adult son, who had arranged to meet him at the suggestion of the prominent butter merchant John Mahony. O'Sullivan enquired if they had arrived:

> The Hotel people know no more of them than their having come over from Glengarriff about 2 o'clock and no sooner had they arrived than they asked if it was there Father John lived and if he were the Father John that killed the Parson, and upon being assured that it was there the identical character lived they ordered a car and drove up to my house.[664]

Nonetheless, there is also an indication, from that same month, that he feared the whole affair had not strengthened his position outside Kenmare:

> Owen wanted I should say a public Mass today in chapel and attack the soupers, but my game now is to keep myself quiet to be able – in case young Mahony should hereafter be going on with the pranks of his father – to say that I made no move, did nothing, said nothing to provoke him or anybody else until the fight was put upon me.[665]

Legend

For some locals, O'Sullivan's fight against Mahony became the stuff of legend. One person told a folklore collector in 1938 that 'when the "soup" was giving out in Kenmare', a young man named James Grady caught Mahony by the collar as he was giving a speech and pulled him off the platform. Grady then fled to O'Sullivan's house. When the police came knocking, O'Sullivan 'took out his book and read over Grady', who thereby became invisible.[666] And did the priest not also prophesise the fate of the Mahonys' residence?

> Fr O'Sullivan foretold that Dromore Castle would yet be without a Mahony and that Mass would be celebrated in the castle. It came to pass. Old Denis Mahony was seen headless in the castle and when a certain Catholic gentleman rented the castle he took Archdeacon Michael O'Sullivan out and he celebrated Mass in the old castle, thereby fulfilling the previous archdeacon's prophesy.[667]

O'Sullivan himself outlived Mahony by more than two decades.

16

Amazon, Slattern or Saint?
Women of Kenmare

She was a 'viper' – the woman who ran a Protestant school in Templenoe to which she invited poor Catholic children. She was a drunk 'of Amazonian prowess' – the woman who 'excited' a crowd of Catholics to resist proselytisers there. She was 'beautiful and saintly' – the celibate woman who managed an educational and spiritual centre in Kenmare.[668]

The biographer John Aubrey thought that Elizabeth Waller, wife of the settler William Petty, was 'a very beautiful and ingenious lady, brown, with glorious eyes'. Petty loved her and 'deputed oversight and management of his scattered Irish concerns to her, especially during his absences in London'.[669] In a nice turn of phrase, he wrote from England to her in Kerry, in 1675, that 'The children are well and to play with them is my great supply of your absence.'[670] Her diary includes a brief description of this able woman's journey from Killarney to Kenmare Bay, 'Thursday I went over the Mangerton [mountain] with the help of Mr Robert Hassett and his gelding, in pain enough; and some danger, but with a guard of seventy or eighty horse, to Phill. Hease's at Ro[u]ghty Bridge.'[671]

However, appearance as much as agency was the concern of some who wrote about contemporary women. Thus, Elizabeth Waller-Petty's daughter Anne Petty seems not to have inherited her mother's good looks and Jonathan Swift – who liked Anne – described her nevertheless as 'most egregiously ugly'.[672] Anne's grandson, the later William Petty, who became 1st Lord Lansdowne in 1784, likewise described her as 'a very ugly woman'.

Class was no divide in that respect. In 1809, a proclamation offered a reward for the capture of one Michael Murphy, who was wanted for the murder of Fitzgerald Tisdall, then rector of Kenmare. It described Murphy's wife, who travelled with him, as 'an uncommonly ugly

Fig. 10–Two women on the road to Killarney. By Theresa Rose Marrable (1862–1936). Private collection. *Thought to have been drawn about 1880.*

woman' whose face was 'much disfigured by her front teeth being knocked out'.[673] More admiringly, an Englishman who came to Kenmare in 1842 wrote of local women, 'In the carriages, among the ladies of Kerry, every second woman was handsome; and there is something peculiarly tender and pleasing in the looks of the young female peasantry, that is perhaps better than beauty.' The author was the anti-Catholic and unionist William Makepeace Thackeray, who also penned pieces for *Punch* – notorious for its crude caricatures of the Irish.[674]

Men had defined the women described above, but it was the daughter of the Paymaster General of the Queen's household who later sketched two fine local women on the road to Killarney. One is seen restraining pigs on a lead. Theresa Rose Marrable also drew, in Kenmare, a poor old woman who had lived through famine times.[675]

Workhouse women

In 1838, when it passed an act for the relief of the destitute poor in Ireland, parliament made it clear that wives, in effect, belonged to their husbands, 'All relief given under this Act to a wife or child shall be considered as given to the person declared by this Act to be liable to maintain such wife or child.'[676] In practice many pauper women found themselves coping alone – their husband dead, away seeking work or absconded. One such woman was Catherine Connolly, whose tragic loss of four children near Kenmare Bay happened to be recorded in some detail, unlike the suffering of so many others (see Chapter 10).

Through the surviving minute books of Kenmare Union, one glimpses the lives of women within it – not only paupers but also female staff. The latter included a schoolmistress and nurse, and the matron Victoria Robertson, who told an enquiry into the death of the Connolly children that she saw their widowed mother in tears at leaving the workhouse.[677] Robertson had to plead for an assistant or seamstress, as found 'in all other' workhouses, to help her in cutting clothing for all the female paupers and shirting for men.[678]

By their nature, the minutes tend to refer only to women who were causing a problem. These included Mary Sullivan, 'discharged from the house for disorderly conduct', and Johanna Lynch, discharged with her children because she was deemed 'an imposter and not an object for workhouse relief'. The guardians also ordered that Norry Sullivan, 'number 660 on register', be discharged for 'improper' behaviour. They later ruled that a woman of the same name be taken before a magistrate because of alleged 'improper' or 'refractory conduct' – its precise nature left unexplained. Four 'disorderly women' were accused of creating disturbances in the dining hall and brought before a special court sitting, which was conducted in the porter's hall by two local justices of the peace, who sentenced the women to one month's imprisonment with hard labour in Tralee jail. An attorney was directed to proceed against Mary Williams because she allegedly pawned items of clothing. Those who damaged or stole workhouse property faced quite severe punishment, including jail.[679]

The pressures of need and displacement on women told. Dr Brennan was paid for his attendance at the women's auxiliary dormitory – over the courthouse in the old barracks in Kenmare town – when a number of the females there were said to have suffered 'paralysis and hysterics'.[680] Women desperate to get relief could be rebuffed simply because their husbands were absent. For example, on one day in July 1848 nine married women and their fourteen children were refused admission to the workhouse or outdoor relief on the grounds that (1) the heads of families did not apply, (2) the wives refused to swear that they had been deserted, (3) they could not or would not state where the men had gone, and (4) they did not appear to be in such an extremely destitute condition as would warrant an order for temporary relief.[681] There were continuing personal tragedies, such as that of the unmarried Nellie Sullivan, who 'had been delivered of a child on Tuesday night – which was conveyed to the privy'. The workhouse medical officer examined the infant 'to see if unfair means had been used to destroy the child' but concluded that the infant was not born alive. A wardswoman, Kate Lynch, was tried at Tralee Assizes as an accessory to concealing the birth.[682]

Men, women and older children had separate dormitories in the workhouses, and these could be far from pleasant. In early 1848 it was ordered that two watchmen be stationed constantly in the women's yard 'for the purpose of preventing the women committing nuisance in the yard which they are in the practice of doing: any person detected in the disgusting practice must be punished.' While that nuisance was not described, a conjoined order mandated the refusal of breakfast to every person sleeping in a ward where the urine buckets were let overflow or were upset upon the floor, 'unless the offender is reported'.[683]

Just coping with numbers at the workhouse meant eating in relays. Informing Chief Secretary for Ireland Sir William Somerville that the treatment of poor people in the workhouse was 'enough to horrify the most hardened', Fr John O'Sullivan wrote:

> To feed such a number the women were roused out of bed before 5 o'clock in the morning three hours before day; after getting seven ounces of meal made into stirabout with a pinch of sugar on it, they bundled up to bed again to try and keep some warmth in their thin, wretched bodies. Batch succeeded batch until by 10 o'clock the breakfast was got through.

He continued:

> The women are in a truly deplorable state, squatted on the naked pavement without employment or occupation, in filth and rags without as much as a stool to sit on. A gentleman passed here last winter and he described them as so many rats in a flood – perched up on the few stools they were allowed, seeking to

escape from the wet that had been driven in through the
windows and with which the whole floor was inundated.[684]

An effort was made to engage some of the girls in spinning flax and
wool, with twenty wheels and four looms ordered, but these were to be
shared with boys.[685] O'Sullivan worried about the spiritual needs of
hundreds of girls in the workhouse.[686]

So bad were the conditions under which inmates lived,
notwithstanding the separation of men and women, that girls who grew
to womanhood in the workhouse were at risk of becoming mentally
disturbed. In 1856 Fr O'Sullivan pointed out that 'there are a great
many young women in the house, and have been there for several years,
equally anxious to be allowed to learn.' He took steps to have a number
trained in lacework.

It was suggested that if they sold their lacework directly, the women
incurred the risk of their being propositioned in Kenmare by tourists
who passed through the town.[687] Some workhouse girls did become
pregnant by men from outside, while a number fell in with criminals.
In 1861 the superintendent of the female section of Mountjoy Prison
in Dublin was to write that the most difficult prisoners to deal with were
young girls who had either been reared or spent a long time in a
workhouse, 'They seem to be amenable to no persuasion, advice or
punishment. When they are corrected, even in the mildest manner, for
any breach of regulations, they seem to lose all control of reason.' She
added that they broke the windows of their cells, tore up bedding,
ripped their clothing with their teeth and used 'absolutely shocking'
language. However, she noted too, 'They are not at all deficient in
intelligence or capacity for better things. They learn quite as quickly,
perhaps more quickly, than the average of prisoners.'[688]

Within the workhouse some women were employed to care for the
female residents, including a matron, nurse and schoolmistress. On 26
August 1848 it was noted that the then 'nursetender' was 'a very
deserving servant' and she was given permission for her children, who
lived in Kenmare town, to attend the school in the workhouse
alongside the children of its residents. Whether this indicates that the
nurse was of a very low social class or that the school in the workhouse
was at that time functioning well is unclear. The following year the
matron took what was deemed to be 'the imprudent step' of concealing
her own marriage to an outdoor relief officer – an event that the vice-
guardians of the workhouse feared 'might interfere with her usefulness
as matron of the workhouse'. Throwing herself on the mercy of the

Poor Law Commissioners, she luckily found that the workhouse guardians supported her because she had hitherto 'conducted herself to the entire satisfaction of the guardians'.[689]

Bitches, bibles and bastards

Individual guardians were not always supportive of workhouse employees. Ellen Corcoran, an assistant nurse at Killowen, complained that one guardian had arrived at Killowen auxiliary workhouse 'in a drunken state', where he made disparaging remarks about Dr Mayberry and another person, neither of whom were present, 'He called the nurse then to know what bed Hurley slept in. When she showed him the bed he called her a blackguard bitch, and repeatedly called her that name.' Corcoran asked the board 'to put a stop to this man of visiting the house in his drunkenness, fearing he might beat me which would cause great annoyance in the house as the women wanted to beat him on the evening he was there'.[690]

In 1849 a special government-funded emigration scheme involved the selection of girls from the Kenmare workhouse aged 14–18, who 'now await inspection by the Government Agent'. Lieutenant Henry, Royal Navy Emigration Agent, duly inspected them and picked thirty – of whom twenty-five were to be fitted out for leaving for Australia via Cork and Plymouth. Tenders were invited for 'black stuff for petticoats', woollen plaid for dresses, stockings, shawls, bonnets and other items, including ribbon. Bibles and prayer books were also supplied. The workhouse schoolmaster was mandated to accompany the girls to Cork in five cars, each car to have a tarpaulin. When they reached Cork, Lieutenant Henry again inspected them and found certain deficiencies in their outfits. These were put right at a cost of £1 13s, for which Kenmare Union was charged. Only recently has the story of Kerry girls who went from Dingle, Killarney, Listowel and Kenmare to Australia, as potential wives, received the kind of attention that it merits.[691]

One category not entitled to outdoor relief was described in 1848 as 'a very extensive class' in Kenmare, this being 'women, with children, whose husbands are gone to America; they are in the greatest distress.'[692] It was understandable that men went abroad in search of work. In 1850 the guardians wrote to the Poor Law Commissioners to explain that the preponderance of females and children in the workhouse since 1846–7 was due to 'the males having died from the hardships they endured in a most inclement winter, from starvation, exposure and work – the wages allowed in the then state of the markets being totally inadequate to support life in a working man – and having stinted themselves to share with their starving families.'[693]

As the memory of famine receded, the guardians of Kenmare workhouse had more time on their hands. In 1856 they decided to adopt their committee's recommendation of setting apart from other women any 'females having illegitimate children or females of abandoned character'. They allocated these women a special 'Penitential Ward' with a separate 'Penitential Stairs' so that 'their shameful society will not be imposed upon those whose character is correct'; this was for a period of at least one year in the case of a first child born outside marriage and three years in other cases. They feared that 'it would be an injustice to the virtuous, while it would be a boon to the vile to allow them at once to bring their polluted character and their bastard children into the company of the other inmates.' Moreover, 'common prostitutes' who gave birth were *never* to be let mingle with other 'inmates of the House', although the guardians noted that, in any event, the such prostitutes usually only came in for hospital treatment in a special small ward allocated to them exclusively and did not stay. The Poor Law Commissioners requested that the term 'Separation Ward' be used instead of 'Penitential Ward', but the guardians thought this 'too mild a character to be given to the ward proposed'. Not wishing to rebuff the commissioners entirely, they agreed to call it the 'Punishment Ward'.[694] The very term 'poor house', used popularly as a synonym for 'workhouse', has echoed down the years as a byword for misery and shame.[695]

Lacemaking

During 1850 the *Cork Examiner* drew attention to Farney, Co. Monaghan, where the remarkable lawyer and land agent Tristram Kennedy had 'introduced various sorts of embroidery, with the greatest success, and hundreds are now remuneratively employed, under his care who otherwise would be inmates of the Carrickmacross Workhouse.' The paper said that others could do likewise.[696] Nonetheless, when Mrs Eliza (née Orpen) Herbert of Roughty and other Protestant ladies around Kenmare attempted to acquire a property in which to open a small industrial school for embroidery at Killowen, Fr John O'Sullivan denounced their initiative and pledged to put it down as proselytising. Herbert protested that proselytism was neither intended nor permitted – that no prayer books of any description were to be used in the school and that the school was 'solely intended for industrial purposes, and with the anxious hope of benefiting poor children'. The attorney Francis Henry Downing, son of Kenmare merchant Eugene Downing, publicly expressed

> deep regret that the getting up of a poor industrial school, and which the Catholic ladies of the parish were invited to assist in, should be tortured into a party question, and that an attempt should be made to revive those religious feuds which have so long made the neighbourhood of Kenmare remarkable, and which I did hope had passed away.[697]

Within a few weeks of the dispute about the Protestant women's initiative erupting, O'Sullivan himself opened an industrial school, meeting all of the preliminary expenses and locating it on Shelburne Street in a two-storey building that he appears to have leased some years earlier.[698] By this time he had already founded eleven national schools in the surrounding district. He designed the curriculum of his new venture as a mixture of 'literary' and industrial courses, with a half-hour of daily religious instruction. There was just one teacher, a young woman. The sole 'industrial' training provided was in sewing, embroidery, crochet and guipure. Guipure was included at the suggestion of Lord Lansdowne, whose family secured an outlet for its sale in London. Reporting on the school's first year of operation, a district inspector used its existence to bolster the argument against what he saw as 'a conviction in the minds of the people that females need little or no education, and may, without injustice done to them, be employed from their tenderest years in domestic service'.[699] Later, when they came to Kenmare, nuns would also train girls in lacemaking.

Fr John's women

Some years after his death, one of the nuns of Kenmare claimed that it was Fr John O'Sullivan's grandmother who instilled into his mind 'a holy ambition for the priesthood', although he did not suggest this in his journal. His mother, out of financial necessity, had wanted him to be placed in some business house. The young O'Sullivan seems to have been possessive of his widowed mother's time. A teacher of Greek and Latin, Fr Dan McCarthy, tutored him at home in the evenings, but 'it would pain me when I would hear my mother pressing him to remain longer.' She, presumably, enjoyed the adult company.[700]

O'Sullivan's reaction to news that his only sister was seriously ill is jarring. He was at that time a clerical student in Maynooth, preparing for examinations, 'I was written to when she was drawing near her end, and I must confess that the fear of the ensuing examinations more than anything else operated with me to solicit leave to come home.' More than anything else? His sister was a successful teacher, running a private school and had been 'getting on rapidly'.[701] Did her imminent death not count for more than academic convenience? Was this a statement on the status of women or just a poor choice of words in his journal?

At Maynooth – unlike later, when servants were employed there for the purpose – students did their own cleaning. But when O'Sullivan became parish priest of Kenmare, he employed two maids. Between them, their services in 1848 cost him about £3 a year, or one fifth of the total salary of his two curates. The maids may have been impoverished country girls who were glad of a chance to live in the relative comfort of a parish priest's house, and help him cope with many demands. We have seen that one of them was not afraid to confront a thief who held in his bloody hand a knife with which he had just slaughtered a sheep.[702]

O'Sullivan's views on women, even pious women, were not always flattering. He criticised Fr Michael Devine of Dingle for not spending more time exciting and rousing the feelings of the faithful against Protestant proselytisers rather than being 'buried in the confessional hearing the scruples of some old hag who has confessed them over twenty times perhaps to somebody else or even to himself'. There was Mrs Connor of Ballyheigue, who kept a house in fine order but who turned out to be 'an old, ugly, wrinkled dame'. There was Mrs O'Reilly Dease, a very rich visitor sent by his friend, the butter merchant John Mahony, who was 'a selfish little hag' who made demands on his time. The wife of his enemy Denis Mahony was, as we have seen, a 'viper'. Embroiled in trying to sort out a family dispute, he refers to one man as 'a half fool' and claims that the man's wife was 'the greatest virago I ever met', while the women in general in that family were 'a set of harpies'. Disturbed by the haste with which Fr Richard Power, 'a steady young man apparently', went to have tea with two women, he asked, 'If priests will make so much of those hussies, is it any wonder that they will assume the airs and the toys these ladies set up for and are so truly unbecoming?'[703] His references to men in his notebooks, including fellow priests, were also frequently sharp and unflattering.

He did not like it when a woman from Caherciveen who had been eight or nine years a nun in Dingle convent asserted herself and insisted on moving to Caherciveen convent:

When she found she would not be indulged [...] she stole out of the Convent, got on the six o'clock car to Tralee and arrived at Walpole's Hotel. The Tralee nuns fortunately heard at once of her being there and they sent for her and have her in Tralee Convent.

O'Sullivan was surprised when the bishop permitted her to proceed to Caherciveen and warned, 'It is very easy to anticipate a good deal of trouble from that young woman, dark, gloomy, distant and reserved she appeared to be – but not without a good deal of intellectuality which makes her more dangerous.' Having thus voiced his concern about this intelligent nun being indulged, he also, in fairness to her, noted that the superior of Caherciveen convent was 'a narrow-minded rigid little woman asking for too much perfection in every one'.[704]

Other women indulged in religion too heartily for his liking, 'The greatest nuisance in any parish is a childless wife or an elderly spinster. When they have no babies at home to wash or to dress or to look after they get a pious turn.'[705]

Yellow Kate

O'Sullivan was vitriolic about Katherine Franks, Denis Mahony's third wife, who ran a proselytising Protestant school in Templenoe. This was the woman whom the parish priest, in his recollections, described as a 'viper' and 'wicked'.[706]

His third wife was an old hidebound Tartar, some fifty-three or fifty-six years of age, the daughter of a Dublin attorney, a tractgoing, biblereading, parsonhunting, yellow, lean, sallow, shrivelled, half-starved-looking, sharp, vinegar-faced, bitter vixen. A repulsive, scowling, faggot she! She had been all her life engaged in proselytism – at least since she began to fade, to grow ancient, for 'tis only then these devils begin to get pious! They take tracts and bibles very easy until they begin to get stale and fear they'll bloom to the end in their virginity. No characters in society so troublesome, so pestiferous or so meddling as these old maids or pious wives without children. Every priest that wishes for peace in his parish should daily pray for their fruitfulness.[707]

The rationale for conversion work by women such as Franks had been earlier spelt out by Charlotte Elizabeth Tonna, who saw it as saving

Catholics from damnation and strengthening the Anglican Church in Ireland, which she felt was under attack. The relationship between such 'meddling' women and priests during the famine has received attention elsewhere.[708] In this case O'Sullivan found Katherine Franks-Mahony not only meddlesome but also 'ugly', just as Captain Ommanney's wife was 'ugly'.

Bound into the volume of O'Sullivan's recollections are two handbills of abusive and spiteful stanzas referring to Katherine, 'Katty' or 'Yellow Kate', 'You're so withered, spent and grey.' John O'Sullivan firmly believed in the power of a ballad or song to move the masses.[709] These misogynistic verses of a personal nature, which O'Sullivan distributed and quite possibly also wrote, were unworthy of any priest. They are said to have drawn a response of the same ilk in which one 'Friar Bullphiz', believed to represent the parish priest, was denounced as 'an unmanly wretch' who 'On woman pours – oh, shame to human kind / The rankling venom of his coward mind.'[710]

No doubt partly due to contemporary invective about her – as well as her offensive proselytising – Katherine Franks gained a notorious reputation in folklore. For example, Jeremiah O'Connor, who was born in 1868, later told a researcher about 'Yellow Kate (Caít Bhuidhe an tSúip – Yellow Kate of the Soup)':

> She was an infamous proselytiser who lived at Dromore Castle. It was the Archdeacon O'Sullivan Parish Priest of Kenmare who added the words souper and souperism to the vocabulary. Caít Bhuidhe sent Catholic children to Dublin but Archdeacon O'Sullivan brought them back again. He held meetings throughout the parish condemning the work of Yellow Kate. *Caít Bhuidhe an tSúip* – her heart was sore as a rotten crab. Fr O'Sullivan foretold that Dromore Castle would yet be without a Mahony.[711]

She and Anne Thompson in Dingle were not the only Protestant women to play leading roles in proselytising in south Kerry. On a visitation to the Beara Peninsula with the bishop, O'Sullivan noticed a cottage with a red-tiled roof that Mrs Puxley was building, 'This woman is the prime mover, the arch promoter of the Soup crusade at Castletown.'[712]

Churching

The pious custom of 'churching' was long practised in Ireland and other Catholic countries. The ceremony consisted of a blessing given by a priest to mothers after their recovery from childbirth, and marked the women's readmission by the priest to the altar. Only a Catholic who had given birth inside marriage – and provided she had not allowed the child to be baptised outside the Catholic Church – was entitled to be churched. Dismissed by some today as an expression of misogyny, churching has also been described as a potentially valuable source for feminist liturgical theology in church communities.[713] Although a custom and not a precept, churching was a valued source of revenue for priests – as the young John O'Sullivan soon discovered as a new curate in Dingle in 1830:

> I was not twenty-four hours there when a woman applied to me to be churched, which I did at once. A second applied and I churched her too. I did the same by a third, and a fourth, and up to twenty. At length a woman I had churched threw herself on her knees and sought to kiss my feet; and – then only – I asked the clerk why she, as well indeed as were all the others, was so thankful. 'Lord Sir' said he, 'because you're churching them all for nothing, and when the Parish Priest comes home, and hears it, he'll be stark staring mad'. Now I declare that up to that moment I never knew there was such a thing as a fee for churching and I think I should have got some hints of the matter before I came on the mission.[714]

O'Sullivan's views on churching were somewhat conflicted. According to him, it was wrong to refuse communion to a woman who had not been churched, but 'a considerable part of the priest's revenue flows from this service', so where women had not been churched, he 'would not blame the priest who would threaten such women occasionally for not being purified'. He thought women who could not afford the fee should be churched anyhow, but it 'should be done as a favour, and not as a matter of course [...] otherwise they will not be grateful for it.' Besides:

> It is infinitely better to be liberal than stingy on such occasions [...] The longer they are unchurched the more careless they become about it. They have very erroneous notions of its importance and it is quite clear those notions would not have been so sedulously instilled if there were not certain emoluments flowing to the Priest from the ceremony. It behoves a Priest certainly to explain to the people what an antient ceremony it is, and how desirable to be observed by all, but the lengths that some have gone.[715]

He certainly felt that women who could afford the fee to be churched should pay one, although any woman who conceived outside marriage should not expect an easy passage. This fact led to an incident involving Jane Maybury, who asked to meet their bishop expressly in the absence of Fr John O'Sullivan. He did not take the request kindly:

> I replied by saying it should only be in my presence. This lady was a virago, a regular *mulier fortis* [Latin: strong woman] from whose family I got much trouble and little gains, none in fact at all. They never paid me as much as one shilling at Christmas or at Easter, tho they came to Mass every Sunday in silks and satins and on a side-car! Their father was a Protestant but died a Catholic five years ago. About two years since a brother of theirs, an attorney, got a child by a dairymaid of his and from his being a Protestant I said nothing about it. He soon after sent the damsel to be churched. When I refused he first began to send word he was ready to pay any sum I require, and finding me inexorable he threatened he would send her to the Parson for the purpose and he did, but to his amazement the Parson only got indignant at a strumpet like her being sent to him when she was rejected by the Priest. Maybury's blackguard sisters then began to circulate that I required £5 for churching her, upon which I had to allude to the whole transaction in the chapel and in consequence the bold attorney would never since as much as look at the same side of the road with me. Miss Jane was married last Shrove twelve-month and I thought they would then make some amends for their former neglect, but the munificent sum of £5-10-0 was all they condescended to give on the occasion. In something more than twelve months Jane presented her lord with a youngster and I was sent for to baptise it and upon having baptised it, to the great dismay of the lot of ladies I refused to church the Madam [Jane] until my dues should be paid.[716]

Bishop Egan appears to have upheld O'Sullivan's decision on that occasion, on the grounds that the Mayburys could afford the fee.

That some priests had little understanding of women, or just lacked common sense, is suggested by an incident that O'Sullivan recalled concerning a confessor who imposed as a penance on an old woman aged 95, 'who had not crossed the street for several years but who in an evil hour gave her scapulars to put on the neck of a neighbour dangerously ill in childbirth', the obligation of 'going fasting three

mornings to give rounds about a church two miles distant – a penance
[...] impossible for her to perform'.[717] It is a doubly interesting
anecdote because it also points to concerns about 'charms', or
superstituous practices. Why else might it be a sin to lend a 'scapular',
that small piece of cloth with devotional significance worn quite often
then as a discreet accoutrement of the faithful?

Nuns

Once, many Irish Catholic parents were proud to see a daughter
become a nun, and it was common for women to do so. Nuns had an
opportunity to manage projects in ways that were not generally open
to women then. One such project was the convent-school that Fr John
O'Sullivan ensured was built at Kenmare. It enabled local women to
advance. When the unaffiliated American missionary Asenath
Nicholson (from a Congregationalist background) visited Ireland
during the famine, she compared unfavourably what she found at a
Protestant school in Ventry with her experience at the local convent in
Dingle, 'Here is a nun spending her whole life in teaching the poor,
without any compensation, and saying, "We don't know what station
God may want them to fill, and we advance them as far as we can."'[718]

O'Sullivan thought quite highly of nuns in general. Mother Mary
Austin (Mrs Johanna Hayden) of Presentation Convent in Tralee was,
he believed, in 1849, a 'plain, sensible shrewd woman to whom I am
much obliged for the last twenty years'.[719] He was to be found in
Killarney attending a special ceremony when Elizabeth, a daughter of
his cousin Anne Walsh and her husband John Murphy of The Square
in Tralee, took her solemn vows at the Presentation Convent.[720] He was
even somewhat intimidated by the piety of nuns and declined to preach
regularly at the convent in Dingle, explaining of the nuns there, 'I knew
every one of them to be so much more perfect and more advanced in
the love of God than I was myself. I felt I would be a real hypocrite
preaching what I did not practise.' This did not stop him complaining
that he had been 'a slave to the same nuns' when ministering to their
needs, nor did he refrain from recording a highly critical opinion of 'a
little woman' who was their superior and who later ran the convent at
Caherciveen. He thought that she was 'as mulish and as stiff-necked
and as wedded to her own opinions as any lady I ever met, with all her
piety and religion'.[721] A case of the pot calling the kettle black?

Bishop Egan expected to be able to call – announced or
unannounced – at convents and have nuns there provide a dinner for

his visitation party and local priests.[722] O'Sullivan expressed reservations about the nuns catering in this manner, although from his journals it is clear that they exacted in return a level of attention to their spiritual requirements that the priests at times found irksome. He wrote:

> I do not like those dinners at convents. I think they are more or less inconsistent with the poverty those religious [nuns] undertake to profess. It is an innovation. Such a thing was unheard of when I was first ordained. It must put those nuns more or less out of their way and I fear for its leading to further innovations.

He objected to the presence of any layman at these dinners, even a brother of the superioress.[723] Nevertheless, O'Sullivan's reservations did not stop him enjoying the hospitality, which at least once in Dingle included 'a capital dinner – pea soup, turbot, sole, John Dory, hake, mullet and trout. Lobster did not come to table from some mishap or other.'[724] The bishop stayed longer in convents as he got older, a practice that his critics apparently used against him in Rome to suggest that he was giving scandal.[725]

O'Sullivan appreciated what nuns did for the people generally, and thought that this social return was worth the investment of a priest's attention to them:

> Peculiar though they be in their habits and in their manners all allowances must be made for their seclusion from the world and the isolation of their ideas and I have been often pained to find men who ought to have more sense, and be above such petty cavilling, descend to unseemly disputes with those poor females who so untiringly and increasingly devote themselves to the glory of God and the furtherance of good morals.[726]

The range of jobs available to women in society was very limited then. Teacher, nun, governess and domestic servant were principal avenues of employment. In 1874 a nun at Kenmare wrote that 'One of Fr John's great objects, and one in which he had our Mother [Superior]'s heartiest and happiest concurrence, was the advancement of girls showing any special talent.'[727] The nuns, for example, cultivated musical abilities, which gave girls confidence. They also built on earlier lacemaking initiatives, providing outlets for the skills of local women. One of the nuns involved wrote later:

The need was, indeed, very great. There was no remunerative occupation of any kind for the women or girls in the neighbourhood and the poverty was extreme. A few girls had made some poor attempts at crochet, showing, at least, their eagerness for employment; and a few had offered their work for sale to the tourists as they passed on the cars.[728]

The nuns saw a moral hazard in girls directly approaching tourists to sell their wares. Besides, in winter there were no tourists. So they decided to support the girls financially until the lacemaking venture could sustain itself. It is said that O'Sullivan shrank back from their becoming so involved, telling the mother superior that 'she would ruin herself'. However, she persisted and promised the girls regular employment if they would work at the convent. It was a strict rule that anyone who went to the tourist cars to sell work would be fired, 'In a very little time the girls got to see what was in their interest [...] and many began to earn from five to eighteen shillings a week.' The nuns paid them as promised, despite the fact that, at first, some of the work was of poor quality and so was financially worthless. This left the nuns with a stock of unsold work, 'and our convent being very poor, and our support depending very much on such donations as we might get, made this outlay a serious embarrassment.' The proprietor of the local hotel promoted the venture by displaying the lacework and by bringing some visitors to the convent to see where it was made, 'and we must also say that English and Protestant tourists have been our principal support.'[729]

Suitable matches

There was a strange interlude in court when the boy James Jones sued the Mahonys of Dromore Castle for seizing clothing he had received when he attended the Protestant school in Templenoe. As 'Yellow Kate' Mahony's maid gave evidence, Mary Laird's marital status, suddenly and for no obvious reason, came under scrutiny. Laird came from Ulster:

Mr Murphy: Now, Miss Laird, don't be angry, 'twill spoil your beauty; allow me to ask you are you married? No.

Would you have any objection? If I got a suitable match.

Are you anxious on that point? No – not in Kerry. If he were from the North I might, but certainly not in Kerry.

Don't you think we live pretty well in Kerry? Cannot say.

Don't you think you may go farther and fare worse? Don't know.

Assistant-barrister [presiding as judge]: I think you are a pretty fair specimen of Kerry living yourself, Mr Murphy (great laughter).[730]

That a woman's marital status could thus be made a matter for random comment and ridicule potentially reduced her value as a witness. That her reluctance to marry locally might be understandable is suggested by the rather glib response O'Sullivan received when he enquired why so many local men were eager to marry young: they wanted someone to wash their shirts.[731]

For Catholic priests the marriage of a parishioner was a chance to earn revenue from the fee paid to them for presiding. Critics claimed that the system put pressure on poor people and that the opportunity to charge fees tempted priests to encourage marriages, or at least not to advise against them, even when a couple had no sustainable interest in land that could support them subsequently. Such pressure, it was thought, increased the likelihood of further subdivisions of already uneconomic holdings. O'Sullivan was critical of high fees.[732]

The question of what a priest should do when called out to an unmarried person who was dying in the presence of a cohabiting partner was also an issue then. Should the 'concubine' be excluded as the last rites were administered, or even sent out of the house? O'Sullivan was ambivalent.[733] Nevertheless, he denounced the cohabitation of his parishioners outside marriage, including where a spouse of one of the parties had been absent for years and that spouse's fate was unknown.[734] Personally, he found attendance at wedding celebrations quite trying:

I don't think I ever went out to one without making an act of resignation. It requires much patience and resignation to come to a country house in the evening with a roaring fire roasting, boiling, baking, cooking in a variety of ways various and sundry joints of fowl, beef, mutton, bacon [and] superintended by a dirty slattern melting from the action of the heat and the steam [...] with so many streams of perspiration oozing from every pore of her body [...] The priest must preside and officiate at the carving for the company. He must make a semblance of eating something; for if he have common sense he will have eaten his dinner at home as usual, and be he ever so hungry, if he have got a glimpse at the cook and her *modus operandi*, I defy him to make much use of the dinner.[735]

When he threw his eyes up to heaven on beholding such scenes, he found there an inspiring model. For he had a devout respect for Mary the mother of Jesus, and a traditional belief in her spiritual power. Yet he disagreed with the pope when it came to church teaching about her.

The 'Immaculate Conception'

Proselytisers who demeaned Mary's status in Catholicism offended him. Nevertheless, he felt that the kind of faith with which he was comfortable did not need new assertions of theoretical dogma to bolster it. When he learnt, in 1854, that a meeting of Kerry priests was being convened to plan local events to mark a jubilee year for the Catholic Church, he reflected on its agenda, which included an item concerning the belief that Mary, mother of Jesus, was exempt from all stain of 'original sin' – the hereditary stain with which all humans were said to be born because of their descent from the first man, Adam:

> This Jubilee is preparatory to defining the Immaculate Conception. That's too bad. I hope it never will be defined: not that I am wanting in respect and honour and love and regard to the ever glorious and blessed Virgin. I think I'd spill my blood for her more readily than hundreds of those who are so loud in her praise, and who I knew myself at the Synod of Thurles to care not as much as a 'thraneen' [Irish: *tráithnín*, or 'blade of grass'] for her; but I cannot understand how it is now that in the nineteenth century we are called upon to make an act of faith in what we never were obliged to before, the more so when the dogma is not impugned by any heretics: were the heretics to question it or anything else regarding her I would be one of the first to pommel the vagabonds, but when no question is raised thereon I don't see why the Church should so come out to gratify the piety of a few enthusiastic, pious devotees. How did it happen that we were allowed to pass through [Maynooth] College without ever having the question discussed? How did it happen that until within the last few years we never heard of such dogma? It certainly startled me when I first heard it, for I never dreamed that anyone believed the Blessed Virgin to have been immaculately conceived until we were called upon some years

ago to recite that office; and let pious and devout souls argue over the […] doctrine – the one that will be always staring them in the face *in quo omnes peccaverunt* [Latin: 'in that all have sinned' (Romans 5:2)]. I for one sincerely hope the dogma won't be defined and I have great hopes the Blessed Virgin will not be the less favourably disposed towards men. I fought harder in one couple of years for her honour and her glory and our holy religion than will the whole of the zealots who are now throwing up their caps for her, during the course of their lives. I hope that Her Immaculate Conception will not be made *de Fide* [Latin: 'of the faith', signifying an essential part of Catholicism].[736]

Pope Pius IX promulgated the dogma in December 1854, with Protestant critics regarding it as an exercise in papal power. It placed Mary on a pedestal – a valiant woman but also now intrinsically different from other women. O'Sullivan was not the only Catholic uneasy about it. More recently, feminists such as Mary Daly have critically examined aspects of the dogma.[737]

17

After the Famine

As Ireland emerged from the trauma of famine, the Catholic Church began to formulate future policies. Priests such as O'Sullivan had their own ideas of what was needed, but the many priests and people who hoped to see him become bishop of Kerry were to be disappointed.

The Synod of Thurles

A meeting of Irish bishops was convened at Thurles in August 1850. It was to prove contentious. Bishop Egan of Kerry had intended to go, and O'Sullivan made preparations for him. He found that Egan had no red cope to wear 'but a shabby old fellow [i.e. cloak] some forty years old in Killarney and he will not allow me to get a red one made. As a last shift he allows me to write to Dr Delany, bishop of Cork, an old acquaintance and fellow student of mine to try and procure the loan for him.'[738] In the event Egan was not well enough to attend the synod. He sent Fr John McEnnery and Fr John O'Sullivan instead, although only one substitute, or 'procurator', for any absent bishop was permitted. As the junior of the two, O'Sullivan felt obliged to stand down. However, each bishop present was allowed a theologian, and when Bishop Thomas Feeny of Killala found himself without one, he let O'Sullivan attend in that capacity.[739]

The new Catholic archbishop of Ireland, Paul Cullen, had ideas about church reform, but O'Sullivan did not like Cullen's approach. Cullen wished to ensure that his institution's external appearance and behaviour was beyond reasonable reproach. He was deeply suspicious of the 'stations', desiring to see the sacraments administered principally in churches or chapels. He wanted to align Ireland with contemporary devotional practices elsewhere in Europe and frowned on local or popular Irish religious practices such as patterns. He aspired to a Catholic university for Ireland instead of the new non-denominational

Queen's Colleges that the government had set up in Cork, Galway and Belfast to provide a secular alternative to Trinity College Dublin. Some dioceses, including Kerry, did not strongly oppose these allegedly 'godless' Queen's Colleges, and at the synod Cullen only narrowly won a motion against Catholic participation in them. O'Sullivan claimed, 'All lengths were gone to in order to coax or to intimidate.'[740] John McEnnery, Bishop Egan's procurator, had been, according to O'Sullivan, 'like a fish out of water, moping about without joining anyone' and 'moping about [...] at the Synod like a fool'. McEnnery switched his vote under what O'Sullivan saw as undue pressure from Cullen.[741] He himself suspected that if the bishops undermined the Queen's Colleges and succeeded in having the state fund a Catholic university, then the existing state endowment for Maynooth College would be removed.[742]

There was disagreement too about national schools, which had been intended to be non-denominational but were being run in many cases as Catholic or Protestant establishments. O'Sullivan regarded ecclesiastical squabbling over these schools as distasteful and unwise, and he tried to address the issue at the synod; however, he was first told by Cullen to wait and then was not called to speak.[743] He felt that Cullen blocked his advocacy. He thought that Cullen, 'with all his piety and all his learning has not in my opinion commonsense nor an ordinary knowledge of men'.[744] O'Sullivan believed that the Church of Ireland made a strategic error in opposing 'mixed' or non-denominational national schools on principle; he thought this left it open to parish priests such as himself to seize the initiative locally and to fill a void that the cannier Presbyterians in Ulster – 'a clever and sharp-witted body', he thought – had not overlooked there. Catholic priests received state aid to build and run schools within their parishes, and he himself built about a dozen. Lord Lansdowne had also erected five schools on his estate – 'at a considerable expense, for he ornamented some of them', noted O'Sullivan.[745]

Proselytism had not disappeared with the worst of the famine, even if it seemed to be less potent when people were not in the greatest need. Of those conversions that faded away when circumstances improved, O'Sullivan once wrote, 'The summer Protestants were becoming harvest Catholics.'[746] The bishops were still concerned. Cullen in particular felt so strongly about proselytism that, writes Kerr, 'his hatred of it is crucial to an understanding of his policy in his early years in Ireland.' An irritated O'Sullivan, long busy against proselytism, thought that Cullen had caused the authorities in Rome 'to charge all the Bishops and priests of Munster with inactivity and indifference to Souperism and obliged them to hold a synod [Thurles] to meet the evil'. If Cullen brought renewed determination to the battle, O'Sullivan felt that, in his own case, he needed no instruction on the topic.[747] He wrote in 1854, 'I defy a man to meet souperism without carrying agitation to its acme.' He then drafted advice to young priests on how to respond to soupers and bible-readers.[748]

The tone of O'Sullivan's response to the violent assault on Denis Mahony appears to have made some senior members of the hierarchy wary of him. He seems to have hoped that the synod might actually adopt a national policy on opposing bible-readers based on what he had done to mock them in his parish. So he felt slighted by Archbishop John MacHale at the Synod of Thurles when the latter misplaced a copy of a press cutting that he had given him concerning the priest's employment of Patrick Connor to dog the steps of bible-readers in Templenoe. MacHale 'told me not only superciliously but insolently that he could not stoop to the preservation of such documents as those and he knew not what became of it'. O'Sullivan wrote that the incident lowered his opinion of MacHale.[749]

Even still, O'Sullivan was publicly mentioned in Munster as a possible coadjutor bishop for Kerry – as someone to help the ailing Cornelius Egan.[750] Such an appointment was usually the stepping-stone to succeeding a bishop in due course. O'Sullivan did not want to be seen to hope too hard for the position, and was perhaps genuinely unsure if he wanted it. He confided in his diary:

> Time will tell what ambition I have for it [...] a greater cross could not possibly come in my way. Few lead a happier, easier, quieter life or have more reasons for passing their time more pleasantly, but it is a subject on which I wish to say as little as possible.[751]

A clash at Maynooth

O'Sullivan was not the most diplomatic person. Having already ruffled feathers at the Synod of Thurles, he now argued with the president of Maynooth College, Laurence Renehan. In February 1851 O'Sullivan was returning from Dublin, intending to spend a few days in Cork 'with my esteemed friend Right Rev. Doctor Delany'. On the way he stopped for dinner in Maynooth, Renehan having hospitably prevailed on him to stay the night. After dinner they adjourned to the president's room, where their host laid on tea, coffee, madeira, port, sherry, whiskey, sugar and hot water. Various topics turned up, including certain diocesan statutes that raised the question of jurisdiction and its exercise within the Catholic Church:

> He asked me had I ever seen the statutes of our diocese published and printed in 1747 by Doctor O'Meara. He could scarcely contain his surprise when I told him I not only had a copy of them but that I was about to get a reprint of them last year and had been in treaty with a bookseller about the matter. Great was his surprise and exceeding great did his indignation wax, and in most pompous, authoritative tones did he tell me that so far from seeking to perpetuate such a production that I should rather strive to destroy every surviving copy thereof […] its being a most unfortunate circumstance that such a thing was ever published, presenting as it did such a picture of the state of discipline in the Diocese of Kerry in them days.[752]

Another man might have nodded his head and let Renehan assume that the priest had been suitably chastened. Not so O'Sullivan:

> My recollections of the said statutes left no other impression on me than their being not much more than a brief synopsis of moral theology without as much as one reserved case from beginning to end, and great was my expectation to hear the mare's nest Renehan had found out. At length he read a passage in which those who dare to carry about the consecrated species [the Holy Communion wafer] in a book, corporal [cloth] or any other than a silver or golden vase are censured. There, said he, slamming the book on the table, is a picture of the laxity of your clergy in them days and no wonder that apostasy should be so rife as it is at present in your diocese. Had I not known Larry of old, and had I not been convinced of his non-intention to insult, I protest I would have walked out of the room. The Madeira etc. satisfied me he did not mean offence, and I know him formerly to be an uncouth, half-savage, ill-tempered, ill-mannered fellow that did not know nor could not bring himself to behave like a gentleman. His attempts at politeness were in truth a caricature of it. Larry must have been of very low origin indeed.

> When he had disburdened himself of his indignation and allowed me to throw in a word or two, my reply was impromptu.

O'Sullivan argued that diocesan statues had been readily made in response to merely a particular or isolated offence that caused great scandal, and that they did not indicate broader misbehaviour:

> The present statutes of our diocese forbade any priest to appear in public at a race course or to carry a female riding behind him on horseback, from which posterity will, like Renehan, infer that these matters are of usual occurrence, whereas no priest in my recollection ever thought of the like, save on one occasion that one priest who was then very obnoxious to the bishop appeared at the races at Killarney, when forthwith the statute against races was made, passed and provided.

He might have wisely left it at that, but did not. Instead, he remarked to Renehan that

> if we were to judge of the state of morality among the clergy by the statutes of the diocese, that his own Cashel would and ought rank among the lowest in Ireland, because it was a matter of suspension *ipso facto* for a man to take a glass of punch in the evening in the house in which the conference dinner had been held that day, or to take spirituous liquor in any shape before dinner – from which by his own rule, it was obvious that the lads after drinking plenty at the conference dinner were wont to adjourn to another room and drink a skinful, and were also tippling during the day. This enraged him beyond measure and he so stuck to me and so bothered me with his arguments and vociferation that I stood up and moved off to my bedroom. He still followed me, took a chair and made himself at home, argued and crossed and was rude and insolent for near another hour, until I had to turn him out by taking up the chamber pot and saying I could not hold out no longer.[753]

Renehan himself was tipped by some to succeed Egan. O'Sullivan wrote of him in his journal, 'A man he is no doubt of much piety and great learning but a man of no experience on the mission, a man knowing very little of the world and its ways [...] God save Kerry from such a Bishop!!'[754] Another person tipped was the man ultimately appointed. This was David Moriarty, who O'Sullivan conceded was no doubt pious and disinterested:

> But Moriarty is a sickly, unhealthy man, without a word of Irish and would in my mind be one of the most unfit men in existence

for the management of this diocese. He is a native of Odorney, has never been on the mission, and I cannot bring myself to think that those men taken from a college can ever have the discretion or the experience necessary for such a position.[755]

O'Sullivan was in effect assessing his competitors for the position of bishop. He wrote astutely in his journal, 'I think I will have the majority of the votes of the priests, [but] still in consequence of my ranking with Dr Murray and his party at the Synod of Thurles, and my known moderation as a politician, Paul Cullen will have me set aside.'[756]

In July 1850, as the famine subsided, O'Sullivan had been confirmed as vicar-general.[757] He was one of two trustees for Bishop Egan, advising him on delicate financial matters concerning Egan's own property as well as properties endowed as gifts for the church and the poor.[758] In late August 1852 he was glad to get home to Kenmare, after seven weeks on the road with his bishop visiting parishes. He was then, he wrote, 'cut up, wasted, exhausted from the daily perspiration in crowded, heated chapels, preaching and catechising in a language [Irish] in which I am so totally and entirely deficient, in a constant state of excitement and uneasiness of mind for fear anything may happen the bishop'. He thought that 'a few weeks quiet here among my flowers and my music will, I trust, soon bring me about again.'[759]

Egan increasingly suffered from ailments and relied heavily on O'Sullivan. By reason of the bishop's approaching old age and infirmities, O'Sullivan expected that Egan had just completed his last visitation.

Praxis parochi

O'Sullivan had started to compose a guide to parish duties for young priests but then had second thoughts when he shared his idea:

> As we went along I took the opportunity of reading some parts of a book I commenced to write some time ago, entitled 'Praxis parochi', with a view to the guidance and direction of young missionaries. I intended publishing it, but I found so many innuendoes and insinuations afloat about it that I determined on keeping it back until after my death, and then let the world judge of it as they please.[760]

Fortunately, the manuscript of Praxis parochi survives, complete with additions that O'Sullivan made to it in 1852 and 1854. It is a rich source of information on a wide range of issues, including his views on the Ten Commandments as kept or broken, holding stations, relations with 'soupers' and other Protestants, establishing national schools, preaching, denunciations, dealing with unmarried cohabitees, the last rites and choosing architecture, painting and furniture for churches. It also includes miscellaneous personal anecdotes and comments on the Synod of Thurles. It merits publication. It is also a valuable insight into the mind of a parish priest at a time when Catholic authorities were trying to assert centralised control. That O'Sullivan himself had an independent intellectual streak is clear from a tantalising reference to him after his death by 'the Nun of Kenmare', who knew and liked him:

> I have seldom met any one with such sublime ideas of God. He used to speak out very plainly about some Roman Catholic devotions which he did not approve, and I often heard him criticise the lessons in the breviary, which all priests are obliged to recite daily, in a way which would have very much astonished the authorities in Rome if they had heard him. He was a great reader of the Bible, and often told me how much he wished it was more read by Roman Catholics. It is certainly no injustice to his memory to say he decidedly discouraged those devotions to the saints which are so popular with priests. Still, when some ladies tried to proselytise some of his flock, by sending a Bible reader amongst them, he took very summary measures to stop them.[761]

He was also sceptical about the proposed dogma of the 'Immaculate Conception' of Mary, mother of Jesus, as seen earlier.

Bishop O'Sullivan?

When O'Sullivan returned to Thurles in September 1853, this time for a synod of only the Munster province's own bishops, he was fearful that he would

> come into collision with some of the powers as I had done at the National Synod, and that such would be made a pretext for representing me in an odious light at Rome – not that I cared three farthings for their power nor for all the mitres in their gift, but still I did not wish to give them a pretext for foisting one of Cullen's nominees on this unhappy diocese.[762]

On 5 October 1853 the priests of Kerry cast their votes for their choice as bishop. In accordance with precedence, they picked three men in order – *dignus* (Latin: worthy), *dignior* (worthier) and *dignissimus* (worthiest) – and the result, or '*terna*', was sent to Rome. The result was John McEnnery (five votes), David Moriarty (eleven) and John O'Sullivan (twenty-four). Four others, including Renehan, got a single vote each, which meant that O'Sullivan had not merely come out on top but did so with an overall majority. He was entertained afterwards in Killarney, at Finn's Hotel ('the Kenmare Arms'), by a party of over thirty diners.[763] That same evening, it was reported that 'every house' in Kenmare was illuminated in celebration, 'The town and surrounding country was beautifully lit up with bonfires.'[764]

O'Sullivan was backed not only by most priests in Kerry but also by the bishops of the Cashel ecclesiastical province, of which Kerry was part, who on 26 October 1853 unanimously agreed that he was the best candidate and informed the Vatican accordingly. They pointed out that Moriarty did not know Irish and so was unsuited to the diocese of Kerry. Nevertheless, Cullen had begun to intervene actively in episcopal appointments, ensuring that relatively fewer parish priests who had spent all or most of their careers 'on the mission' – and fewer Maynooth men too – were made bishops.[765] He thought that O'Sullivan was, from what he had seen of him, someone who was 'most unfit to be a bishop, a boisterous, rough man'. Instead he backed Moriarty, who was 'fond of order, a disciplinarian', although some priests thought that Moriarty was not 'Irish' enough and claimed he had 'apostate' or 'souper' relatives.[766] Cullen exercised his considerable influence, writing to the Vatican on 18 November 1853, 'Father O'Sullivan, having been a parish priest for a long time, will not be disposed to put into effect the reforms prescribed by the Synod [of Thurles] with regard to the administration of the sacraments.'[767] Cullen wrote:

> The first among these candidates is John O'Sullivan. He assisted at the Synod of Thurles, where I had occasion to come to know him well enough to say that he does not have the qualities that are really required in Irish bishops. He does not have a gentle or kindly manner, he is fond of noise, and seems little given to spiritual things. He was sent by his bishop to the National Synod to support the cause of the Queen's Colleges, and if he is nominated bishop now, the supporters of that mixed system of teaching will cry about having obtained a victory.[768]

Cullen wrote to Kirby too, referring to O'Sullivan:

> The first candidate does not appear suitable – some priests of
> the diocese have written me that he is very fond of dogs, that
> when he rides he places a puppy behind him on the saddle, and
> that he has taught this dog to smoke tobacco, and do a thousand
> tricks.[769]

O'Sullivan also heard a rumour that his threat, in 1843, to refuse the
sacraments to those who broke Fr Mathew's temperance pledge was
used to discredit him.[770] In 1847 Mathew himself had been passed over
when the priests of Cork selected him as their choice for bishop; this
may have been at least partly because he (like O'Sullivan) supported
the proposed government endowment of Catholic clergy.[771]

O'Sullivan thought that Cullen 'carried out what he threatened at
Thurles in 1850 for when my name did go to Rome he did put the
broad R [reject] upon it, and that with a vengeance'. He continued:

> They say he represented me there as an idle scamp that did
> nothing but go about the country with a pipe in my mouth (I
> never smoked in my life) and a fine cap on my head, beating
> parsons and smashing church windows! And that's the way
> bishops are made by an infallible Church!!!

He thought that Cullen had made him pay a price 'as I would not
crouch to him at the Synod of Thurles'. He consoled himself:

> However I may be disbelieved, few rejoice at the result more than
> I do myself. I am a happier man and feel more at my ease in my
> garden or playing my piano or making a sundial, aye by Jove or
> even teaching my dog to fetch than if I were a Cardinal Bishop,
> to say nothing of a poor, troubled, pelted bishop in Kerry.[772]

David Moriarty was appointed bishop instead, protesting belatedly that
he did not want the job – 'for which my past habits of life, my
inexperience of the mission and my ignorance of the language of the
Diocese completely unfit me'. O'Sullivan would have agreed with him
if asked, for he was scathing of Moriarty in his journals.[773] He remained
unapologetic for the manner in which he himself had fought
proselytism:

> Now I am no agitator [...] [Yet] if Souperism were to invade my
> parish in the morning, before evening would Father John
> become the greatest agitator in the country. He would be a

Tenant Right man, a Defence Association man, a Repealer, Anything, Everything, to stir up and excite the people. Prayers and Rosaries and Missions and Forty Hours [organised devotion] [...] are the only weapons Dr Cullen depends on [...] Rome knows very little and Dr Cullen seems to know less of what a priest on a country mission must recur to in order to meet Soupers.[774]

He claimed that Cullen was prepared to alienate every bishop individually to get his way, 'Bravo, brave Cullen [...] Take it for granted there is not a pious, nor a zealous, nor an active bishop in the Church but yourself or some of your choosing.'[775]

Moriarty, as bishop – with John O'Sullivan accompanying him – began again the rounds of annual visitations. Once more O'Sullivan's journal includes colourful impressions of priests and tales of encounters along the way. Then his notes stop suddenly. Did this man who wrote so extensively between 1843 and 1855 cease recording his ideas and observations, or were some manuscripts lost or destroyed? His last notes, on 9 August 1855, start by reporting that during the night a rat had woken him while dragging from the priest's portmanteau a large sea biscuit – one of two that O'Sullivan brought on that particular visit, along with 'a glass of brandy to regale ourselves' on the way. The priest was transported at one point in a four-wheeled vehicle pulled by 'a wretched pony' that made the journey long, 'I had full time to imbibe the whole flood of perspiration with which I had been reeking.' His last recorded impressions were as vivid as ever.

Dancing, art and reading

O'Sullivan was said to be 'an excellent Latin scholar' – 'though he did not have the advantage of a cultured style, he made a translation of Bellarmine's well-known *Commentary on the Psalms*, and won approval for his rugged exactness and force of diction' when it was published.[776]

For his times, he was not the most censorious of priests. He tolerated the card playing and pipe music in Ballyferriter that outraged the priest whose house he and his friends were visiting. As a boy in Tralee he had swum naked with friends, and he drew a distinction between the attitude of the 'peasant' towards nudity (being '*in puris naturalibus*', as he put it) and that of 'those in a more civilised sphere', ostensibly the bourgeoisie.[777] It is clear from his *Praxis parochi* that he shared conventional attitudes of his day towards sexual relations. But given more recent instances of scandal, it is worth noting that he felt strongly that in those cases where priests acted improperly (and such cases were rare, he thought), the priest should not be let simply continue in ministry – even if there was nobody else available to say Mass, 'I am of opinion that such persons are too easily dealt with, and let off too lightly by those to whom they confess […] I for one would send such a character about his business […] let him turn his thoughts to other pursuits.'[778]

He approved of dancing, but not at all times or places. When Bishop Egan was evidently disappointed after they encountered people dancing 'vigorously' at a crossroads in Templenoe, in the priest's own parish, O'Sullivan asked, 'What harm is there in the people thus amusing themselves in the face of day? Prevent them and you drive them to public houses, to lanes and alleys and lonesome fields where a much greater amount of sin may be committed.' He added, 'They footed it away manfully as we passed along.' Such dancing in the open air was long a feature of country life. He remarked on another occasion, when they found people dancing in a field near the bridge at Listry chapel (between Killarney and Killorglin), 'High treason this was some time ago.' Yet he reserved the right to determine what was appropriate entertainment for his parishioners, for he added in his diary, 'I never prevent the people from dancing save in jig-houses at night which I always denounce.'[779]

On another occasion he wrote, 'With regard to dancing, hurling and such outdoor amusements, so far from prohibiting them on Sundays, I am always glad to see them going on, 'tho I will take no part in furthering them.' He added:

> Such amusements are in truth necessary for the lower orders. After a week's toil they need some relaxation, and by tolerating them in the day time they will have less reason for so engaging themselves at night. Those amusements are tolerated, nay encouraged in all Catholic countries and I cannot at all understand the dark stoicism of many priests who denounce so violently the very innocent amusement of dancing that seems so congenial […] If John the Baptist lost his head by reason of the dancing of Herodias' daughter, is that a reason that poor people should not be allowed to dance? As well may they prevent the use of wine, to the excess of which it is more likely is to be attributed the rash oath of Herod than to the girl's dancing. I never danced a step in my life, still I like to see young people

dancing, it causes them to forget all the labours and troubles of the week. It puts them in good humour with themselves and with the whole world, and by bringing them together it prevents and anticipates a vast amount of sin they would otherwise perhaps have fallen into. I would much rather see a dance than a goal, for at the latter they often get excited and strike each other. But the priest should with all his might and main put down all night dances and meetings and denounce them constantly. I would not have him go to the houses in which they are held with a stick in his hand, unless he be a person of very cool temper, and having great command of himself. Zeal on such occasions very often lapses into fury and ill-temper and very unseemly collisions.[780]

Bishop Egan actually liked to hear music, although people who feared that he might disapprove of it had to be persuaded to play the accordion or fiddle in his presence.[781] O'Sullivan played the piano at home, but what he played is unknown. He toyed with the idea of starting a choir in Kenmare, 'but the notion of being bored with their discord put me off.' After one excruciating performance elsewhere, he wrote that he often recalled a favourite phrase of Fr John Casey, which he translated as 'I'd rather hear an old stone ditch falling.' O'Sullivan added, 'It does not tell in English but in Irish one fancies he hears the stones rattling about his heels.' He thought that 'these country choirs do well for a while, and *that* a very short while.'[782] He had once heard the great contralto Marietta Alboni sing – possibly during the week in which he gave evidence to a select committee of the House of Commons in March 1849, for she appeared in London in Rossini's *Cinderella* then. He described her in his colourful way as 'a huge unsightly woman, whose beastly appearance nearly spoils the witchery of her beautiful voice'.[783]

His aesthetic interests extended beyond music. Accompanying his bishop on one of the recurrent visitations that involved the latter meeting parish priests and conducting the ceremony of confirmation with young people, O'Sullivan came in 1851 to Duagh, which lies about 9 kilometres south-east of Listowel in north Kerry. An old and simple church building stood there. He mocked the efforts of its parish priest, Tim Hartnett, to bring colour into the parishioners' lives. He had known Hartnett since they were boys in Tralee:

Heavens preserve us, what a chapel and how ludicrous the caricatures he had got painted on it – on the walls, every bit of them, ceiling, over the altar, the altar itself, the very panels of the little sacristy doors, every one possible spot on which an angel or a saint or a cherubim or anything in the shape of anything dreamed of in the Apocalypse could be stuffed – painted in all shapes and sizes in all the gaudiest colours of the rainbow all over the chapel [...] from Genesis to Revelations was there, no one subject that Father Tim's strolling painter did not touch upon.[784]

Nor did O'Sullivan pass up the opportunity to torture Hartnett a little. His behaviour was reminiscent of when he and his school friends used to bait new swimmers in Tralee, or when he and his adult friends descended on the scholarly Fr John Casey in the 1830s to play cards and pipes despite Casey's view of such activities. O'Sullivan went back from the church to Hartnett's house:

I began to praise the paintings in the chapel and to enquire for the artist to the no small satisfaction of Father Tim [Hartnett] who proceeded with the greatest complacency (poor simple man!) to tell me the whole negotiation, and from what chapel in Waterford the design had been taken when the bishop came in and peremptorily ordered every one of them to be whitewashed over as scandalous, wretched daubs. Father Tim saw immediately I had been humbugging him, looked daggers at me and in a spirit of the purest resignation and obedience said of course he would, but I am sure it will cost him many a bitter tear and pang.[785]

Hartnett was not off the hook yet. For O'Sullivan continued by praising the unfortunate priest's 'musical powers', suggesting that these qualified Hartnett to officiate as subdeacon at the opening of the cathedral in Killarney ('poor Tim was a second time imposed upon').[786]

Even as a clerical student in Maynooth, O'Sullivan had had an interest in the decoration of churches. While there, he had some commissions from the country, presumably for a small fee, to go into Dublin city and select new vestments for distant parishes. There was at that time, he wrote, just one establishment in the city for the sale or manufacture of vestments, run by the Misses Dowlings:

I never went there without being invited after making my purchases to a neighbouring room where a table was regularly laid out with luncheon, cold meat, cakes, wine etc. which seemed to

be a regular everyday matter-of-course business for all the
customers as well as for me, but I dare say they made the customers
pay for it! There are now [in the 1850s] six or seven large shops
in Dublin for the sake of vestments and church furniture.[787]

O'Sullivan believed that it was important for priests to know what
constituted quality in church art, 'I would venture to say that through
the whole diocese there is not even as much as one, one solitary priest,
competent to pronounce on the merits of a painting.'[788]

Bishop Egan asked him to take on the task of determining how each
church in the diocese should be fitted with a baptismal font. Priests
had hitherto made do with makeshift arrangements such as a basin in
the chapel, or even with bottles when going out on the stations.
O'Sullivan drew a prototype sketch of a font. A stone font that he
himself carved survives in Kenmare, although removed from the
church to a nearby garden, where it is used to support a statue of Mary.
He also designed a cupboard for vestments (to protect them from
smoking hearths), a tin box for wax candles (to deter mice and rats)
and a *cratis* (a portable confessional screen, from the Latin for 'grill'),
with sketches of these interleaved in his *Praxis parochi*.[789]

On 5 November 1851 O'Sullivan was admitted as a member of the
Kilkenny Archaeological Society.[790] Yet his reaction to the establishment
of a 'national reading room' in Kenmare was discouraging and even
snobbish. He was convinced that Fenians or other revolutionaries were
behind it and that going there might get young parishioners into
trouble. His paternalism was socially calibrated:

> I can understand lads destined for the bar, for [...] parliament,
> for clergy men, exercising themselves in debate [...] but for
> tradesmen and shopboys to turn to spouting is really too
> ridiculous [...] When chaps take up a subject for argument, what
> a better class would discuss dispassionately becomes a matter of
> vital importance and they become partisans.

That day, being in what a reporter described as one of his 'smashing
moods', the priest also let fly at *Moore's Melodies* and at people obsessed
with their ancestry – among other targets.[791]

Such paternalism was not uniquely Catholic, with Protestant
landlords sometimes employing 'moral agents' to patrol their tenants.
Lansdowne's agent William Steuart Trench ejected one married couple
on the grounds that they had 'committed fornication' by cohabiting
for a year before they wed.[792] O'Sullivan's attitude towards reading

presaged the strict censorship that became a feature of the Irish state after its foundation in 1922. Seventy years after O'Sullivan's death, Irish senators were to support strongly the banning of books, including Kate O'Brien's *Land of Spices* and Eric Cross's *The Tailor and Ansty*, the latter an innocuous account of fireside chat by an octogenarian tailor and his wife in rural west Cork.[793]

Hunting with the natives

William Steuart Trench, land agent for the Lansdowne estate, wrote a memorable description of a seal hunt on which he and his son Townsend Trench (who was to succeed him as Lansdowne's agent) and one John Clementi from London embarked in Kerry in September 1856. The hazardous expedition by sea into a deep cave opposite Scariff Island had the killing of a seal in its lair as its objective. To achieve this, they hired a boat crew of local Irish-speaking men. Once the three men and the crew had rowed to a certain point, some members of the party had to slip into the cold water and swim through a narrow passage in order to reach the seal. Of the three who did so, one was a local guide (or 'native', as Trench describes him) and the others were Townsend Trench and Clementi. Once deep inside the cave, Townsend Trench wielded his club and the seal's skull 'shattered like an eggshell'. Trench's son, 'trembling with excitement and cold', was exhausted when pulled into the boat afterwards.[794]

Trench senior's account of the expedition smacks of the big-game hunt, a favoured colonial activity. He makes the analogy himself when he writes at the end of his proud narrative of events – a narrative illustrated by six drawings by his son – that 'it is not necessary to go to Africa to obtain that excitement in sport which is now so greedily sought. It may be obtained much nearer home in the wild caves of Derrynane.' The dress of one 'native' puts him in mind of an 'American Indian chief'. The mastering of Gaelic Ireland and its habitats, as represented by the ideologue Macaulay and lived by the landlord class that Trench typified, was part of a broader colonial enterprise – even if Ireland's position within the United Kingdom has led to the authors of one twentieth-century study of environment and empire defensively excluding it from their work because it was 'essentially European in character'.[795] Kerry, experiencing continued emigration, was now home to a decreasing number of natives, but it remained a romantic destination for tourists and game-hunters and an asset for absentee landlords.

William Steuart Trench and Fr John

Trench was of a higher social class than James Hickson, whom he replaced, and more professional in his style of management. He was in favour of educating Protestants and Catholics together, as the government had sought to do when establishing the new national primary schools and the Queen's Colleges. He clashed with O'Sullivan when the priest invited nuns to found a school and convent in Kenmare. Some other Kerry towns had already seen such institutions established earlier in the nineteenth century.

Trench wished to improve the appearance of Kenmare in a number of ways. He transformed it to the extent that Lyne has described him as the 'architect' of the modern town – although it had assumed its basic shape during the first half of the nineteenth century.[796] Among his projects was the completion of St Patrick's Church, belonging to the Church of Ireland, at a commanding location between the town and the suspension bridge. Both his son Townsend and Denis Mahony's son Richard were later to turn their backs on that church and embrace the Plymouth Brethren. The elder Trench caused great resentment among settled Protestant families in Kenmare through the high-handed manner in which he allocated pews for seating within St Patrick's.[797]

Trench and O'Sullivan wrangled about the convent and church, the appropriate salary for O'Sullivan as chaplain to the workhouse, and the fencing of Catholic graveyards in the area – and even about the remains of the old Catholic chapel in Kenmare, which to the disgust of the priest, was being used as a ball alley. Had O'Sullivan forgotten that he had earlier written in his journal that he and his school friends 'played ball at the old chapel' in Tralee?[798] He and Trench also disagreed about the value of the prospective public reading room in the town.[799] Trench complained that O'Sullivan was 'endeavouring to hunt and worry' out of Kenmare both himself and his son Townsend.[800] Further details of the strained relationship between the agent and the parish priest during this period may be found in Gerard Lyne's discrete account of the Lansdowne estate in Kerry under W.S. Trench between 1849 and 1872,

Partly because of their business-like manner, but also because of a perceived lack of compassion, the Trench family was disliked locally. When Charles Russell MP, the future Lord Chief Justice of England and Wales (and the first Catholic ever to hold that office), visited the Lansdowne estate in Kerry in 1880, after O'Sullivan's death, he reported that he could find only one man in hundreds who praised in any way the Lansdowne management, and that man turned out to be 'a special pet and protégé of the Lansdowne bailiff'.[801]

The Kenmare convent school

Not content with building a dozen local national schools, O'Sullivan set about attracting nuns to Kenmare to form a convent, having seen in Dingle and elsewhere in the diocese what useful work nuns were doing.[802] In 1851 he broached the possibility with Bishop Egan, who demurred.[803] Nonetheless, funding was later found, and by 1859 some sisters of the Presentation Order arrived and started to teach local children. They would not consent to a schedule that O'Sullivan wished them to follow, and such was the level of disagreement that all but one of the nuns withdrew from Kenmare. He then persuaded seven sisters of the Poor Clare Order to come from Newry in Ulster. They set up a school that eventually had more than five hundred pupils on its rolls.[804] One of the nuns from Newry later suggested that the problem with the Presentation nuns was that 'their teaching was not considered up to the mark' by O'Sullivan.[805]

When the Poor Clare sisters began teaching, they first held classes in the big old brewery building that had served as an auxiliary workhouse during the famine, especially for children. Some idea of the conditions in which children had managed and sometimes died there may be gleaned from one nun's description of it when she arrived, 'It had a general appearance of instability which, however, fortunately proved deceptive; and though we daily expected a crash, it remained firm until it was taken down eventually to make way for the church [of the Most Holy Cross, built beside the convent].' She continued, 'The stairs, which led to a very large room where the classes were assembled, [were] held together by a most uncertain tenure, and required wary walking [...] The room, though very large, was exceedingly low and dark.' She thought that Fr John was 'all for the altar and the poor', and was a man of deep feeling that was 'for the most part hidden by a singular sternness and abruptness of manner'. He gave advice to the nuns 'in plain and emphatic terms – and those who knew him know how well he could use such language.'[806]

The new school opened at the convent on 1 May 1862. It was another bad year for crops, with more severe distress than at any time since 1847. Fr John was reported to have refused a public dinner because so many farmers were 'very much dispirited, many of them

smashed'.[807] So Catholics welcomed the opening of the nuns' school.
A narrative of the convent's foundation was published in 1876. It was
a posthumous tribute to its first mother superior, Mary O'Hagan, a
sister of Thomas O'Hagan; Thomas, in 1868, became the first Roman
Catholic to be appointed Lord Chancellor of Ireland since the reign
of James II. One suspects that the judge paid for the publication.[808]

Among the nuns who had come from Newry was Margaret Anna
Cusack, an author who was once an evangelical Protestant but
converted. She was horrified by the poverty in Kerry. Her writings
helped to finance the convent, and she became known as 'the Nun of
Kenmare'. She later left Ireland and became a Methodist. In recent
decades she has been portrayed as a proto-feminist and social reformer
persecuted by arrogant superiors; alternatively, she has been perceived
as a self-aggrandising neurotic.[809] In her autobiography, she suggested
that there might have been a certain strategic reason why O'Sullivan
went north and ensured that the nuns from Newry came to Kenmare:

> Father John, as Archdeacon O'Sullivan was always called, had a
> weakness, who has not? He saw that Miss O'Hagan's brother was
> a rising man, and rising rapidly. He was not then a 'Lord', but
> he was on a fair way to become one. It was the policy of the
> English government to advance a few men like Mr. O'Hagan,
> who had just enough nationality to be popular to a certain extent
> with the Irish people, and who had quite sufficient care for their
> own advancement to make their nationality subservient to their
> personal interests. Miss O'Hagan was then just the person to suit
> the good archdeacon's views in every way, and as he was a man
> of business and quick action, he decided to come himself [to
> Newry] and secure his object.[810]

The new convent was an asset to the area and, like many others in
Ireland then, helped to improve the knowledge and skills of a Catholic
population that had long been oppressed. In 1867 Sir Patrick Keenan,
Chief Inspector of National Schools and himself a Catholic, pointed
out that in its first five years the convent had 'already sent forth,
through its monitorship, twelve competent – indeed accomplished –
teachers to do service in National Schools'. This was exactly equal to
the aggregate number of female teachers that had issued from the
monitorships of model schools in a dozen named Irish towns during
the previous twelve years. Keenan was responding to Presbyterian
criticism of the influence of Catholic institutions on the provision of

education nationally. The growing number of Catholic schools throughout the country helped to ensure that education would remain denominational in Ireland.[811]

Meanwhile, O'Sullivan was involved in a wrangle about both the reduction in size of the area allocated at the workhouse for saying Mass and the moving of his special altar there into a press or cupboard. Changes had been made to accommodate troops in part of the workhouse, and in 1867 O'Sullivan published the extensive correspondence on the matter. He believed that he was defending the dignity and religious rights of the paupers.[812]

Holy Cross Church opens

John O'Sullivan – on whom, in 1857, his bishop conferred the honorary title 'Archdeacon of Aghadoe'[813] – lived to see the completion of a fine new Catholic church at Kenmare, beside the convent. He managed to have it erected and fitted at no financial burden to his parishioners, thanks to his deft use of private donations and diocesan trusts. It was the crowning achievement of a life partly spent building schools and chapels. Its opening in 1864 was a remarkable and striking moment. A local history group has published a fine illustrated volume commemorating its one hundred and fiftieth anniversary. Three of its stained-glass windows feature representations of St John the Baptist, patron saint of earlier places of worship in Kenmare and Killowen. The Star of David features prominently in its wall and floor tiles, perhaps an intended tribute to those Jewish bankers of the British Association in London – especially David Salomons – who had welcomed O'Sullivan to their meetings and sent vital aid to Kenmare in 1847. Some parishioners believe that the black horse with a red bridle held by a Roman soldier close to the crucified Christ – in the big window behind the main altar – represents famine. That is how the apocalyptic black horse in the Book of Revelation (6: 1–8) is often understood. The red of the bridle is also the colour of the fluid with which workhouse clothing in Kenmare was marked.[814]

O'Sullivan had a long-standing interest in church fixtures and design, and he admired the work of the Pugins architects. Unable to afford certain items for Holy Cross at their first asking price in London, he persuaded Kerry craftsmen to make copies of old pieces elsewhere. Unfortunately, two of the most striking examples were later removed unnecessarily during a modernisation that followed the Second Vatican Council. One was the pulpit, which, as a correspondent wrote when the church opened, 'as a work of art, to us appears the gem [...] a most beautiful and intricate work of art'. The writer explained that O'Sullivan, relying on Dollman's *Examples of Ancient Pulpits Existing in England* (published in London in 1849), had had the pulpit and its stairs made by 'native tradesmen' for less than a third of the cost that had been estimated in England. They were modelled after an example in Somerset dated about 1450. The other item removed had hung in the baptistery, being a 'most remarkable' wooden cover said to be based on one in Norfolk from the reign of Richard II, 'this exquisite piece of carving was executed in Tralee, at the establishment of Mr John Murphy, in the Square'. Murphy was a cabinet-maker and the husband of Fr John O'Sullivan's first cousin Anne Walsh (and the great-great-grandfather of this present author).[815]

On the spire of this new church, O'Sullivan placed a metal cock. The cock was a symbol of the resurrection of Jesus, commonly used in the decoration of penal crosses when people's faith had been suppressed by law and by force.[816]

Holy Cross Church was consecrated on the feast day of the Exaltation of the Cross, 14 September 1864, one of the two annual feast days dedicated to remembering the cross on which Jesus was crucified. On those feast days there had once been pattern celebrations at old Kenmare cemetery, across the sound. For the first time, to mark the opening, a High Mass was now celebrated in Kenmare. The impression that the singing of 'Mozart's Mass no. 12' made on parishioners unaccustomed to hearing such a work performed locally may be imagined. A choir was accompanied by the singing of children from the convent school.[817] Prominent among guests was that 'rising man' Thomas O'Hagan, brother of the Kenmare convent's mother superior and now both Attorney-General for Ireland and a member of parliament for Tralee. Afterwards, at dinner in the Lansdowne Arms, he made a speech praising O'Sullivan.[818]

O'Sullivan brought to the new building the statues of Moses and Aaron that had stood in Kenmare chapel on Shelburne Street; they were erected on each side of the high altar.[819] The biblical tale of the two brothers and patriarchs may have had a special meaning for O'Sullivan, a man whose own brother could have been more of a help and less of a hindrance to him. A photograph of O'Sullivan in later life, with patriarchal beard and wearing vestments, survives.[820]

Two chiefs: J.A. Froude and Oscar Wilde

From 1868 until 1871, the English historian James Anthony Froude rented Derreen House on the Beara Peninsula; it was situated on former O'Sullivan land that Lord Lansdowne repossessed in 1856 from a relation of the Mac Finin Dubh Ó Súilleabháins, who had lived there for centuries. Froude had first visited Kenmare about 1840 and now wrote sentimentally of changes wrought by a great famine that he thought had paralysed if not extinguished 'the humour and the fun which made the boy that carried your game-bag, or fishing-basket the most charming of companions'.[821] He was in the process of completing his controversial three-volume *apologia* entitled *The English in Ireland in the Eighteenth Century*. He is said to have done much of his writing near Derreen by an ancient *gallán*, or standing stone, overlooking Kilmackillogue and Kenmare Bay, at a spot that became known as 'Froude's seat'.[822]

Froude frowned on those descendants of Cromwellian and other English settlers whom he termed 'habitual absentees' from their estates in Ireland. This was an implicit criticism of the Lansdownes themselves. Such absentees stunted, he thought, 'the small beginnings of civilised life' that had been made, 'and so long as their rents were regularly paid, they asked no questions, and troubled themselves with no responsibilities.' Froude cited Macaulay in praising the 'brilliant defence' made by Petty's English settlers against Irish 'insurgents' at Kenmare Bay; in common with many of his contemporaries, he believed that the English had a right and even a moral duty to attempt to control and 'civilise' other peoples. He sought to justify the treatment of Ireland by colonisers such as Sir William Petty – while chiding settler descendants for being too weak.[823] He thought that the English generally had not gone far enough in implementing their Irish colonial project; as Oscar Wilde put it, 'Mr Froude admits the martyrdom of Ireland, but regrets that the martyrdom was not completely carried out. His ground of complaint against the Executioner is not his trade but his bungling.'[824] Although Froude had earlier referred to 'English prejudice and English ignorance' towards Ireland and condemned England's narrow commercial exploitation of the island, critics have frequently seen him as prejudiced against both Catholicism and the Gaelic Irish.[825]

Froude's later novel set on the Beara Peninsula was entitled *The Two Chiefs of Dunboy: or, An Irish Romance of the Last Century* and appeared in London in 1889. Its theme was the clash between the descendant of a

Cromwellian settler family and a local Gaelic O'Sullivan chief whose character was based on Murtaí Óg Ó Súilleabháin (c.1710–1754). The settler too had a real prototype: John Puxley, who took up his abode at Dunboy, the former O'Sullivan Beare castle, in about 1730. Daphne du Maurier's 1943 novel *Hungry Hill* would later be partly based on Puxley's descendants.[826]

Reviewing Froude's novel for the *Pall Mall Gazette*, Oscar Wilde dismissed it as 'often false in its lights and exaggerated in its shadows'. He summed it up:

> The interest of the tale, such as it is, centres round two men, Colonel Goring and Morty Sullivan, the Cromwellian and the Celt [...] The first represents Mr. Froude's cure for Ireland. He is a resolute 'Englishman, with strong Nonconformist tendencies', who plants an industrial colony on the coast of Kerry, and has deep-rooted objections to that illicit trade with France which in the last century was the sole method by which the Irish people were enabled to pay their rents to their absentee landlords. Colonel Goring bitterly regrets that the Penal Laws against the Catholics are not rigorously carried out.

Wilde added that England in the eighteenth century had 'tried to govern Ireland with an insolence that was intensified by race hatred and religious prejudice', and during the nineteenth sought to rule Ireland 'with a stupidity that is aggravated by good intentions'.[827]

O'Sullivan's death

In November 1874 John O'Sullivan died in bed, in the shadow of the new convent and church.[828] He had lived long enough to be laid out in his Holy Cross Church. Two photographs of his remains in the coffin were placed in the United Kingdom's national archives.[829] Mary Hickson, the Protestant and unionist Kerry historian, had her second series of extracts from old records passing through the press at the time of O'Sullivan's death; she thought it would be worthwhile to have the printer insert a tribute to him at the end of that volume, noting especially his provision of clothing and food to poor children in latter years and concluding that 'Archdeacon O'Sullivan was on the whole an excellent specimen of a type of Irish priest, with something of the virtues and faults of a Columba in him, now it is to be feared nearly stamped out in Ireland.' She praised him for building national schools, not least because it gave the order of Christian Brothers no 'settlement' within his parish, and she wrote that 'throughout his long life [he] has been most deservedly respected by men of all creeds and classes in his native county. His exertions for his flock in the disastrous famine years were immense, and saved innumerable lives.'[830]

Protestant gentry and clergymen were among those who attended his funeral. Bishop Moriarty delivered a eulogy, referring to O'Sullivan's achievements in having founded both the convent and Holy Cross Church, and praising 'his great exertions in the cause of education, religion, and charity'. The bishop gracefully acknowledged that O'Sullivan had been chosen by a majority of the clergy of Kerry to become bishop, adding that 'while the burden of office had been cast on himself, theirs was the gain, in Father John continuing amongst them.'[831]

Two years earlier the unionist Moriarty had found himself on the wrong side of history when, at a Kerry by-election in 1872, he opposed the successful Home Rule candidate Rowland Ponsonby Blennerhassett.[832] The rising Home Rule and land reform movements reflected a changing balance of power between classes and religious denominations in Ireland; over the following half century, these changes led to the victory of Sinn Féin at the general election of 1918 and the foundation of the Irish Free State in 1922. So opposed to land reform was Henry Petty-Fitzmaurice, 5th Marquess of Lansdowne, that in July 1880 he resigned from Gladstone's government in protest at the Compensation for Disturbance (Ireland) Bill. This proposed a modest measure of protection for tenants – or 'a little morsel of justice to us', as one Kerryman reportedly put it.[833]

Burials

In the area surrounding Kenmare Bay, as elsewhere in Ireland, are scattered the unmarked burial places of children once excluded from Christian cemeteries because they died before being baptised in a church. In the late 1860s Froude came across one such *cillín* near Lansdowne's Derreen House as he wandered up a glen on the Beara Peninsula that had been densely inhabited before the great famine 'and had suffered terribly in consequence'. Just one fourth of the former population remained there, 'Ruined cottages in all directions showed where human creatures had once multiplied like rabbits in a warren.' Froude found the *cillín* adjacent to an ancient *ráth*, of which he saw ten or twelve in the glen:

We pass a singular mound covered with trees at the roadside, with a secluded field behind it sprinkled over with hawthorns. The field is the burying place of the babies that die unbaptised, unconsecrated by the Church, but hallowed by sentiment, and treated seemingly with more reverence than the neglected graveyard.[834]

It is not known how many children died unbaptised out in the countryside during the great famine. The remains of some children who were baptised and who died in Kenmare workhouse were placed in the famine pit in old Kenmare cemetery. In 1975 a local historian, Danny Moriarty, erected there a simple memorial to all buried in it. Four decades later a low wall was constructed around the pit, or plot, with children of schools across the old Kenmare Union area contributing the stones used to build it.

John O'Sullivan's remains were buried in Holy Cross Church, beneath an altar inscribed in his memory.[835]

18

Kenmare Today

Kenmare survived the vicissitudes of the nineteenth century and is today an established centre of business and tourism.

Founded in the late 1700s, the small town saw its slow growth stunted by a great famine in the 1840s and its agricultural hinterland subsequently drained by decades of emigration. Once almost overwhelmed by desperate and starving people who thronged to its workhouse for assistance, and some of whom dropped dead on its streets, Kenmare now presents a very different aspect. Its pavements are lined with busy shops, pubs and restaurants. Between Sheen Falls and Sneem, a wide range of accommodation for visitors still includes the town's Lansdowne Arms Hotel, where Fr John O'Sullivan sometimes dined.

In the 1890s the Great Southern Hotel was built to coincide with the arrival of the railway in Kenmare. Its extensive refurbishing and reopening as the luxurious Park Hotel during the 1980s was a sign of the Republic of Ireland's growing prosperity when national development programmes and membership of the European Economic Community began to bear fruit. Migration has been substantially reversed, with Kenmare now, for example, having its own Polish community.

Kenmare's history is a story of survival, and the author of this volume – with the help of local people – has explored, in particular, events between 1600 and 1900. The fact that those living in the area care about its past is reflected too, since 2013, in the annual publication of the *Kenmare Chronicle*. Its issues have mainly included pictorial and narrative records of Kenmare in the twentieth century, while also recalling the role that its people have played overseas in global events such as two world wars.

Kenmare was of course touched by the Irish War of Independence and by the civil war that subsequently erupted in 1922. The bitterness of those years left an unpleasant aftertaste. But there was healing too, and the 6th Marquess of Lansdowne – great-grandson of the 3rd Lord Lansdowne, local Kerry landlord and leader of the House of Lords with whom O'Sullivan dealt during the great famine – became a senator of the new Irish Free State in the 1920s.

Even during the dark 1840s, Kerry had a range of local newspapers that included the *Kerry Examiner, Kerry Evening Post* and *Tralee Chronicle.* Today, titles such as the *Kerryman* and *Kerry's Eye* continue that tradition. The monthly *Kenmare News* also appears. Today such papers are available not only in print but also online, serving Kenmare people who work abroad as well as the descendants of emigrants from the area.

Visitors to Kenmare can begin their exploration with a trip to the town's heritage centre, located where the court sat in Fr John O'Sullivan's day. The centre includes a small exhibition of lace. Embroidery and lacemaking by local young women were first encouraged by Eliza Herbert, Fr John O'Sullivan and the order of Poor Clare nuns. The educational infrastructure that O'Sullivan and the nuns and others built at primary and secondary level contributed significantly to Kerry's advancement and became part of the foundation of what is now a complex national educational system. Without the efforts and achievements of clergy such as Fr John O'Sullivan, the impact of the great famine would have been even worse and the creation of a sustainable independent Irish state even more problematic than it was.

As the independent state found its feet, new social services gradually emerged. After 1921 county homes and county hospitals were built. Local councils amalgamated and subsumed the functions of the poor law union districts. The old Kenmare Union workhouse on the outskirts of the town was demolished. On 31 January 1936, the *Kerry News* reported from Kenmare, 'That the old Union is almost gone. That it is replaced by a very pretty hospital.' The opening of that district hospital early the following month was celebrated as a modernising initiative. If anything was said at the opening ceremony about the paupers who once walked the site of the workhouse on which the 'cottage hospital' now stood, it went unreported. The Irish Free State had its own problems.

The *Kerry News* also reported from Kenmare that day, 'That the poor are hard hit. That a large number of our young people are leaving for England. That they can get nothing to do at home.' People did not wish to dwell on past miseries. On 11 April 1936 a Tralee paper, *The Liberator,* informed its readers that a suggestion by the Kerry Board of Health and Public Assistance that 'certain of the buildings of the old Kenmare workhouse be not demolished' was brushed aside by the relevant government minister, 'who saw no reason for altering the contract' in order to retain structures not already removed. The current mood had earlier found expression in a reference to similar remnants of the workhouse in Tralee, where a county hospital was erected; on 25 April 1933 *The Liberator* noted that the secretary of the Kerry Board of Health had said that 'If the relics, as well as the taint of the old workhouse are to disappear, the front buildings must be demolished and the forbidding high wall in front be removed.' Nevertheless, the former fever hospital adjacent to Kenmare workhouse was spared, and became a private residence.

Kenmare workhouse and fever hospital can be seen on the extreme right of a photograph, taken about the year 1900, that appears on the front of this book. Invisible and almost forgotten except for a memorial in old Kenmare cemetery are the paupers who once sought refuge there, their shame exacerbated by red dye marked on workhouse clothing lest inmates abscond with it. The old woman whom Theresa Rose Marrable sketched at Kenmare about 1880 (see Fig. 11) may well have been a resident in Kenmare Union workhouse during the great famine, her furtive look over her shoulder a haunted backward glance. Many of those who lived through the 1840s did not relish recalling what they had witnessed. For the famine was a traumatic event, and after it the population of Ireland continued to decline until the 1960s. The population of the island had stood at 45 per cent that of Britain by the 1840s, but it is barely 10 per cent that of Britain today. Not just famine but also general economic and political underdevelopment made statehood a mighty challenge.

There is no shame in being poor due to circumstances beyond one's control, and the story of Kenmare's past is Ireland's story. It is that of a whole nation engulfed, to various degrees, by misfortune – as any nation may be. Fr John O'Sullivan, as we have seen, told a select committee of members of parliament at Westminster that the poor should not have to rely on the transient good will and exertions of individuals such as himself but that they ought to have 'an established right to relief'. The challenge to which he rose in his own unique way in trying to ameliorate the circumstances of the very poor and the desperately ill is a universal and recurring challenge. His story and that of Kenmare are testimony to a people's ultimate survival and recovery.

Fig. 11–Old Woman in Kenmare. By Theresa Rose Marrable (1862–1936). Private collection. *Thought to have been drawn about 1880.*

Acknowledgements

I am grateful to the following, amongst others, for their assistance: Ann McCabe Hickey of Killowen, Kenmare, without whose help this book would not have been completed. Retired from teaching in Tuosist, she has maintained a keen interest in history that her own teacher Sister Philomena McCarthy inspired in her in her youth. Ann generously shared her knowledge and library with this author. Thanks also to Tom Hickey; Jerry and Geraldine Riney; Caitríona McCarthy O'Neill; Pat Quinlan; Kathlyn O'Brien; Anne-Marie Cleary; Sister Concepta of the Sisters of Saint Clare, Kenmare; Fr Tom Crean; Mary O'Neill of Blackwater; Síle O'Shea; Rachael McHugh; Prof. John Breslin of NUI, Galway; Myles McCionnaith; Conor Graham; and the late Nial Osborough.

I am also grateful to the president of St Patrick's College, Maynooth, for permission to reproduce the portrait of Domhnall O'Sullivan Beare; Holy Cross 150 History Group; Fr Nicholas Flynn, Kerry Diocesan Secretary, and his team, who were very obliging in facilitating my special Covid-compliant access to diocesan archives in Killarney for the purpose of writing this book; Michael Lynch, archivist, Kerry Library, who also overcame Covid difficulties to share indispensible minutes of the Kenmare workhouse; the late Annette Murphy-Kenny and her late daughter Kathleen Kenny-Kelly, who kept in my father's family a handwritten copy of a printed letter from Fr John O'Sullivan that sparked my interest in this subject; the late Danny Moriarty and Liam Cousins, whose work to preserve the history of Kenmare and of its paupers has not been forgotten; Bernie Metcalfe, National Library of Ireland; Sara W. Duke, Curator, Popular & Applied Graphic Art, Prints and Photographs Division, Library of Congress; Steve Taylor, for his 'Views of the Famine' website; and of course Ronan Colgan at Eastwood Books for his unflagging support.

As ever, the staff of my local library in Bray were also helpful – as were those of the National Library of Ireland, King's Inns Dublin, the Royal Irish Academy, Newcastle University, Dublin City University, Trinity College Dublin, Maynooth University and University College Dublin. My wife Catherine Curran too deserves thanks for her support, and my sons Oisín, Conor and Sam for their encouragement.

Bibliography

Manuscripts

Bowood House
Most of the Lansdowne political papers are now in the British Library, but the family's estate and family papers remain at its Bowood House in Wiltshire, England. Unfortunately, the archives are described by Bowood as not fully catalogued (and no catalogue is available electronically) and the estate charges a notable £200.00 plus £40.00 VAT access fee per six-hour 'day' – plus an administration fee 'added to cover the time spent in searching for material requested' of £56.00 per hour plus VAT, and a registration fee of £40.00.

Prof. Tyler Anbinder wrote ('From famine to Five Points', p. 365, n. 34) that due to the cost of searching it, he dispensed with the archive by relying on other sources. While random and perhaps necessarily lengthy searches in an archive that has been only partly catalogued might yield relevant documents, the present author too – for practical reasons relating to uncertain cost and Covid restrictions, and because he found adequate resources elsewhere – did not visit Bowood.

Capuchin Archives
CA/FM/RES/1/9: Copy letter of Fr. Theobald Mathew OSFC to David O'Meara, his secretary, affirming that he is attending to his sick brother in Kenmare, Co. Kerry. 30 Jan. 1848. Typescript, 1p. Online: http://www.capuchinfranciscans.ie/wp-content/uploads/2018/07/5.-Descriptive-List-Web-Fr.-Theobald-Mathew-Research-and-Commemorative-Papers.pdf (consulted 7 March 2021).

Friends Historical Library, Dublin
Report of Edmund Richards and Edward Fitt, 5–6 May 1847, as transcribed by Kay Caball at https://mykerryancestors.com/great-famine-kerry-1847/ (consulted 7 March 2021).

Kerry County Library, Tralee
Kenmare BGMB: Kenmare Union Board of Guardians Records: Minute Books, 1840–1921 (119 vols).

Kerry Diocesan Archives
Archdeacon John O'Sullivan papers. These principally include journals, written between 1843 and 1852. Although some researchers give these as 'diaries', they are here named as O'Sullivan himself named them:
(1) 'Random Recollections and Effusions' ('Recollections'), 9 Oct. 1843–10 July 1849 (270 pages, unpaginated, including a short opening narrative of his early life). Possibly assembled by transcribing original but no longer extant dated notes, with additions.
(2) 'Notes of a Visitation in Kerry by a Queer Fellow' ('Notes'), 2 vols, 19 July 1850–9 Aug. 1855 [and] 'typescript of same by Canon John McKenna in 1 volume'.
(3) *Praxis parochi*, 1849–1852. 2 vols. Advice to young priests and personal notes and observations.

National Archives (UK)
COPY 1/27/423. Photograph of the remains of Archdeacon O'Sullivan lying in state in the Roman Catholic Chapel, Kenmare.

National Library of Ireland
MS GO 107, Grants and Confirmations E: 1803–48, pp. 15–16, 'Hickson Mahony'.
MS 24,445, Reports of Dingle Colony: Charles Gayer, 'My Dear Christian Friends' (Dingle, 26 Sept. 1839).
MS 2022, British [Relief] Association Minute Book 1847–48.
MS 35,700/2 and 4, NLI McCarthy Papers, Material relating to Mary Downing ('Christabel').
MS 28,901. Ulster King of Arms. James Hampston, notes on an O'Sullivan lineage.

Newcastle University, UK
Trevelyan (Charles Edward) Archive. Letters to O'Sullivan:
CET/1/12 p.209–211 (25 Feb. 1847) Cause of delay of 'Adventure' – Sir H. Pigot. To remain on station at Kenmare.
CET/1/13 p.115–116 (20 March 1847) Proposal to sell seed to proprs.

on credit.

CET/1/14 p.162 (29 April 1847) To Mr Rathbone – Balance of produce of seed.

CET/1/14 p.164–165 (30 April 1847) Establishment of depot at Kenmare.

CET/1/15 p.297–8 (6 July 1847) Supplies for sick under the Provisions of the Fever Act.

CET/1/18 p.153 (7 Dec. 1847) Effective operation of poor law and Kenmare Store.

CET/1/18 p.186–187 (13 Dec. 1847) Fund of the British Relief Association: approval of their present mode of applying it.

CET/1/21 p.264 (15 June 1848) Wish to be examined as a witness before Poor Law Committee.

CET/1/22 p.158–159 (12 Aug. 1848) Site for School at Bear Island (one sentence acknowledging an application).

CET/1/23 p.237 (19 Dec. 1848) Public document shall be sent.

CET/1/26 p.239 (24 June 1850) Remission on legacy duty on convent money.

CET/1/27 p.186 (2 May 1851) No Irish Blue Book published this session.

CET/1/28 p.193 (25 Feb. 1852) Sum due by Mr Byrne.

CET/1/30 p.167 (20 Dec. 1852) O'Sullivan's sister-in-law's passage for Grenada.

Royal Irish Academy

Ordnance Survey of Ireland: Letters, Kerry, 1841, 14/C/30/14 (ii). Online: http://www.askaboutireland.ie/aai-files/assets/ebooks/OSI-Letters/KERRY_14%20C%2030.pdf (consulted 7 March 2021).

Trinity College Dublin

'The Kenmare Committee', J.D. White Collection of slip ballads, Trinity College Dublin, at https://digitalcollections.tcd.ie/collections/sf2685934?locale=en (consulted 7 March 2021).

University College Dublin

National Folklore Collection, The Schools' Collection, at https://www.ucd.ie/folklore/en/collections/schoolscollectionduchas/ (consulted 7 March 2021).

Parliamentary papers and other official publications

Accounts and Papers of the House of Commons, 54 (1847–1848): Relief of Distress (Ireland).

Calendar of Convert Rolls 1703–1838, ed. Eileen O'Byrne (Dublin: Irish Manuscript Commission, 2005).

Correspondence from July 1846 to January 1847 relating to the Measures Adopted for the Relief of Distress in Ireland.

Dev. Comm. Ev., part 2: Report from Her Majesty's Commissioners of Inquiry into the State of the Law and Practice in Respect to the Occupation of Land in Ireland. Minutes of Evidence. part 2, H.C. 1845 (616) xx.

Eighth Report of the Commissioners of Irish Education Inquiry: Roman Catholic College of Maynooth (London, June 1827).

H.C. Deb. and *H.L. Deb.*, Hansard, *House of Commons/Lords Debates.*

Papers Relating to Proceedings for the Relief of Distress and State of the Unions and Workhouses in Ireland, 5th series (London, 1848).

Parliamentary Papers 52 (19 Jan.–23 July 1847).

Register Book of Marriages, Parish of St George, Hanover Square, Middlesex, 1824–1837 (London, 1897).

Report of the Commissioners Appointed to Take the Census of Ireland for the Year 1841 (Dublin: Thom, 1843).

Report from the Select Committee on Bribery and Intimidation at Elections, together with Extracts from the Minutes of Evidence Shewing the Intimidation Practised by the Priests in Ireland (London, [1837])

Reports from Commissioners: Poor Laws (Ireland), Appendix E (1836).

[*Select Committee 1849*] *Reports from Select Committees of the House of Commons and Evidence, Poor Laws (Ireland)*, vol. 33, *Third Report, with Minutes of Evidence* (London: HMSO, 1849, and http://www.dippam.ac.uk/eppi/documents/12537/page/155874).

Books and articles

'An anti-conspirator', *Supplement to the Trials of the Rev. Robert Morritt* (Cork: *s.n.*, 1819).

Anbinder, Tyler, *Five Points: The 19th Century New York City Neighbourhood That Invented Tap Dance, Stole Elections, and Became the World's Most Notorious Slum* (New York and London: Plume, 2002).

Anbinder, Tyler, 'From famine to Five Points: Lord Lansdowne's Irish tenants encounter North America's most notorious slum', *American Historical Review*, vol. 107, no. 2 (April 2002), pp. 351–87.

Andrews, K.R., N.P. Canny and P.E.H. Hair (eds), *The Westward Enterprise: English Activities in Ireland, the Atlantic and America 1480–*

1650 (Detroit: Wayne State University Press, 1979).

Anon. [Mary Francis Cusack], *In Memoriam Mary O'Hagan: Abbess and Foundress of the Convent of Poor Clares Kenmare* (London: Burns, 1876).

Anon. (ed.), *Persecution of Protestants in the Year 1845, As Detailed in a Full and Correct Report of the Trial at Tralee on Thursday, March 20, 1845 for a Libel on the Rev. Charles Gayer*, based on reports in the *Tralee Chronicle* (Dublin: Philip Dixon Hardy, 1845).

Anon., 'Suspension bridge over Kenmare Sound', *The Civil Engineer and Architect's Journal* (Oct. 1837–Dec. 1838), pp. 316–17.

Anon., 'Theiner's works: materials for Irish history', *The Dublin Review*, vol. 18 (March 1845), pp. 205–30.

Anon. [John Wilson Croker?], *A Sketch of the State of Ireland, Past and Present* (Dublin: Mahon, 1808).

Aubrey, John, *'Brief Lives', Chiefly of Contemporaries, Set Down by John Aubrey, Between the Years 1669 & 1696*, ed. Andrew Clark, 2 vols (Oxford: Clarendon, 1898).

B.B.G., 'Kilcrohane', *Kerry Archaeological Mag.*, vol. 3, no. 14 (1915), pp. 119–22.

Beckett, J.C., *The Making of Modern Ireland 1603–1923*, 2nd ed. (London: Faber, 1981).

Beinart, William, and Lotte Hughes, *Environment and Empire* (Oxford: Oxford University Press, 2007)

Bennett, William, *Narrative of a Recent Journey of Six Weeks in Ireland* (London: Charles Gilpin, 1847).

Berger and Spoerer, 'Economic crises and the European revolutions of 1848', *Journal of Economic History*, vol. 61, no. 2 (2001), pp. 293–326.

Binns, Jonathan, *The Miseries and Beauties of Ireland*, 2 vols (London: Longman, 1837).

Bland, F.C., 'Description of a remarkable building, on the north side of Kenmare River, commonly called Staigue Fort', *RIA Transactions*, 14 (1825), pp. 17–27.

Borlase, William C., *The Dolmens of Ireland*, 3 vols (London: Chapman and Hall, 1897).

Bowen, Desmond, *The Protestant Crusade in Ireland 1800–70* (Dublin: Gill and Macmillan, 1978).

Bowen, Desmond, *Souperism: Myth or Reality? A Study of Catholics and Protestants during the Great Famine* (Cork: Mercier Press, 1970).

British Association for the Relief of The Extreme Distress in Scotland and Wales, *Report with Correspondence etc.* (London: British

Association, 1849).

Breen, Colin, *The Gaelic Lordship of the O'Sullivan Beare: A Landscape Cultural History* (Dublin: Four Courts Press, 2005).

Bric, Maurice J. (ed.), *Kerry: History and Society* (Dublin: Geography Publications, 2020).

Brunton, Deborah, *The Politics of Vaccination: Practice and Policy in England, Wales, Ireland and Scotland 1800–1874* (Rochester, NY: University of Rochester Press, 2008).

Burke, Bernard, *A Genealogical and Heraldic History of the Landed Gentry of Great Britain and Ireland*, 6th ed., 2 vols (London: Harrison, 1879).

Burke, Helen, *The People and the Poor Law in Nineteenth Century Ireland* (Littlehampton, UK: Women's Education Bureau, 1987).

Burke, John, *A General and Heraldic Dictionary of the Peerage and Baronetage of the British Empire*, 12th ed. (London: Henry Colburn, 1850).

Burke, John, *A General and Heraldic Dictionary of the Peerage and Baronetage of the British Empire*, 5th ed. (London: Henry Colburn, 1838).

Caball, Kay Moloney, *The Kerry Girls: Emigration and the Earl Grey Scheme* (Dublin: History Press, 2014).

Caball, Marc, *Kerry, 1600–1730: The Emergence of a British Atlantic County* (Dublin: Four Courts, 2017).

Carleton, William, *Traits and Stories of the Irish Peasantry*, 2 vols (Dublin: William Curry, 1830 and new edition 1843–44).

Carr, John, *The Stranger in Ireland: A Tour in the Southern and Western Parts of That Country in the Year 1805* (Hartford, CT: Hudson, Goodwin *et al.*, 1806).

Carroll, William George, *The Lansdowne Irish Estates and Sir William Petty*, 2nd ed. (Dublin: Gill, 1881)

Chatterton, H.G., *Rambles in the South of Ireland During the Year 1838*, 2nd ed., 2 vols (London: Saunders and Otley, 1839).

Cole, Grenville, *Memoir and Map of Localities of Minerals of Economic Importance and Metalliferous Mines in Ireland* (Dublin: Stationery Office, 1922).

Cowman, Des, 'Two Kerry lead-silver mines: Kenmare and Castlemain', *Journal of the Mining Heritage Trust of Ireland*, vol. 8 (2008), pp. 39–46.

Connolly, S.J., *Religion and Society in Nineteenth-Century Ireland* (Dundalk: Dundalgan Press, 1985).

Connolly, S.J., *Priests and People in Pre-Famine Ireland 1780–1845* (Dublin:

Gill & Macmillan, 1982).

Corish, Patrick J., *Maynooth College 1795–1995* (Dublin: Gill & Macmillan, 1995).

Crawford, E. Margaret (ed.), *Famine – The Irish Experience, 900–1900: Subsistence Crises and Famines in Ireland* (Edinburgh: John Donald, 1989).

Crolly, George, *A Life of the Most Rev. Doctor Crolly, Archbishop of Armagh* (Dublin: Duffy, 1807).

Crowley, John, W.J. Smyth and Mike Murphy (eds), *Atlas of the Great Irish Famine* (Cork: Cork University Press, 2012).

Crowley, John and John Sheehan, *The Iveragh Peninsula: A Cultural Atlas of the Ring of Kerry* (Cork: Cork University Press, 2009).

Cusack, Margaret Anna [also known as Mary Francis], *The Nun of Kenmare: An Autobiography* (London: Hodder and Stoughton, 1889).

Cusack, Mary F. ('The Nun of Kenmare' as 'Sister Mary Francis Clare'), *The Life of Father Mathew: The People's Soggarth Aroon* (Dublin: James Duffy, 1874).

Cusack, Mary F. (as 'The Nun of Kenmare'), *A History of the Kingdom of Kerry* (London: Longmans, Green, 1871).

Daly, Mary, *Pure Lust: Elemental Feminist Philosophy* (London: The Women's Press, 1984).

de Brún, Pádraig, 'A Census of the Parish of Ferriter, January 1835', *Jn. Kerry Arch. and Hist. Soc.*, vol. 7 (1974), pp. 37–70.

de Brún, Pádraig, 'John Windele and Father John Casey: Windele's visit to Inis Tuaisceart in 1838', *Jn. Kerry Arch. and Hist. Soc.*, vol. 7 (1974), pp. 71–196.

Delay, Cara, 'Meddlers amongst us: women, priests, and authority in Famine-era Ireland', in Christine Kinealy, Jason King and Ciarán Reilly (eds), *Women and the Great Hunger* (Hamden, CT: Quinnipiac University Press, 2016), pp. 71–82.

Delay, Cara, 'The devotional revolution on the local level: parish life in post-famine Ireland', (U.S.) *Catholic Historian*, vol. 22, no. 3, special Irish edition (2004), pp. 41–60.

de Selincourt, Ernest, *The Letters of William and Dorothy Wordsworth*, ed. Alan Hill, 2nd ed., 5 vols (Oxford: Oxford University Press, 1979).

DIB: Dictionary of Irish Biography, ed. James McGuire and James Quinn for the Royal Irish Academy (Cambridge, UK: Cambridge University Press, 2009), with online updates.

DNB: Dictionary of National Biography (Oxford University Press, online).

Doheny, Michael, *The Felon's Track* (Dublin: Gill, 1914).

Donnelly, James S., *Captain Rock: The Irish Agrarian Rebellion of 1821–1824* (Wisconsin: University of Wisconsin Press, 2009).

Donnelly, James S., 'The administration of relief, 1847–51', in W.E. Vaughan (ed.), *A New History of Ireland, v: Ireland under the Union part I, 1801–70* (Oxford: Clarendon, 1989), pp. 316–31.

Downey, Declan, 'Insights into Kerry and the Habsburg Imperium, *c.* 1500–*c.* 1800', in Bric (ed.), *Kerry History and Society*, pp. 183–200.

Doyle, Aidan, *A History of the Irish Language: From the Norman Invasion to Independence* (Oxford: Oxford University Press, 2015).

Duffy, P.J., 'Colonial spaces and sites of resistance: landed estates in 19th century Ireland', in L.J. Proudfootand M.M. Roche, (eds), *(Dis)Placing Empire: Renegotiating British Colonial Geographies* (Aldershot: Ashgate, 2005), pp. 15–40.

Durell, Penelope and Cornelius Kelly, *The Grand Tour of Kerry* (Allihies, Co. Cork: Cailleach, 2001).

Fetherstonhaugh, A.J., 'The true story of the two chiefs of Dunboy: an episode in Irish history', *Jn. Royal Soc. Antiquaries of Ireland*, 5th s., vol. 4, no. 1 (1894), pp. 35–43.

FitzGerald, Garret, 'Irish-speaking in the pre-Famine period: a study based on the 1911 census data for people born before 1851 and still alive in 1911', *Proc. Royal Irish Academy*, vol. 103C (2003), pp. 191–283.

FitzGerald, Garret, 'Estimates for baronies of minimum level of Irish-speaking amongst successive decennial cohorts: 1771–1781 to 1861–1871', *Proc. Royal Irish Academy*, vol. 84C (1984), pp. 117–55.

FitzGibbon, John (1st Earl of Clare), *The Speech of the Right Honourable John, Earl of Clare, Lord High Chancellor of Ireland, in the House of Lords of Ireland, 10 Feb. 1800* (Dublin: Milliken, 1800).

Foley, Kieran, 'The Killarney Poor Law guardians and the great famine', in Bric (ed.), *Kerry History and Society*, pp. 349–66.

Foster, Thomas Campbell, *Letters on the Condition of the People of Ireland* (London: Chapman and Hall, 1846).

Fraser, James, *A Handbook for Travellers in Ireland* (Dublin: William Curry, 1844).

Froude, James A., *The Two Chiefs of Dunboy: or, An Irish Romance of the Last Century* (London: Longmans, Green, 1889).

Froude, James A., *The English in Ireland in the Eighteenth Century*, 3 vols (New York: Scribner, 1885).

Froude, James A., 'A fortnight in Kerry', no. 1 (1869) and no. 2 (1870), in Froude, *Short Studies on Great Subjects* (New York: Scribner, 1872), pp. 178–201, 344–81.

Gillissen, Christophe, 'Charles Trevelyan, John Mitchel and the historiography of the great famine', *Revue Française de Civilisation Britannique*, vol. 19, no. 2 (2014), pp. 195–212.

Goddard, Stanley E., *All Roads Lead to Kenmare* (Victoria, BC: Trafford, 2006, 'written in 1983').

Godkin, James, *Ireland and Her Churches* (London: Chapman and Hall, 1867).

Gray, Peter, *The Irish Famine* (London: Thames and Hudson, 1995 and 2010).

Gray, Peter, *Famine, Land and Politics: British Government and Irish Society, 1843–1850* (Dublin: Irish Academic Press, 1999).

Gray, Peter, 'Famine relief in comparative perspective: Ireland, Scotland and Northwestern Europe, 1845–49', *Éire-Ireland*, vol. 32, no. 1 (1997), pp. 86–108.

Gray, Sara, *Dictionary of British Women Artists* (Cambridge: Lutterworth, 2009).

Haines, Robin, *Charles Trevelyan and the Great Irish Famine* (Dublin: Four Courts Press, 2014).

Hall, Anna Maria and Samuel Carter Hall, *Ireland: Its Scenery, Character, &c.*, 3 vols (London: How and Parsons, 1841).

Hamell, P.J., *Maynooth Students and Ordinations Index 1795–1895* ([Birr, Co. Offaly], 1982)

Hickson, Mary Agnes, *Selections from Old Kerry Records* (London: Watson and Hazell, 1st series 1872, 2nd series 1874).

Holy Cross Church Kenmare 150 (1864–2014): A Social and Local History, ed. Holy Cross 150 History Group (Kerry: Holy Cross 150 History Group, 2014).

Hussey, S.M., *The Reminiscences of an Irish Land Agent*, being those of S.M. Hussey compiled by Home Gordon (London: Duckworth, 1904).

Hutton, Annie (ed. and trans.), *The Embassy in Ireland of Monsignor G.B. Rinuccini 1645–1649* (Dublin: Thom, 1873).

Jordan, Thomas, *Ireland's Children: Quality of Life, Stress and Development in the Famine Era* (Westport, CT: Greenwood, 1998).

Joyce, Patrick W., *Irish Names of Places*, 3 vols (Dublin: Phoenix, [1863–1913]).

Kalendarium Saint Patrick's College Maynooth 2018–2019 (Maynooth: St Patrick's College, 2018).

Kenny, Colum, *Tristram Kennedy and the Revival of Irish Legal Training*

1835–1885 (Dublin: Irish Academic Press, 1996).

Kenny, Mary, 'Tug-of-love dilemma: Seumas O'Kelly poignantly portrayed a child-care conflict', *Irish Independent*, 24 Nov. 2018, magazine, p. 8.

Kerr, Donal A., *'A Nation of Beggars': Priests, People and Politics in Famine Ireland 1846–1852* (Oxford: Clarendon Press, 1994).

Kinealy, Christine, 'The British Relief Association and the great famine in Ireland', *Revue Française de Civilisation Britannique: French Journal of British Studies*, vol. 19, no. 2 (2014), pp. 49–65.

Kinealy, Christine, *Charity and the Great Hunger in Ireland: The Kindness of Strangers* (London: Bloomsbury, 2013).

Kinealy, Christine, Jason King and Gerard Moran (eds), *Children and the Great Hunger in Ireland* (Cork: Cork University Press, 2018).

Kinealy, Christine, *The Great Irish Famine: Impact, Ideology and Rebellion* (Basingstoke, UK: Palgrave, 2002).

Knodel, Natalie, 'Reconsidering an obsolete rite: the churching of women and feminist liturgical theology', *Feminist Theology*, vol. 14 (1977), pp. 106–25.

Laborde, Abbé Jean Joseph, *The Impossibility of the Immaculate Conception as an Article of Faith* […] (Philadelphia: Herman Hooker, 1855, from the French).

Lansdowne, (sixth) Marquess of (Henry William Petty-Fitzmaurice), *Glanerought and the Petty-Fitzmaurices* (London: Oxford University Press, 1937).

Larkin, Emmet, 'Economic growth, capital investment and the Roman Catholic Church in nineteenth century Ireland', *Am. Hist. Rev.*, vol. 72, no. 3 (April 1967), pp. 852–84.

Larkin, Emmet, *The Making of the Roman Catholic Church in Ireland 1850–1860* (Chapel Hill: University of North Carolina Press, 1960).

Larkin, Emmet, *The Pastoral Role of the Roman Catholic Church in Pre-Famine Ireland, 1750–1850* (Dublin: Four Courts, 2006).

Lewis, Samuel, *A Topographical Dictionary of Ireland*, 2 vols (London: Lewis, 1837, and 2nd ed. 1849).

Lucas, A.T. and H.G. Tempest, '"Penal" crucifixes', *Jn. Co. Louth Arch. Soc.*, vol. 13 (1954), pp. 145–74.

Luddy, Maria and Mary O'Dowd, *Marriage in Ireland 1660–1925* (Cambridge, UK: Cambridge University Press, 2020).

Lyne, Gerard, *Murtaí Óg Ó Súilleabháin (c.1710–54): A Life Contextualised* (Dublin: Geography Publications, 2017).

Lyne, Gerard, *The Lansdowne Estate in Kerry under the Agency of William*

Steuart Trench 1849–72 (Dublin: Geography Publications, 2001).

Lyne, Gerard, 'An enterprising Cromwellian family: the Taylors of Dunkerron', *Jn. Kerry Arch. and Hist. Soc.*, vol. 17 (1984), pp. 61–76.

Lyne, Gerard, 'Lewis Dillwyn's visit to Kerry, 1809', *Jn. Kerry Arch. and Hist. Soc.*, vol. 15/16 (1982–3), pp. 87–9.

Lyne, Gerard, 'Landlord-tenant relations on the Shelburne estate in Kenmare, Bonane and Tuosist, 1770–75: with a rental of the estate for 1783', *Jn. Kerry Arch. and Hist. Soc.*, vol. 12 (1979), pp. 19–62.

Lyne, Gerard, 'Land tenure in Kenmare, Bonane and Tuosist 1720–70: with lists of the tenants and their holdings', *Jn. Kerry Arch. and Hist. Soc.*, vol. 11 (1978), pp. 25–55.

Lyne, Gerard, 'Land tenure in Kenmare and Tuosist 1696–*c.*1716: with notes on the tenants and their holdings', *Jn. Kerry Arch. and Hist. Soc.*, vol. 10 (1977), pp. 19–54.

Lyne, Gerard, 'Daniel O'Connell, intimidation and the Kerry elections of 1835', *Jn. Kerry Arch. and Hist. Soc.*, vol. 4 (1971), pp. 74–97.

Macaulay, Thomas B., *The History of England from the Accession of James II*, 5 vols (Philadelphia: Porter and Coates, 1890).

MacCarthy, Robert, *The Trinity College Estates, 1800–1923* (Dundalk: Dundalgan Press, 1992).

MacMahon, Bryan, *Faith and Fury: The Evangelical Campaign in Dingle and West Kerry, 1825–1845* (Dublin: Eastwood, 2021).

MacMahon, Bryan, *The Great Famine in Tralee and North Kerry* (Cork: Mercier Press, 2017).

MacNeill, Máire, *The Festival of Lughnasa: A Study of the Survival of the Celtic Festival of the Beginning of Harvest* (Dublin, 1982).

McAuliffe, Mary, 'O'Connor Kerry of Carrigafoyle: history and memory in Iraghticonor', *Béaloideas*, vol. 82 (2014), pp. 100–15.

McCabe, Anne, 'John O'Sullivan of Cappanacuss Castle', *Kenmare Journal* (1982), pp. 30–2.

McCarthy, Philomena, *Poor Clare Convent Kenmare: The Women Who Did Not Sit and Wait* (Kenmare: Presentation Convent, 1999).

McCarthy, Philomena, *Holy Cross Church, Kenmare* (Kenmare: Holy Cross Church, 2000).

McCarthy, Philomena, *Kenmare and its Storied Glen* (Kenmare: Presentation Convent, 1993).

McCarthy, S.T., 'The Mahonys of Kerry', *Kerry Archaeological Mag.*, vol. 4, no. 19 (Oct. 1917), pp. 171–90, and no. 20 (April 1918), pp. 223–55.

McCarthy, S.T., 'The Clann Carthaigh', *Kerry Archaeological Mag.*, vol.

3, no. 13 (1914), pp. 55–72.

McLoughlin, Dympna, 'Workhouses', in *The Field Day Anthology of Irish Writing*, vol. 5, Irish Women's Writing and Traditions, ed. Angela Bourke *et al.* (New York: NYU Press, 2002), pp. 722–35.

Meehan, C.P., *The Rise and Fall of the Irish Franciscan Monasteries*, 5th ed. with appendices (Dublin: Duffy, n.d., after 1877).

Moraghan, Seán, *Days of the Blackthorn: Faction Fighters of Kerry* (Cork: Mercier Press, 2020).

Moran, P.F., *Historical Sketch of the Persecutions Suffered by the Catholics of Ireland* (Dublin: Gill, 1907).

Moriarty, Danny, 'Early years of Kenmare', *Kenmare Journal* (1982), pp. 13–27.

Moriarty, Danny, 'Trinity College Estate in Kenmare Parish', *Kenmare Journal* (1982), pp. 108–14.

Murphy, Cliona, 'The trial at Tralee: the Reverend Charles Gayer and *The Kerry Examiner*, proselytism or persecution?', in Bric, *Kerry: History and Society*, pp. 407–30.

Murphy, Cliona, '"The destruction of the Protestant Church and dismemberment of the empire": Charlotte Elizabeth, Evangelical Anglican in Pre-Famine Ireland', *Women's Studies*, vol. 30, no. 6 (2001), pp. 741–61.

Murphy, J.A., *The Church of Ireland in Co. Kerry: A Record of Church and Clergy in the Nineteenth Century* (lulu.com, 2012).

Murphy, John A., 'O'Connell and the Gaelic World', in Nowlan and O'Connell (eds), *O'Connell*, pp. 32–52.

Murray, Alice E., *History of the Commercial and Financial Relations between England and Ireland from the Period of the Restoration* (London: King, 1903).

Ní Chinnéide, Sile, 'A new view of eighteenth century life in Kerry', *Jn. Kerry Arch. and Hist. Soc.*, vol. 6 (1973), pp. 83–100.

Ní Mhóráin, Brighid, *Thiar sa Mhainistir atá an Ghaoluinn Bhreá: Meath na Gaeilge in Uíbh Rathach* [Over in Mainister they speak lovely Irish: The decline of Irish in Iveragh] (An Daingean: An Sagart, 1997).

Nicholson, Asenath, *Ireland's Welcome to the Stranger, or, An Excursion Through Ireland in 1844 and 1845 for the Purpose of Personally Investigating the Condition of the Poor* (London: Charles Gilpin, 1847).

Nowlan, K.B. and Maurice R. O'Connell (eds), *Daniel O'Connell: Portrait of a Radical* (New York: Fordham University Press, 1985).

O'Brien, Gerard, 'Workhouse management in pre-Famine Ireland', *Proc. Royal Ir. Acad.*, vol. 86C (1986), pp. 113–34.

O'Carroll, Gerald, 'Mary Agnes Hickson and writing the histories of Kerry', in Bric, *Kerry: History and Society*, pp. 221–42.

Ó Casaide, Seamus, 'Latin in County Kerry', *Kerry Archaeological Mag.* vol. 3, no. 16 (1916).

Ó Cathaoir, Breandán, 'The Kerry "Home Rule" by-election, 1872', *Jn. Kerry Arch. and Hist. Soc.*, vol. 3 (1970), pp. 154–70.

O'Connell, Mary Anne Bianconi (Mrs Morgan John O'Connell), *The Last Colonel of the Irish Brigade, Count O'Connell, and Old Irish Life at Home and Abroad, 1745–1833*, 2 vols (London: Kegan Paul, 1892).

O'Connell, Maurice R. (ed.), *The Correspondence of Daniel O'Connell*, 8 vols (Shannon: Irish University Press, 1972–77).

O'Donoghue, D.J., 'A neglected Kerry poetess [Christabel]', *Evening Press*, 5 Dec. 1891.

O'Donovan Rossa, Jeremiah, *Rossa's Recollections 1838 to 1898* (New York: O'Donovan Rossa, 1898).

O'Donovan Rossa, Jeremiah, 'The Fenian movement: an account of its origins, progress and temporary collapse', in the *Brooklyn Eagle*, 7–28 June 1885.

O'Donovan Rossa, Jeremiah, *Prison Life: Six Years in Six English Prisons* (New York: Kenedy, 1874).

O'Ferrall, Fergus, 'The rise of the Catholic middle class: O'Connellites in County Longford, 1820–50', in Fintan Lane (ed.), *Politics, Society and the Middle Class in Modern Ireland* (Basingstoke, UK: Palgrave Macmillan, 2010), pp. 48–64.

O'Flaherty, Eamon, 'Urban Kerry: the development and growth of towns, c.1580–1840', in Bric, *Kerry: History and Society*, pp. 243–275.

O'Flanagan, J. Roderick, *The Irish Bar* (London: Sampson Low *et al.*, 1879).

Ó Gráda, Cormac, T. Anbinder and S. Wegge, 'Assisted emigration as Famine relief: lessons from the Lansdowne Estate', in Bric, *Kerry: History and Society*, pp. 367–90.

Ó Gráda, Cormac, *Black '47 and Beyond: The Great Irish Famine in History, Economy and Memory* (Princeton, NJ: Princeton University Press, 1999).

Ó Gráda, Cormac, *Ireland before and after the Famine: Explorations in Economic History 1800–1925* (Manchester: Manchester University Press, 1988, 2nd ed. 1993).

O'Hart, John, *Irish Pedigrees: or, The Origin and Stem of the Irish Nation*, 5th ed., 2 vols (Dublin: Duffy, 1892).

O'Leary, Eileen (ed.), *Changing Times: Blackwater and Templenoe Social*

History (Kerry: Blackwater Women's Group, 2009).

Ó Mainnín, Mícheál, 'A post-mortem on the Protestant Crusade in Dingle', *Jn. Kerry Arch. and Hist. Soc.*, vol. 29 (1996), pp. 99–118.

Ó Nualláin, Seán, 'A survey of stone circles in Cork and Kerry', *Proc. RIA*, vol. 84C (1984), pp. 1–77.

Ó Nualláin, Seán, 'The stone circles of Co. Kerry', *Jn. Kerry Arch. and Hist. Soc.*, vol. 4 (1971), pp. 5–27.

Opie, Redvers, 'A neglected English economist: George Poulett Scrope', *Quarterly Journal of Economics*, vol. 44, no. 1 (1929), pp. 101–37.

O'Rourke, John, *The Great Irish Famine* (Dublin: Duffy, 1874, and abridged ed., Veritas, 1989).

Orpen, Goddard Henry, *The Orpen Family, Being An Account of the Life and Writings of Richard Orpen of Killowen, Co. Kerry, Together with Some Researches into his Forbears in England and Brief Notices of the Branches of the Orpen Family Descended from Him* (Somerset and London: privately published, 1930).

[Orpen, Richard], *An Exact Relation of the Persecutions, Robberies, and Losses, Sustained by the Protestants of Killmare* [= Kenmare], *in Ireland* […] (London: Thomas Bennet, 1689), 30pp. Rare, but now at Early English Books Online.

O'Shea, Kieran, 'David Moriarty (1814–1877): The making of a bishop', *Jn. Kerry Arch. and Hist. Soc.*, vol. 3 (1970), pp. 84–98, and vol. 4 (1971), p. 108.

O'Sullivan (Friar), 'Ancient history of the kingdom of Kerry'. See Prendergast below.

[O'Sullivan, John], *The Altar Turned Out and Turned in Again; or, Crowbar Practice in Kenmare* (Dublin, 1867).

O'Sullivan, John, *Commentary on the Book of Psalms* (Dublin: Duffy, 1866).

O'Sullivan, Niamh, 'Mass in a Connemara cabin', *Éire-Ireland*, vol. 40, nos 1 and 2 (2005), pp. 126–39.

Ó Tuathaigh, Gearóid, *I mBéal an Bháis: The Great Famine and the Language Shift in Nineteenth Century Ireland* (CT: Quinnipiac University Press, 2015).

Owens, Gary, '"A moral insurrection": faction fighters, public demonstrations and the O'Connellite campaign, 1828', *Irish Historical Studies*, vol. 30, no. 120 (1997), pp. 513–41.

Palmer, A.H. Herbert, *A Genealogical and Historical Account of the Family of Palmer of Kenmare, Co. Kerry, Ireland* (London: privately printed, 1872).

Parliamentary Gazetteer of Ireland, Adapted to the New Poor-Law [...] *1844–45*, 3 vols (Dublin, London and Edinburgh: Fullarton, 1846).

Petty, William, *A Political Anatomy of Ireland* (London: Brown and Rogers, 1691).

Phelan, Mary, *Irish Speakers, Interpreters and the Courts, 1754–1921* (Dublin: Four Courts, 2019).

Póirtéir, Cathal (ed.), *The Great Irish Famine* (Cork: RTE/Mercier, 1995).

Powell, Geraldine, *A Want of Inhabitants: The Famine in Bantry Union* (Dublin: Eastwood, 2021).

Powell, John, 'The third Marquess of Lansdowne', *Parliamentary History*, vol. 22, no. 1 (2003), pp. 57–73.

Prendergast, F. Jarlath (ed.), 'Ancient history of the kingdom of Kerry, by Friar O'Sullivan, of Muckross Abbey', *Jn. Cork Hist. and Arch. Soc.*, vols 4–6, nos 38–47 (1898–1900).

[Pückler-Muskau, Hermann] A German Prince, *Tour in England, Ireland, and France, in the Years 1826, 1827, 1828, and 1829* [...] (Philadelphia: Carey, Lee and Blanchard, 1833).

Quinn, John F., *Fr Mathew's Crusade: Temperance in Nineteenth Century Ireland and Irish America* (Amherst and Boston: University of Massachusetts Press, 2002).

Rafferty, Oliver, 'David Moriarty's episcopal leadership in the diocese of Kerry, 1854–77', in Bric, *Kerry: History and Society*, pp. 391–406.

Ralls, Walter, 'The Papal Aggression of 1850: a study in Victorian anti-Catholicism', *Church History*, vol. 43, no. 2 (1974), pp. 242–56.

Reid, Thomas, *Tour of Ireland in the Year 1822* (London: Longman, Hurst, 1823).

Russell, Charles, *'New Views on Ireland', or, Irish Land: Grievances: Remedies* (London: Macmillan, 1880).

Salmon's *Modern Gazetteer: or, a Short View of the Several Nations of the World*, 4th ed. (Dublin: Wilson and James, 1757).

Sayre, G. 'Biographical sketch of Thomas Taylor', *Journal of Bryology*, vol. 14 (1987), pp. 415–27.

Sloan, Robert, *William Smith O'Brien and the Young Ireland Rebellion of 1848* (Dublin: Four Courts, 2000).

Smith, Charles, *The Ancient and Present State of the County of Kerry* (Dublin: unidentified publisher, 1774, being a reprinting of a private publication of *c.*1756).

Somerville-Large, Peter, *From Bantry Bay to Leitrim* (London: Arena, 1986).

Strickland, W.G., *A Dictionary of Irish Artists* (Dublin and London:

Maunsel, 1913).

Sullivan, Robert E., *Macaulay* (Cambridge, Mass.: Belknap/Harvard University Press, 2009).

Thackeray, William M. (under pseudonym M.A. Titmarsh), *The Irish Sketch Book*, 2nd ed., 2 vols (London: Chapman and Hall, 1845).

Thompson, Mrs D.P., *A Brief Account of the Rise and Progress of the Change in Religious Opinion Now Taking Place in Dingle* [...] (London: Seeley, Burnside and Seeley, 1845).

Trench, William Steuart, *Realities of Irish Life*, 3rd ed. (London: Longmans, Green, 1869).

Trevelyan, C.E., *The Irish Crisis* (London: Longman, Green and Longmans, 1848).

Turner, Michael, 'The French connection with Maynooth College, 1795–1855', *Studies: An Irish Quarterly Review*, vol. 70, no. 277 (Spring, 1981), pp. 77–87.

Vaughan, W.E., *Landlords and Tenants in Mid-Victorian Ireland* (Oxford: Clarendon Press, 1994).

Walsh, T.J., 'Through Kerry, Cork and Limerick with Rinuccini', *Capuchin Annual* (1963), pp. 145–65.

Weld, Isaac, *Illustrations of the Scenery of Killarney and the Surrounding Country* (London: Longman *et al.*, 1807).

Wendling, Karina Bénazeck, '"A City Upon a Hill": The "Dingle Colony" of converts and disruption of traditional communities in mid-19th-century Ireland', *Études Irlandaises*, vol. 44, no. 2 (2019), pp. 77–93.

Whelan, Irene, *The Bible War in Ireland: The 'Second Reformation' and the Polarization of Protestant-Catholic Relations, 1800–1840* (Dublin: Lilliput Press, 2005).

Whelan, Kevin, 'An underground gentry? Catholic middlemen in eighteenth-century Ireland', *Eighteenth-Century Ireland*, vol. 10 (1965), pp. 7–68.

Whyte, J.H., 'The appointment of Catholic bishops in nineteenth-century Ireland', *Catholic Historical Review*, vol. 48, no. 1 (1962), pp. 12–32.

Wilde, Oscar, 'Mr Froude's Blue Book', *Pall Mall Gazette*, 13 April 1889, also available free as an Apple podcast from Librivox.

Windele, John, 'Dunkerron Castle', *Jn. Kilkenny and South-East of Ireland Arch. Soc.*, n.s. vol. 2, no. 2 (1859), pp. 292–301.

Windele, J., *Historical and Descriptive Notices of the City of Cork and* [...] *Killarney* (Cork: Bolster, 1839).

Witte, John (ed.), *Sharing the Book: Religious Perspectives on the Rights and Wrongs of Proselytism* (Eugene, OR: Wipf and Stock, 1999).

Wolf, Nicholas, 'The Irish-speaking clergy in the nineteenth-century: education, trends, timing', *New Hibernia Review*, vol. 12, no. 4 (2008), pp. 68–83.

Wood, Herbert, 'Sir William Petty and his Kerry Estate', *Journal of the Royal Society of Antiquaries of Ireland*, vol. 4, no. 1 (1934), pp. 22–40.

Young, Arthur, *A Tour in Ireland*, 2 vols (Dublin: Whitestone *et al.*, 1780).

Notes

Chapter 1

1 O'Sullivan, 'Random Recollections and Effusions', 1843–49, Kerry Diocesan Archives MSS, John O'Sullivan Papers, box 1, unpaginated but with dates [*hereafter* **Recollections**], 20 April 1849.
2 Recollections, 7 April 1849.
3 Recollections, 20 April 1849.
4 *Kerry Evening Post*, 14 and 18 April 1849.
5 Recollections, 7 April 1849; Lyne, *Lansdowne Estate*, p. 369 n. 47.
6 Recollections, 10 and 17 April 1849.
7 Recollections, 7 and 20 April 1849.
8 Kenmare Union Board of Guardians Minute Books [*hereafter* **Kenmare BGMB**], 6 April 1849.
9 Kenmare BGMB, 28 February 1846.
10 Crowley, Smyth and Murphy, *Atlas of the Great Irish Famine, passim.*
11 Crawford, *Famine: The Irish Experience 900–1900*, pp. 11–27.
12 Berger and Spoerer, 'European revolutions of 1848', pp. 293–326; Gray, 'Famine relief policy in comparative perspective', pp. 86–108.
13 *Select Committee 1849*, p. 133; *Parliamentary Gazetteer*, vol. 2, p. 345 and vol. 3, p. 336 show the totals for Kenmare and Templenoe together in 1834 as having been 9,052 Catholics and 372 Protestants.
14 *Select Committee 1849*, pp. 131–3; *Twelfth Annual Report of the Poor Law Commissioners* (London: Charles Knight, 1846), p. 308.
15 Hall, *Ireland*, vol. 1, pp. 161–2; Binns, *Miseries and Beauties of Ireland*, vol. 2, pp. 328, 331–4; O'Sullivan, 'Ancient history of the kingdom of Kerry', vol. 4, no. 40 (1898), p. 260n cites an old manuscript that suggests many families once went to Spain from Kerry annually to 'spend the summer in begging and wandering up and down along the northern side of that kingdom'.
16 Powell, 'Third marquess of Lansdowne', p. 57.
17 Gray, *Famine, Land and Politics: British Government and Irish Society, 1841–1850*, p. 320n, citing O'Sullivan to Twistleton, 10 Dec. 1848 and O'Sullivan to Trevelyan, 5 Feb. 1849, Treasury Papers, T64/366A; *Kerry Evening Post*, 28 Sept. 1850, editorial.
18 Lyne, *Lansdowne Estate*, pp. 345–51.
19 Breen, *Gaelic Lordship of the O'Sullivan Beare*, pp. 37–214; Somerville-Large, *From Bantry Bay to Leitrim, passim.*
20 Lyne, 'Landlord-tenant relations on the Shelburne estate in Kenmare', pp. 20–37.

21 FitzGibbon, *Speech*, p. 22.
22 McCarthy, *Mahonys of Kerry*, p. 234; Beckett, *Modern Ireland*, p. 213; Coquebert de Montbret, cited at Ní Chinnéide, 'A new view', p. 87. See Prendergast, 'Ancient history of the kingdom of Kerry' for an extensive treatment of the O'Sullivans around Kenmare Bay.
23 *Tralee Chronicle*, 6 Dec. 1861; Lewis, *Ireland*, vol. 2, p. 611; Windele, 'Dunkerron Castle', pp. 292–301; McCabe, 'John O'Sullivan', pp. 30–2; 'Sullivan, John William', by Stuart Reid, in Oxford *Dictionary of National Biography* [**hereafter DNB**].
24 O'Hart, *Irish Pedigrees*, vol. 1, pp. 244–5, 334–6.
25 RIA MS OSI: Letters, Kerry, 1841, 14/C/30/14 (ii), pp. 184–5; Ó Nualláin, 'The stone circles of Co. Kerry', p. 5; Ó Nualláin, 'A survey of stone circles in Cork and Kerry', pp. 8, 26–7, 63 (Killowen circle as drawn in 1841); O'Leary, *Changing Times*, pp. 224–7; McCarthy, *Kenmare*, pp. 2–12. All are shown on the first Ordnance Survey 6-inch map of 1842, as is the 'site of (the little) chapel' in Killowenbeg and another *gallán* east of the Killowen Church of Ireland burial ground. No sign of the chapel or stone circle east of Kenmare remains, with a local woman telling this author that she recalls that in about 1950 her father 'threw a fit about gallauns being blasted out the Killowen road just because some farmer wanted to clear rocks off his land'. Borlase, *Dolmens of Ireland*, vol. 1, p. 7 gives the Reennagappul circle 'in a field called Parknagullane' (Irish *páirc* + *gallán*: pasture-field + pillar stones).
26 Bland, 'Staigue Fort', pp. 17–27; *Holy Cross Church 150*, pp. 5–7.
27 Lyne, *Murtaí Óg*, pp. 63–85, 89–103; Breen, *Gaelic Lordship of the O'Sullivan Beare*, esp. pp. 85, 118–21; O'Sullivan, 'Ancient history of the kingdom of Kerry', vol. 4, no. 38 (1898), pp. 115–7 and vol. 6, no. 45 (1900), pp. 16–17; Downey, 'Insights into Kerry', pp. 183–200; Caball, *Kerry, 1600–1730, passim*.
28 Ní Chinnéide, 'A new view', p. 85.
29 Weld, *Illustrations*, pp. 165–6; De Selincourt, *Letters of William and Dorothy Wordsworth*, vol. 5, pp. 135–6.
30 Reid, *Tour of Ireland*, p. 272; Carr, *The Stranger in Ireland*, pp. 215, 237. For this traffic see also Weld, *Illustrations*, pp. 163–6, 190.
31 Pückler-Muskau, *Tour in England, Ireland, and France*, pp. 375–92.
32 Anon., 'Suspension bridge', pp. 316–17; *Kerryman*, 5 Jan. 1935.
33 Hall, *Ireland*, vol. 1, pp. 161–2, possibly influenced by Binns, *Miseries and Beauties of Ireland*. Also Young, *Tour of Ireland*, vol. 2, pp. 83–4.
34 *Parliamentary Gazetteer*, vol. 2, p. 346.

Chapter 2
35 Lansdowne, *Glanerought*, pp. 8, 37.
36 Hickson, *Old Kerry Records*, 2nd series, p. 117.
37 Aubrey, *'Brief Lives'*, vol. 2, p. 142; Hickson, *Old Kerry Records*, 2nd series, pp. 39–42, 117.
38 Published in William Petty, *Hiberniae delineatio* (London, 1685).
39 Aubrey, *Brief Lives*, vol. 2, pp. 142–3, who also states that 'He had his patent for earl of Kilmore [...] which he stifled during his life to avoid envy.' A farthing was a quarter of a penny, a half-crown was worth thirty pennies.
40 Lansdowne, *Glanerought*, pp. 12–35.
41 Cole, *Minerals and Metalliferous Mines in Ireland*, pp. 43–4, 127 for mining in the area.

42 Lansdowne, *Glanerought*, p. 48 suggests that 'most of the Kenmare "colonists" found their way back to County Kerry' when the war between William and James ended, but Orpen does not support this.

43 Lansdowne, *Glanerought*, pp. 10, 50–2, 55.

44 Lyne, 'Land tenure in Kenmare and Tuosist 1696–*c.*1716: with notes on the tenants and their holdings'; Orpen, *Orpen*, pp. 57–60, 75–6.

45 Petty, *Political Anatomy of Ireland*, pp. 99–100.

46 'Macaulay, Thomas Babington, Baron Macaulay', by William Thomas, in *DNB*.

47 *Cork Examiner*, 20 Aug. 1849 and *Westmeath Independent*, 25 Aug. 1849.

48 Sullivan, *Macaulay*, pp. 331–4.

49 Sullivan, *Macaulay*, pp. 260–7.

50 Hussey, *Reminiscences*, p. 3.

51 Rinuccini, letter from Limerick and report, at Hutton, *The Embassy in Ireland*, pp. 84, 489.

52 Anon., 'Theiner's works: materials for Irish history', pp. 219–21.

53 Anon., 'Theiner's works: materials for Irish history', p. 222; Walsh, 'Though Kerry ... with Rinuccini', pp. 151–2. Walsh deduces (note 5) that the nuncio disembarked near the present bridge at Kenmare sound; Moran, *Persecutions Suffered by the Catholics of Ireland*, p. 488; Meehan, *Irish Franciscan Monasteries*, pp. 348–55; 'My Irish campaign', in *Catholic Bulletin*, vols 6–10 (1916–27).

54 Andrews *et al.*, *The Westward Enterprise, passim*.

55 Lansdowne, *Glanerought*, pp. 14–15, 25, 158.

56 Orpen, *Orpen*, pp. 58–9, citing a report by Lord Herbert of Cherbury on the state of Kerry, dated 27 May 1673; McCarthy, *Kenmare and its Storied Glen*, p. 37.

57 RIA MS OSI: Letters, Kerry, 1841, 14/C/30/14 (ii), pp. 184–5.

58 Hickson, *Old Kerry Records*, 1st series, p. 270.

59 Sullivan, *Macaulay*, pp. 6–7.

60 Orpen, *An Exact Relation, passim*.

61 Sullivan, *Macaulay*, pp. 330–6, citing Macaulay's manuscript journals.

62 'Macaulay', by William Thomas, in *DNB*.

Chapter 3

63 Smith, *Kerry*, pp. 86–7.

64 See https://www.bowood.org/bowood-house-gardens/bowood-house/family-history/. The 3rd marquess died in 1863 and was buried at Bowood.

65 'Petty [formerly Fitzmaurice], William', by John Cannon, in *DNB*; Lyne, 'Landlord-tenant relations on the Shelburne estate', pp. 21–46.

66 Smith, *Kerry*, p. 84; Orpen, *Orpen*, p. 75. At Killowen today stands the ruin of its second Church of Ireland place of worship (1814–1858, on the site of its first Protestant church); this was used until St Patrick's Church was opened in Kenmare on the road to the suspension bridge (*Holy Cross Church 150*, p. 263).

67 Lyne, 'Landlord-tenant relations on the Shelburne estate', pp. 20–1, 28–41.

68 Smith, *Kerry*, p. 84.

69 Joyce, *Irish Names of Places*, vol. 1, p. 490.

70 McCarthy, *Kenmare*, pp. 2 (photo of 'Finn's Cradle'), 6, 13–14; Joyce, *Names of Places*, vol. 1, p. 490. Joyce points out (p. 31) that 'Fionn' may also signify 'white' or 'fair', as in Finnahy, Co. Tipperary.

71 O'Sullivan, 'Ancient history of the kingdom of Kerry', vol. 6, no. 47 (1900), p. 153. According to a contributor to the National Folklore Collection, Schools' Collection, Volume 0465, Page 022, 'Fionn's Cradle' was about a quarter mile

'from the present cinema hall [1939]' in Kenmare 'and is supposed to have been at one time the hiding place of the Fianna'.

72 *Cork Examiner*, 16 Aug. 1858; Lyne, *Lansdowne Estate*, p. 355.

73 RIA MS OSI: Letters, Kerry, 1841, 14/C/30/14 (ii), pp. 182–3, including a detailed description of the ruined church.

74 RIA MS OSI: Letters, Kerry, 1841, 14/C/30/14 (ii), pp. 184–5; O'Sullivan, 'Ancient history of the kingdom of Kerry', vol. 4, no. 39 (1898), p. 210n; Lansdowne, *Glanerought*, p. 71n.

75 Salmon's *Modern Gazetteer*, at 'Kenmare'.

76 O'Flaherty, 'Urban Kerry: the development and growth of towns', pp. 243–52.

77 Lansdowne, *Glanerought*, p. 65.

78 Taylor to Shelburne, 5 July 1773, quoted at Lyne, 'Landlord-tenant relations on the Shelburne estate', p. 27.

79 Lansdowne, *Glanerought*, pp. 60–71.

80 Lansdowne, *Glanerought*, pp. 65–7n; 'Petty [formerly Fitzmaurice], William', by John Cannon, in *DNB*.

81 Young, *Tour in Ireland*, vol. 2, p. 84.

82 Lyne, 'Lewis Dillwyn', pp. 87–9; *Freeman's Journal*, 10 Oct. 1923.

83 Windele, *Historical and Descriptive Notices*, p. 287; *Parliamentary Gazetteer*, vol. 2, p. 345.

84 For example, Mike Guihan (aged 83), 'How Kenmare – Neidín – got its name, or Fionn mac Cooil and the Gruagac leah coach ruadh' (NFC, The Schools' Collection, vol. 0463, pp. 193–4) and (informant uncertain), 'Fionn the Giant from Kenmare' (NFC, The Schools' Collection, vol. 0461, pp. 100–2).

85 See Logainm: https://www.logainm.ie/en/1416504?s=Neid%c3%adn.

86 Lansdowne, *Glanerought*, pp. 66–71.

87 Recollections, 10 Oct. and 15 Nov. 1843; Ní Chinnéide, 'Eighteenth century life in Kerry', *Kerry Arch Jn.*, vol. 6 (1973), p. 86, citing Bibliothèque Nationale de France, Département des Manuscrits: NAF 20098-20100, Charles-Étienne Coquebert de Montbret, Carnets de voyage en Irlande, 1790–1791.

88 Weld, *Illustrations*, pp. 146–7, 221–2; Lyne, 'Lewis Dillwyn', pp. 87–9.

89 Recollections, 10 Oct. 1843.

90 Recollections, 15 Nov. 1843.

91 *Cork Examiner*, 4 Jan. 1858; Lyne, *Lansdowne Estate*, pp. xxxiv–viii.

92 Powell, 'Third marquess of Lansdowne', p. 72. See also Grey, *Famine, Land and Politics*.

93 Lansdowne, *Glanerought, passim*.

94 *Freeman's Journal*, 30 Sept. 1817; *Freeman's Journal*, 3 March 1825 for Eugene and other Kenmare Downings paying O'Connell's 'Catholic Rent'.

95 Lyne, *Lansdowne Estate*, pp. 457–60; McCarthy, *Kenmare*, pp. 72–7.

96 OS map 1842; Lewis, *Ireland*, vol. 2, p. 611; Lewis, *Ireland*, 2nd ed., vol. 6, at Kenmare; Kenmare BGMB, 17 May 1850; *Cork Examiner*, 17 July 1920; Lansdowne, *Glanerought*, p. 71 n. 1. It was gutted by fire in 1920 but later partly restored.

97 Lewis, *Ireland*, vol. 2, pp. 37–8; Windele, *Notices of Cork and Killarney*, p. 287; *Kerry Evening Post*, 30 Dec. 1840. See Hall, *Ireland*, vol. 1, p. 162 and Goddard, *All Roads Lead to Kenmare*, pp. 8–9 for the old suspension bridge.

98 *Census of Ireland 1851: Part VI, General Report*, p. 276. *Census of Ireland 2011* found 841 private households in Kenmare.

Chapter 4

99 Recollections, 18, 26 May and 10 Dec. 1847, 10–11 Jan. and 18 April 1849 (x2) – writing on the last date to Catherine, wife of Dan McCartie of Headfort, Co. Kerry, and daughter of his father's close friend Daniel 'Splinter' O'Connell; *Holy Cross Church 150*, pp. 18–20, 129–30.

100 O'Hart, *Irish Pedigrees*, vol. 1, pp. 334–5, giving 'E. Mahony' as Walsh's first wife 'by whom he had five daughters' but also giving an Eleanor Mahony as Anne's mother.

101 *House of Commons (Ire.) Jn.*, 16 (Dublin, 1774) p. 77 lists among the officers of his majesty's customs service a 'boatman in the cruising barge' at Dingle whose name was Nicholas Connolly.

102 O'Hart, *Irish Pedigrees*, vol. 1, pp. 334–6 gives a third sibling of his mother, this being Mary, who married Dingleman Thomas O'Connor of the O'Connors of Carrigafoyle, from whom descended Arthur O'Connor MP (born 1844). For that old but dispossessed Kerry family, see McAuliffe, 'O'Connor Kerry of Carrigafoyle'.

103 Recollections, 11 Jan. 1849.

104 Recollections, opening narrative.

105 Recollections, 7 and 19 May, 24 June 1849 and 19 May 1849.

106 O'Sullivan, 'Notes of a Visitation in Kerry by a Queer Fellow', 1850–55, 2 vols, Kerry Diocesan Archives MSS, John O'Sullivan Papers, box 4 [*hereafter* **Notes**], pp. 538, 544 (1852); O'Sullivan, *Praxis parochi*, 1849–52, two hardback volumes numbered sequentially, Kerry Diocesan Archives MSS, John O'Sullivan Papers, boxes 2(a) and 3 [*hereafter Praxis*], p. 915; Cusack, *History of the Kingdom of Kerry*, pp. 381–2, n. 1. See n. 97 above for Mahonys.

107 Notes, pp. 97–8 (19 July 1851).

108 Recollections, 18 and 21 April 1849. Splinter's daughter Catherine was 'as eccentric as her father and mother' (Recollections, 21 Apr. 1849).

109 On 3 June 1809 Stephen Walsh (d. before 1840), cabinet-maker and auctioneer of The Square, Tralee, married Gobinet (Arabella) Hawkins. The couple had children: Stephen, Francis, Ann, Elizabeth, Maria and Jane (Church and civil records, retrieved 7 Sept. 2020 at irishgenealogy.ie); Recollections, 9 Feb. 1849; *Kerry Examiner*, 4 March 1842; *Kerry Evening Post*, 10 Feb. 1849; O'Hart, *Irish Pedigrees*, vol. 1, p. 335).

110 Hickson, *Old Kerry Records*, 2nd series, p. 322.

111 Recollections, opening narrative; Notes, p. 225 (27 July 1851).

112 Downey, 'Insights into Kerry', pp. 190–1; *Cork Advertiser*, 30 Aug. 1808, cited at Ó Casaide, 'Latin in County Kerry', pp. 301–2.

113 *Kerry Evening Post*, 20 April 1841; *Kerry Examiner*, 20 April 1840; *Cork Examiner*, 31 Dec. 1849.

114 *Praxis*, pp. 768–71; Recollections, 28 June 1849; Burke, *Landed Gentry*, vol. 2 (1879), pp. 1583–4.

115 Notes, pp. 377–8 (11 Aug. 1851).

116 Notes, pp. 358–60 (8 Aug. 1851).

117 Recollections, opening narrative.

118 Recollections, opening narrative.

119 Recollections, opening narrative.

120 Recollections, 11 May 1849.

121 Notes, p. 57 (27 July 1851). The prefix 'Mr' instead of 'Fr' was sometimes then used for Catholic priests.

[122] Hamell, *Maynooth Students and Ordinations*, p. 147 gives O'Sullivan's matriculation date as 25 August 1824.

[123] Crolly, *Life of Dr Crolly*, p. xxiii; Beckett, *Modern Ireland*, pp. 256–7, 329; Turner, 'The French connection with Maynooth College', pp. 78, 83–4.

[124] Larkin, 'Economic growth, capital investment and the Roman Catholic Church in nineteenth century Ireland', pp. 865, 1254.

[125] *Praxis*, pp. 5, 838–9; p. 80; Turner, 'The French connection with Maynooth College', pp. 77–87, 79–80; *Eighth Report of the Commissioners of Irish Education Inquiry: Roman Catholic College of Maynooth* (London, June 1827); Corish, *Maynooth College*, pp. 73–80.

[126] Recollections, 2 June 1849; Notes, pp. 606–7 (11 Aug. 1852).

[127] Recollections, opening narrative; Notes, pp. 133–4 (22 July 1851); 'Callan, Nicholas Joseph', by William Reville, in Cambridge/RIA *Dictionary of Irish Biography* [*hereafter DIB*].

[128] *Praxis*, p. 329; Anon, *In Memoriam*, p. 230; McCarthy, *Kenmare*, pp. 100, 117–19, with photographs of his coils and font.

[129] Recollections, opening narrative; Pigot's *Commercial Directory 1824*, p. 31.

[130] Recollections, opening narrative and 23 May 1847; Recollections, 7 May 1849.

[131] *Eighth Report of the Commissioners of Irish Education Inquiry*, pp. 8, 11.

[132] Egan to O'Connell, 20 Jan. 1827, cited at de Brún, 'Census', p. 42.

[133] Recollections, opening narrative; Notes, p. 12 (19 July 1850); Corish, *Maynooth*, p. 75; *Tralee Mercury*, quoted at *US Catholic Miscellany*, 3 Oct. 1829.

[134] Church and Civil Records, retrieved 7 Sept. 2020 at irishgenealogy.ie; Recollections, 4 Jan. and 9 Feb. 1849; Notes, p. 91 (8 Aug. 1851); *Kerry Evening Post*, 10 Feb. 1849; *Kerry Examiner*, 13 Feb. 1849; O'Hart, *Irish Pedigrees*, vol. 1, p. 335. Anne and John Murphy's son Edward (b. 1847) was the present author's great-grandfather.

Chapter 5

[135] *Praxis*, pp. 10–11, 839.

[136] Notes, pp. 405–6 (19 Aug. 1851); *Praxis*, p. 12.

[137] Burke, *Peerage*, 12th ed., p. 1007. Early editions of Burke did not give De Moleyns as a variant of the old family name Mullins (*Peerage*, 5th ed., p. 985).

[138] Recollections, 28 June 1849; Notes, pp. 405–10 (19 Aug. 1851); *Parliamentary Papers, Miscellaneous Papers: Ireland, April–November 1820*, vol. 9, p. 310 showed Mullins not resident at Killiney 'but under monition [instruction] to reside, and to build a glebe-house' there.

[139] Recollections, opening narrative; Lewis, *Ireland*, vol. 1, pp. 460–2.

[140] Notes, pp. 304–6 (3 Aug. 1851).

[141] Recollections, 14 April 1849.

[142] Recollections, 11 April 1849.

[143] Fraser, *Handbook for Travellers*, p. 349; Whelan, *Bible War in Ireland 1800–1840*, pp. 254–60; NLI MS 'My Dear Christian Friends' (Dingle, 26 Sept. 1839), p. 1 for a contemporary printed drawing of the settlement.

[144] Thompson, *Religious Opinion in Dingle*, p. 7.

[145] Burke, *Landed Gentry* (1879), vol. 2, pp. 1583–4; Thompson, *A Brief Account*, *passim*; Notes, pp. 562–3 (21 July 1854). For more recent perspectives on the controversy, see Wendling, '"A City Upon a Hill": The "Dingle Colony"', pp. 77–93; Ó Mainnín, 'A post-mortem on the Protestant Crusade in Dingle', pp. 99–118.

[146] Thompson, *Brief Account*, p. 47; Hussey, *Reminiscences*, pp. 52–4.

[147] National Folklore Collection (UCD), The Schools' Collection, Volume 0461, Pages 443–4 (from Jeremiah O'Connor, aged 67, of Rock Lane Kenmare on 16 Jan. 1935).

[148] Notes, pp. 239–40 (28 July 1851).

[149] NLI MS 'My Dear Christian Friends' (Dingle, 26 Sept. 1839), p. 1.

[150] Anon., *Persecution of Protestants in the Year 1845*, pp. 23–4; de Brún, 'Census', pp. 59, 62. Also see Murphy, 'The trial at Tralee'.

[151] Anon., *Persecution of Protestants in the Year 1845*, p. 24.

[152] MacMahon, *Faith and Fury*, *passim*.

[153] Bowen, *Souperism*, pp. 11–21, 79–87 for Dingle. On the jacket of the book Bowen is said to have served curacies in Kenmare and Crosshaven (perhaps on summer relief work?). For a sceptical review of Bowen's thesis, see Peadar O'Curry, 'Soupers', *Irish Times*, 5 Mar. 1971.

[154] 'Fitzgerald, Maurice', by Patrick Geoghegan, in *DIB*; 'Fitzgerald, Maurice (1774–1849) of Ballinruddery, Co. Kerry', by P.J. Jupp at historyofparliamentonline.org (consulted 6 March 2021).

[155] Recollections, opening narrative.

[156] *The Times*, 27 Oct. 1835; *Report from the Select Committee on Bribery and Intimidation at Elections, together with Extracts from the Minutes o Evidence Shewing the Intimidation Practised by the Priests in Ireland* (London, [1837]), pp. 15–16.

[157] Lyne, 'Daniel O'Connell, intimidation and the Kerry elections of 1835', pp. 74–97.

[158] *Praxis*, pp. 768–71, 940; *Gentleman's Magazine*, April 1849, pp. 423–5.

[159] Notes, p. 429 (21 Aug. 1851).

[160] *Freeman's Journal*, 24 and 25 Oct. 1809; Chatterton, *Rambles in the South of Ireland*, vol. 1, pp. 288–90; Hickson, *Old Kerry Records*, 2nd series, pp. 210–11, 239 for these Hicksons and pp. 169–76 for some other cargoes that came to Dingle.

[161] *Select Committee 1849*, p. 134.

[162] *Freeman's Journal*, 11 Jan. 1822; Burke, *Landed Gentry* (1879), vol. 1, pp. 149, 783–4, but only Agnes is given also by Burke under Mahony of Dromore at vol. 2, p. 1049; Hickson, *Old Kerry Records*, 2nd series, pp. 211, 313; National Library of Ireland, GO MS 107, pp. 15–16, under 'Hickson Mahony', shows one of John and Barbara's sons, also Christened John, allowed to assume the surname Mahony after his uncle Richard Mahony of Dromore died. His grant includes a coloured Mahoney coat of arms and confirmation of the Mahony family motto '*Lasair romhuin a buadh*', which Burke, *Landed Gentry* (1879), vol. 2, p. 1049 translates as 'blazes before us to victory'. At the time of Griffith's valuation, 'John M. Hickson' was occupying Tubbrid House, parish of Templenoe, which appears to have been built by the [O']Mahony-Hickson family (Landed Estates Database, retrieved 2 Dec. 2020 at http://landedestates.ie/LandedEstates/jsp/property-show.jsp?id=1795).

[163] Notes, p. 36 (23 July 1850), p. 558 (20 July 1854). Neligan was licensed as an apothecary in 1803.

[164] Chatterton, *Rambles in the South of Ireland*, i, 127–8.

[165] Notes, pp. 436–8 (23 Aug. 1851).

[166] Notes, pp. 417–22 (20 Aug. 1851); de Brún, 'John Windele and Fr John Casey', p. 84n mistakenly dates the account in O'Sullivan's 'diary' (i.e. Notes) as 1850.

[167] de Brún, 'John Windele and Fr John Casey', *passim*.

[168] Nicholson, *Ireland's Welcome*, p. 375.

[169] Notes, pp. 418–23 (20 Aug. 1851); Nicholson, *Ireland's Welcome*, p. 375 wrote that these were cannon balls that 'Cromwell had left in besieging the place'.

[170] Chatterton, *Rambles in the South of Ireland*, vol. 1, pp. 144–5.

[171] Notes, pp. 418–23 (20 Aug. 1851).

[172] de Brún, 'John Windele and Fr John Casey', p. 90.

[173] Notes, pp. 421–2 (20 Aug. 1851).

[174] Notes, pp. 424–5 (20 Aug. 1851).

[175] de Brún, 'John Windele and Fr John Casey', p. 88.

[176] Notes, pp. 286–7 (2 Aug. 1851). For Naughten also see Notes, pp. 578, 800–2.

[177] Notes, pp. 36–7 (23 July 1850).

[178] Notes, pp. 74–5 (10 July 1851), pp. 108–9 (20 July 1851), pp. 129 and 142 (22 July 1851), p. 37 (23 July 1850), p. 223 (27 July 1851).

[179] Murphy, 'O'Connell and the Gaelic World', p. 39.

[180] *Census of Ireland 1851: Part VI, General Report*, pp. xlvii–iii, Fitzgerald, 'Estimates for baronies', pp. 123, 127–9, 133, 152; Fitzgerald, 'Irish-speaking in the pre-Famine period', pp. 202, 276–80.

[181] For a comparative context, see O'Ferrall, 'The rise of the Catholic middle class: O'Connellites in County Longford, 1820–50', pp. 48–64.

[182] Connolly, *Priests and People in Pre-Famine Ireland*, pp. 135–48.

[183] Finn/Fionn is said to have named Loch Br(a)inn in O'Sullivan's parish of Templenoe 'Bran's Lake' (National Folklore Collection [UCD], The Schools' Collection, Volume 0465, Page 032 [from Thade Morley, aged 55, Gearha South, near Sneem, Co. Kerry, May 1936]).

[184] Notes, pp. 59–60 (28 July 1850).

[185] MacNeill, *Festival of Lughnasa*, pp. 101–5, 449–50, 459–70, 482–5, 594–5, 598.

[186] Recollections, 26 April 1849.

[187] *Praxis*, pp. 180–2.

[188] Recollections, 18 May 1847; Notes, pp. 78, 82 (16 and 18 July 1851); Notes, p. 708 (19 July 1850); *Praxis*, pp. 716–18.

Chapter 6

[189] Anon, *A Sketch of the State of Ireland*, pp. 30–1

[190] *Reports from Commissioners: Poor Laws (Ireland)*, Appendix E (1836), pp. 211–13.

[191] See also *Freeman's Journal*, 10 Jan. and 8 and 12 Feb. 1822.

[192] *Parliamentary Gazetteer*, vol. 1, pp. cxliv.

[193] *Report of the Commissioners, Census 1841*, p. xiv.

[194] *Report of the Commissioners, Census 1841*, pp. xvi–xvii. The term 'family' was defined to include servants, resident apprentices and labourers who used the same kitchen and boarded under the same roof as a head who supported them. If someone lived independently under the same roof on his or her own means of support, then that person constituted a separate family.

[195] Foster, *Letters on the Condition of the People of Ireland*, p. 388. The text of this book consists of his articles in the *Times*, with some additions.

[196] Weld, *Illustrations*, p. 163n.

[197] Foster, *Letters on the Condition of the People of Ireland*, pp. 388–9.

[198] *Ibid.*, p. 390.

[199] *Select Committee 1849*, p. 143.

[200] Kenmare BGMB, 3 Jan. 1846.

[201] Trench, *Realities*, pp. 111–13.

[202] *Ibid.*

203 Notes, p. 431 (21 Aug. 1851).

204 Lansdowne, *Glanerought*, pp. 61–4; Palmer, *Palmer*, p. 12.

205 Owens, 'Faction fighters, public demonstrations and the O'Connellite campaign, 1828'; Moraghan, *Days of the Blackthorn, passim.*

206 *Dublin Journal*, 11 April 1809.

207 Pückler-Muskau, *Tour in England, Ireland, and France*, pp. 375–6.

208 *Praxis*, pp. 231–2.

209 Pückler-Muskau, *Tour in England, Ireland, and France*, pp. 375–92.

210 Murphy, 'O'Connell and the Gaelic World', pp. 42–3.

211 *Census of Ireland 1851: Part VI, General Report*, p. xlii; *Tralee Chronicle and Killarney Echo*, 6 Dec. 1861.

212 Lansdowne, *Glanerought*, p. 106.

213 Ó Gráda, *Ireland before and after the Famine*, pp. 78–82.

214 Trinity College Dublin MS, 'The Kenmare Committee'.

215 *Praxis*, pp. 941–3.

216 Lansdowne, *Glanerought*, p. 10.

217 Whelan, 'An underground gentry?', pp. 7–68 for an overview of the class; Hickson, *Old Kerry Records*, 2nd series, p. 152; Lyne, *Lansdowne Estate*, pp. 527–67.

218 'Búrdúin Bheaga', ed. T. F. O'Rahilly, in *The Irish Monthly*, vol. 51, no. 600 (1923), pp. 296–7, citing Royal Irish Academy MS 12 E 24, p. 37.

219 Lansdowne, *Glanerought*, p. 128.

220 Murray, *History of the Commercial and Financial Relations between England and Ireland*, p. 362.

221 *Dev. Comm. Ev.*, part 2, pp. 917–18.

222 Lyne, 'Landlord-tenant relations on the Shelburne estate'.

223 Lansdowne, *Glanerought*, pp. 116–17.

224 MacCarthy, *Trinity College Estates*, p. 5.

Chapter 7

225 Recollections, opening narrative.

226 O'Hart, *Irish Pedigrees*, vol. 1, pp. 243–5.

227 O'Sullivan, 'Ancient history of the kingdom of Kerry', vol. 6, no. 45 (1900), p. 17; Hickson, *Old Kerry Records*, 2nd series, p. 117.

228 RIA MS OSI: Letters, Kerry, 1841, 14/C/30/14 (ii), pp. 418–20.

229 'The Wants of Ireland', *Dublin Review*, 10 (February–May 1841), pp. 218–48, cited at Larkin, *Pastoral Role*, pp. 177–8.

230 Recollections, 1 June 1847.

231 Recollections, 18 May 1847.

232 Recollections, 18 May and 5 June 1847; O'Leary, *Changing Times*, pp. 55–64, 393; *Holy Cross Church 150*, pp. 208, 256.

233 *Kerry Evening Post*, 20 April 1841; *Kerry Examiner*, 20 April 1841.

234 Notes, p. 75 (10 July 1851).

235 *Praxis*, pp. 587–8; Kenmare BGMB, 22 Nov. 1845.

236 Doyle, *History of the Irish Language*, pp. 107–58; Ó Tuathaigh, *I mBéal an Bháis*; Ní Mhóráin, *Thiar sa Mhainistir, passim.*

237 Notes, pp. 2–3 (19 July 1850). The Latin phrase may refer to Virgil, *Bucolics*, Eclogue 5 (i).

238 Notes, pp. 2–3 (19 July 1850).

239 Notes, pp. 8–11 (19 July 1850).

240 *Praxis*, pp. 717–18.

[241] Notes, pp. 226–30 (27 July 1851).

[242] *Praxis*, pp. 20–169, 841–6 for an extensive discussion of stations (reference at p. 76 to the old and 'naked'); Larkin, *Pastoral Role of the Roman Catholic Church*, Ch. 4 'The Rise of Stations in Ireland', pp. 189–258; Carleton, *Traits and Stories of the Irish Peasantry* (1830 ed.), vol. 2, pp. 211–304; *Ibid.* (1843 ed.), vol. 1, pp. 145–79 (including illustrations) – a jaundiced view somewhat toned down in later editions. Also see O'Sullivan, 'Mass in a Connemara cabin' for Aloysius O'Kelly's later painting of an Irish station.

[243] *Select Committee 1849*, p. 157.

[244] Recollections, 13 Oct. 1843 and 10 Sept. 1848.

[245] 'An anti-conspirator', *Supplement to the Trials of the Rev. Robert Morritt*, p. 26; Donnelly, *Captain Rock*, pp. 192, 194; *Register Book of Marriages, Parish of St George, Hanover Square, Middlesex, 1824–1837* (London, 1897), p. 134 gives Rev. George Hely Hutchinson married Alicia Margaret Morritt on 13 July 1830.

[246] Recollections, 10 Sept. 1848.

[247] *Kerry Examiner*, 4 March 1842.

[248] Recollections, opening narrative, ostensibly written in 1843. For more of his views on the conditions of priests in earlier days, see *Praxis*, pp. 715–18.

[249] Recollections, 10 Oct. 1843. He lists 'Callaghan McCarthy and his curate Dan O'Sullivan, Tuosist [Beara]; Mick Walshe, Ballybog [Sneem]; John O'Kane, Kilgarvan; Mike Enright, Bonane'.

[250] Recollections, 10 Oct. 1843; *Tralee Mercury*, 23 May 1829 reports Fitzmaurice chairing a meeting at Kenmare to express gratitude to Daniel O'Connell for Catholic emancipation.

[251] Recollections, 10 Oct. 1843.

[252] Recollections, 10 Oct. 1843.

[253] Thackeray, *The Irish Sketch-Book, 1842*, vol. 1, pp. 194, 222–3; Lewis, *Ireland*, vol. 1, pp. 161–2.

[254] Recollections, 11 Oct. 1843.

[255] Recollections, 11 Oct. and 15 Nov. 1843

[256] *Dev. Comm. Ev.*, part 2, pp. 910–23 (7 Sept. 1844) and 942–3 (7 Sept. 1844).

[257] Recollections, 23 March, 3 April and 15 May 1848.

[258] Recollections, 28 May 1849.

[259] Recollections, 26 April 1849. See also 7 May 1849.

[260] Recollections, O'Sullivan to John Murphy, 4 June 1849.

[261] Recollections, 18 May 1847.

[262] Notes, p. 754 (10 March 1854), 776 (18 April 1854).

[263] Recollections, 11 Oct. 1843.

[264] Recollections, 10 Sept. 1848.

[265] Recollections, 15 June 1849 for anticipated expenses; Larkin, *Pastoral Role of the Roman Catholic Church*, pp. 240–42.

[266] Notes, p. 799 (28 July 1855).

[267] Notes, p. 833 (8 Aug. 1855); *Praxis*, pp. 185–93.

[268] Notes, p. 428 (21 Aug. 1851).

[269] Recollections, 11 Oct. 1843.

[270] Recollections, 11 Oct. 1843; Notes, pp. 750–1 (10 March 1854).

[271] *Kerry Evening Post*, 20 April 1841; *Kerry Examiner*, 20 April 1840.

[272] 'Mathew, Theobald', by Thomas O'Connor, in *DIB*.

[273] Recollections, 11 Oct. 1843.

[274] *Kerry Examiner*, 17 Feb. 1843.

[275] Recollections, 11 Oct. 1843.

[276] Recollections, 11 Oct. 1843; Quinn, *Fr Mathew's Crusade*, pp. 4–7, 112–15.

[277] Cusack ('Clare'), *Life of Father Mathew, passim.*

[278] Cusack ('Clare'), *Life of Father Mathew*, pp. 127–9 for examples of Mathew browbeating those who wished to be released from the pledge.

[279] *Kerry Examiner*, 23 Dec. 1845.

[280] Recollections, 26 April 1849, 25 Jan. 1848; Capuchin Archives, Theobald Mathew OSFC to David O'Meara, his secretary, affirming that he is attending to his sick brother in Kenmare (30 Jan. 1848).

[281] Recollections, 15 June 1849 for anticipated expenses; Larkin, *Pastoral Role of the Roman Catholic Church*, pp. 240–2.

Chapter 8

[282] *Select Committee 1849*, pp. 143–4.

[283] Burke, *People and the Poor Law*, pp. 1–16.

[284] Ó Gráda, *Black '47 and Beyond*, p. 50; O'Brien, 'Workhouse management in pre-Famine Ireland', pp. 115–18.

[285] Poor Relief (Ireland) Act 1838, sections 20–4, 61–4.

[286] *Holy Cross Church 150*, pp. 45–81 for extracts 1845–56 from the workhouse minutes now archived at Kerry County Library in Tralee.

[287] *Select Committee 1849*, pp. 151–2.

[288] William Mahony and Peter McSweeny were rejected as 'valuators' in favour of James Mayberry and James McClure (Kenmare BGMB, 25 Jan.–13 Nov. 1841, esp. 21 April).

[289] Kenmare BGMB, 13 Nov. 1841, 8 and 22 Feb. 1845, 28 Feb. 1846; Brunton, *The Politics of Vaccination*, pp. 106–121 ('Ireland: The failure of Poor Law vaccination 1840–50').

[290] O'Brien, 'Workhouse management', p. 113.

[291] Hall, *Ireland: Its Scenery and Character*, vol. 3, pp. 344–6.

[292] Kenmare BGMB, 11 Feb. 1843.

[293] *Select Committee 1849*, pp. 134–5.

[294] Kenmare BGMB, 25 Oct. 1845 (compare 2 March 1849).

[295] Burke, *The People and the Poor Law in Nineteenth Century Ireland*, pp. 79–100.

[296] Kenmare BGMB, 15 Nov. 1845 (also see 8 and 29 Nov. 1845).

[297] Kenmare BGMB, 29 Nov., 6 and 13 Dec. 1845, 2 May 1846.

[298] *Tralee Chronicle*, 10 June 1848, tabulated at Ó Gráda, Anbinder and Wegge, 'Assisted emigration', p. 379.

[299] Kenmare BGMB, 29 Nov. 1845; *Kerry Evening Post*, 17 Dec. 1845. He later had an altar erected in the dining hall, as in other workhouses. In 1849 the Poor Law Commissioners increased his salary to £80 p.a. so long as he should be required to perform certain additional duties. A local 'Relieving Officer' then was paid £50 p.a. (Kenmare BGMB, 4 and 11 April 1846, 9 Feb., 13 and 20 April 1849).

[300] Kerry Diocesan Archives, O'Sullivan Papers, box 1, printed letter (two slightly different editions/versions), O'Sullivan to Denis Mahony, 22 Dec. 1848. A transcript at McCarthy, *Kenmare*, pp. 85–95.

[301] Kenmare BGMB, 11 and 18 July 1846, 16 Oct. 1847.

[302] Kenmare BGMB, 16 Oct. 1847, 17 Jan. 1851.

[303] Kenmare BGMB, 11 April, 2 May, 25 July, 8 and 29 Aug., 3 Oct. 1846.

[304] Kenmare BGMB, 1 Aug. 1846.

[305] *Kerry Examiner*, 15 Sept. 1846.

306 *Kerry Examiner*, 15 Sept. 1846.

307 Kenmare BGMB, 12 Sept. 1846.

308 Donnelly, 'The administration of relief, 1847–51', pp. 316–31.

309 *Kerry Examiner*, 16 Oct. 1846, 12 Jan. 1847.

310 *Kerry Examiner*, 15 Sept. 1846; Kenmare BGMB, 26 Sept. and 19 Dec. 1846, 30 Jan. 1847.

311 Kenmare BGMB, 10 and 24 Oct., 7 and 21 Nov. 1846; 22 Nov. 1850; 3 Jan. 1851.

312 *Kerry Evening Post*, 11 Nov. and 16 Dec. 1846.

313 O'Connell, *Correspondence of Daniel O'Connell*, vol. 8, p. 156.

314 *Kerry Evening Post*, 16 Dec. 1846.

315 Kenmare BGMB, 12 and 19 Dec. 1846 (and 27 Feb. 1847 for a recommendation that barley water be given when milk was unavailable).

Chapter 9

316 Recollections, 18 May 1847.

317 *Kerry Examiner*, 2 Feb. 1847; *Select Committee 1849*, p. 134.

318 Recollections, back references at 18 May 1847.

319 *Select Committee 1849*, p. 134.

320 *Kerry Evening Post*, 30 Jan. 1847.

321 Kenmare BGMB, 7 Nov. 1846 and 2 Jan. and 27 Feb. 1847; Lyne, 'Taylors of Dunkerron'; Sayre, 'Biographical sketch of Thomas Taylor'; Burke, *Landed Gentry*, vol. 2, p. 993 suggests that Taylor's grandmother too was Indian – 'the daughter of an Indian Rajah'.

322 Kenmare BGMB, 9 and 30 Jan. 1847. See also 2 and 23 Jan., 6, 13 and 20 Feb. and 6, 13 and 20 March 1847.

323 Kenmare BGMB, 9 and 16 Jan. and 27 Feb. 1847.

324 *Select Committee 1849*, p. 135.

325 Notes, p. 430 (21 Aug. 1851); *Praxis*, p. 905.

326 *Select Committee 1849*, p. 134, which has a comma before the word 'unless'; Recollections, back reference made at 18 May 1847.

327 Kinealy, *Charity and the Great Hunger*, p. 171; Kinealy, 'The British Relief Association', pp. 49–65; *Cork Examiner*, 31 Dec. 1849.

328 Dobree to CET, 12 Dec. 1847, Trevelyan Papers, Irish Relief, PRO, T64/369A/2 cited at Haines, *Trevelyan*, p. 384.

329 *Correspondence from July 1846 to January 1847, relating to Measures Adopted for the Relief of Distress in Ireland*, p. 502 (Sir R. Routh to Trevelyan, 19 Jan. 1847).

330 National Library of Ireland, British Association Minute Book, on 4, 9 and 18 Jan. 1847.

331 National Library of Ireland, British Association Minute Book, on 2 Feb. 1847.

332 National Library of Ireland, British Association Minute Book, on 4 Feb. 1847.

333 *Tralee Chronicle*, 29 Dec. 1849.

334 *Praxis*, p. 905.

335 *Parliamentary Papers 52 (1847): Relief of Distress Ireland*, pp. 166–7 (John O'Sullivan, vicar-general, to Trevelyan, February 1847).

336 *Parliamentary Papers 52 (1847): Relief of Distress Ireland*, p. 196 (Rear-Admiral Sir Hugh Pigot to the Secretary of the Admiralty, 27 Feb. 1847, and Commodore H.E. Wingrove to Pigot, 25 Feb. and to Captain Hamilton, 27 Feb. 1847).

337 Newcastle University (UK) MSS, Trevelyan (Charles Edward) Archive, CET/1/12 pp. 209–211 (Trevelyan to O'Sullivan, 25 Feb. 1847) re cause of delay; CET/1/14 pp. 164–165 (Trevelyan to O'Sullivan, 30 April 1847) re a depot at

Kenmare; CET/1/18 p. 153 (Trevelyan to O'Sullivan, 7 Dec. 1847) re operation of Poor Law and Kenmare depot; CET/1/18 pp. 186–7 (13 Dec. 1847) re Poor Law and mode of applying the funds of the British Relief Association.

338 Cowman, 'Two Kerry lead-silver mines', pp. 39–40; *Kerry Examiner*, 23 March 1847; *Kerry Evening Post*, 16 April 1847; *Dublin Evening Packet*, 7 April 1847.

339 *Dublin Evening Packet*, 7 April 1847.

340 *Kerry Examiner*, 19 Feb. and 23 March 1847; Kenmare BGMB, 26 Feb. 1848 refers to 'jobbing'.

341 'The Kenmare Committee', J.D. White Collection of slip ballads, Trinity College Dublin, at https://digitalcollections.tcd.ie/collections/sf2685934?locale=en

342 Kenmare BGMB, 3, 10, 17 and 24 April 1847.

343 Bennett, *Narrative of a Recent Journey in Ireland*, pp. 128–9, 175–6.

344 Bennett, *Narrative*, pp. 130, 175–6.

345 Lyne, *Lansdowne Estate*, p. xxxii.

346 MacMahon, *Great Famine in Tralee and North Kerry*, *passim*; Foley, 'Killarney Poor Law Guardians and The Great Famine', *passim*.

347 *Kerry Examiner*, 30 April 1847. See also Foley, 'Killarney Poor Law guardians', *passim*.

348 Recollections, 15 Nov. 1847.

349 Recollections, 21 May 1847.

350 Report of Richards and Fitt, 5–6 May 1847. From Quaker archives, transcribed by Kay Caball (https://mykerryancestors.com/great-famine-kerry-1847/)

351 Kenmare BGMB, 22 May 1847.

352 Recollections, 1 June 1847.

353 Recollections, 1–4 June 1847.

354 Recollections, 12 July 1847.

355 Recollections, 29 Oct. 1847.

356 'The wild flower of Mangerton or a Kerry peasant child'. See frontispiece above.

357 Strickland, *Dictionary of Irish Artists*, at both 'Royal Irish Art Union' and 'Matthew Wood'.

358 Kenmare BGMB, 10 April 1847.

359 Kenmare BGMB, 28 Aug. 1847. See also 29 June, 10, 24 and 31 July, 7 and 21 Aug. 1847; Recollections, 1 June 1847.

360 Recollections, 15 Nov. 1847.

361 Recollections, 15 Nov. 1847.

362 *Select Committee 1849*, p. 134.

363 Recollections, 29 Nov. 1847.

364 *Act for the Temporary Relief of Destitute Persons in Ireland* (10 Vic., c. 7); Notes, p. 45 (*s.d.*, Dec. 1845); *Kerry Evening Post*, 14 April 1847 and 6 Oct. 1847.

365 Newcastle University (UK) MS, Trevelyan (Charles Edward) Archive, CET/1/18 p. 153 (Trevelyan to O'Sullivan, 7 Dec. 1847) re Poor Law and Kenmare depot. There is a pencil line through this paragraph in the letter book and the words 'Omit in copy' are in the margin.

366 *Connaught Telegraph*, 24 March 1847; *Accounts and Papers of the House of Commons*, 54 (1847–48), Relief of Distress (Ireland), p. 35.

367 'Ommanney, Sir Erasmus (1814–1904)', by L.G.C. Laughton, revised by Andrew Lambert, in *DNB*. The entry is almost one thousand words, of which just twenty-five refer to his time in Ireland.

368 Recollections, Dec. 1847.

369 Newcastle University (UK) MS, CET/1/18 p. 153 (Trevelyan to O'Sullivan, 7

Dec. 1847) re operation of Poor Law and Kenmare depot.

[370] Recollections, 3–20 Dec. 1847; Kenmare BGMB, 21 and 22 Jan. 1848, 26 Aug. 1848; *Accounts and Papers of the House of Commons*, 54 (1847–48), Relief of Distress (Ireland), p. 41.

[371] *Papers Relating to the Relief of Distress and State of the Unions and Workhouses in Ireland* (1848), p. 514.

[372] British Association, *Report*; Notes, p. 383 (13 Aug. 1851).

[373] *Accounts and Papers of the House of Commons*, 54 (1847–48), Relief of Distress (Ireland), p. 35.

Chapter 10

[374] Haines, *Trevelyan*, pp. 440–1, citing National Archive correspondence.

[375] *Papers Relating to the Relief of Distress and State of the Unions and Workhouses in Ireland* (1848), p. 520.

[376] *Ibid.*, pp. 525–6.

[377] *Ibid.* The 'highroad' here probably signifies the coastal road from Kenmare to Castletown-Bearhaven, off which (as the Ordnance Survey map of 1842 shows) a track or 'green road' led to Loch Inchiquin, immediately east of which are Gleninchiquin and Cooryeen townlands.

[378] *Ibid.*, p. 525; *Dublin Evening Post*, 11 Jan. 1848.

[379] *Papers Relating to the Relief of Distress and State of the Unions and Workhouses in Ireland* (1848), pp. 520, 525 (where in evidence she corrects Tuesday to Wednesday, and Mucksna to adjacent Killaha, and where a typographical error gives 'Floreamore'). She was also known as 'Honora' or 'Norry'.

[380] *Ibid.*, pp. 520, 525–6, 529.

[381] *Papers Relating to the Relief of Distress and State of the Unions and Workhouses in Ireland* (1848), p. 526; O'Flanagan, *The Irish Bar*, pp. 224–31 for a witty account of Henn.

[382] *Papers Relating to the Relief of Distress and State of the Unions and Workhouses in Ireland* (1848), p. 530.

[383] *Ibid.*, p. 528.

[384] *Ibid.*, pp. 533, 538; Kenmare BGMB, 21 and 22 Jan. and 5 Feb. 1848; Recollections, 12 and 20 Jan. 1848. (Ommanney acted briefly as vice-guardian pending Robinson's arrival.)

[385] Haines, *Trevelyan*, pp. 439–43.

[386] *Papers Relating to the Relief of Distress and State of the Unions in Ireland* (1848), p. 537.

[387] *Cork Examiner*, 1 May 1848; Kenmare BGMB, 13 May and 17 June 1848.

[388] Kenmare BGMB, 3 July 1847, 17 Jan., 5 Feb., 17 June and 29 July 1848; *Kerry Examiner*, 18 Feb. 1848; Lyne, 'Taylors of Dunkerron', p. 72.

[389] Kenmare BGMB, 11 and 25 March 1848.

[390] Kenmare BGMB, 11 March and 22 April 1848.

[391] Kenmare BGMB, 12 Feb., 8 April and 9 Dec. 1848.

[392] Kenmare BGMB, 22 and 29 April 1848.

[393] Kenmare BGMB, 25 Nov. and 9 Dec. 1848, 26 Oct. 1849, 12 Nov. 1850, 2 May 1851; Recollections, 26 Oct. 1849.

[394] *Select Committee 1849*, p. 154; Kenmare BGMB, 24 June 1848, 6 April and 19 Oct. 1849.

[395] *Cork Examiner*, 28 April and 1 and 5 May 1848.

[396] Sloan, *William Smith O'Brien and the Young Ireland*, p. 239.

[397] Doheny, *The Felon's Track*, p. 256.

398 Notes, pp. 449–52 (26 Aug. 1851); *Cork Examiner,* 7, 12–16 Feb. 1849 for another account of these fugitives in Kerry.

399 O'Donoghue, 'A neglected Kerry poetess'.

400 Doheny, *The Felon's Track,* pp. 251–2; McCarthy, 'The Clann Carthaigh', p. 66; Lewis, *Ireland,* vol. 2, p. 96.

401 O'Donoghue, 'A neglected Kerry poetess', including a poem referencing her 'beloved Kilfadimore [*sic*]'; McCarthy Papers, NLI MS 35,700/2; McCarthy, *Kenmare,* pp. 72–7 ('The Downings in Kenmare'). For her poem on the death of her mother-in-law Helena McCarthy, see *Tralee Mercury,* 7 Aug. 1830 and *Limerick Chronicle,* 10 July 1830.

402 Kenmare BGMB, 26 Aug. 1848

403 Kenmare BGMB, 26 Aug., 2 and 9 Sept. and 4 Nov. 1848, 20 Jan. 1849.

404 Kenmare BGMB, 25 Nov. 1848.

405 This letter in the *Dublin Evening Post* was republished in the *Cork Examiner,* 1 Jan. 1849.

406 Recollections, 31 Dec. 1848.

407 Kenmare BGMB, 30 Dec. 1848, 6 Jan. 1849.

408 Kenmare BGMB, 21 Feb. 1851.

Chapter 11

409 *Select Committee 1849,* pp. 131–64.

410 *Accounts and Papers of the House of Commons, 43 (1849), Papers relating to the aid afforded to the distressed unions of the West of Ireland,* p. 46 (Clarke to Poor Law Commissioners, 18 Dec. 1848).

411 Recollections, 19 April 1849.

412 Recollections, 4 Jan. 1849.

413 Kenmare BGMB, 6 Jan. 1849; *Select Committee 1849,* pp. 152–3, 155.

414 Kenmare BGMB, 4 Nov. and 2 and 9 Dec. 1848, 20 Jan. 1849.

415 *Select Committee 1849,* p. 135.

416 *Accounts and Papers of the House of Commons, 43 (1849), Papers relating to the aid afforded to the distressed unions of the West of Ireland,* pp. 46–8 (Clarke to Commissioners, 8 Jan. 1849).

417 *Ibid.*

418 *Ibid.*

419 *Ibid.,* p. 100 (Clarke to Commissioners, 23 Jan. 1849).

420 *Ibid.,* p. 101.

421 Recollections, 20 Feb. 1849.

422 Recollections, Jan. 1849.

423 *H.L. Deb.,* 30 May 1848; Newcastle University, CET/1/21 p. 264 (Trevelyan to O'Sullivan, 15 June 1848).

424 Recollections, 1 March 1848.

425 Recollections, 26 March 1849.

426 Recollections, 26 April 1849, O'Sullivan to Mother Mary Austin (Mrs Johanna Hayden).

427 *Select Committee 1849,* pp. 139, 148.

428 *Select Committee 1849,* pp. 148, 150, 155.

429 *Select Committee 1849,* p. 156.

430 *Select Committee 1849,* p. 152.

431 *Select Committee 1849,* pp. 152, 159.

432 *Select Committee 1849,* p. 152.

[433] *Select Committee 1849*, p. 140.

[434] *Select Committee 1849*, pp. 153–4, 158.

[435] *Select Committee 1849*, pp. 163–4.

[436] Recollections, 26 March 1849.

[437] *Select Committee 1849*, p. 154.

[438] *Select Committee 1849*, p. 132.

[439] *Select Committee 1849*, pp. 134, 144.

[440] *Select Committee 1849*, pp. 158–62.

[441] *Select Committee 1849*, p. 159; *Dev. Comm. Ev.*, part 2, p. 918; MacCarthy, *Trinity College Estates, passim;* Moriarty, 'Trinity College Estate in Kenmare Parish', *passim; Tralee Mercury*, 7 Oct. 1829 for a colourful account of a legal dispute about Trinity's management of its local woods.

[442] *Select Committee 1849*, pp. 144–5, 157–62.

[443] Recollections, 28 March 1849, O'Sullivan to the Reporter, Committee Room no. 17.

[444] Recollections, 26 April 1849, 7 March 1851; Kenmare BGMB, 11 May 1849; *Cork Examiner*, 10 March 1851.

[445] Recollections, 2 April 1849.

[446] Recollections, 17, 21 and 26 April 1849.

[447] Recollections, 26 April 1849.

[448] *Cork Examiner*, 30 April 1849.

[449] Recollections, 30 April 1849.

[450] Recollections, 9 April 1849. Also O'Sullivan to Somerville, at Recollections, 30 April 1849. Recollections, 13 May 1849.

[451] Recollections, 30 April 1849.

[452] Recollections, 30 April 1849; *Holy Cross Church 150*, pp. 129–30.

[453] Recollections, 8 and 9 June 1849.

[454] Recollections, 1, 4, 6 (from John Murphy), 14 and 15 June 1849.

[455] Recollections, 24 June 1849, O'Sullivan to Lansdowne; Kenmare BGMB, 10 and 17 April 1847, 29 June 1849.

[456] *Waterford News and Star*, 29 June 1849; *Cork Examiner*, 6 July 1849; *Kerry Evening Post*, 7 July 1849.

[457] *Limerick Chronicle*, 29 Sept. 1849.

[458] Kenmare BGMB, 27 April, 29 June and 12 Oct. 1849, 22 March 1850 for examples of the workhouse debts.

[459] Kenmare BGMB, 10 Aug. 1849, 21 Sept., 30 Nov. 1849.

[460] Kenmare BGMB, 30 Nov. 1849; Recollections, 28 March 1849.

[461] Trench, *Realities*, p. 134.

[462] Trench, *Realities*, p. 116.

[463] *Kerry Examiner*, 19 July 1850.

Chapter 12

[464] Kenmare BGMB, 18 Jan. 1850.

[465] Kenmare BGMB, 15 March 1850.

[466] Jordan, *Ireland's Children in the Famine Era*, p. 1; Kinealy *et al.*, *Children and the Great Hunger in Ireland, passim.*

[467] Recollections, 29 June 1849.

[468] Recollections, 14 and 16 July 1849.

[469] *Praxis*, pp. 659–60.

[470] Froude, 'A Fortnight in Kerry, 2', p. 200.

471 Trench, *Realities*, pp. 118–20.

472 *Ibid.*

473 *Ibid.*, p. 115.

474 *Ibid.*, pp. 114, 134.

475 Anon., 'A Picture of The West of Cork, and Kerry', dated Kenmare, 27 Feb. 1849, addressed to 'my dear William' (unidentified printed report bound into O'Sullivan's Recollections).

476 *Ibid.*; Powell, *The Famine in Bantry Union, passim.*

477 *Select Committee 1849*, p. 157.

478 *Select Committee 1849*, pp. 157–8.

479 Recollections, 3 May 1849, pp. 139–40.

480 *Select Committee 1849*, p. 92.

481 *Select Committee 1849*, pp. 142–4.

482 Recollections, 6 May 1849, p. 142.

483 Kenmare BGMB, 23 Aug. and 15 Nov. 1850.

484 Kenmare BGMB, *passim*; *Holy Cross Church 150*, p. 385 for the union's census figures 1821–1911. In spring 1851 enumerators found 3,353 people in the workhouse buildings (*Census of Ireland 1851: Part VI, General Report*, pp. 276–80).

485 Kenmare BGMB, 6 Dec. 1850.

486 Trench, *Realities*, pp. 122–4.

487 Trench, *Realities*, pp. 124–5, 127; Kenmare BGMB, 28 Feb. 1851.

488 Trench, *Realities*, pp. 122–7.

489 Anbinder, *Five Points*, p. 135.

490 Anbinder, 'Famine to Five Points', pp. 351–87; Anbinder, *Five Points*, p. 449 n. 21.

491 Trench, *Realities*, p. 125.

492 Lyne, *Lansdowne Estate*, p. 115. See also Ó Gráda, Anbinder and Wegge, 'Assisted emigration as Famine relief', *passim.*

493 Trench, *Realities*, p. 127.

494 Recollections, 8 Jan. and 1 Sept. 1848.

495 Recollections, 30 Dec. 1848.

496 Recollections, 30 Dec. 1848.

497 Recollections, January and 1 March 1849.

498 Recollections, 26 March 1849.

499 Recollections, 3 May 1849.

500 Recollections, 8–10 May 1849.

501 Recollections, 3 May 1849.

502 Recollections, 7 May and 19 May 1849.

503 Recollections, 20 May 1849.

504 Recollections, 20 May 1849.

505 Recollections, 7 and 20 May 1849.

506 Recollections, 7 and 20 May 1849, located just after the Murphy letters.

507 Recollections, 19 June 1849, from C.E. Hussey.

508 Recollections, 22 June 1849.

509 Recollections, 24 June and 16 July 1849.

510 Recollections, 24 June 1849. Also see Notes, p. 532 (13 July 1852).

511 Recollections, 24, 25 and 28 July 1849.

512 Notes, p. 545 (17 July 1852).

513 Recollections, 28 July 1849.

514 Recollections, 21 June 1849.

Chapter 13

515 *Select Committee 1849*, p. 160.

516 *Praxis*, pp. 413–15.

517 Recollections, back reference on 18 May 1847.

518 Haines, *Trevelyan*; Gillissen, 'Charles Trevelyan', pp. 195–217.

519 Trevelyan, *The Irish Crisis*, pp. 183–4, where the article was reprinted under his name.

520 Sullivan, *Macaulay*, p. 265; Gray, *Famine, Land and Politics*, p. 331.

521 *Select Committee 1849*, p. 134; Recollections, 18 May 1847.

522 Recollections, 30 Dec. 1848, p. 56; Haines, *Trevelyan*, pp. 358–9, 383, 439–44, 503–4, 513, 533–9.

523 Clarendon to Russell, 16 Sept. 1847, Clarendon Deposit, Bodleian Library, Irish Letterbooks, vol. 1, cited at Haines, *Trevelyan*, p. 342.

524 Haines, *Trevelyan*, pp. 440–2.

525 Kerr, *'Nation of Beggars'*, pp. 50–1; Fitzpatrick to the editor, *The Tablet*, 20 March 1847.

526 Recollections, 24 June 1849, O'Sullivan to John Buckley of the *Dublin Evening Post*; Recollections, 19 May 1849, O'Sullivan to Arundel.

527 *Kalendarium Saint Patrick's College Maynooth 2018–2019*, Ch. 10 'Appointments from 1795 to date', p. 234.

528 Recollections, 18 and 21 May 1847.

529 *Select Committee 1849*, p. 134; Recollections, 18 May 1847.

530 Recollections, 29 Nov. 1847.

531 *H.C. Deb.*, 21 July 1848.

532 Recollections, 1 Sept. 1848.

533 *H.C. Deb.*, 24 Aug. 1848, Tyrell on the Diplomatic Relations with the Court of Rome Bill.

534 *H.C. Deb.*, 24 Aug. 1848; *Kerry Evening Post*, 30 Aug. and 18 Oct. 1848.

535 *H.C. Deb.*, 24 Aug. 1848.

536 Recollections, 20 May 1849.

537 *Dublin Evening Post*, 7 Sept. 1848; *Kerry Evening Post*, 9 Sept. 1848.

538 Recollections, 10 Sept. 1848.

539 *Belfast Newsletter*, 1 Sept. 1848.

540 Kerr, *'Nation of Beggars'*, pp. 186–7.

541 Recollections, 15 Nov. 1843.

542 Recollections, 18 and 21 May and 29 Nov. 1847.

543 Recollections, 29 Nov. 1847.

544 Clarendon to Russell, 4 Oct. 1848, Clarendon Papers, Letterbook 3, cited at Kerr, *'Nation of Beggars'*, p. 186.

545 Recollections, 20 Feb. and 26 March 1849.

546 Recollections, April 1849.

547 Recollections, 26 March 1849.

548 Recollections, 2–3 May 1849; *Cork Examiner*, 17 Jan. 1851 for Fitzpatrick in Skibbereen.

549 Recollections, 26 March 1849; 'Salomons, Sir David, baronet', by Geoffrey Alderman, in *DNB*.

550 *Select Committee 1849*, p. 157.

551 Recollections, 24 June 1849, O'Sullivan to John Buckley of the *Dublin Evening Post*; Recollections, 19 May 1849, O'Sullivan to Arundel.

552 Recollections, 30 April 1849.

[553] Recollections, 28 April and 2–3 May 1849; 'Scrope, George Julius Poulett', by Marin Rudwick, in *DNB*; R. Opie, 'Scrope', pp. 101–37.

[554] Recollections, 26 March 1849.

[555] Recollections, 28 March 1849.

[556] Recollections, 28 March and 2 April 1849; Notes, p. 416 (20 Aug. 1851); Gray, *Famine, Land and Politics*, p. 312n, citing O'Sullivan to Trevelyan, 2 April 1849, Treasury Papers T64/366A.

[557] Recollections, 30 April 1849.

[558] Recollections, 2 and 27 April 1849; Notes, pp. 384–5 (13 Aug. 1851).

[559] Recollections, 10 and 19 July 1849.

[560] Recollections, 18 and 19 May 1849.

[561] *Kerry Evening Post*, 16 Sept. 1848. A 'shoneen' is a person who apes English attitudes and ways.

[562] *Kerry Evening Post*, 28 Sept. 1850.

[563] *Cork Examiner*, 15 Nov. 1850.

[564] Recollections, 19 May 1849.

[565] Notes, pp. 484–5, 506–7, 522–5, 532–3.

[566] Notes, p. 533 (13 July 1852). Also see Notes, pp. 524–5 and 'O'Connell, Maurice Daniel', by Patrick Maume, in *DIB*.

[567] *Cork Examiner*, 31 Dec. 1849; Haines, *Trevelyan*, pp. 533–8, citing the *Tralee Chronicle*, 29 Dec. 1849.

[568] *Cork Examiner*, 31 Dec. 1849; Haines, *Trevelyan*, pp. 533–8, citing the *Tralee Chronicle*, 29 Dec. 1849.

[569] *Kerry Evening Post*, 29 Dec. 1849.

[570] *The Irishman*, 11 Jan. 1862.

[571] O'Donovan Rossa, *Rossa's Recollections*, pp. 142, 156–7.

[572] *Freeman's Journal*, 5 Nov. 1858; *Kerry Evening Post*, 30 Oct. 1858.

[573] O'Donovan Rossa, 'The Fenian Movement'. The letters appear to have been first published in the New York *Irish Republic*, from which they were reproduced in *The Nation*, 9 Oct. 1869. O'Donovan Rossa had also published them in his 1874 book *Prison Life* (pp. 15–19), but without explaining then how he had obtained them.

[574] O'Donovan Rossa, *Rossa's Recollections*, pp. 142, 156–7, and *Prison Life*, p. 11.

[575] *Belfast Newsletter*, 12 March 1859; *Freeman's Journal*, 27 Dec. 1858; *Nenagh Guardian*, 28 Dec. 1858.

[576] See note 57.

[577] O'Donovan Rossa, 'The Fenian Movement'; O'Donovan Rossa, *Prison Life*, p. 15.

[578] O'Donovan Rossa, 'The Fenian Movement'.

Chapter 14

[579] Recollections, 18 May 1847.

[580] Lewis, *Ireland*, vol. 1, p. 210 and vol. 2, p. 611.

[581] Burke, *Landed Gentry*, 6th ed., vol. 2, p. 1049.

[582] O'Connell, *Last Colonel of the Irish Brigade*, vol. 1, p. 51; McCarthy, 'Mahonys of Kerry', esp. p. 229.

[583] Froude, *English in Ireland*, vol. 1, pp. 454–6; Hickson, *Old Kerry Records*, 2nd series, pp. 137–8, 157–64; McCarthy, 'Mahonys of Kerry', p. 230.

[584] *Calendar of Convert Rolls*: 'Denis Mahony, Blackwater, Co. Kerry, gent.' Date of certificate, 24 Nov. 1747 / Enrollment, 16 May 1748. Also Honora Mahony,

Templeno[e], spinster, 8 May 1750/11 Sept. 1750.

585 Burke, *Landed Gentry*, 6th ed., vol. 2, p. 1049; McCarthy, 'Mahonys of Kerry', esp. p. 234.

586 O'Connell, *The Last Colonel*, p. i, p. 53.

587 Burke's *Peerage and Baronetage* (5th ed., London, 1838), p. 420; McCarthy, 'Mahonys of Kerry', pp. 234–5. Margaret Day's brother Robert was a leading judge.

588 Recollections, 18 May 1849; Murphy, *Church of Ireland in Kerry*, pp. 112, 194.

589 Donnelly, *Captain Rock*, pp. 61, 269–70. This church was deconsecrated in 1993 and was later a restaurant.

590 Lewis, *Ireland*, vol. 2, p. 611.

591 Recollections, 11 Oct. 1843. McCarthy, 'Mahonys of Kerry', pp. 234–5 does not refer to the death of Richard or to his ever having the estate.

592 Godkin, *Ireland and Her Churches*, p. 217.

593 *Praxis*, pp. 875–6.

594 Recollections, for handbill of verses 'Dromore Pastorals–No. 2' bound within it; Recollections, 20 June 1849, O'Sullivan to Fr Thomas Lee.

595 Lyne, *Lansdowne Estate*, pp. 649, 682 references information from the Catholic baptismal registers for Kenmare conveyed to Lyne.

596 *Praxis*, pp. 390–2.

597 *Kerry Evening Post*, 3 May 1845.

598 *Praxis*, p. 876.

599 Recollections, 18 May 1847.

600 Recollections, 23 and 24 May 1847.

601 Recollections, 29 Oct. 1847.

602 Recollections, 30 Nov. 1847; *Praxis*, p. 878.

603 Recollections, for a copy of the handbill bound within.

604 Recollections, 30 Nov. 1847.

605 *Waterford Mail*, 9 Sept. 1848; *The Post Office Directory 1851*, for Ifield, West Sussex. Hansard gives the name Peton, evidently an error for Pipon.

606 Recollections, 19 May 1849, and verses bound within.

607 *Kerry Evening Post*, 18 Oct. 1848.

608 *Kenmare Examiner*, 8 Sept. 1848.

609 *Kerry Evening Post*, 9 Sept. 1848.

610 *Kerry Evening Post*, 9 Sept. 1848.

611 Recollections, 10 Sept. 1848; *Cork Examiner*, 15 Nov. 1850.

612 *Cork Examiner*, 15 Nov. 1850; Bowen, *Souperism*, pp. 20, 142–3; Witte, *Sharing the Book*, p. xiv.

613 McCarthy, pp. 84–101; Kerry Diocesan Archives, O'Sullivan Papers, box 1 includes printed copies of two slightly different versions of the letter.

614 Recollections, 26 Dec. 1848.

615 Recollections, 21 April 1849.

616 Lyne, *Lansdowne Estate*, p. 648.

617 Recollections, 20 Feb. 1849; *Holy Cross Church 150*, pp. 113–15.

618 *Select Committee 1849*, p. 160.

619 Recollections, 28 March 1848; 7 April 1849.

620 Recollections, 28 April 1849.

621 Recollections, 18 May 1849.

622 *Cork Examiner*, 15 Nov. 1850.

Chapter 15

[623] Notes, pp. 743–4 (10 March 1854); Notes, p. 753 (10 March 1854).

[624] *Cork Examiner*, 15 Nov. 1850.

[625] Notes, p. 386 (13 Aug. 1851).

[626] Kerr, *'Nation of Beggars'*, p. 212.

[627] *Praxis*, pp. 195–6.

[628] Recollections, 25 April 1849.

[629] Recollections, 14 June and 7 and 12 July 1849.

[630] Recollections, 30 June 1849 (final page of entries); *Praxis*, pp. 420–6, 889–97, 905–6.

[631] *Praxis*, pp. 905–6; *Kerry Evening Post*, 26 Nov. 1849.

[632] Bowen, *Protestant Crusade*, pp. 74–5.

[633] Recollections, 19 July 1849, O'Sullivan to Thomas Redington.

[634] Recollections, 25 July 1849.

[635] Notes, pp. 49–50 (25 July 1850); Recollections, 7 and 12 July 1849; *Cork Examiner*, 15 Nov. 1850.

[636] *Cork Examiner*, 13 Aug. 1849.

[637] *Cork Examiner*, 16 July 1849.

[638] *Cork Examiner*, 15 Aug. 1849.

[639] *Cork Examiner*, 13 Aug. 1849 and *Freeman's Journal*, 15 Aug. 1849 for an account of the day.

[640] *Kerry Evening Post*, 18 Aug. 1848; *Waterford Evening News*, 17 Aug. 1849; *Cork Examiner*, 24 Aug. 1848.

[641] *Cork Examiner*, 13 Aug. 1849; *Tralee Chronicle*, 18 Aug. 1849; Lyne, *Lansdowne Estate*, pp. 649–50.

[642] National Folklore Collection (UCD), The Schools' Collection, Volume 0461, Pages 443–4 (from Jeremiah O'Connor, aged 67, of Rock Lane Kenmare on 16 Jan. 1935).

[643] *Cork Examiner*, 11 Jan. 1850.

[644] *Cork Examiner*, 15 Nov. 1850.

[645] *Cork Examiner*, 11 Jan. 1850.

[646] *Cork Examiner*, 20 and 29 March 1850.

[647] *Cork Examiner*, 30 Sept. 1850, reprinted *Kerry Evening Post*, 2 Oct. 1850.

[648] *Kerry Evening Post*, 28 Sept. 1850.

[649] *Ibid.*; *Cork Examiner*, 30 Sept. 1850, reprinted *Kerry Evening Post*, 2 Oct. 1850.

[650] *Kerry Evening Post*, 28 Sept. 1850, editorial.

[651] *Cork Examiner*, 15 Nov. 1850.

[652] Notes, p. 753 (10 March 1854).

[653] *Praxis*, pp. 913–14.

[654] *Praxis*, p. 405; *Cork Examiner*, 15 Nov. 1850.

[655] *Praxis*, pp. 915–17.

[656] *Cork Examiner*, 28 March 1851.

[657] Kinealy, *Great Irish Famine*, pp. 177–8. See also Ralls, 'Papal Aggression of 1850', pp. 242–56.

[658] *Praxis*, pp. 915–17; *Cork Examiner*, 29 Sept. 1851.

[659] *Cork Examiner*, 30 Sept. 1850.

[660] Notes, p. 754 (10 March 1854).

[661] *Praxis*, pp. 917–18.

[662] *Praxis*, p. 918.

[663] Notes, p. 224 (27 July 1851).

[664] Notes, p. 386 (13 Aug. 1851).

[665] Notes, p. 445 (24 Aug. 1851).

[666] National Folklore Collection (UCD), The Schools' Collection, Volume 0461, Page 043 (from Seán Ó Buachalla, aged 60, of Coolnagoppog on 3 March 1938).

[667] National Folklore Collection (UCD), The Schools' Collection, Volume 0461, Pages 443–4 (from Jeremiah O'Connor, aged 67, of Rock Lane Kenmare on 16 Jan. 1935).

Chapter 16

[668] Recollections, 29 Oct. 1847; Letter from 'A Protestant', *Cork Examiner*, 30 Sept. 1850; Anon., *In Memoriam*, p. 390.

[669] 'Petty, Sir William', by Toby Barnard, in *DNB*.

[670] Aubrey, *Brief Lives*, vol. 2, pp. 142–3; Lansdowne, *Glanerought*, p. 21.

[671] Wood, 'Sir William Petty and his Kerry Estate', p. 30.

[672] Carroll, *The Lansdowne Irish Estates and Sir William Petty*, p. 32.

[673] Orpen, *Orpen*, p. 62; *Freeman's Journal*, 22 April 1809.

[674] Thackeray, *The Irish Sketch-Book, 1842*, vol. 1, pp. 222–3.

[675] Gray, *Dictionary of British Women Artists*, p. 182. The present author found these undated sketches – and another by her of High Street, Killarney, on market day – in a bookship in Shrewsbury alongside others of England by the same artist dated late 1870s.

[676] *Poor Relief (Ireland) Act*, sections 54, 58.

[677] *Papers Relating to Proceedings for the Relief of Distress and State of the Unions and Workhouses in Ireland*, 5th series (London, 1848), pp. 519–38 (January–February 1848) at pp. 525–6.

[678] Kenmare BGMB, 24 May 1850.

[679] Kenmare BGMB, 14 and 28 Feb., 3 Oct. and 28 Nov. 1846, 8 Jan. and 24 June 1848 and 21 Sept. 1849; McLoughlin (ed.), 'Workhouses', pp. 722–35.

[680] Kenmare BGMB, 17 June 1848.

[681] Kenmare BGMB, 22 July 1848.

[682] Kenmare BGMB, 8 Feb. 1850.

[683] Kenmare BGMB, 26 Feb. 1848.

[684] Recollections, 30 April 1849.

[685] Kenmare BGMB, 26 Aug. and 9 Sept. 1848.

[686] Recollections, 16–17 June 1849.

[687] Anon., *In Memoriam*, p. 307; Kenmare BGMB, 18 April 1856.

[688] Delia Lidwill, cited at McLoughlin (ed.), 'Workhouses', pp. 730–2.

[689] Kenmare BGMB, 16 Nov. 1849.

[690] Kenmare BGMB, 8 March 1850.

[691] Kenmare BGMB, 31 Aug., 26 Oct., 9, 23 and 30 Nov. and 21 Dec. 1849; Caball, *Kerry Girls, passim*.

[692] *Papers Relating to the Relief of Distress and State of the Unions in Ireland* (1848), p. 531.

[693] Kenmare BGMB, 15 Nov. 1850.

[694] Kenmare BGMB, 23 and 28 May 1856; *Holy Cross Church 150*, pp. 80–1 for the committee's report.

[695] See, for example, Mary Kenny, 'Seumas O'Kelly poignantly portrayed a child-care conflict', p. 8.

[696] *Cork Examiner*, 7 Aug. 1850 and 10 Sept. 1851. For Kennedy's initiative, see Kenny, *Tristram Kennedy and the Revival of Irish Legal Training*, pp. 28–32, 41, 45.

[697] *Kerry Evening Post*, 6 and 20 Dec. 1851; *Cork Examiner*, 17 and 24 Dec. 1851; McCarthy, *Kenmare*, p. 105.

[698] McCarthy, *Kenmare*, p. 104.

[699] *Tralee Chronicle*, 23 Dec. 1853 for 'Special Report on the Kenmare Industrial School, for 1852', by Thaddeus MacNamara, District Inspector, Killarney, January 1852.

[700] Anon., *In Memoriam*, p. 260; Recollections, opening narrative.

[701] Recollections, opening narrative.

[702] Recollections, 7 April 1849; Larkin, *Pastoral Role*, p. 241.

[703] Notes, p. 45 (26 July 1850), pp. 412–14 (20 Aug. 1850), p. 171 (24 July 1851), p. 234 (27 July 1851), p. 387 (13 Aug. 1851).

[704] Notes, pp. 454–5 (27 Aug. 1851).

[705] *Tralee Chronicle and Killarney Echo*, 6 Dec. 1861.

[706] Recollections, 29 Oct. 1847 and 17 May 1849.

[707] *Praxis*, pp. 876–7.

[708] Murphy, 'Charlotte Elizabeth', p. 742; Delay, 'Meddlers amongst us', pp. 71–82.

[709] Notes, p. 768 (13 April 1854).

[710] Lyne, *Lansdowne Estate*, pp. 647–9 referencing copies of this poem simply as being 'in Orpen Papers, National Library of Ireland', but the National Library has been unable to identify their location today; *Tralee Chronicle*, 27 Feb. and 2 March 1850, 13 Sept. 1851.

[711] National Folklore Collection (UCD), The Schools' Collection, Volume 0461, Pages 443–4 (from Jeremiah O'Connor, aged 67, of Rock Lane Kenmare on 16 Jan. 1935).

[712] Notes, pp. 627–8 (16 Aug. 1854).

[713] Knodel, 'The churching of women and feminist liturgical theology', pp. 106–25.

[714] *Praxis*, p. 11.

[715] *Praxis*, pp. 331–3.

[716] Notes, pp. 496–8 (27 June 1852); *Praxis*, pp. 330–2.

[717] *Praxis*, p. 150.

[718] 'Nicholson, Asenath', by Deirdre Bryan, in *DIB*; Nicholson, *Ireland's Welcome to the Stranger*, pp. 372–3.

[719] Recollections, 25 April 1849; *The Pilot*, vol. 28, no. 2 (14 Jan. 1865), p. 3.

[720] *Freeman's Journal*, 27 Nov. 1863.

[721] Notes, pp. 662–4 (22 Aug. 1850).

[722] Notes, pp. 35–6, 38 (21 July 1850). Also Notes, p. 529 (1852).

[723] Notes, p. 22 (21 July 1850).

[724] Notes, p. 56 (27 July 1850).

[725] Notes, pp. 717–23 (Aug. 1853) and p. 734 (Sept. 1853).

[726] Notes, pp. 100–1 (19 July 1851).

[727] Anon., *In Memoriam*, p. 270; Cusack, *The Nun of Kenmare*, pp. 49ff.

[728] Anon., *In Memoriam*, p. 307.

[729] Anon., *In Memoriam*, pp. 308–11.

[730] *Cork Examiner*, 11 Jan. 1850.

[731] Luddy and O'Dowd, *Marriage in Ireland*, p. 229.

[732] Luddy and O'Dowd, *Marriage in Ireland*, p. 80.

[733] *Praxis*, p. 652. See *Praxis*, pp. 682–714 for marriage generally.

[734] *Praxis*, pp. 699–700.

[735] *Praxis*, pp. 708–9.

[736] *Praxis*, pp. 956–8.

[737] See, for example, Laborde, *The Impossibility of the Immaculate Conception as an Article of Faith*, from the French; The *Catholic Layman*, vol. 44, no. 39 (March 1855), p. 26; Daly, *Pure Lust: Elemental Feminist Philosophy, passim.*

Chapter 17

[738] Notes, pp. 19–20 (19 July 1850).

[739] *Praxis*, pp. 404, 803; Larkin, *Making of the Roman Catholic Church in Ireland*, Appendix A, for a list of the complete attendance in an official capacity at the national Synod of Thurles, 22 Aug. to 10 Sept., 1850.

[740] Notes, pp. 724–7 (13 Feb. 1854).

[741] Notes, pp. 724–5 (13 Feb. '1854', out of sequence?); *Praxis*, pp. 811, 819; Notes, p. 478 (2 Feb. 1852); Kerr, *'Nation of Beggars'*, pp. 227, 232–4.

[742] *Praxis*, p. 944.

[743] *Praxis*, pp. 375–6. More generally for the synod, see *Praxis*, pp. 802–36, and for his views on national school policy, see *Praxis*, pp. 431–4.

[744] *Praxis*, pp. 834, 926–37.

[745] *Praxis*, pp. 381, 431–4; *Select Committee 1849*, p. 159.

[746] *Cork Examiner*, 15 Nov. 1850.

[747] Notes, pp. 749–53 (10 March 1854); Kerr, *'Nation of Beggars'*, pp. 206–14, 324.

[748] *Praxis*, pp. 860–922, 938.

[749] *Praxis*, pp. 896–8. See also Notes, pp. 183–4 (24 July 1851).

[750] Notes, p. 73 (10 July 1851) referencing an unidentified newspaper.

[751] Notes, pp. 352–4 (7 Aug. 1851).

[752] Notes, pp. 206–17 (26 July 1851); O'Sullivan Papers, Kerry Diocesan Archives, box 6 includes the Latin work *Constitutiones Ecclesiasticae pro Unitis Dioecesibus Ardfertensi & Aghadoensi* [etc] [Ecclesiastical Constitution for the united diocese of Ardfert and Aghadoe] (Caldwell, Waterford, 1747).

[753] Notes, pp. 208–12 (26 July 1851).

[754] Notes, pp. 218–19 (26 July 1851).

[755] Notes, pp. 352–4 (7 Aug. 1851).

[756] Notes, pp. 709–10 (30 Aug. 1852).

[757] Notes, p. 27 (21 July 1850).

[758] Notes, p. 713 (July 1853).

[759] Notes, pp. 708–9 (30 Aug. 1852).

[760] Notes, p. 397 (17 Aug. 1851).

[761] Cusack, *Autobiography*, pp. 80–1.

[762] Notes, pp. 723–4 (13 Feb. 1854).

[763] Notes, pp. 734–6 (5 Oct. 1853); Larkin, *Making of the Roman Catholic Church in Ireland*, p. 213. See also O'Shea, 'David Moriarty (1814–1877): The making of a bishop', vol. 3 (1970) p. 96 and vol. 4 (1971), p. 108.

[764] *Tralee Chronicle*, 7 Oct. 1853.

[765] Whyte, 'Catholic bishops in nineteenth century Ireland', pp. 27–30.

[766] Notes, pp. 737–42 (26 Oct. 1853–3 Feb. 1854); The Papers of Tobias Kirby, Archives of the Irish College Rome, cited at Larkin, *Making of the Roman Catholic Church in Ireland*, pp. 210–11.

[767] Whyte, 'Catholic bishops in nineteenth century Ireland', p. 29.

[768] Archives of the Society for the Propagation of the Faith (*Propaganda Fide*), Piazza d'Espagna Rome, Irish Correspondence, vol. 218, fols 10–11, Cullen to Fransoni, 18 Nov. 1853, cited at Larkin, *Making of the Roman Catholic Church in Ireland*, p. 213.

769 The Papers of Tobias Kirby, Archives of the Irish College Rome, cited at Larkin, *Making of the Roman Catholic Church in Ireland*, p. 214.

770 Notes, pp. 750–1 (10 March 1854).

771 'Mathew, Theobald', by Thomas O'Connor, in *DIB*.

772 *Praxis*, pp. 937–8; Notes, pp. 749–50 (10 March 1854).

773 Notes, pp. 752, 756–63 (10 March–13 Apr. 1854). See Rafferty, 'David Moriarty' for the latter's episcopal career.

774 Notes, pp. 767–8 (13 April 1854); Kerr, *'Nation of Beggars'*, p. 212.

775 Notes, pp. 761–2 (10 March 1854).

776 Cusack, *Autobiography*, pp. 49–50; Killarney Diocesan Archives, box 6, for a copy of O'Sullivan, *Commentary on the Book of Psalms*, with a press clipping from *Tralee Chronicle and Killarney Echo* (1 June 1866) that includes its endorsement by Bishop Moriarty.

777 *Praxis*, p. 238.

778 *Praxis*, pp. 244–6.

779 Notes, pp. 399–400 (17 Aug. 1850).

780 *Praxis*, pp. 219–21.

781 Notes, pp. 650–1 (20 Aug. 1852) and p. 830 (7 Aug. 1855) for a dancing master and 'exquisite' fiddle player named Silvani, on Iveragh.

782 Notes, pp. 809–10 (2 Aug. 1855).

783 Notes, p. 831 (7 Aug. 1855).

784 Notes, pp. 267–71 (1 Aug. 1851).

785 Notes, pp. 61–8 (28 July–1 Aug. 1850).

786 Notes, pp. 274–5, 282 (1 Aug. 1851).

787 *Praxis*, pp. 839–40.

788 *Praxis*, p. 484.

789 *Praxis*, pp. 307, 325–8, 555, 850–5, 954.

790 *Transactions of the Kilkenny and South-East of Ireland Archaeological Society*, 2, pt. 2 (1853), p. 183; Notes, p. 424 (12 July 1852).

791 *Tralee Chronicle and Killarney Echo*, 6 Dec. 1861.

792 Duffy, 'Landed estates in 19th century Ireland', pp. 24–7.

793 *Seanad Éireann debates*, 18 Nov. 1942.

794 Trench, *Realities*, chapter 10 'The Seal Hunt', pp. 153–69. Lansdowne, *Glanerought*, p. 139 wonders if this and other incidents in Trench's book were indeed 'realities'.

795 Beinsart and Hughes, *Environment and Empire*, pp. 5–6.

796 Lyne, *Lansdowne Estate*, p. 475; Moriarty, 'Early years', pp. 19–27 with map.

797 Lyne, *Lansdowne Estate*, pp. 678–81; *Holy Cross Church 150*, pp. 116–28.

798 Notes, pp. 377–8 (11 Aug. 1851).

799 Lyne, *Lansdowne Estate*, pp. 650–81, 687, 691–9; McCarthy, *Kenmare*, p. 97.

800 Trench to Lansdowne, 23 May 1867 (Bowood Papers, Kerry: Miscellaneous 1865–1900), cited at Lyne, *Lansdowne*, p. 674.

801 Russell, *'New Views on Ireland'*, p. 37.

802 Notes, pp. 100–1 (19 July 1851).

803 Notes, pp. 348–9 (7 Aug. 1851).

804 *Praxis*, p. 375.

805 Cusack, *Autobiography*, p. 50.

806 Anon., *In Memoriam*, pp. 222–4, 228, 262, 308; McCarthy, *Kenmare*, pp. 98, 106.

807 Lyne, *Lansdowne Estate*, pp. 499, 511.

808 'O'Hagan, Thomas', by Patrick Geoghegan, and 'O'Hagan, Mary', by Georgina

Clinton and Sinéad Sturgeon, in *DIB*.

809 'Cusack, Margaret Anna', by Patrick Maume, in *DIB*.

810 Cusack, *Autobiography*, pp. 50–1.

811 *Freeman's Journal*, 10 May 1867.

812 [John O'Sullivan], *The Altar Turned Out and Turned in Again; or, Crowbar Practice in Kenmare* (Dublin, 1867).

813 *Kerry Evening Post*, 21 Feb. 1857; *Cork Examiner*, 22 Feb. 1858.

814 *Holy Cross Church 150*, *passim*; Kenmare BGMB, 28 Feb. 1846; Interview with Ann McCabe Hickey, Killowen.

815 *Tralee Chronicle and Killarney Echo*, 13 Sept. 1864. Murphy was also the present author's great-great-grandfather. That wooden cover is stored at Holy Cross Church.

816 Lucas, '"Penal" crucifixes', pp. 152–3, 163–4.

817 *Tralee Chronicle and Killarney Echo*, 13 Sept. 1864 refers to the children as 'sinners', presumably a typographical error for 'singers'!

818 *Freeman's Journal*, 19 Sept. 1864; *Cork Examiner*, 16 and 17 Sept. 1864, including reference to some older chapels as 'barn-like buildings which are relics of an untoward past'; *Kerry Evening Post*, 17 Sept. 1864; *Holy Cross Church 150*, pp. 145–71.

819 *Holy Cross Church 150*, p. 165. The two statues were later removed to the church at Templenoe, built in the 1840s, and are said to have been buried there about 1959, when that church was being reconstructed.

820 *Holy Cross Church 150*, pp. 16, 226.

821 Froude, 'A fortnight in Kerry, 1', pp. 178, 201; Lyne, *Lansdowne Estate*, pp. 211–15.

822 Froude, *The English in Ireland*, vol. 1, pp. 454–6; Lansdowne, *Glanerought*, p. 187.

823 Froude, *The English in Ireland*, vol. 1, pp. 454–6; Froude, 'A fortnight in Kerry, 1', pp. 179, 199.

824 Wilde, 'Mr Froude's Blue Book'. This lively review is also available free as an Apple podcast from Librivox.

825 Froude, 'A fortnight in Kerry, 2', pp. 244, 377–9.

826 Fetherstonhaugh, 'The true story of the two chiefs of Dunboy', *passim*. It is difficult to see value in an abridged or edited version of Froude's novel published in 1969.

827 Wilde, 'Mr Froude's Blue Book'.

828 Anon., *In Memoriam*, pp. 318, 330–5; Cusack, *Autobiography*, pp. 142–3.

829 National Archives (UK), Ireland, Copy 1/27/423 (5 Dec. 1874). See also *Holy Cross Church 150*, p. 27.

830 Hickson, *Old Kerry Records*, 2nd series, pp. 310, 321–3; O'Carroll, 'Mary Agnes Hickson', p. 232.

831 *Freeman's Journal*, 19 Nov. 1874; *Irish Times*, 19 Nov. 1874; *Tralee Chronicle*, 20 Nov. 1874.

832 Ó Cathaoir, 'The Kerry "Home Rule" by-election, 1872', *Jn. Kerry Arch. and Hist. Soc.*, vol. 3 (1970), pp. 157–8.

833 'Fitzmaurice, Henry Charles Keith Petty', by Patrick Geoghegan, in *DIB*; *Dundalk Democrat*, 18 Sept. 1880.

834 Froude, 'A fortnight in Kerry, 1', pp. 201–2.

835 *Holy Cross Church 150*, pp. 27–9.

Index